TRIAGE X

Shouji Sato #25

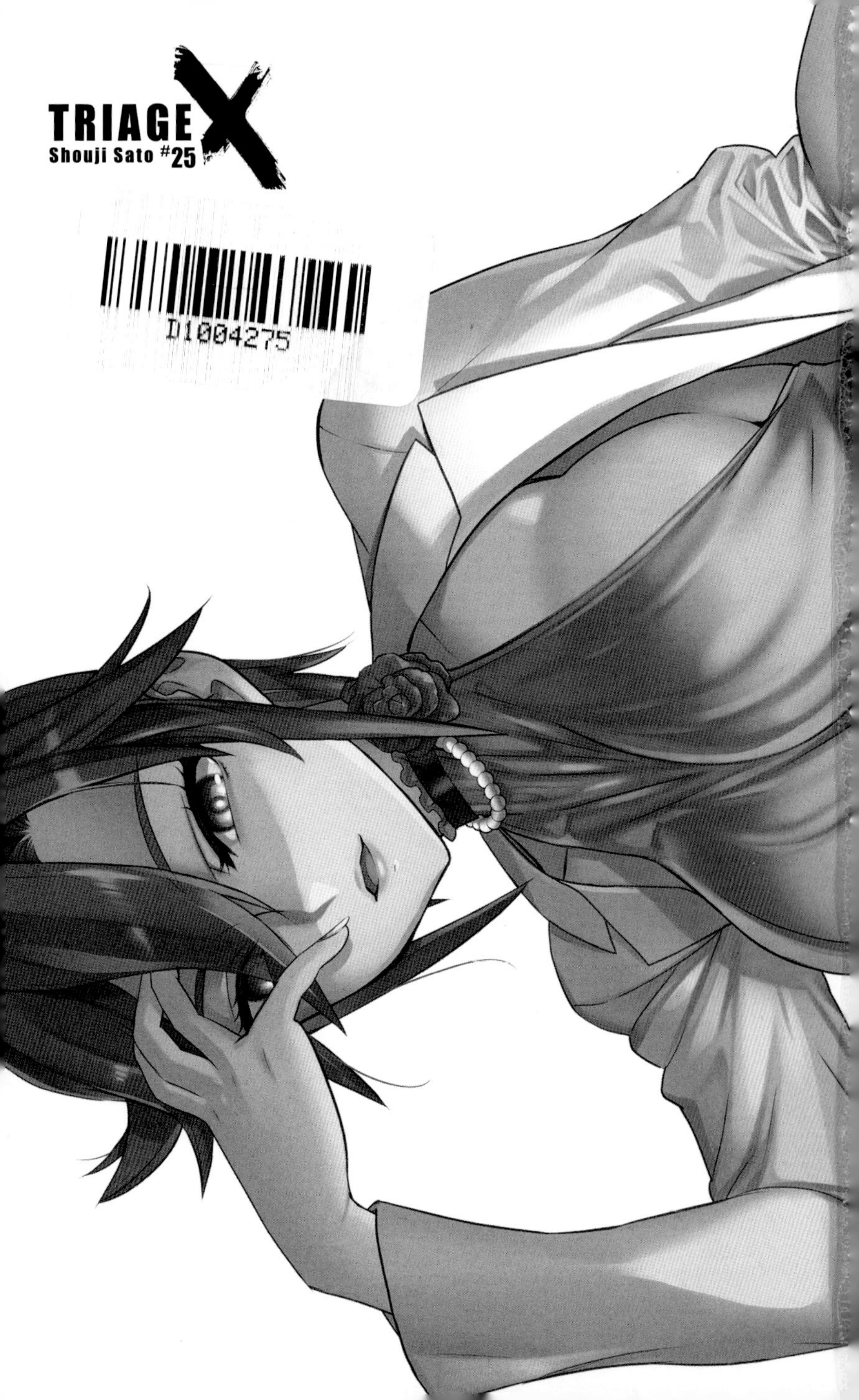

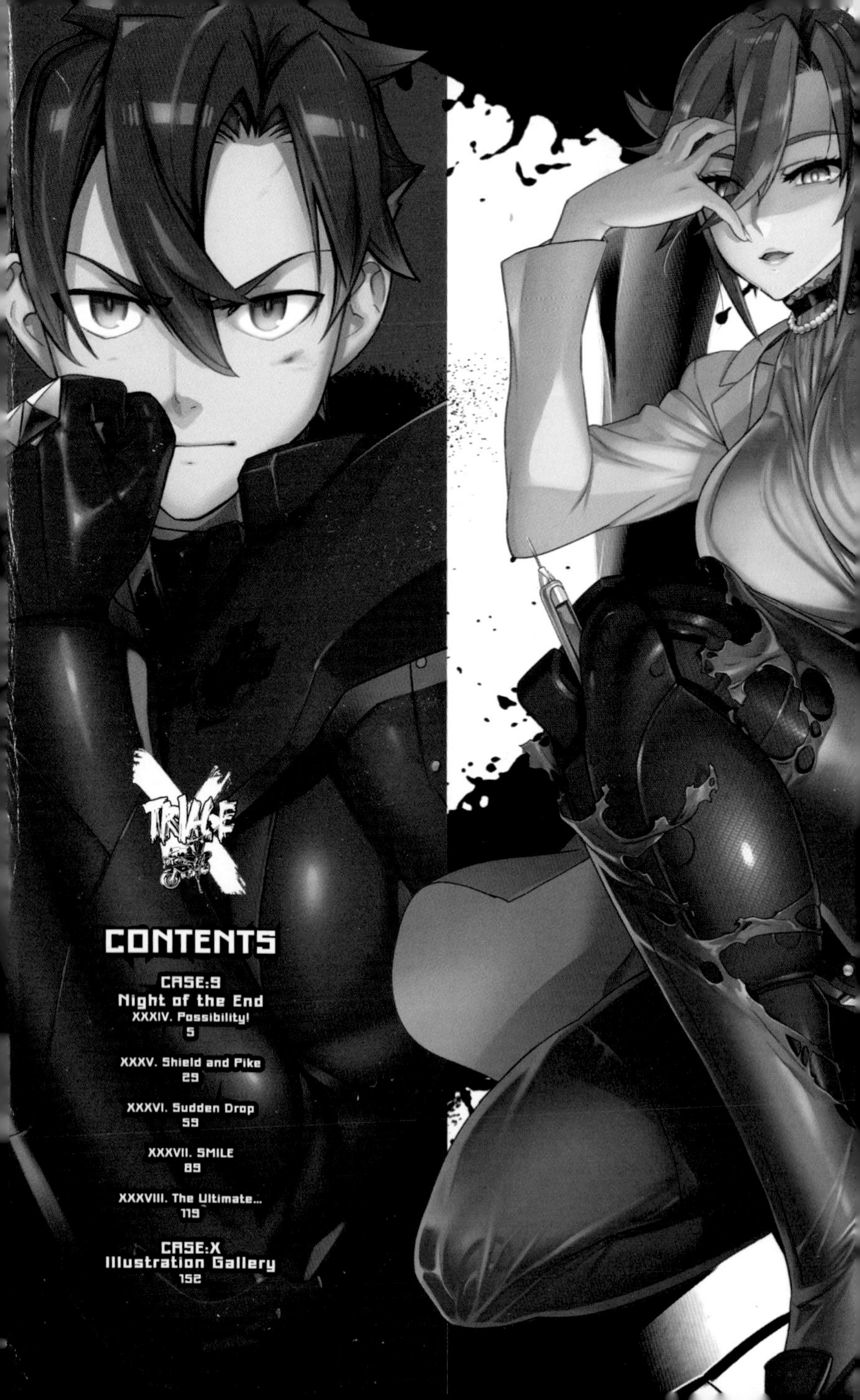

CONTENTS

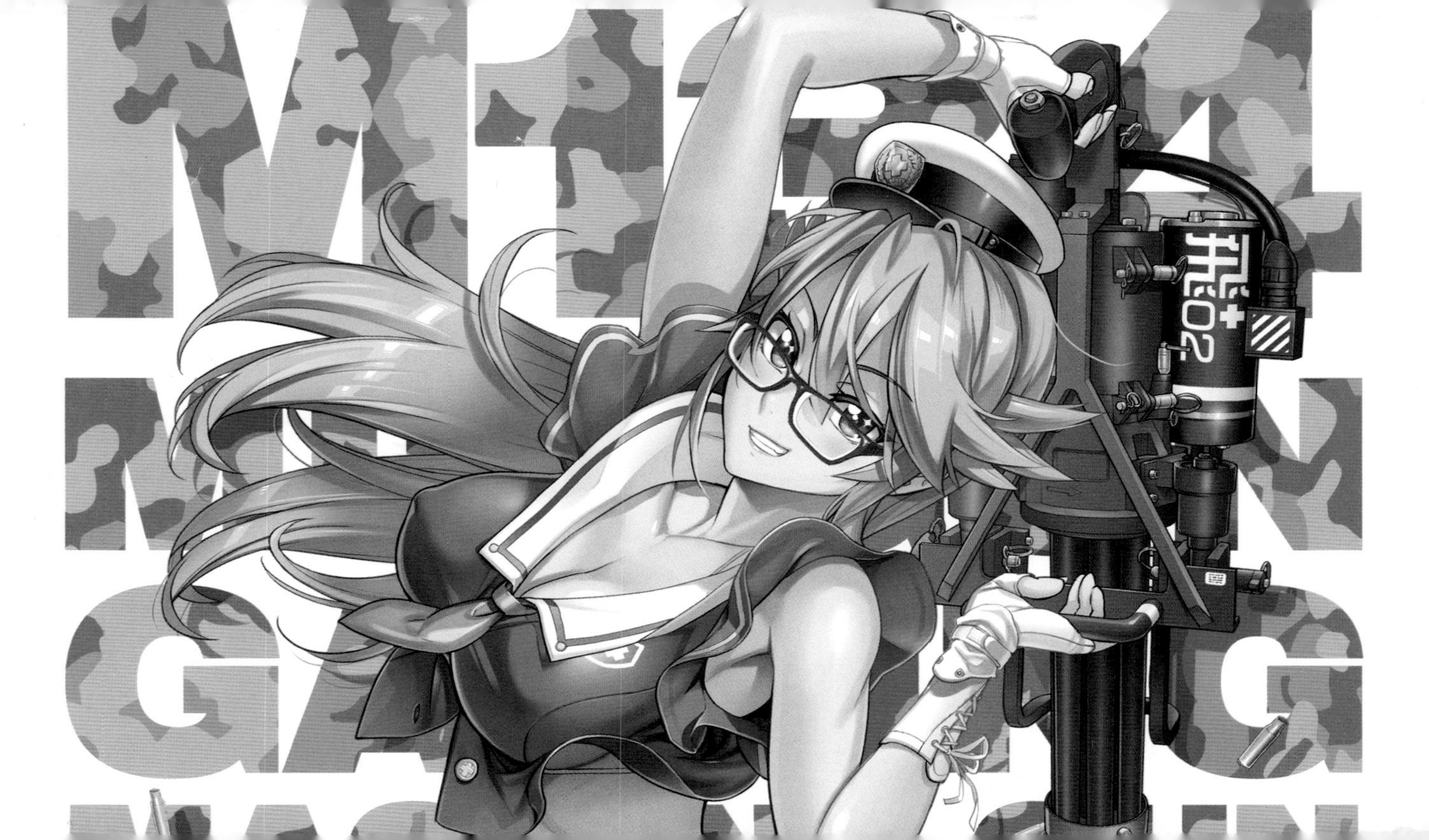

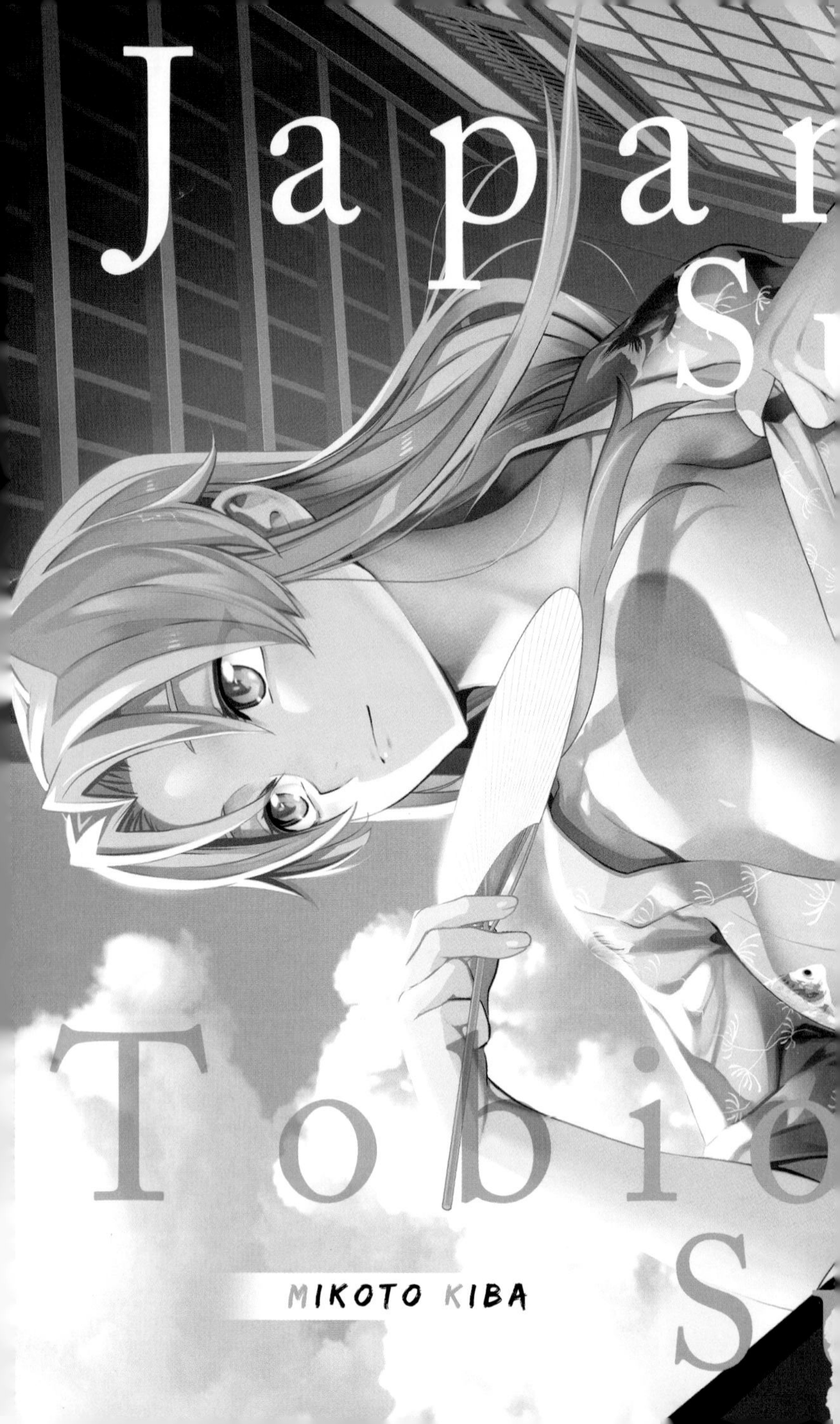
MIKOTO KIBA

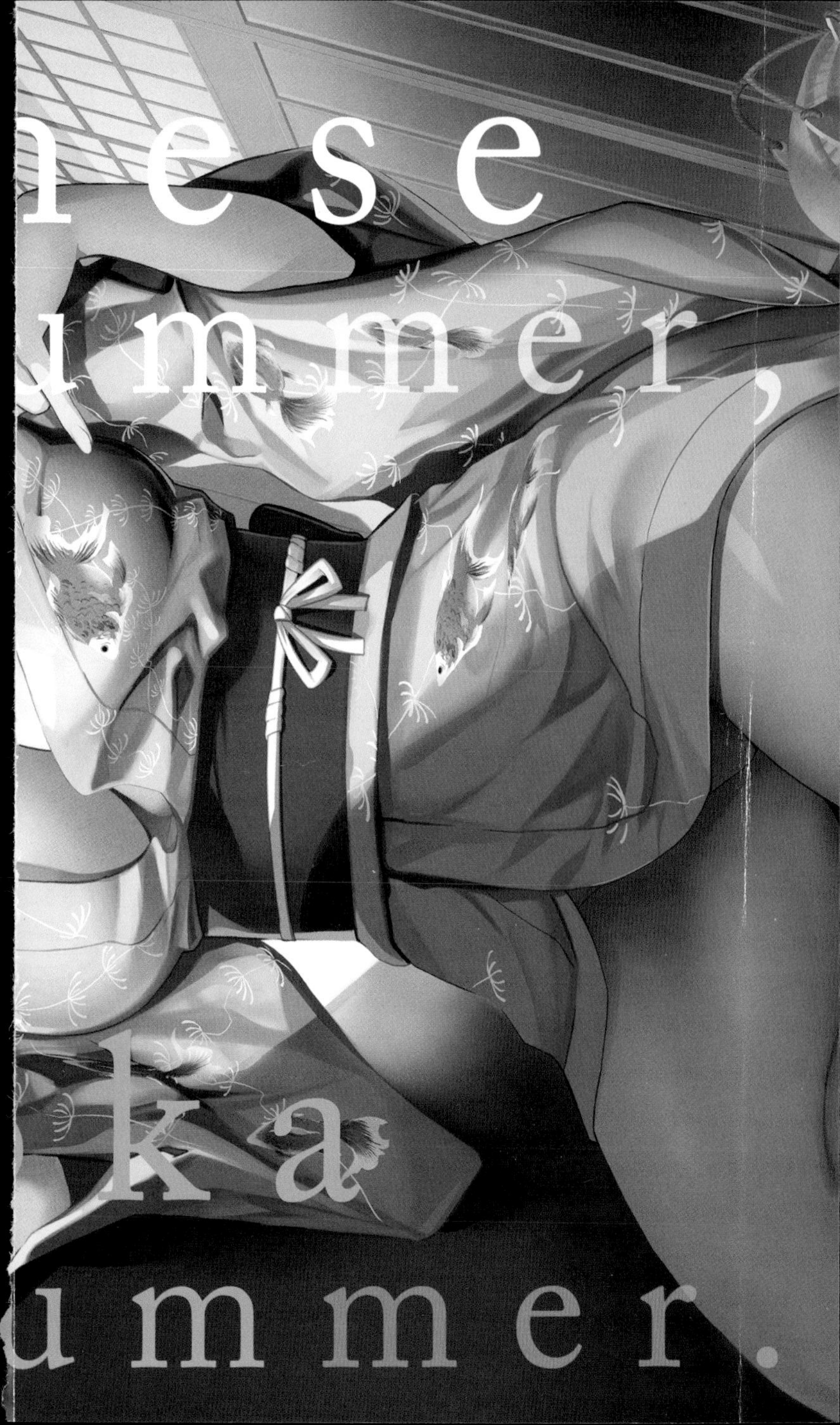
nese
ummer,
ka
ummer.

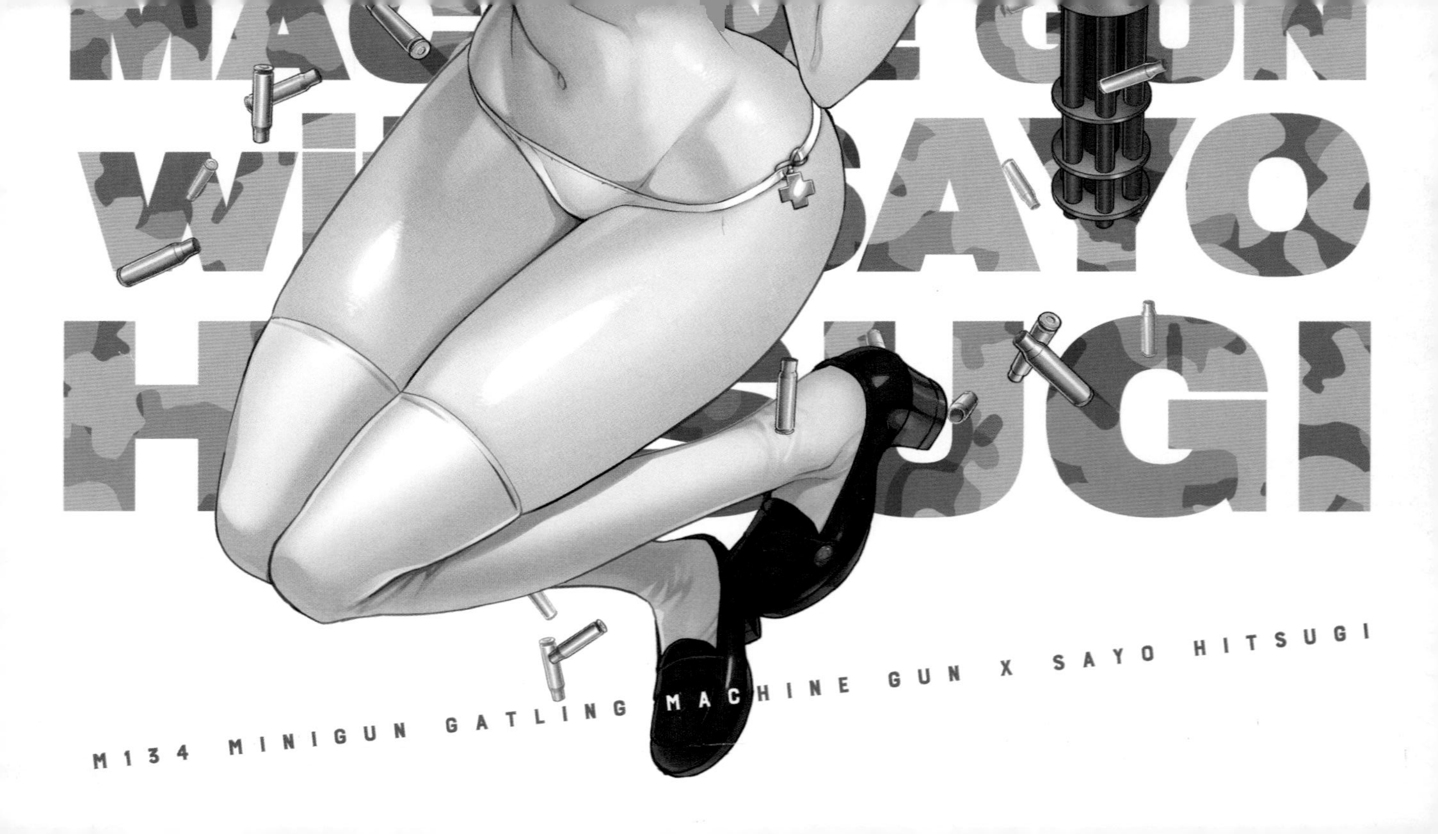
M134 MINIGUN GATLING MACHINE GUN X SAYO HITSUGI

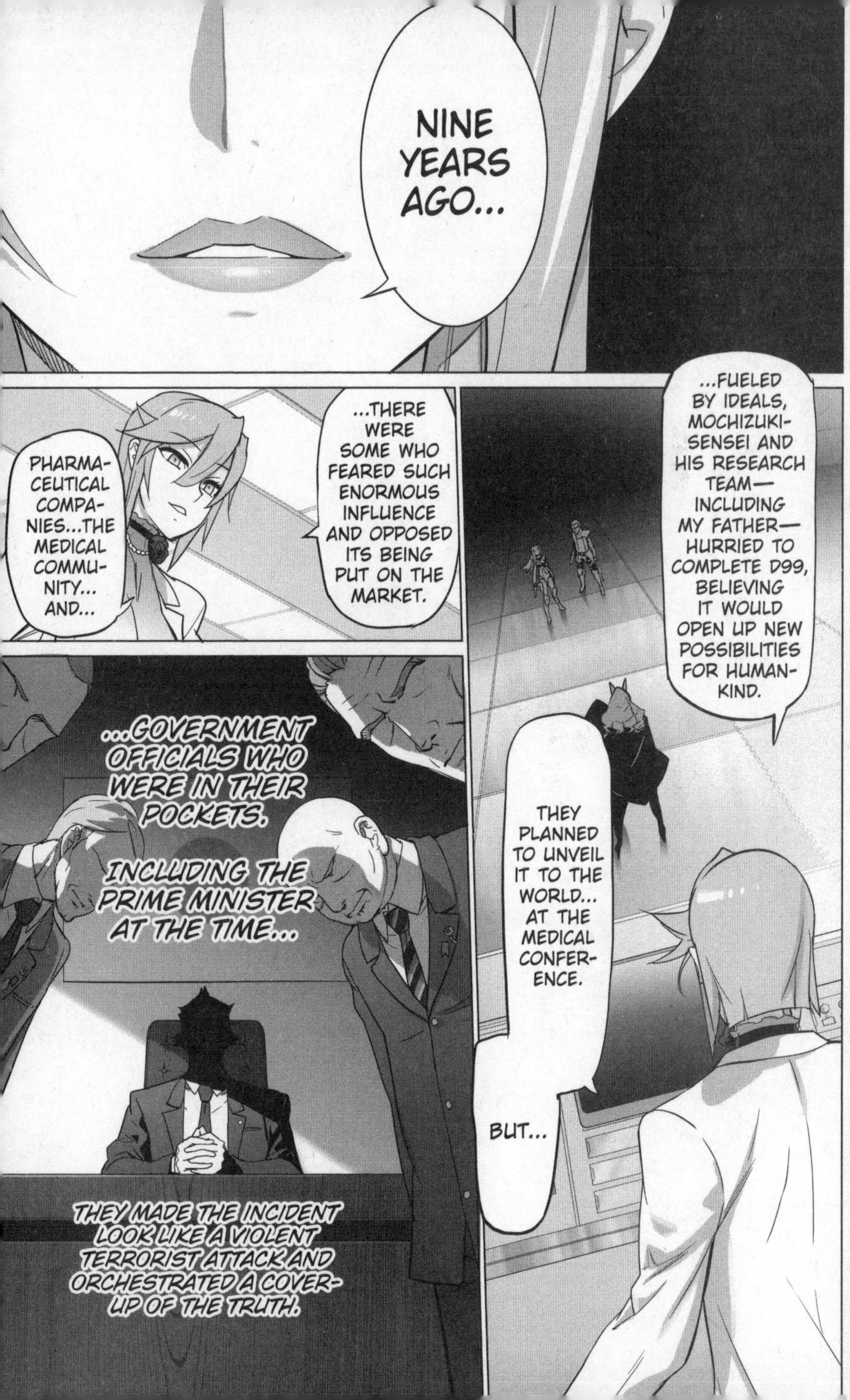
NINE YEARS AGO...
...FUELED BY IDEALS, MOCHIZUKI-SENSEI AND HIS RESEARCH TEAM—INCLUDING MY FATHER—HURRIED TO COMPLETE D99, BELIEVING IT WOULD OPEN UP NEW POSSIBILITIES FOR HUMANKIND.
THEY PLANNED TO UNVEIL IT TO THE WORLD... AT THE MEDICAL CONFERENCE.
BUT...
...THERE WERE SOME WHO FEARED SUCH ENORMOUS INFLUENCE AND OPPOSED ITS BEING PUT ON THE MARKET.
PHARMACEUTICAL COMPANIES...THE MEDICAL COMMUNITY... AND...
...GOVERNMENT OFFICIALS WHO WERE IN THEIR POCKETS.
INCLUDING THE PRIME MINISTER AT THE TIME...
THEY MADE THE INCIDENT LOOK LIKE A VIOLENT TERRORIST ATTACK AND ORCHESTRATED A COVER-UP OF THE TRUTH.

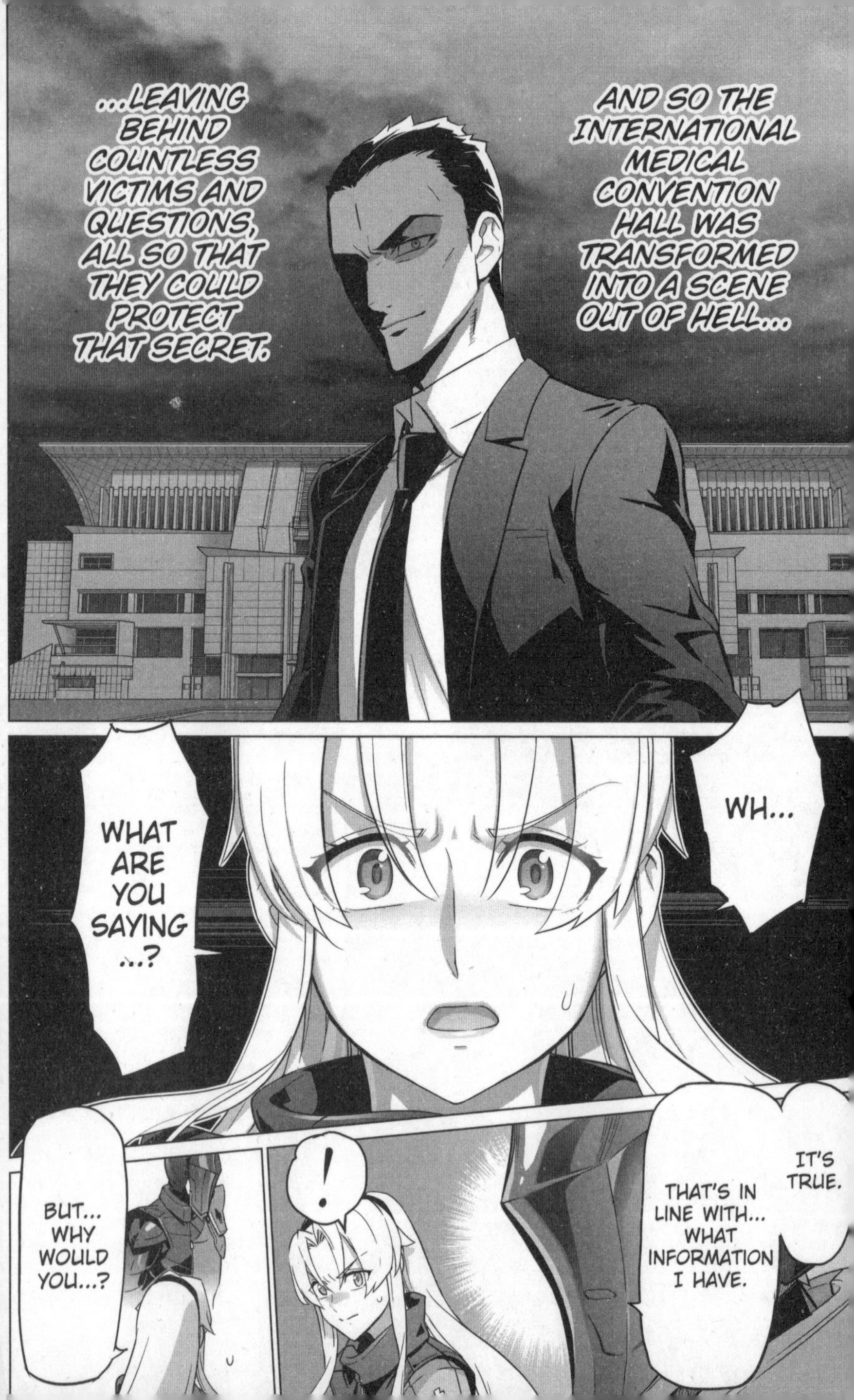
AND SO THE INTERNATIONAL MEDICAL CONVENTION HALL WAS TRANSFORMED INTO A SCENE OUT OF HELL...
...LEAVING BEHIND COUNTLESS VICTIMS AND QUESTIONS, ALL SO THAT THEY COULD PROTECT THAT SECRET.
WH...
WHAT ARE YOU SAYING ...?
IT'S TRUE.
THAT'S IN LINE WITH... WHAT INFORMATION I HAVE.
!
BUT... WHY WOULD YOU...?

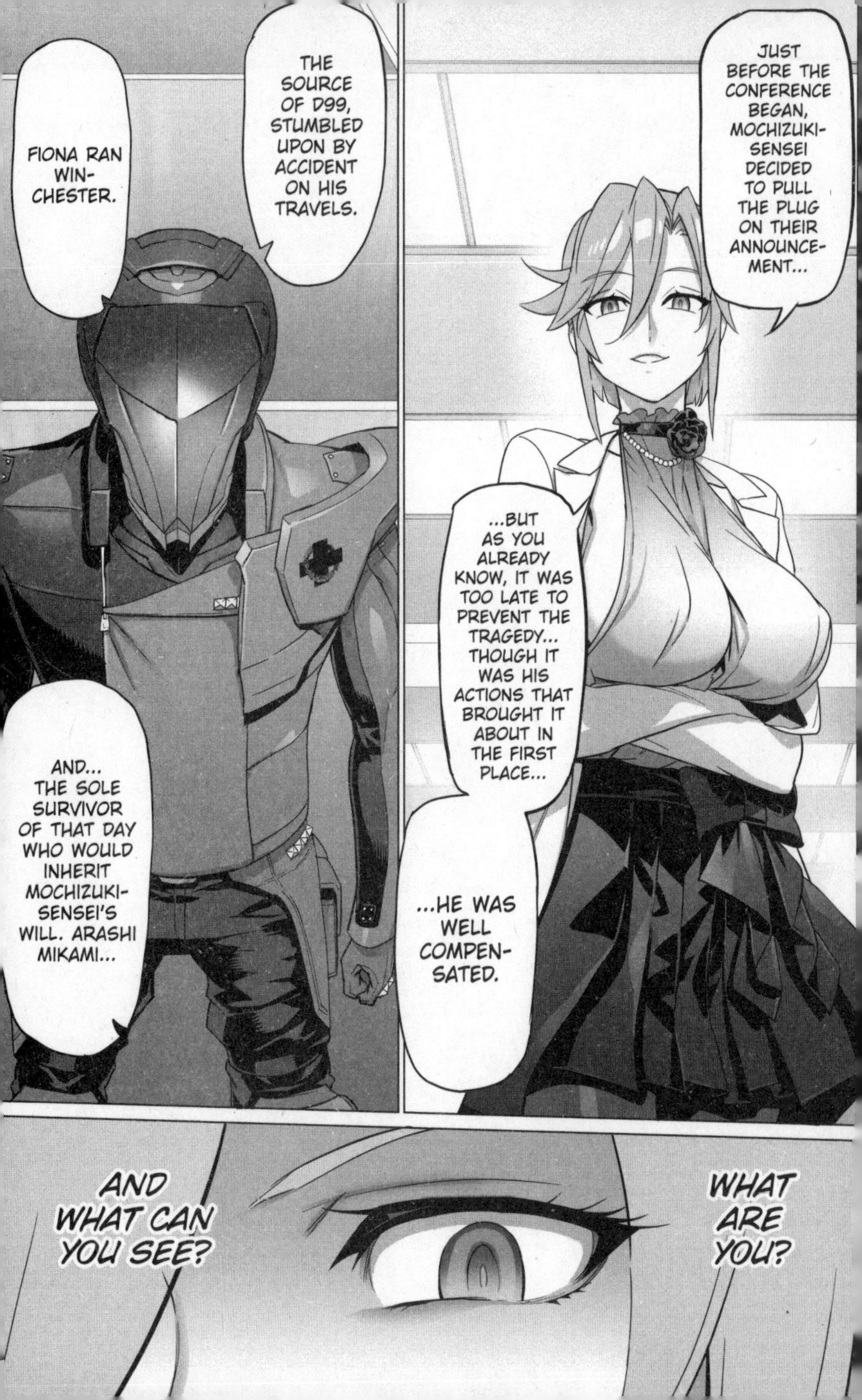
JUST BEFORE THE CONFERENCE BEGAN, MOCHIZUKI-SENSEI DECIDED TO PULL THE PLUG ON THEIR ANNOUNCEMENT...
...BUT AS YOU ALREADY KNOW, IT WAS TOO LATE TO PREVENT THE TRAGEDY... THOUGH IT WAS HIS ACTIONS THAT BROUGHT IT ABOUT IN THE FIRST PLACE...
...HE WAS WELL COMPENSATED.
THE SOURCE OF D99, STUMBLED UPON BY ACCIDENT ON HIS TRAVELS.
FIONA RAN WIN-CHESTER.
AND... THE SOLE SURVIVOR OF THAT DAY WHO WOULD INHERIT MOCHIZUKI-SENSEI'S WILL. ARASHI MIKAMI...
WHAT ARE YOU?
AND WHAT CAN YOU SEE?

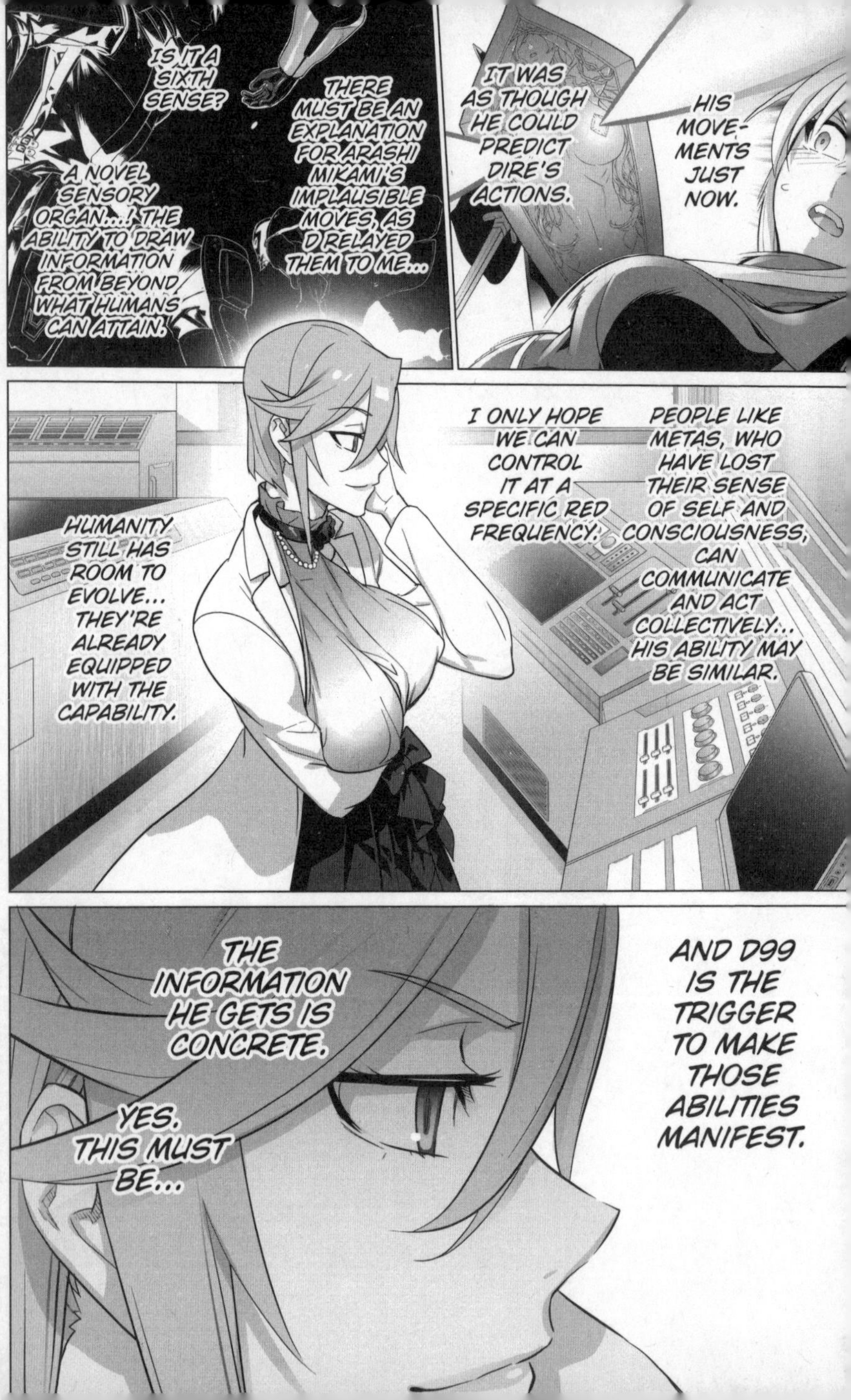
HIS MOVEMENTS JUST NOW.
IT WAS AS THOUGH HE COULD PREDICT DIRE'S ACTIONS.
THERE MUST BE AN EXPLANATION FOR ARASHI MIKAMI'S IMPLAUSIBLE MOVES, AS D RELAYED THEM TO ME...
IS IT A SIXTH SENSE?
A NOVEL SENSORY ORGAN...! THE ABILITY TO DRAW INFORMATION FROM BEYOND WHAT HUMANS CAN ATTAIN.
PEOPLE LIKE METAS, WHO HAVE LOST THEIR SENSE OF SELF AND CONSCIOUSNESS, CAN COMMUNICATE AND ACT COLLECTIVELY... HIS ABILITY MAY BE SIMILAR.
I ONLY HOPE WE CAN CONTROL IT AT A SPECIFIC RED FREQUENCY.
HUMANITY STILL HAS ROOM TO EVOLVE... THEY'RE ALREADY EQUIPPED WITH THE CAPABILITY.
AND D99 IS THE TRIGGER TO MAKE THOSE ABILITIES MANIFEST.
THE INFORMATION HE GETS IS CONCRETE.
YES. THIS MUST BE...

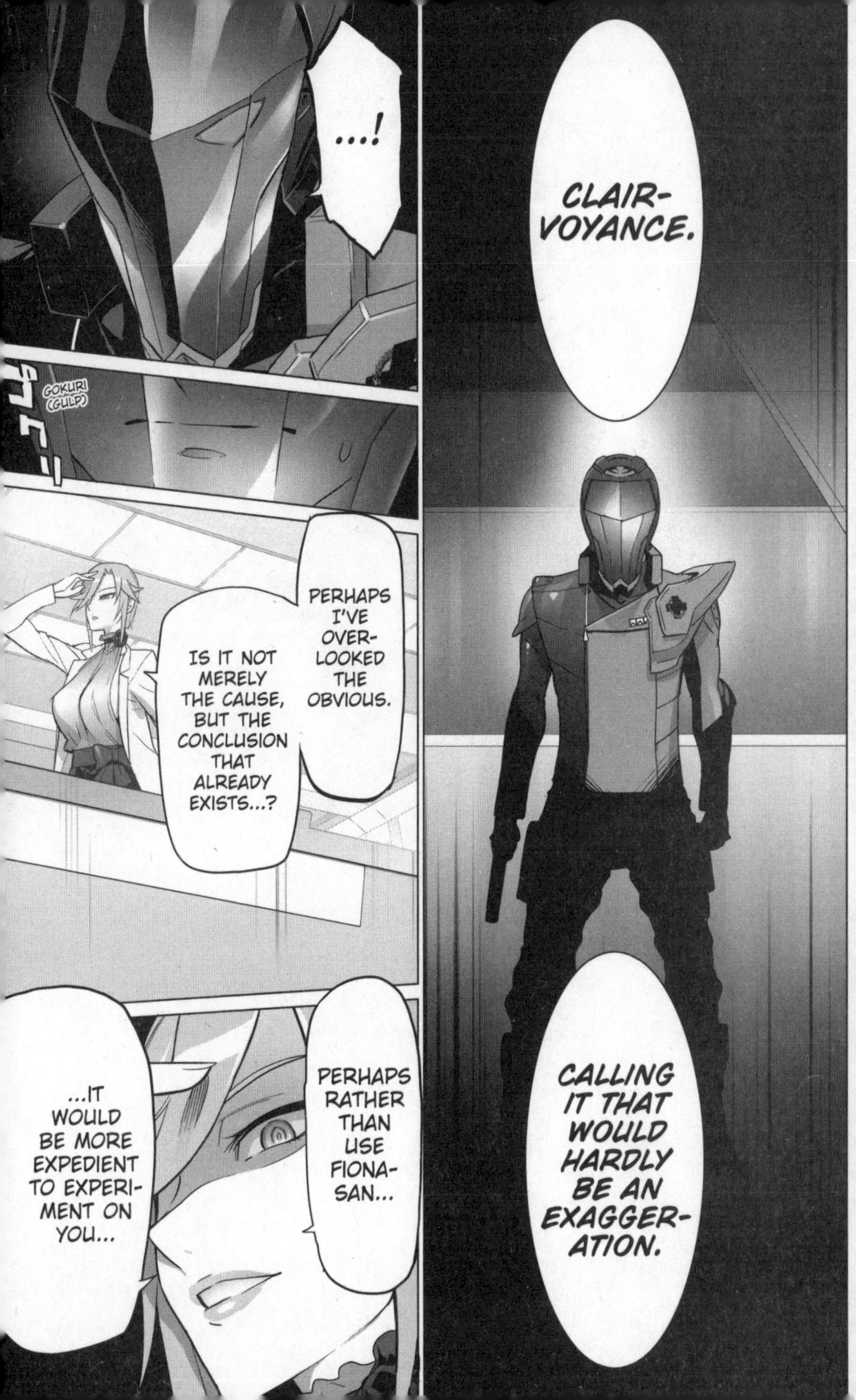
CLAIR-VOYANCE.
CALLING IT THAT WOULD HARDLY BE AN EXAGGERATION.
...!
GOKURI (GULP)
PERHAPS I'VE OVERLOOKED THE OBVIOUS.
IS IT NOT MERELY THE CAUSE, BUT THE CONCLUSION THAT ALREADY EXISTS...?
PERHAPS RATHER THAN USE FIONA-SAN...
...IT WOULD BE MORE EXPEDIENT TO EXPERIMENT ON YOU...

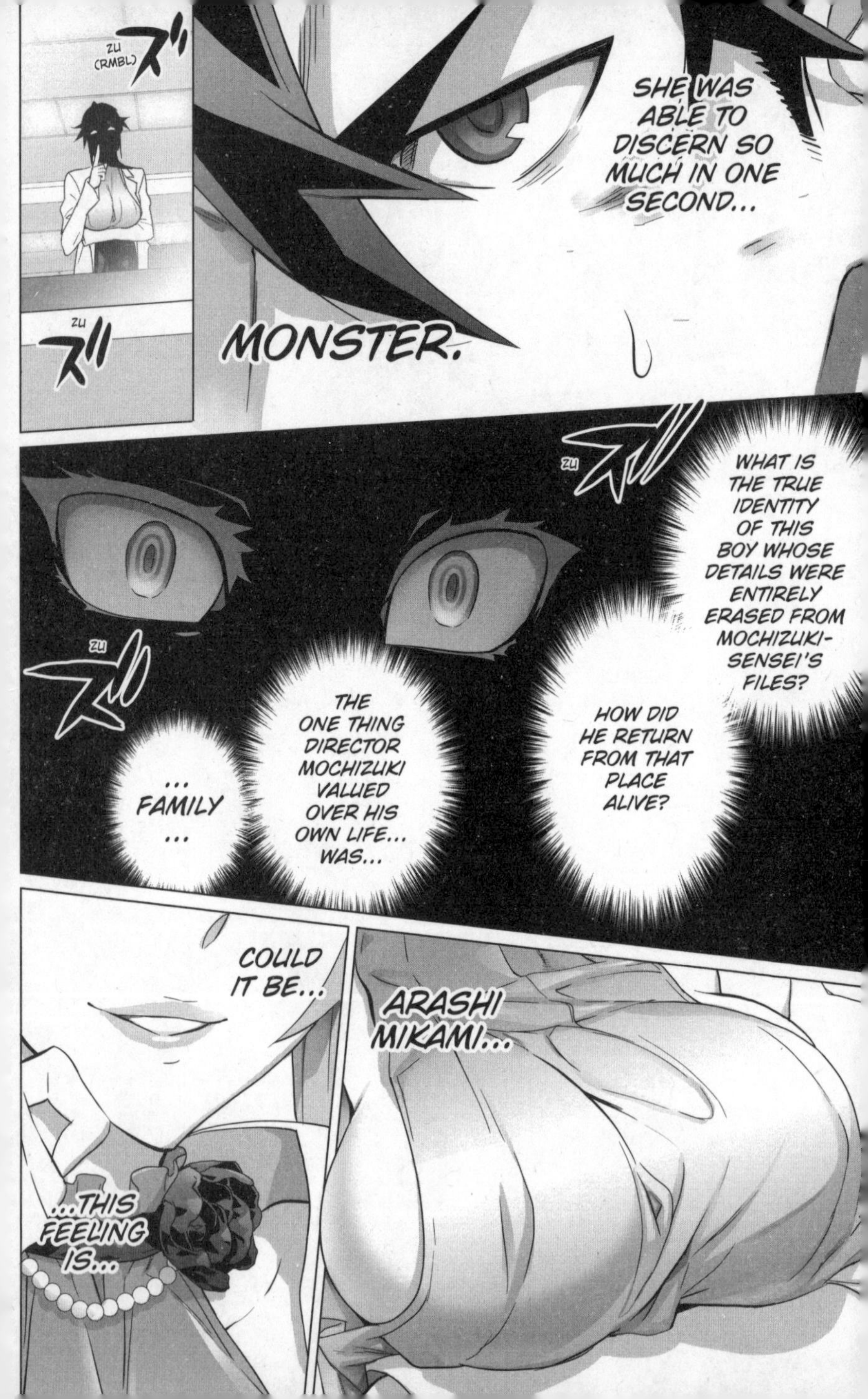
SHE WAS ABLE TO DISCERN SO MUCH IN ONE SECOND...
MONSTER.
ZU (RMBL)
ZU
ZU
WHAT IS THE TRUE IDENTITY OF THIS BOY WHOSE DETAILS WERE ENTIRELY ERASED FROM MOCHIZUKI-SENSEI'S FILES?
HOW DID HE RETURN FROM THAT PLACE ALIVE?
THE ONE THING DIRECTOR MOCHIZUKI VALUED OVER HIS OWN LIFE... WAS...
ZU
... FAMILY ...
ARASHI MIKAMI...
COULD IT BE...
...THIS FEELING IS...

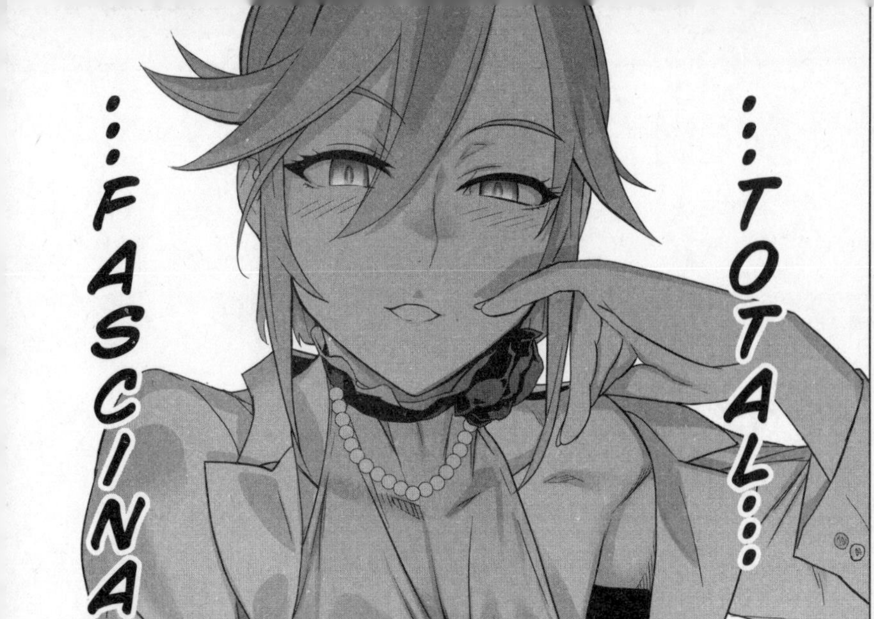
...TOTAL...
...FASCINATION?♥
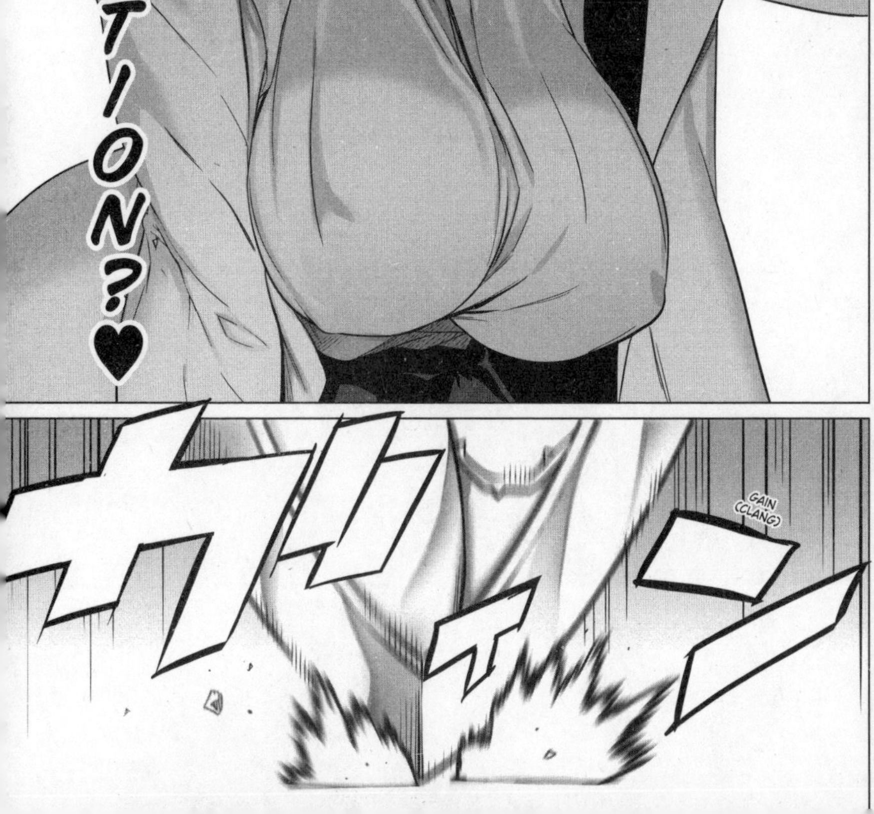
GAIN
(CLANG)

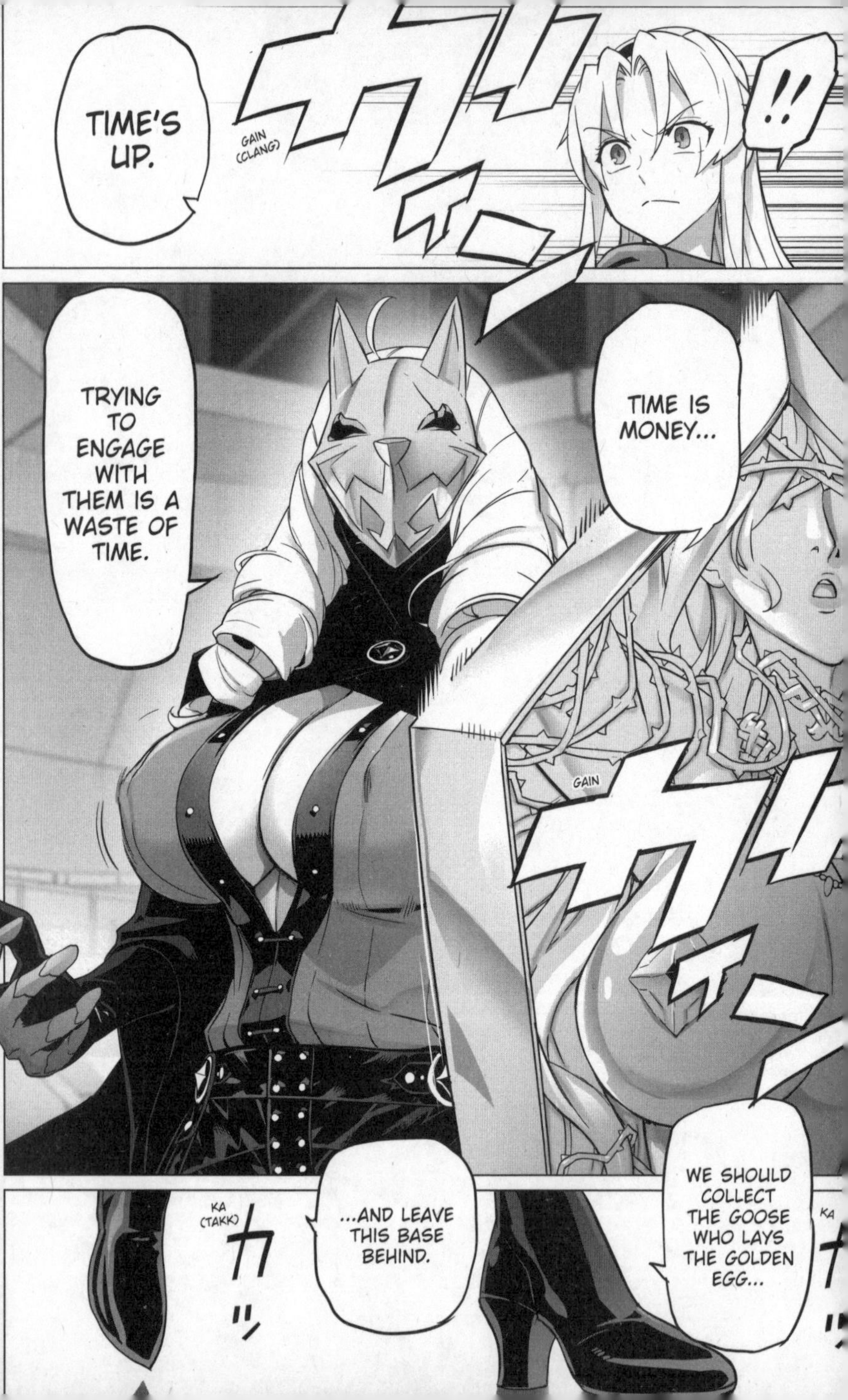
!!
GAIN (CLANG)
TIME'S UP.
TIME IS MONEY...
GAIN
TRYING TO ENGAGE WITH THEM IS A WASTE OF TIME.
KA
WE SHOULD COLLECT THE GOOSE WHO LAYS THE GOLDEN EGG...
...AND LEAVE THIS BASE BEHIND.
KA (TAKK)

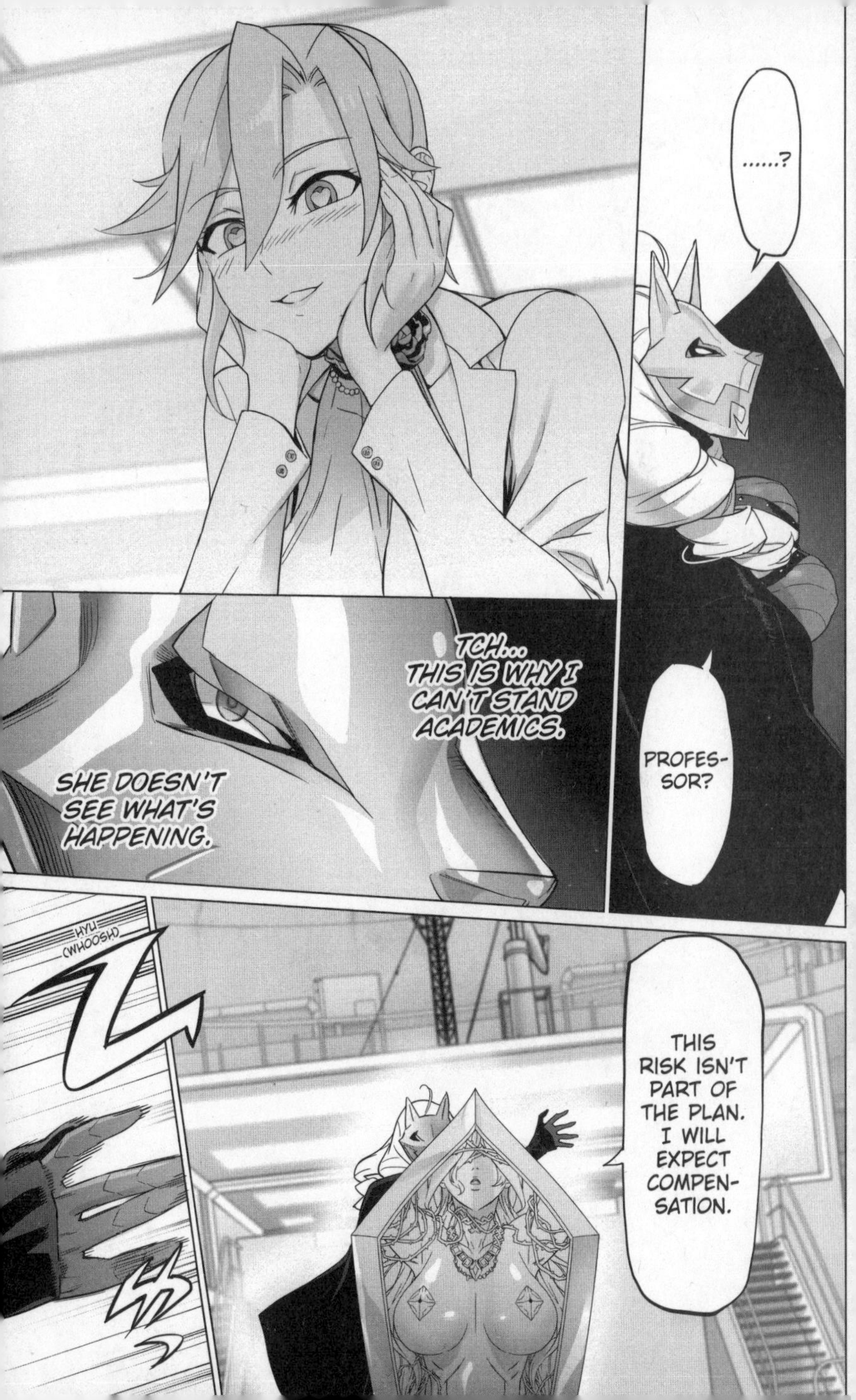
......?
PROFES-SOR?
TCH... THIS IS WHY I CAN'T STAND ACADEMICS.
SHE DOESN'T SEE WHAT'S HAPPENING.
THIS RISK ISN'T PART OF THE PLAN. I WILL EXPECT COMPEN-SATION.
HYU
(WHOOSH)

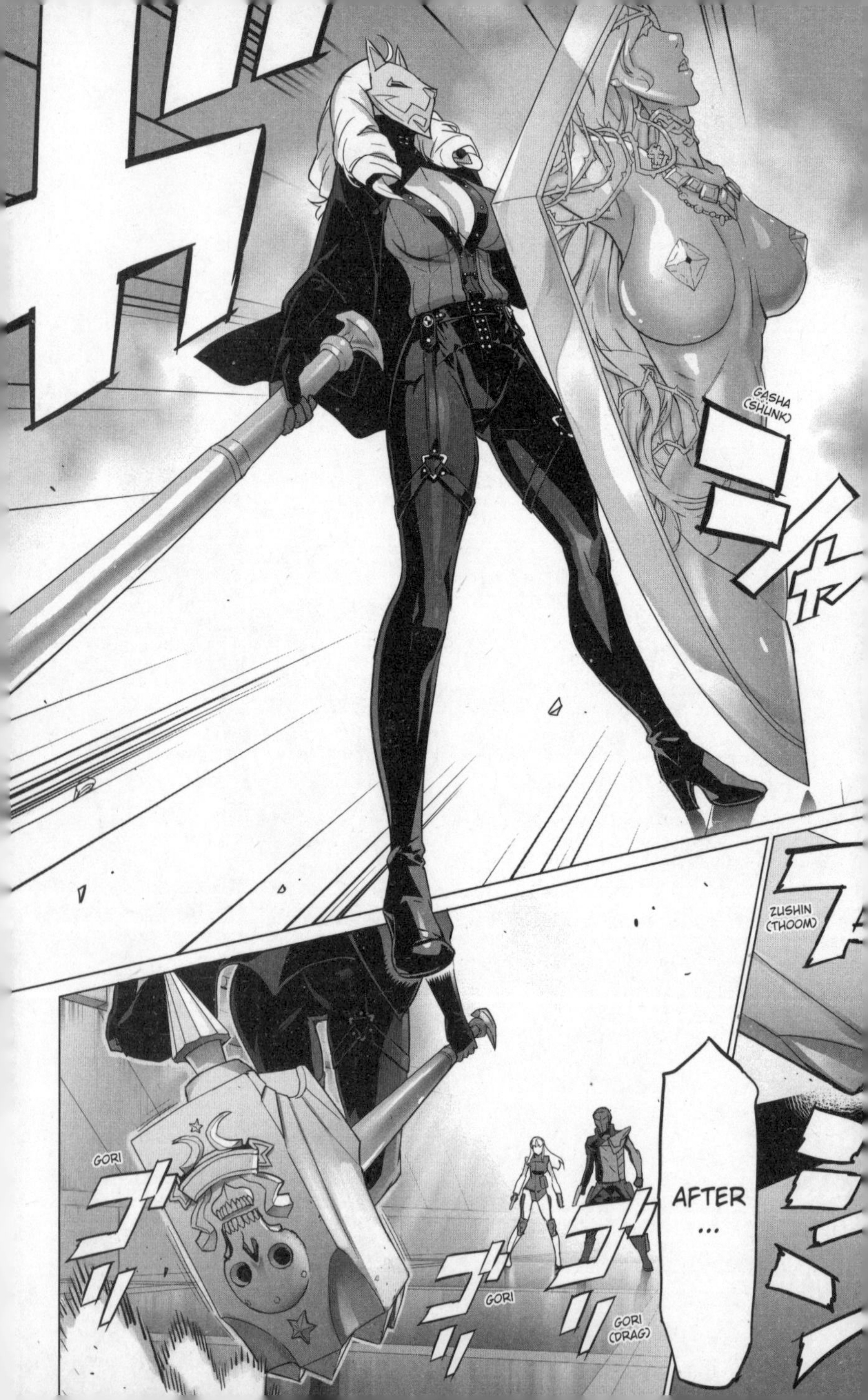
GASHA (SHUNK)
ZUSHIN (THOOM)
AFTER ...
GORI (DRAG)
GORI
GORI

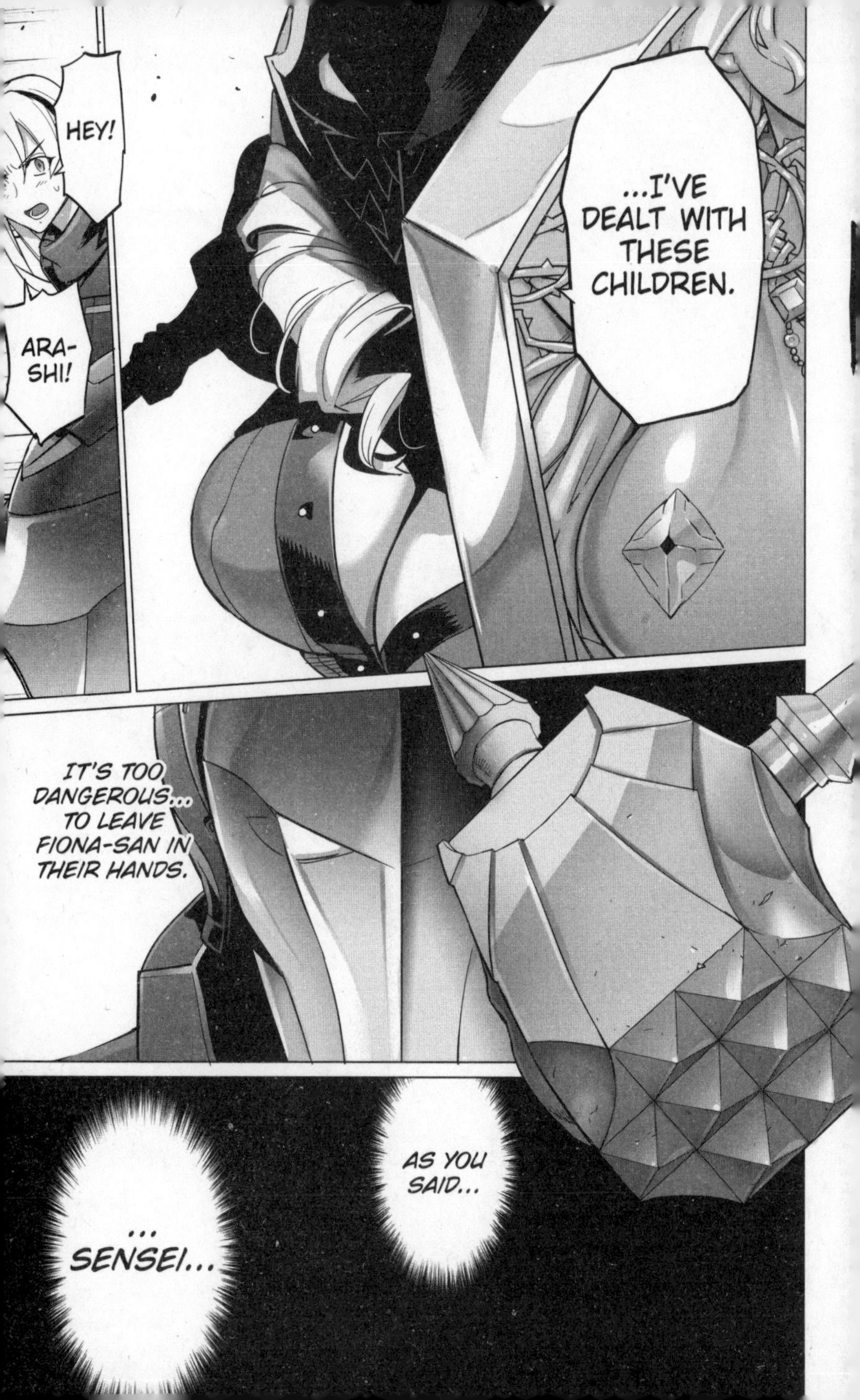
...I'VE DEALT WITH THESE CHILDREN.
HEY!
ARA-SHI!
IT'S TOO DANGEROUS... TO LEAVE FIONA-SAN IN THEIR HANDS.
AS YOU SAID...
...SENSEI...

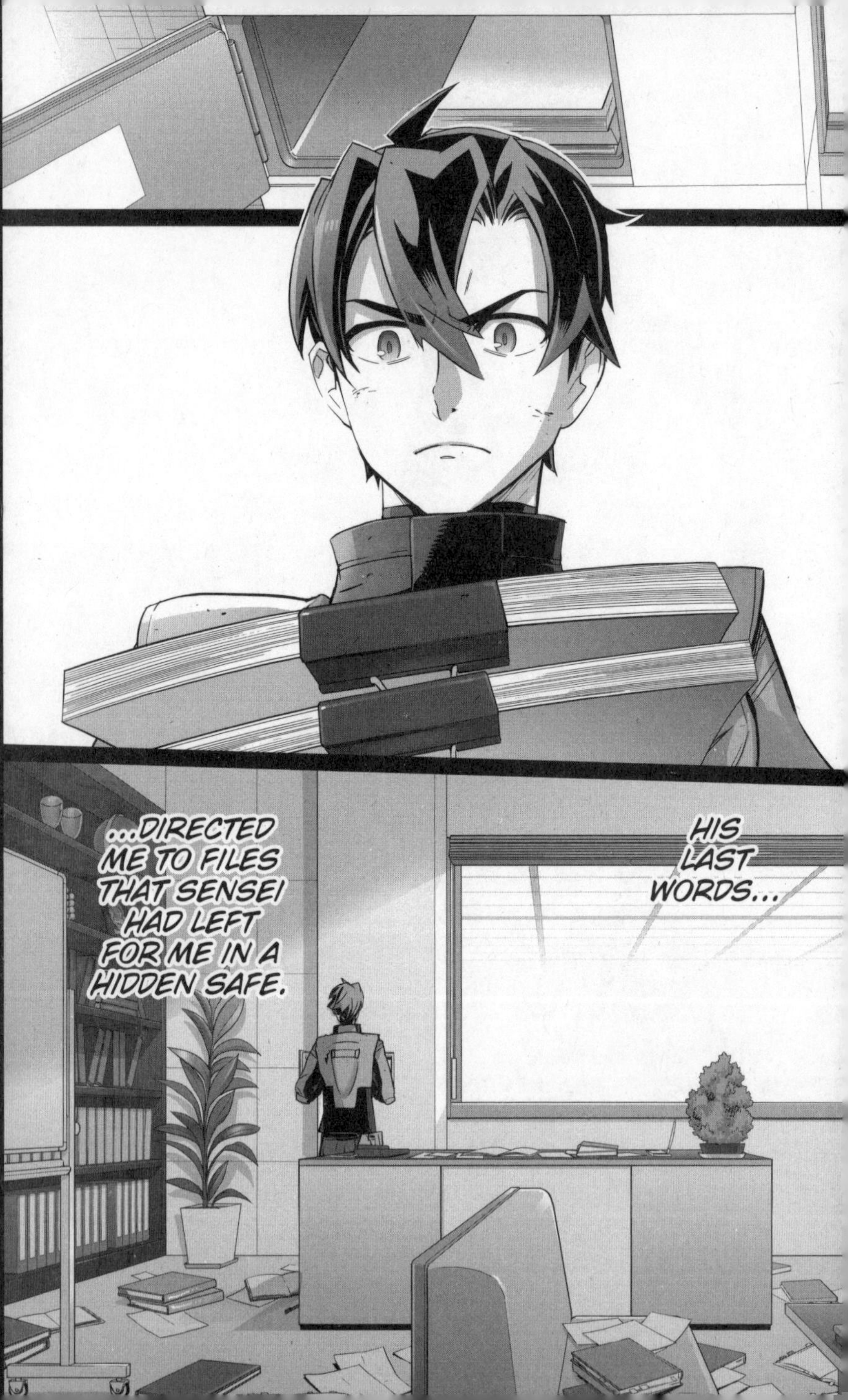
HIS LAST WORDS...
...DIRECTED ME TO FILES THAT SENSEI HAD LEFT FOR ME IN A HIDDEN SAFE.

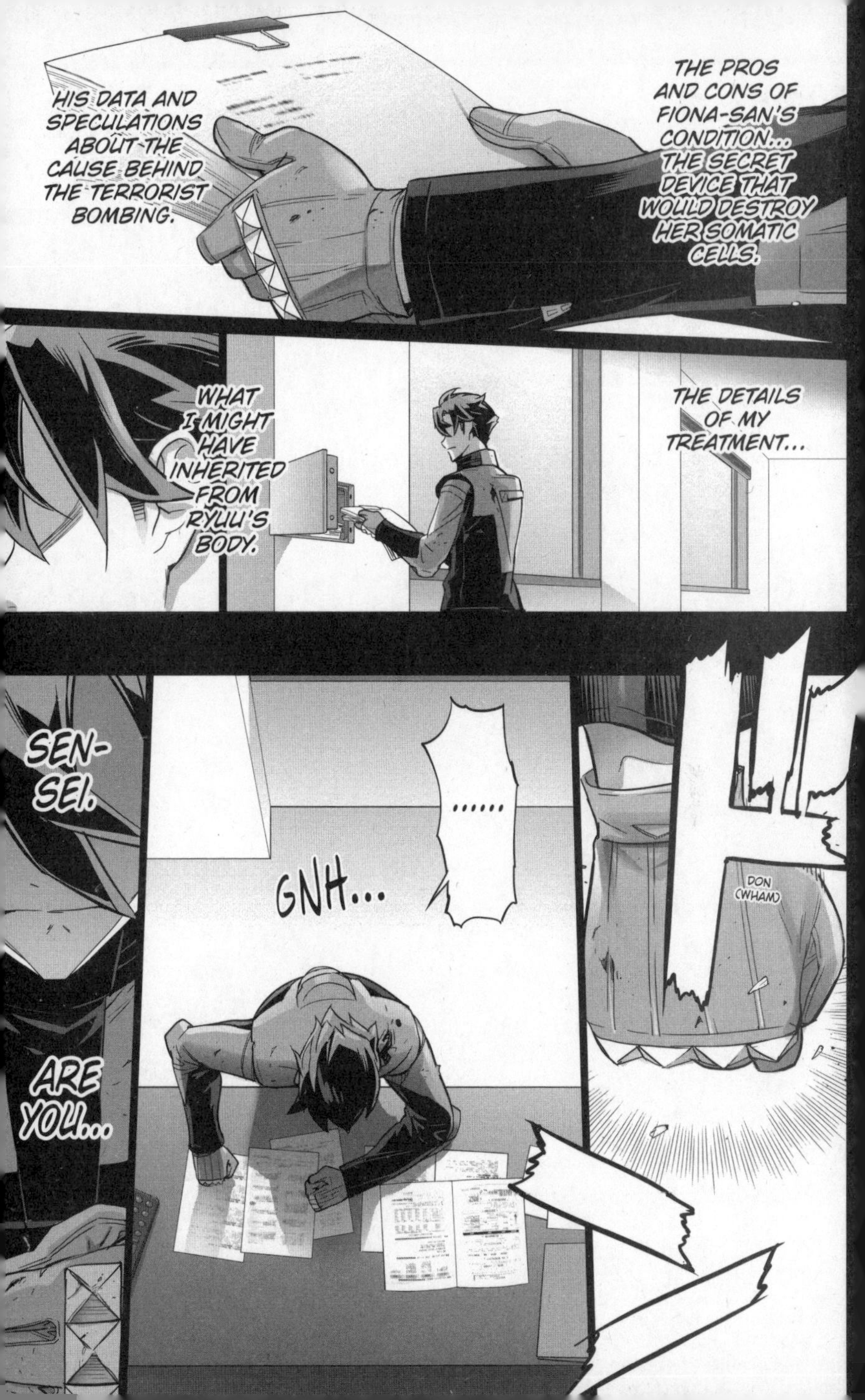
THE PROS AND CONS OF FIONA-SAN'S CONDITION... THE SECRET DEVICE THAT WOULD DESTROY HER SOMATIC CELLS.
HIS DATA AND SPECULATIONS ABOUT THE CAUSE BEHIND THE TERRORIST BOMBING.
THE DETAILS OF MY TREATMENT...
WHAT I MIGHT HAVE INHERITED FROM RYUU'S BODY.
DON (WHAM)
......
GNH...
SEN-SEI.
ARE YOU...

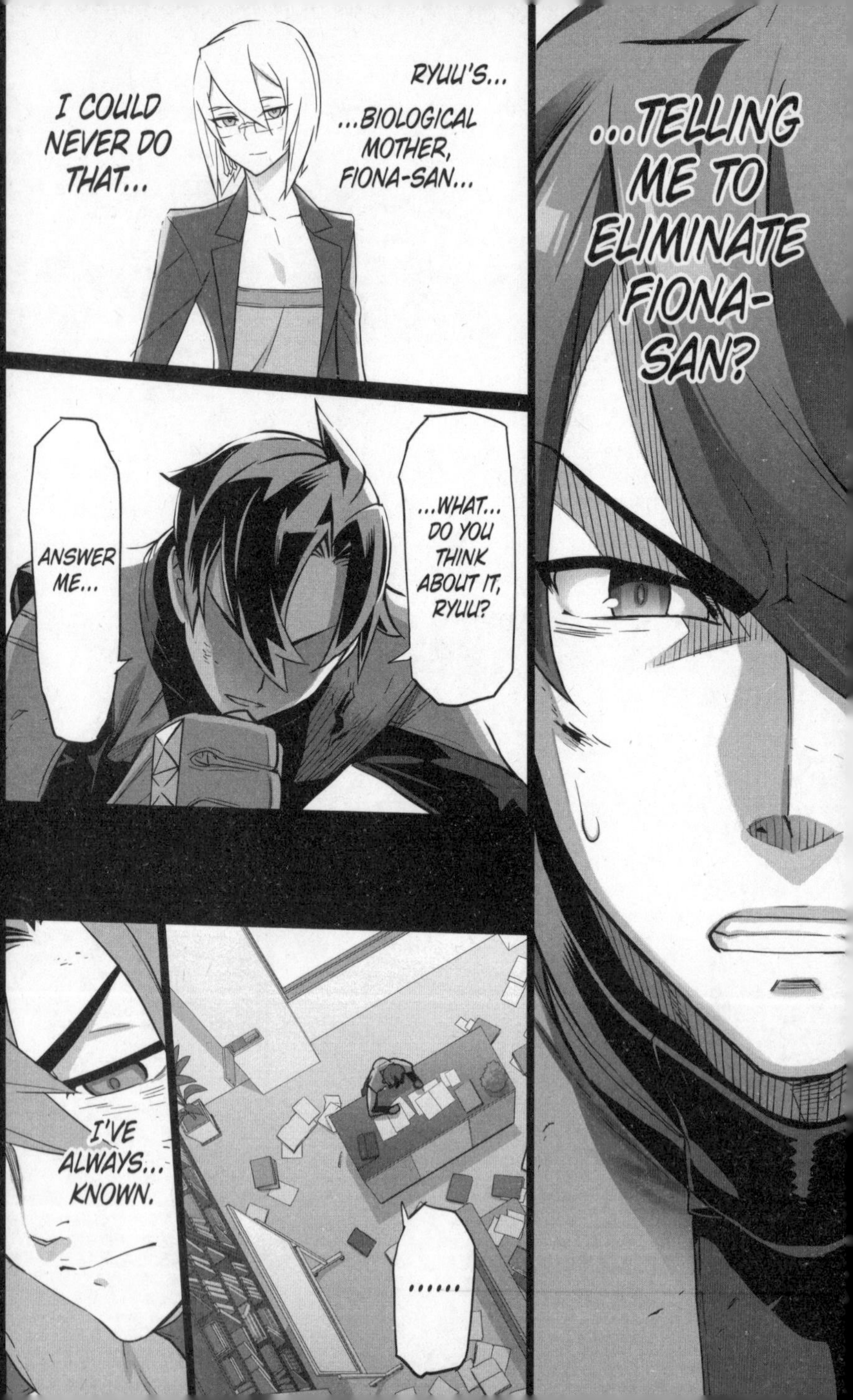
...TELLING ME TO ELIMINATE FIONA-SAN?
RYUU'S...
...BIOLOGICAL MOTHER, FIONA-SAN...
I COULD NEVER DO THAT...
...WHAT... DO YOU THINK ABOUT IT, RYUU?
ANSWER ME...
......
I'VE ALWAYS... KNOWN.

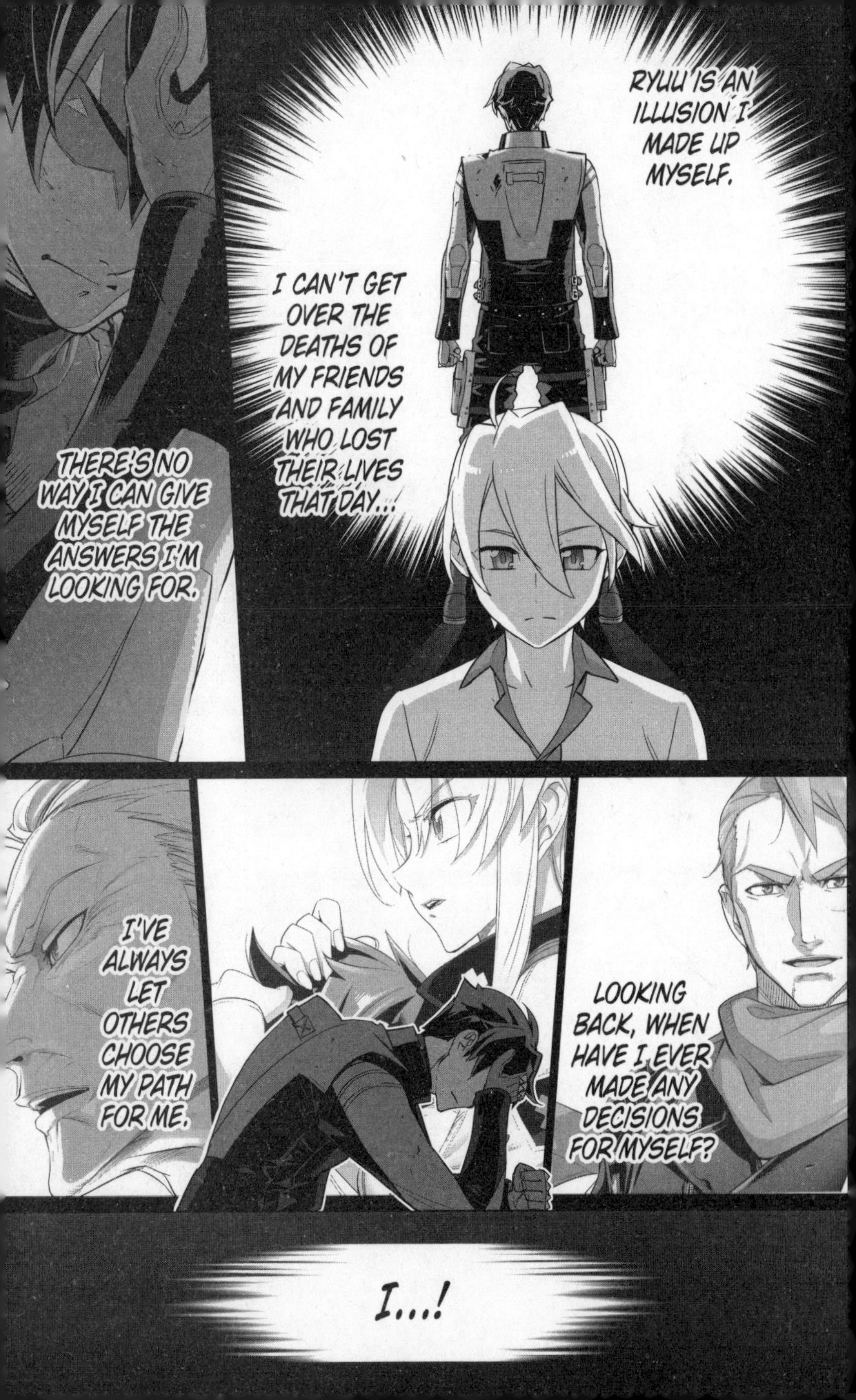
RYUU IS AN ILLUSION I MADE UP MYSELF.
I CAN'T GET OVER THE DEATHS OF MY FRIENDS AND FAMILY WHO LOST THEIR LIVES THAT DAY...
THERE'S NO WAY I CAN GIVE MYSELF THE ANSWERS I'M LOOKING FOR.
LOOKING BACK, WHEN HAVE I EVER MADE ANY DECISIONS FOR MYSELF?
I'VE ALWAYS LET OTHERS CHOOSE MY PATH FOR ME.
I...!

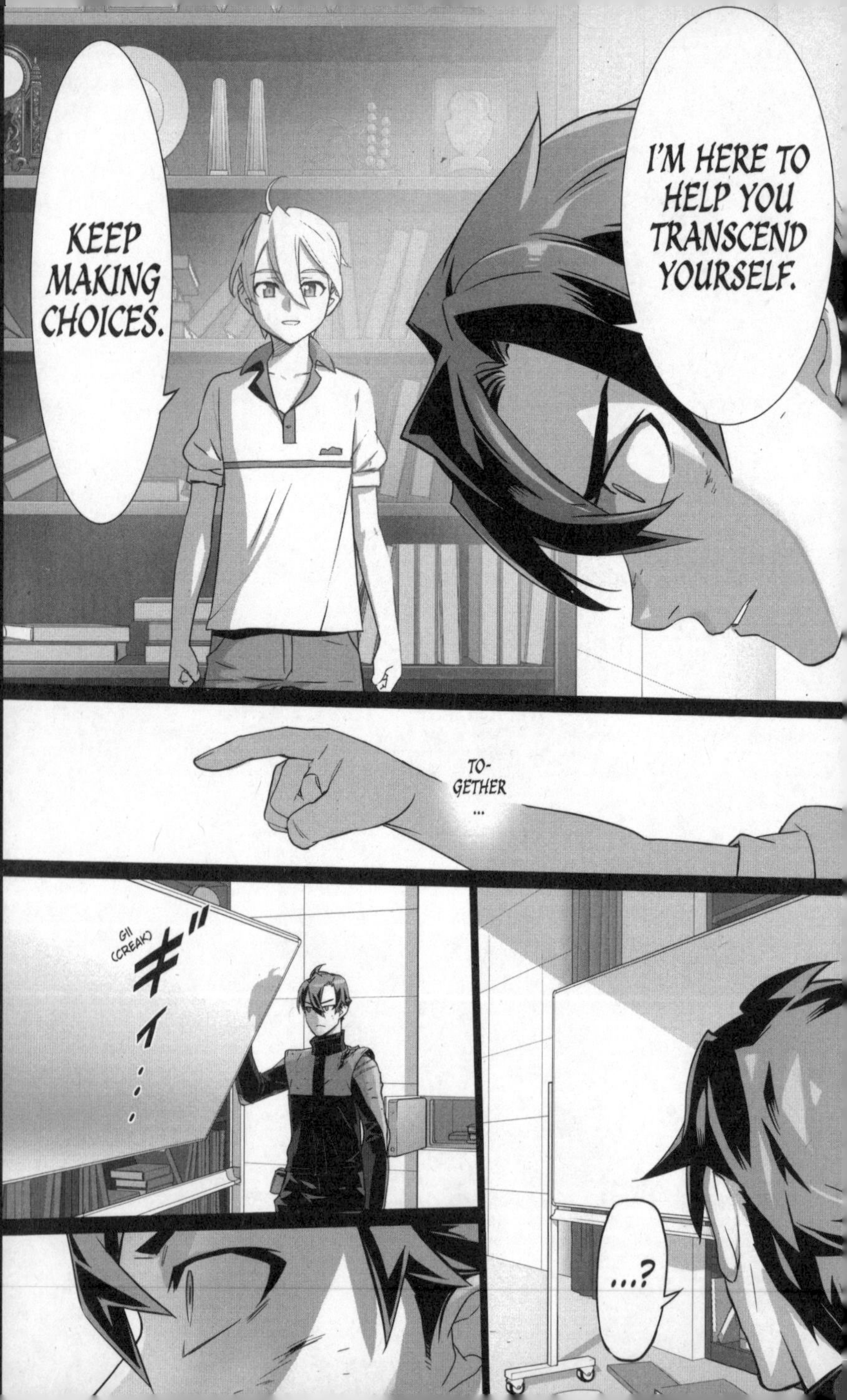
I'M HERE TO HELP YOU TRANSCEND YOURSELF.
KEEP MAKING CHOICES.
TO-GETHER ...
...?
GII (CREAK)

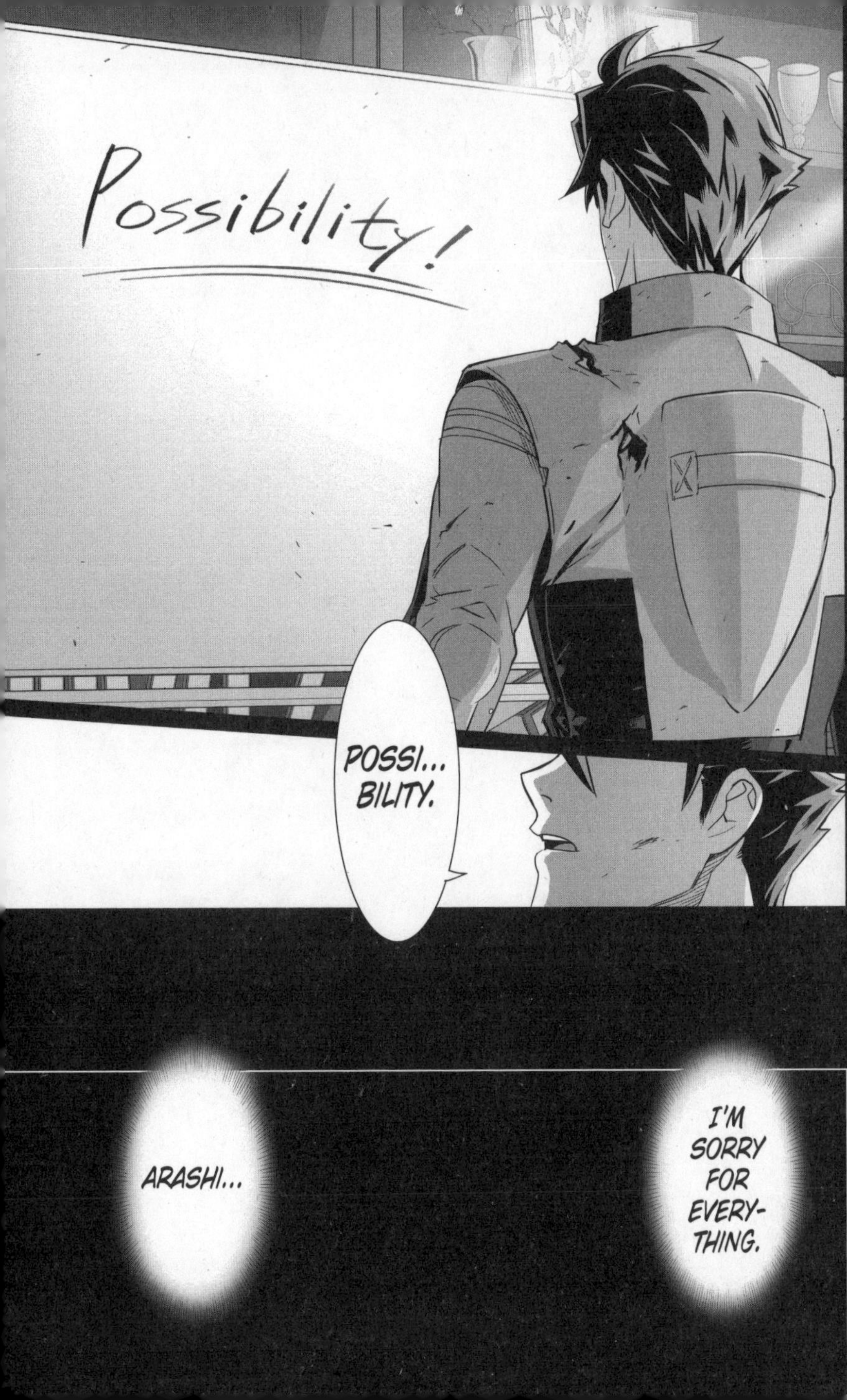
Possibility!
POSSI... BILITY.
I'M SORRY FOR EVERY-THING.
ARASHI...

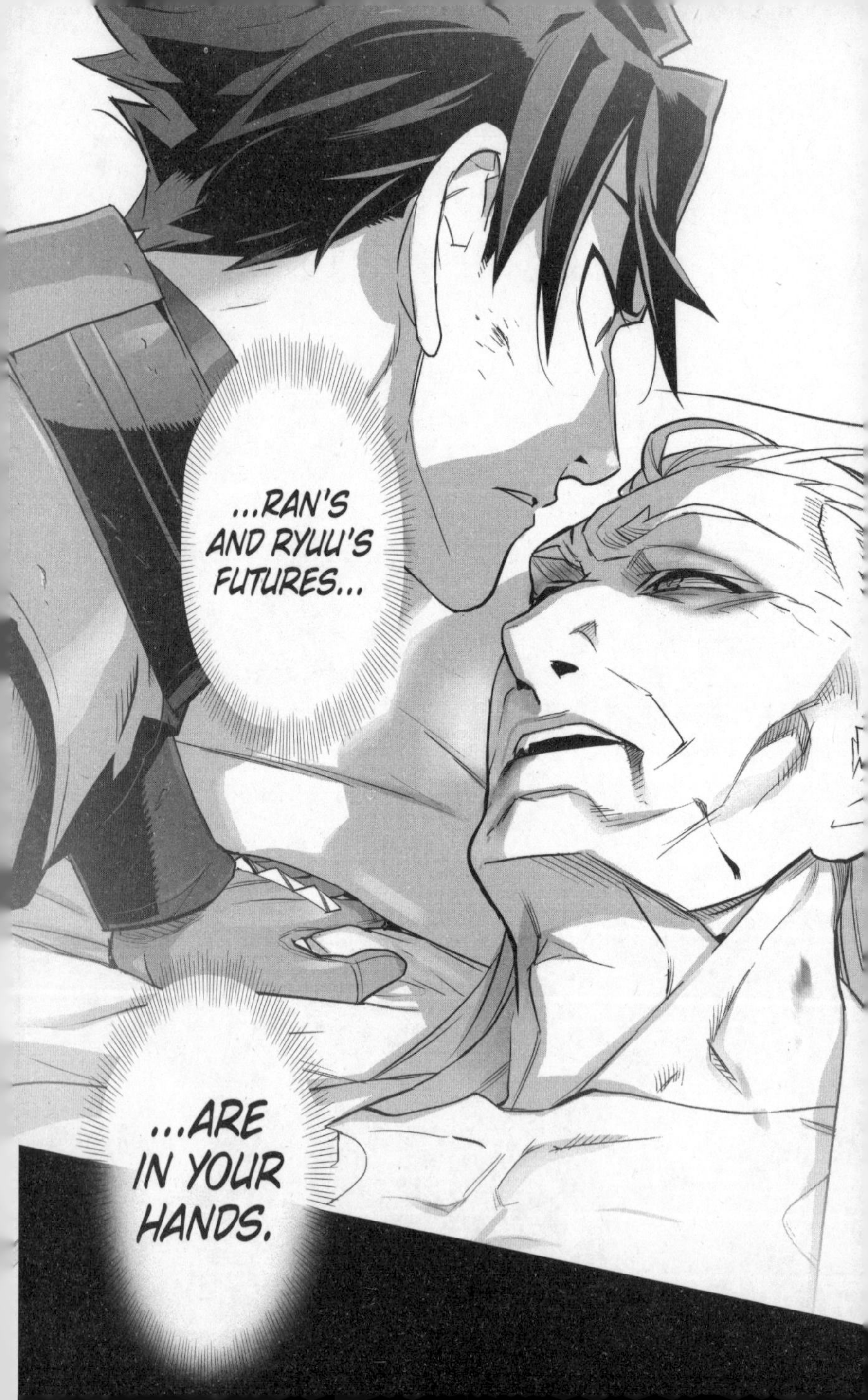
...RAN'S AND RYUU'S FUTURES...
...ARE IN YOUR HANDS.

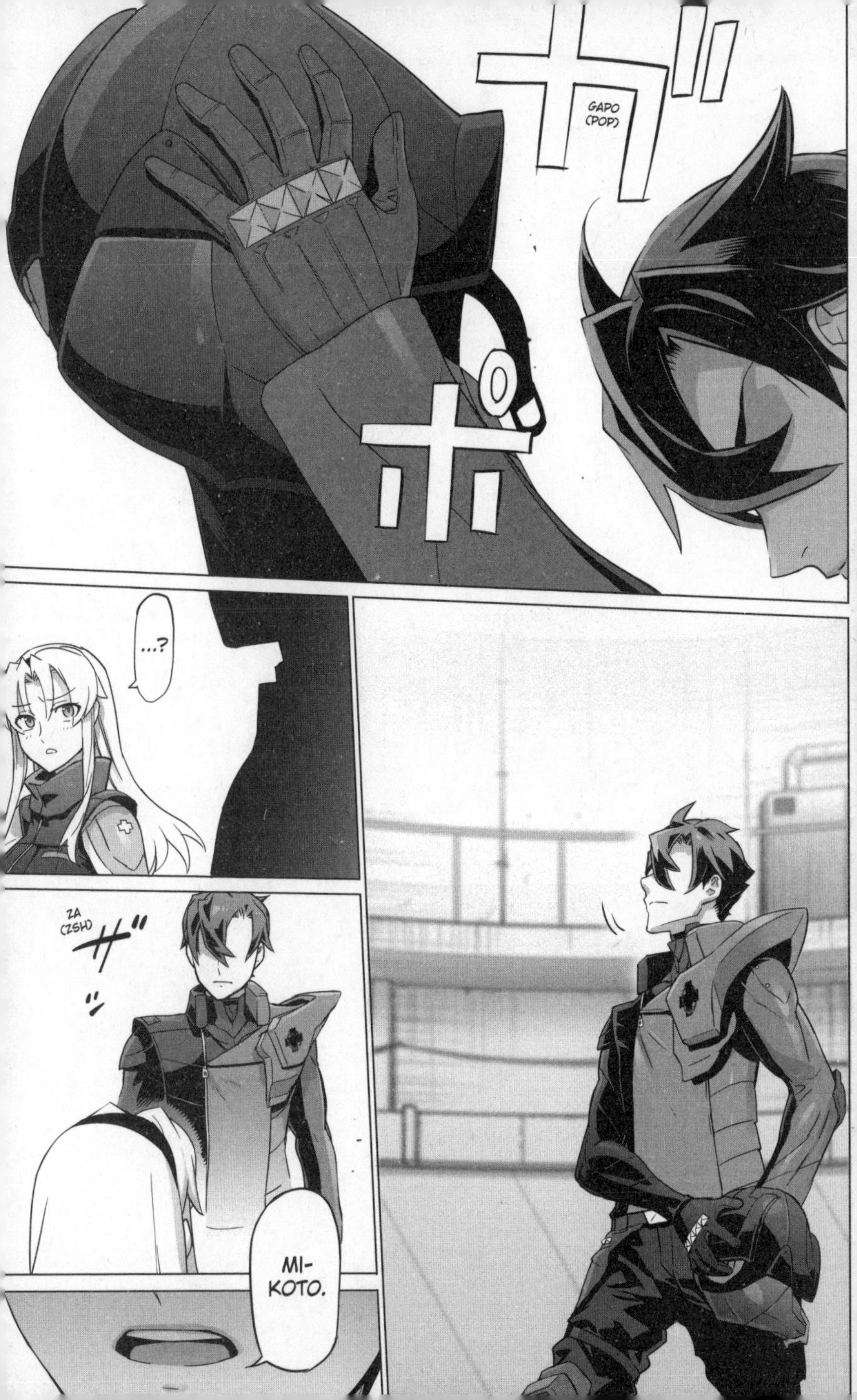
ガポ
GAPO (POP)
...?
ザッ
ZA (ZSH)
MI-KOTO.

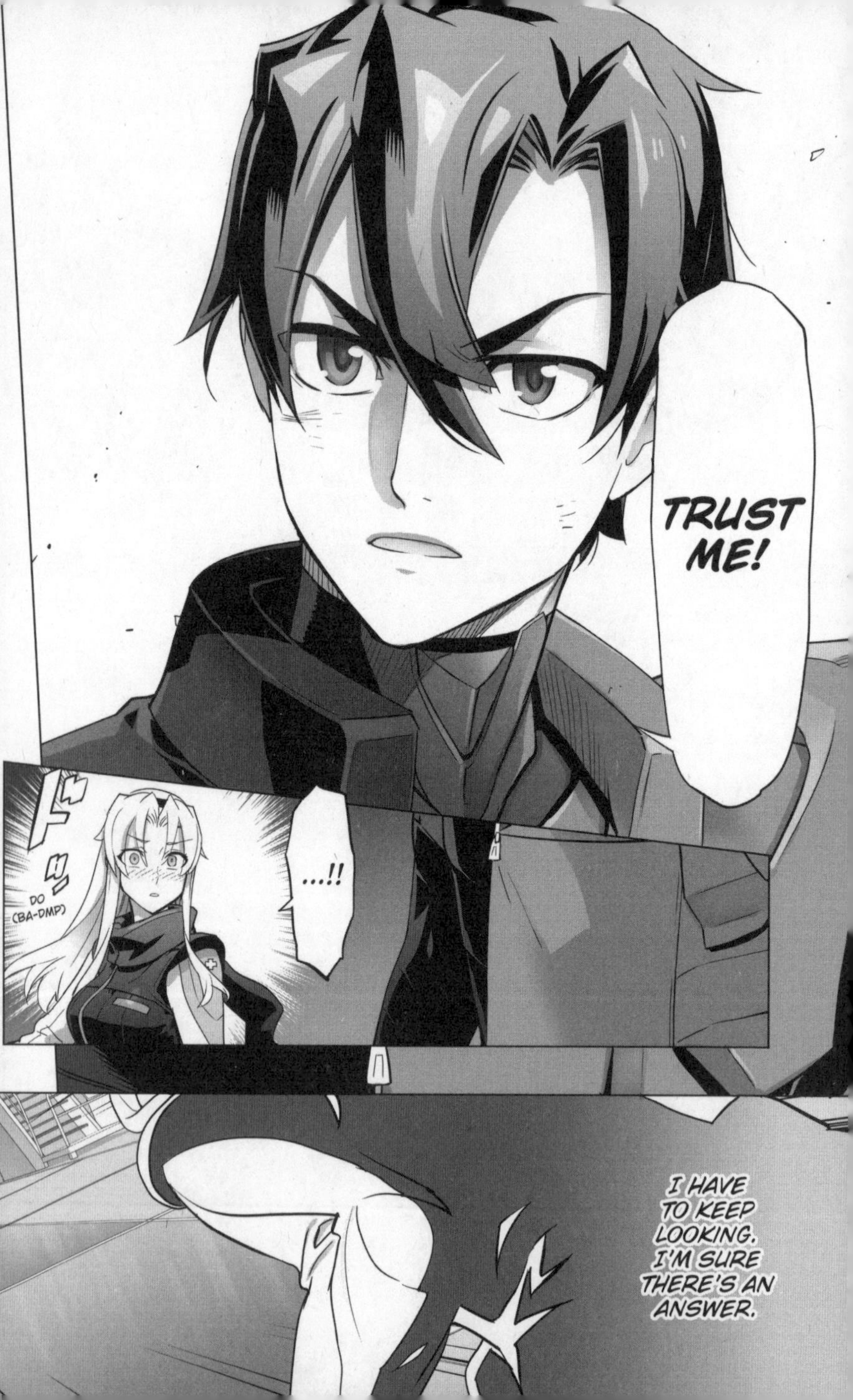
TRUST ME!
...!!
DO (BA-DMP)
I HAVE TO KEEP LOOKING. I'M SURE THERE'S AN ANSWER.

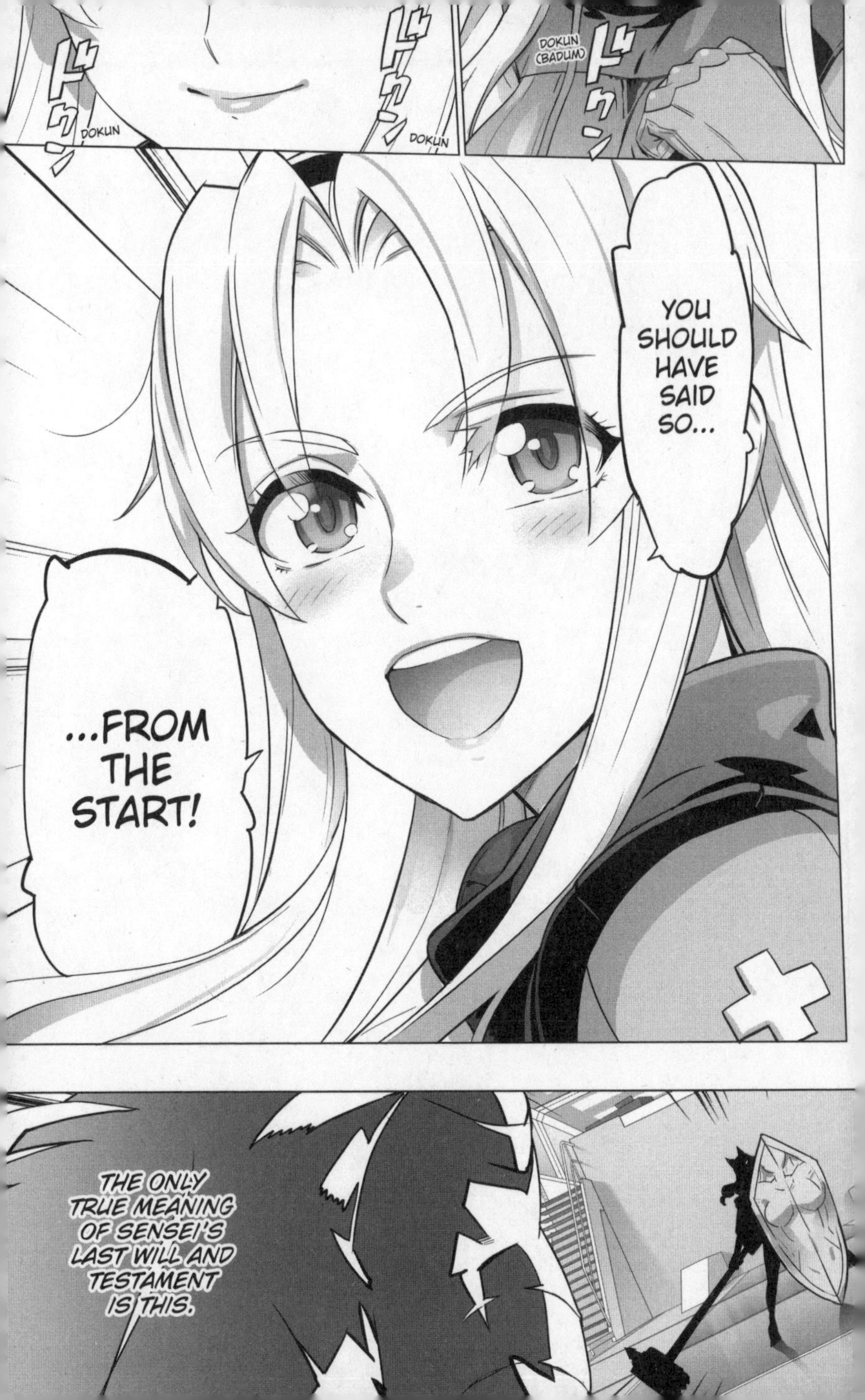
DOKUN (BADUM)
DOKUN
DOKUN
YOU SHOULD HAVE SAID SO...
...FROM THE START!
THE ONLY TRUE MEANING OF SENSEI'S LAST WILL AND TESTAMENT IS THIS.

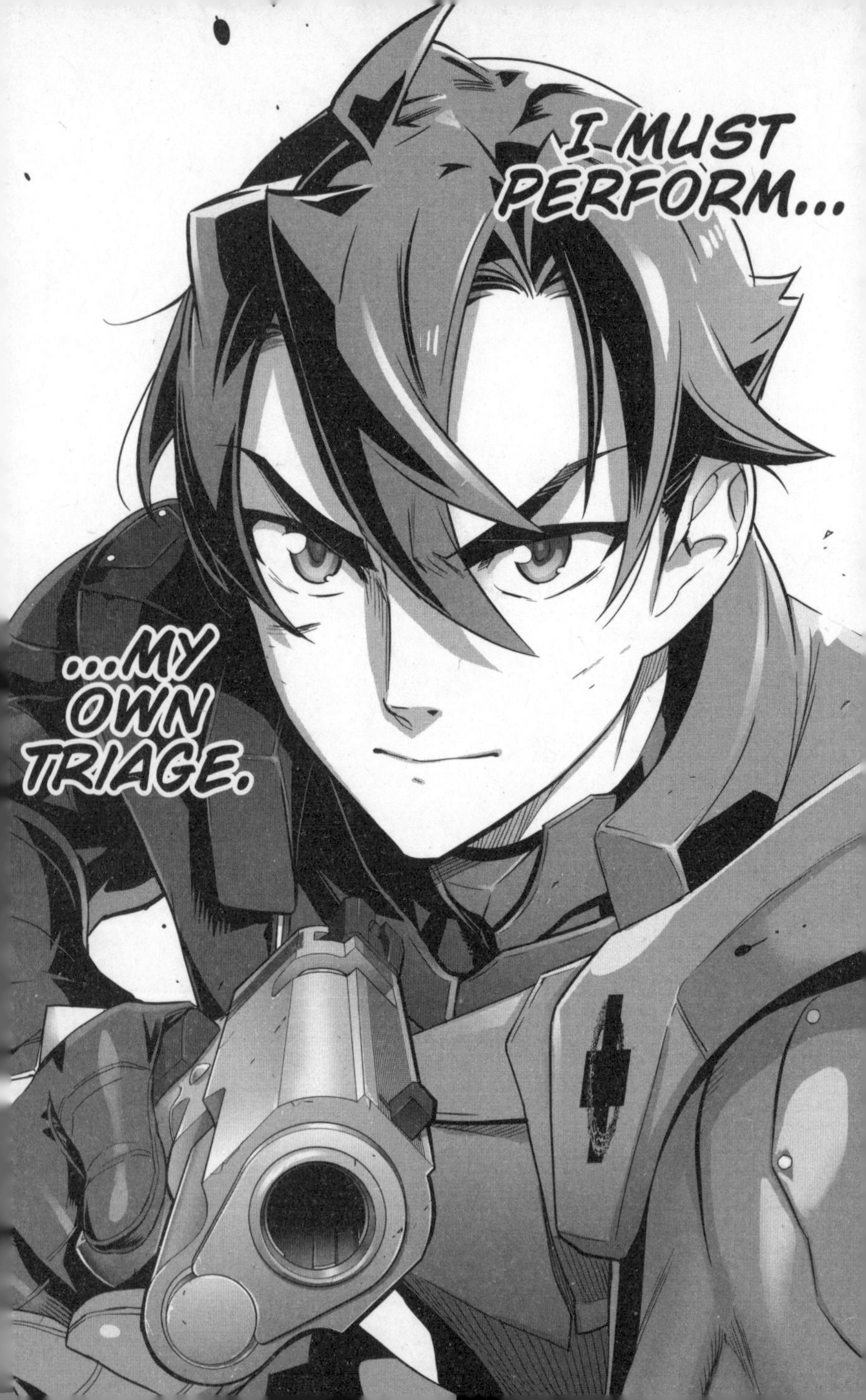
I MUST PERFORM...
...MY OWN TRIAGE.

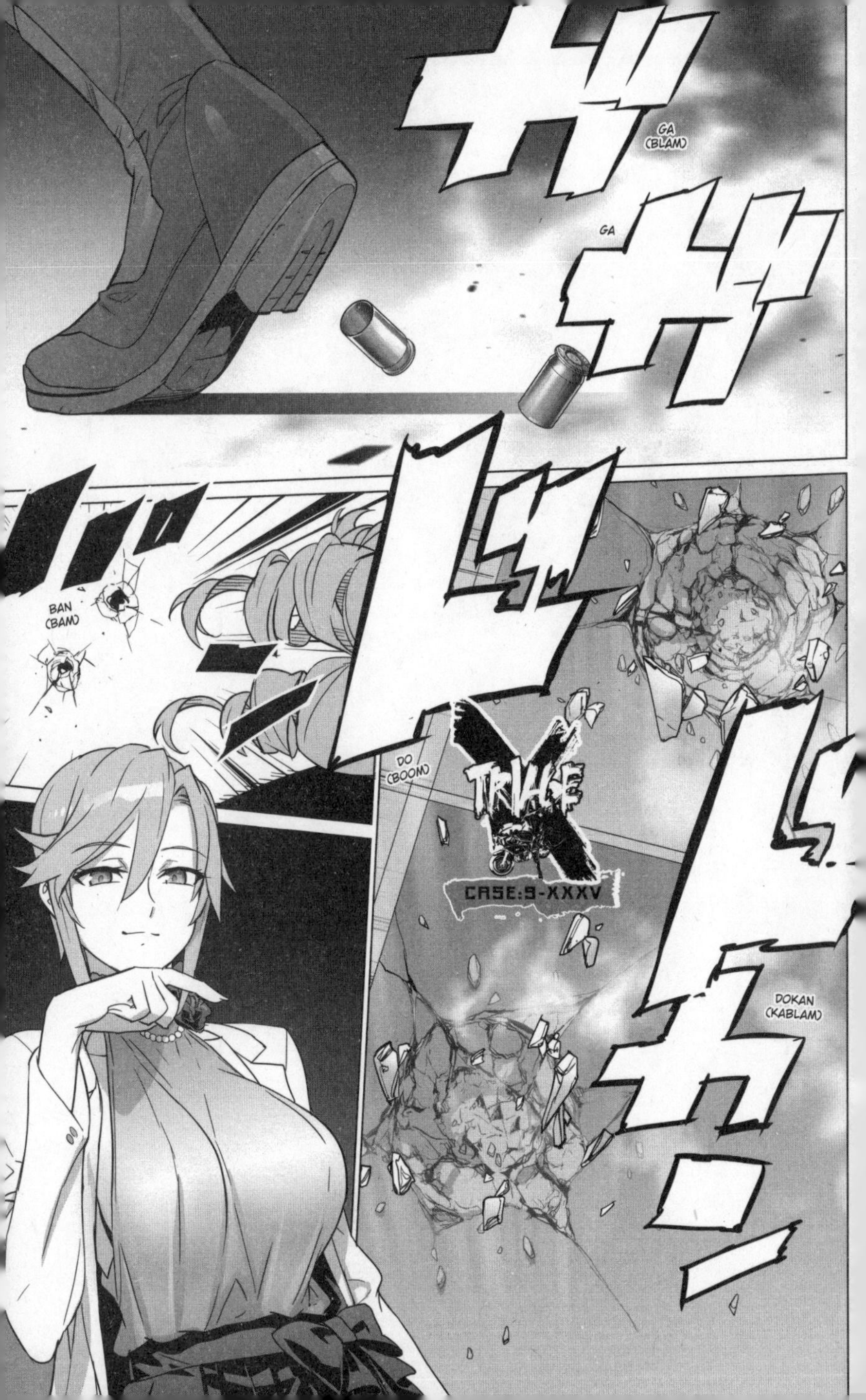
GA (BLAM)
GA
DO (BOOM)
TRIAGE X
CASE:9-XXXV
DOKAN (KABLAM)
BAN (BAM)

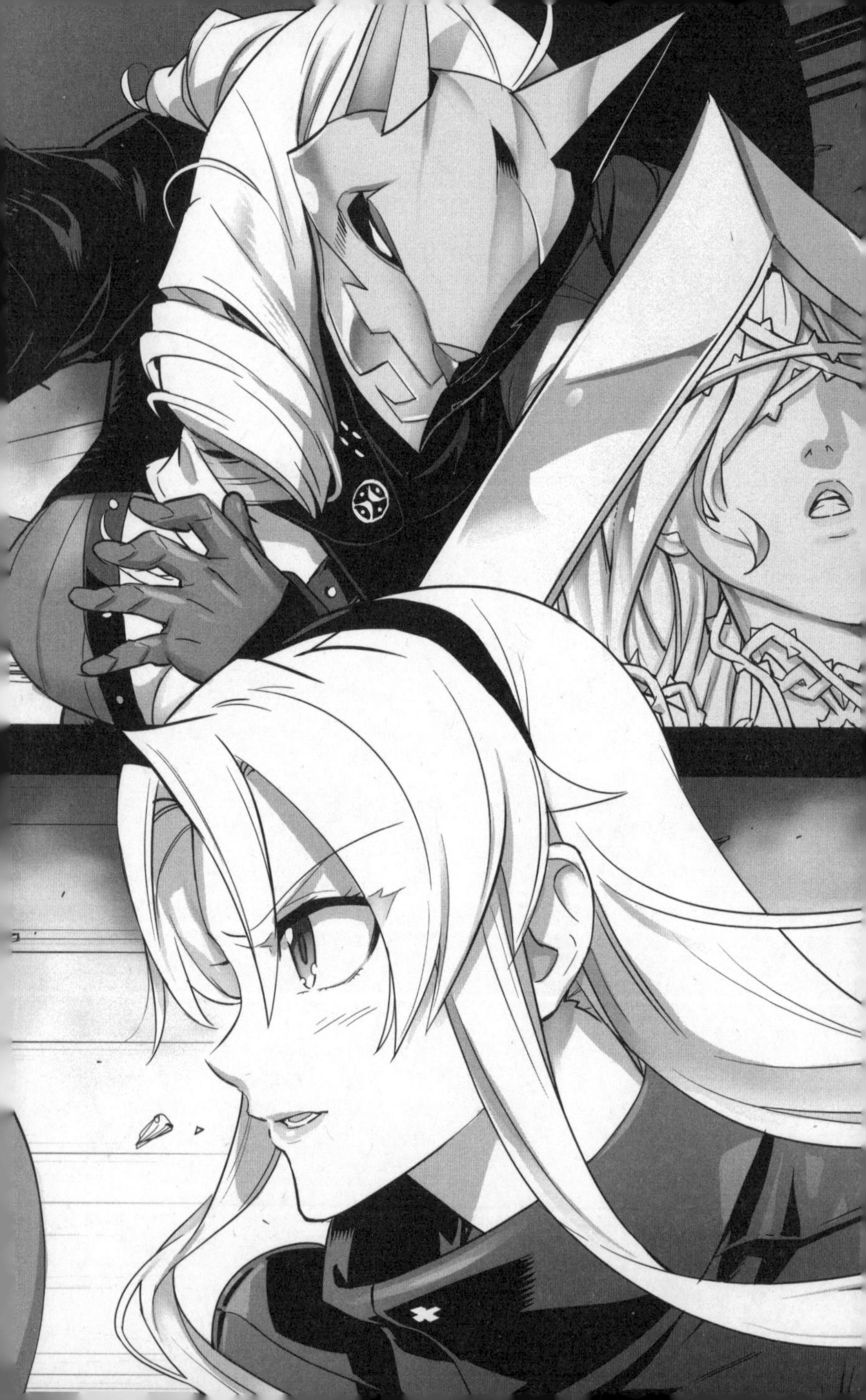

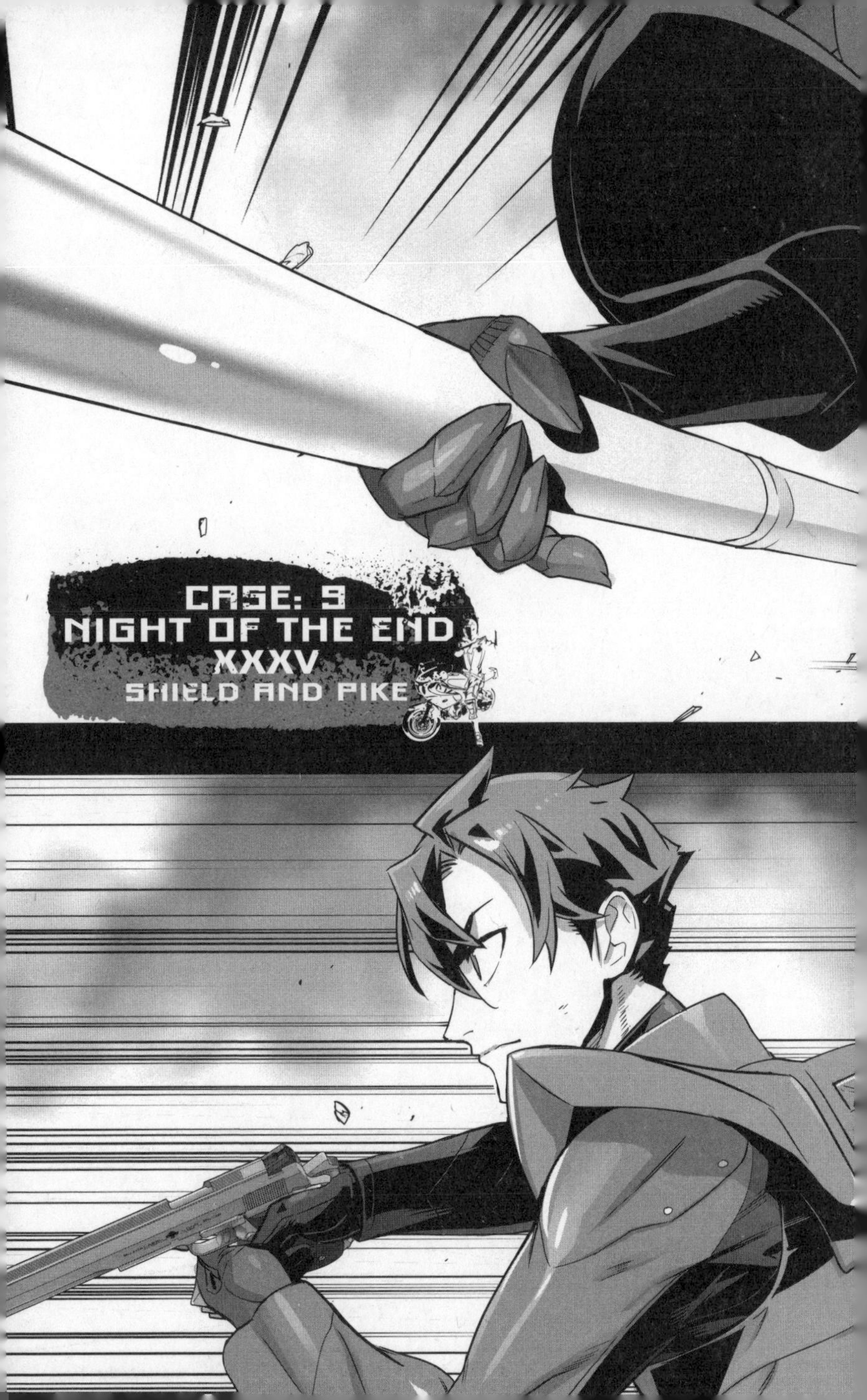
CASE: 9
NIGHT OF THE END
XXXV
SHIELD AND PIKE

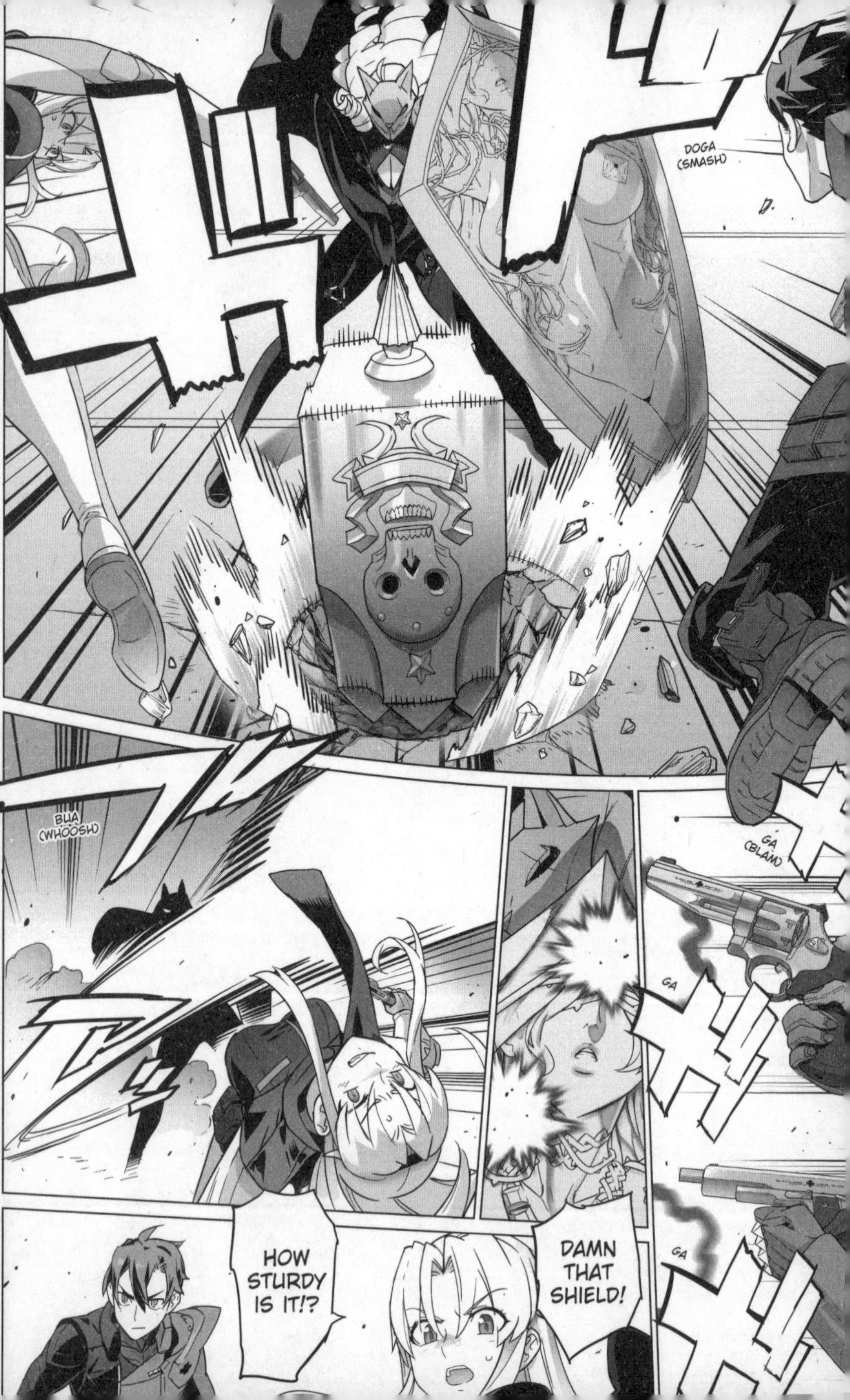
DOGA (SMASH)
GA (BLAM)
GA
GA
BUA (WHOOSH)
DAMN THAT SHIELD!
HOW STURDY IS IT!?

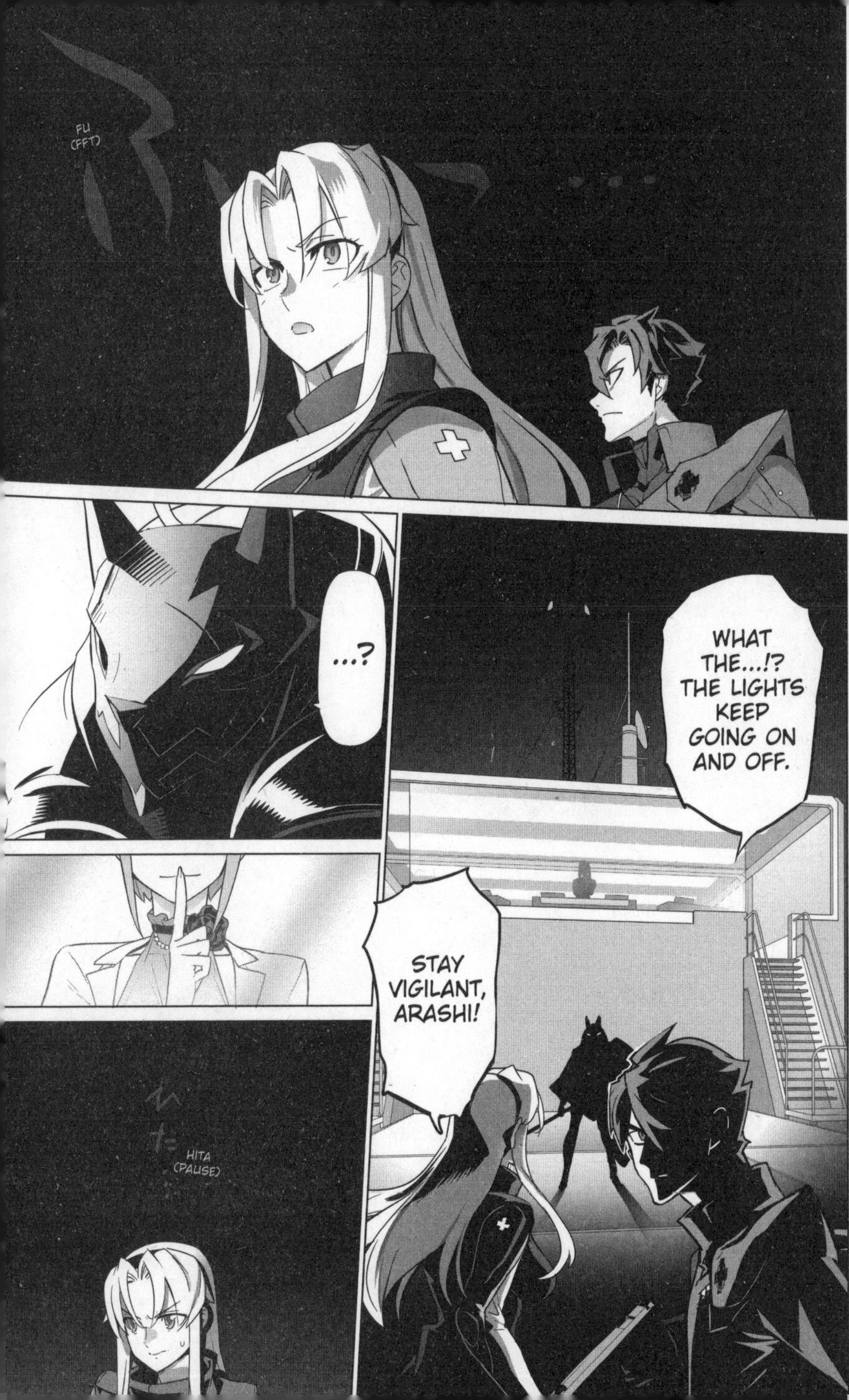
FU (FFT)
WHAT THE...!? THE LIGHTS KEEP GOING ON AND OFF.
STAY VIGILANT, ARASHI!
...?
HITA (PAUSE)

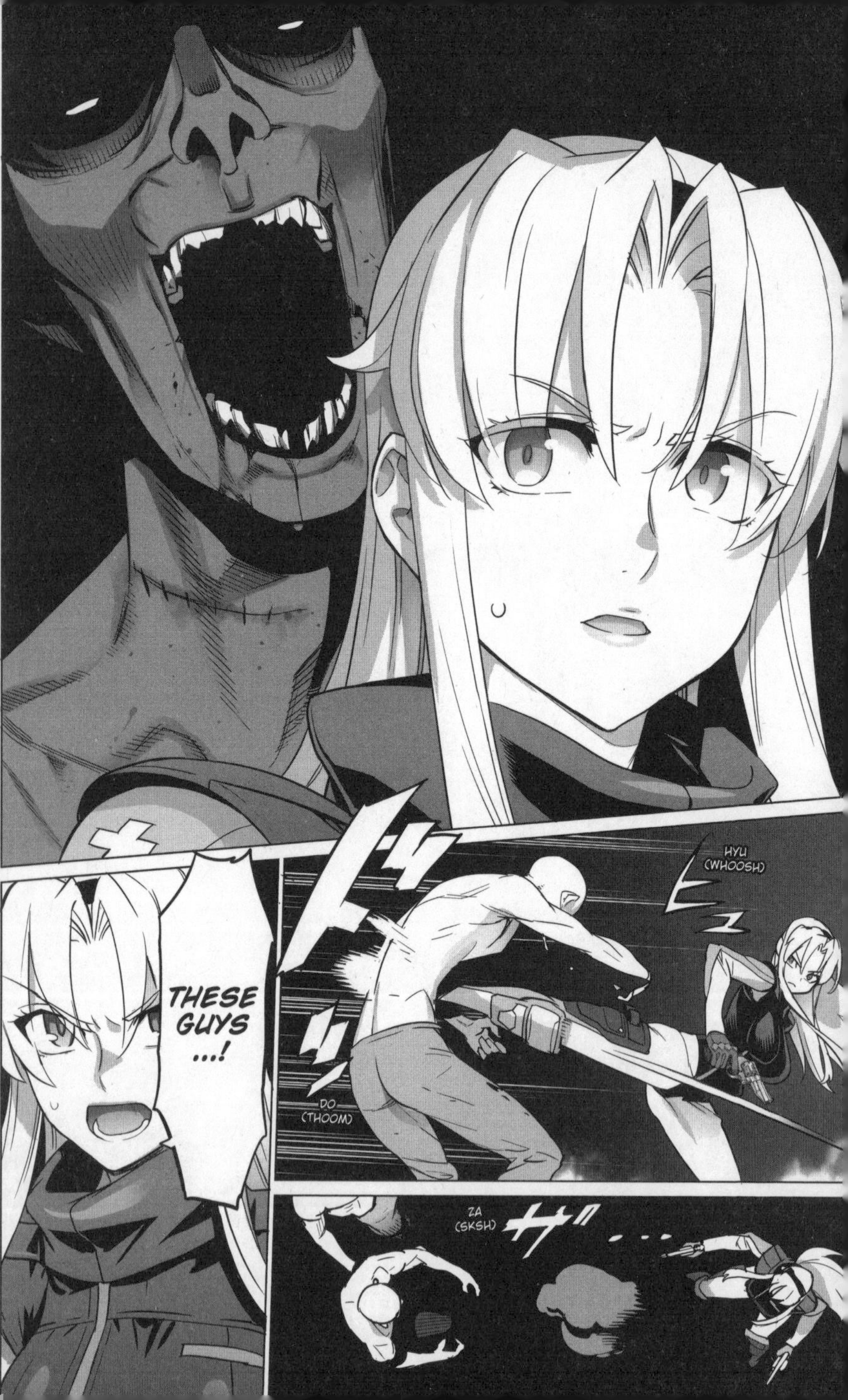
HYU
(WHOOSH)
DO
(THOOM)
ZA
(SKSH)
THESE GUYS ...!

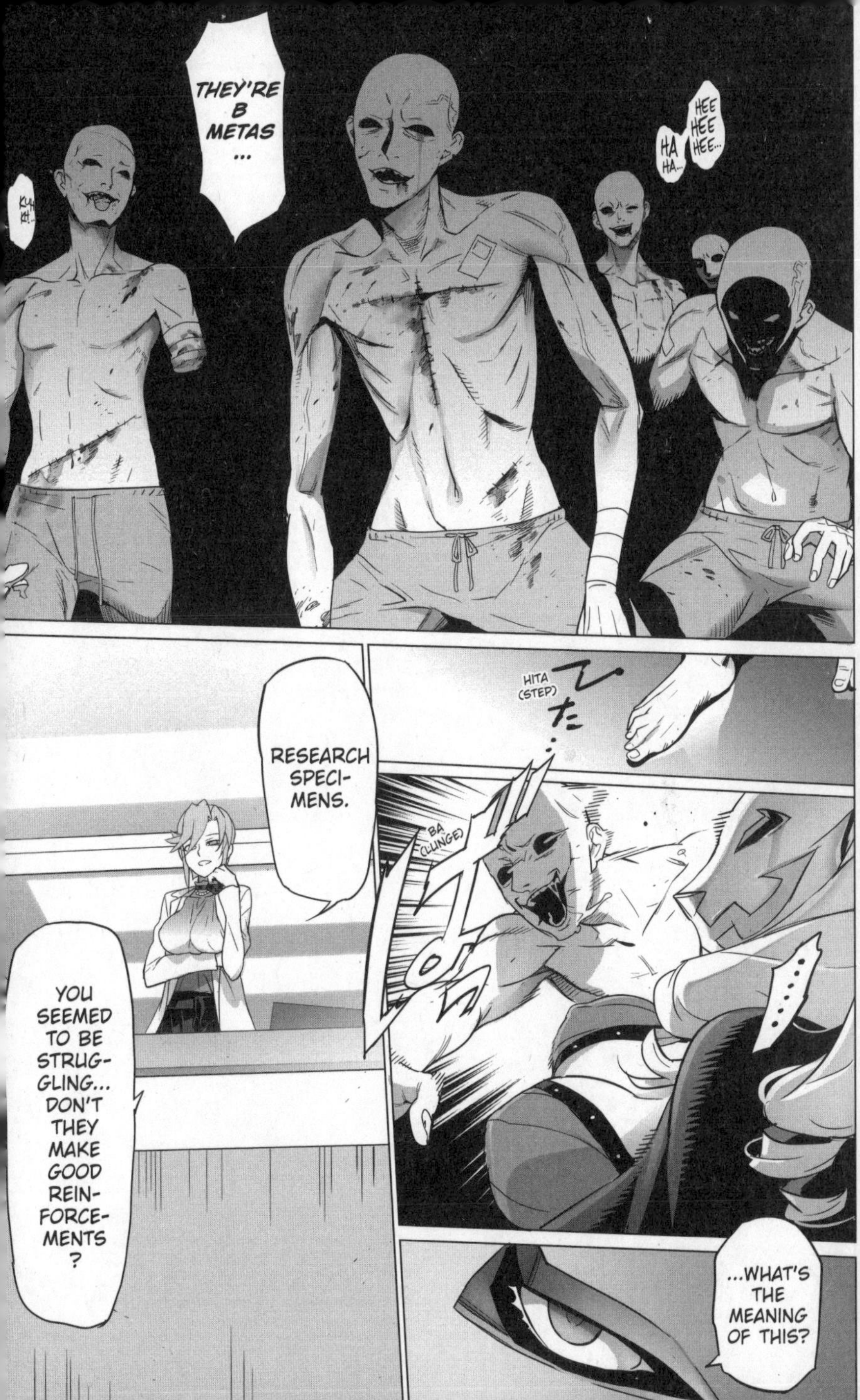
HEE HEE HEE...
HA HA...
THEY'RE B METAS...
KUH KH...
HITA (STEP)
BA (LUNGE)
......
...WHAT'S THE MEANING OF THIS?
RESEARCH SPECIMENS.
YOU SEEMED TO BE STRUGGLING... DON'T THEY MAKE GOOD REINFORCEMENTS?

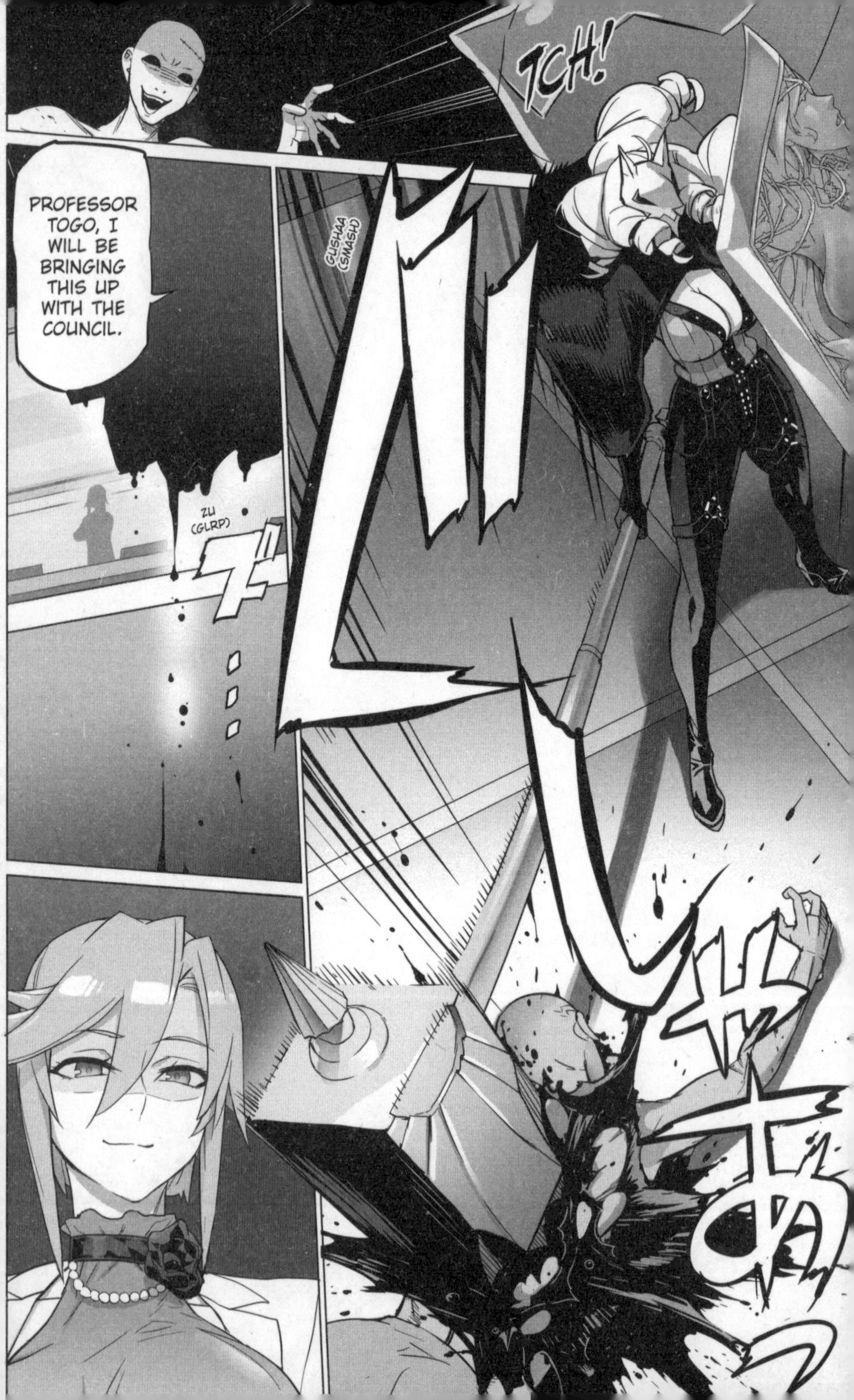
TCH!
PROFESSOR TOGO, I WILL BE BRINGING THIS UP WITH THE COUNCIL.
GUSHAA (SMASH)
ZU (GLRP)

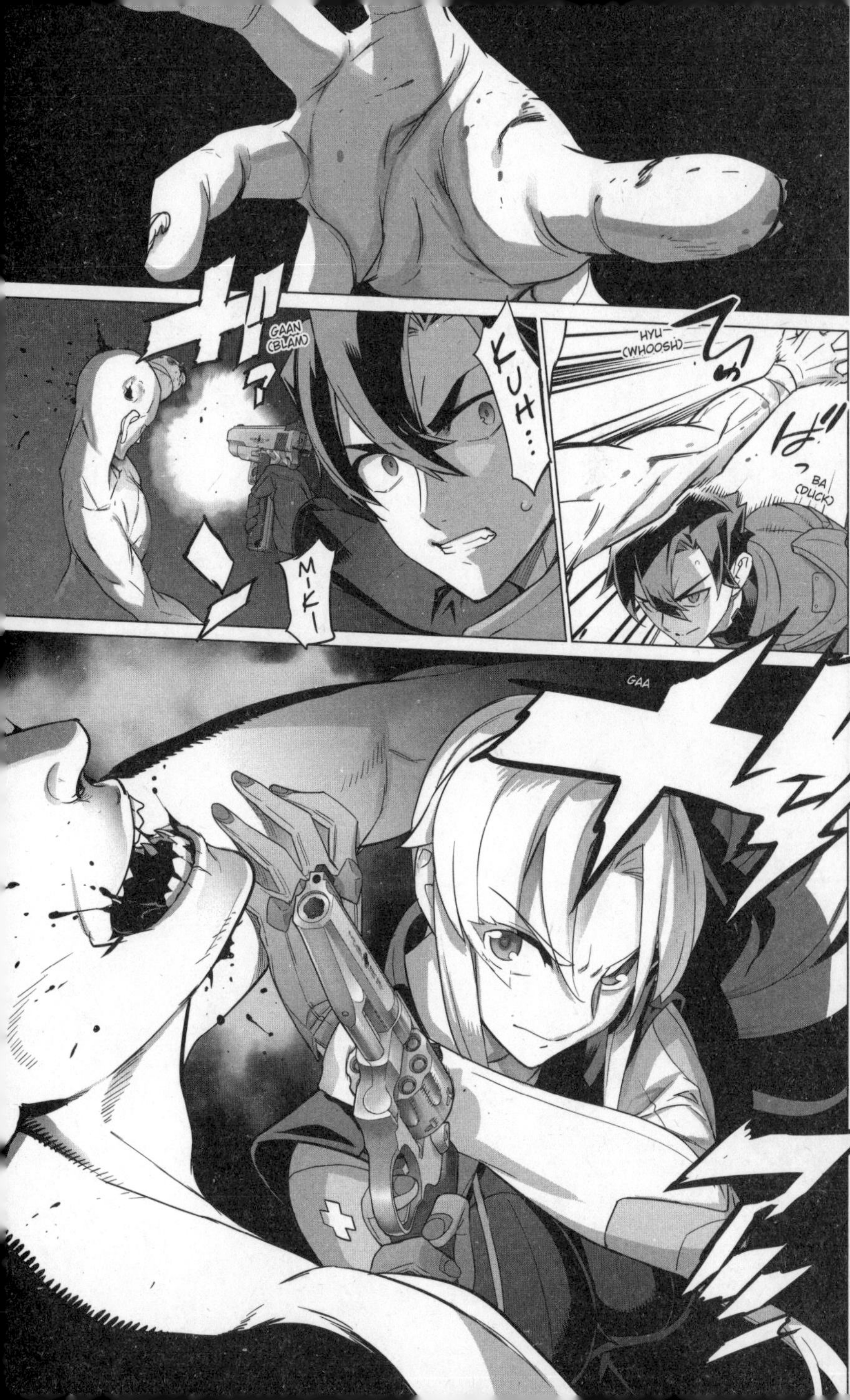
HYU
(WHOOSH)
BA
(DUCK)
KUH...
GAAN
(BLAM)
MIKI
GAA

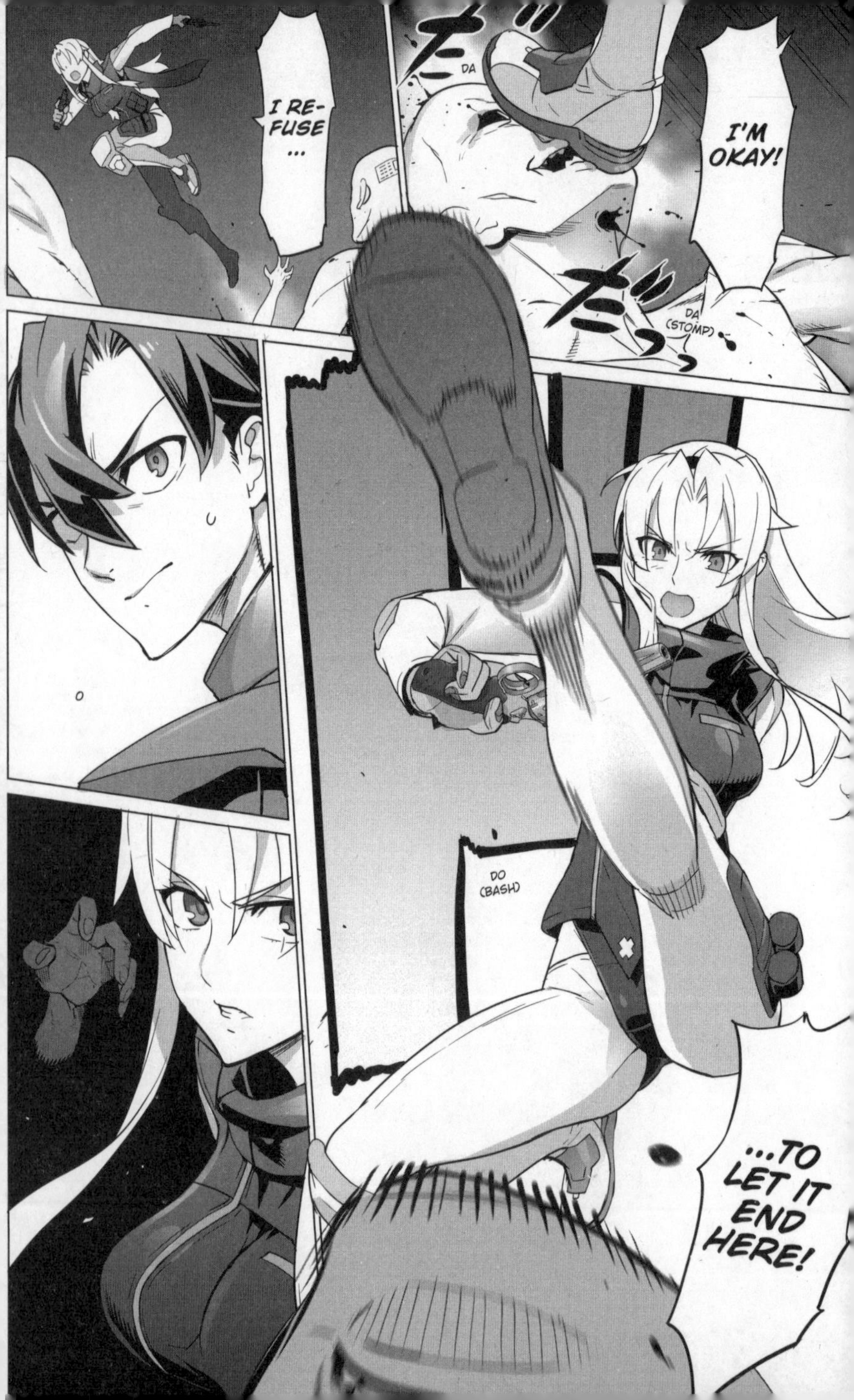
DA
I'M OKAY!
DA (STOMP)
I RE-FUSE ...
DO (BASH)
...TO LET IT END HERE!

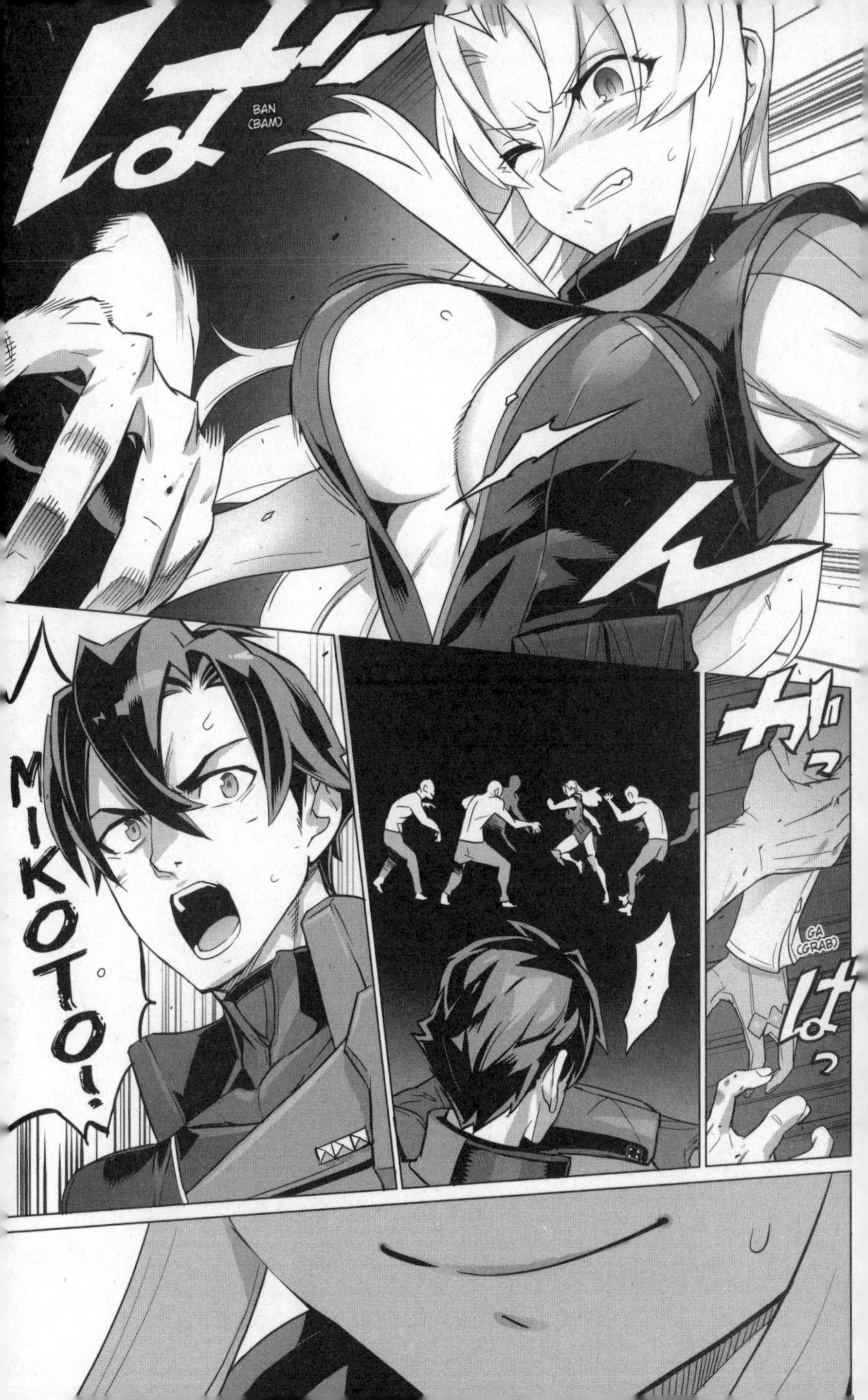

BAN (BAM)
MIKOTO!
GA (GRAB)

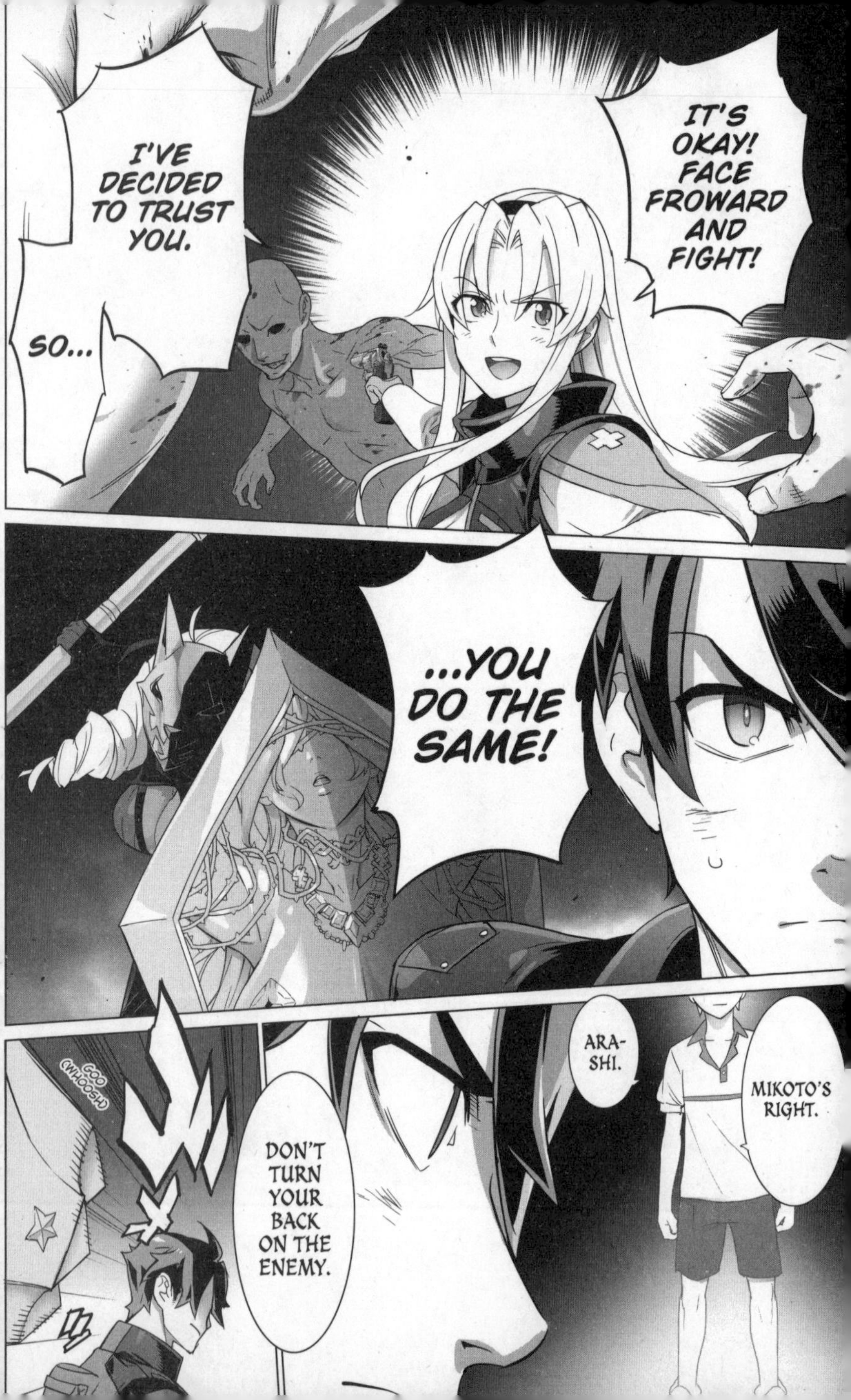
IT'S OKAY! FACE FROWARD AND FIGHT!
I'VE DECIDED TO TRUST YOU.
SO...
...YOU DO THE SAME!
MIKOTO'S RIGHT.
ARA-SHI.
DON'T TURN YOUR BACK ON THE ENEMY.
GOO (WHOOSH)

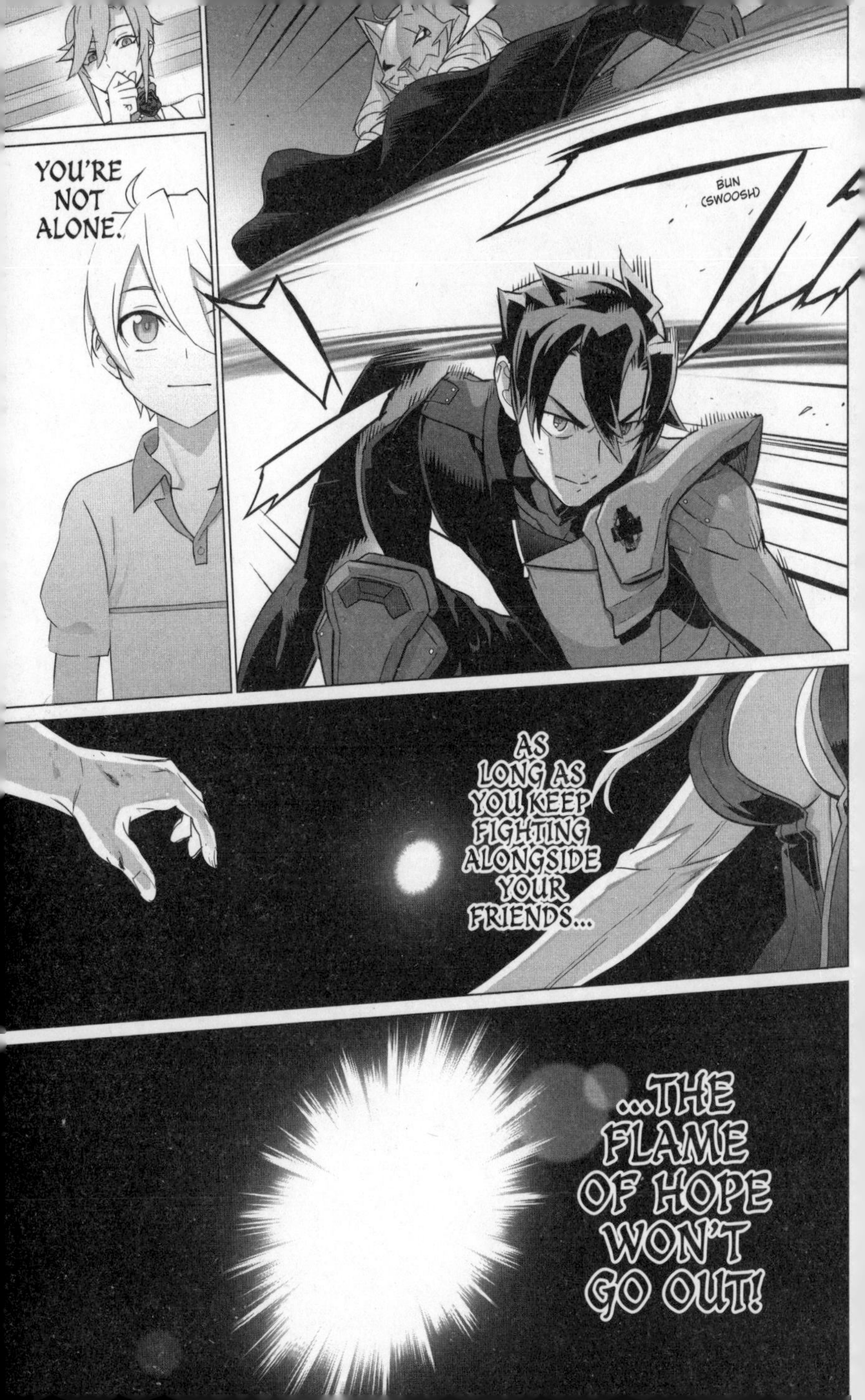
BUN (SWOOSH)
YOU'RE NOT ALONE.
AS LONG AS YOU KEEP FIGHTING ALONGSIDE YOUR FRIENDS...
...THE FLAME OF HOPE WON'T GO OUT!

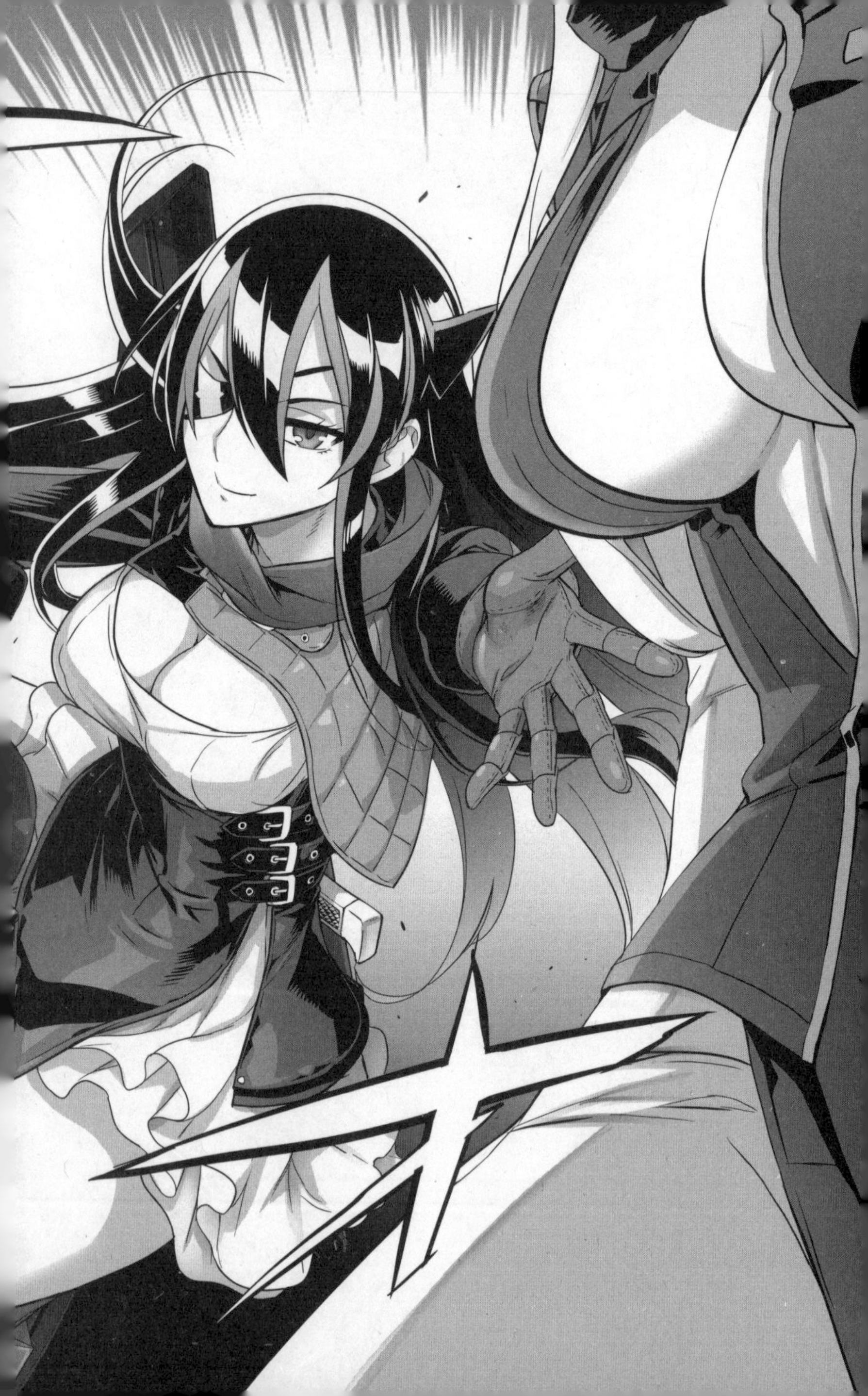

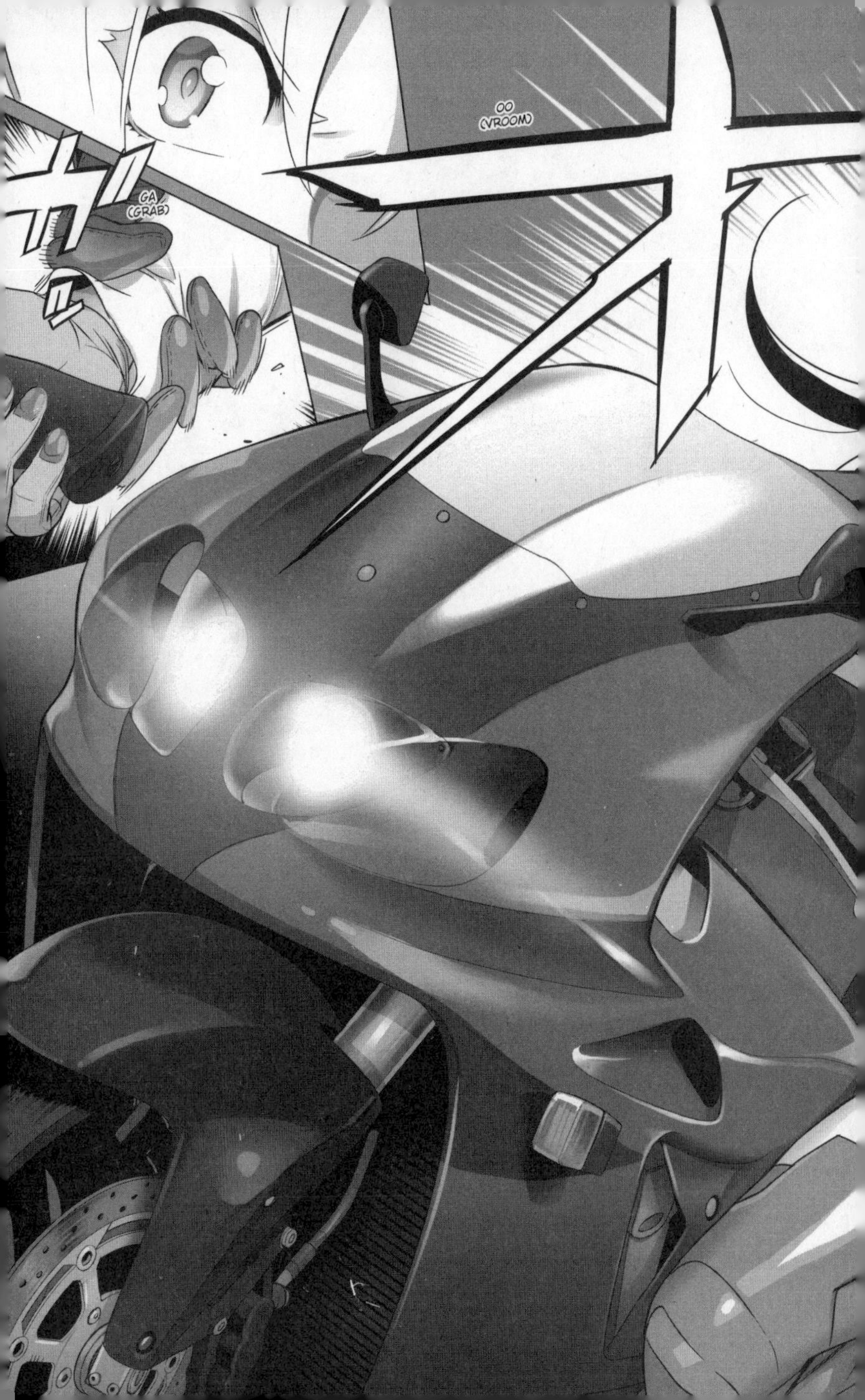
OO
(VROOM)
GA
(GRAB)

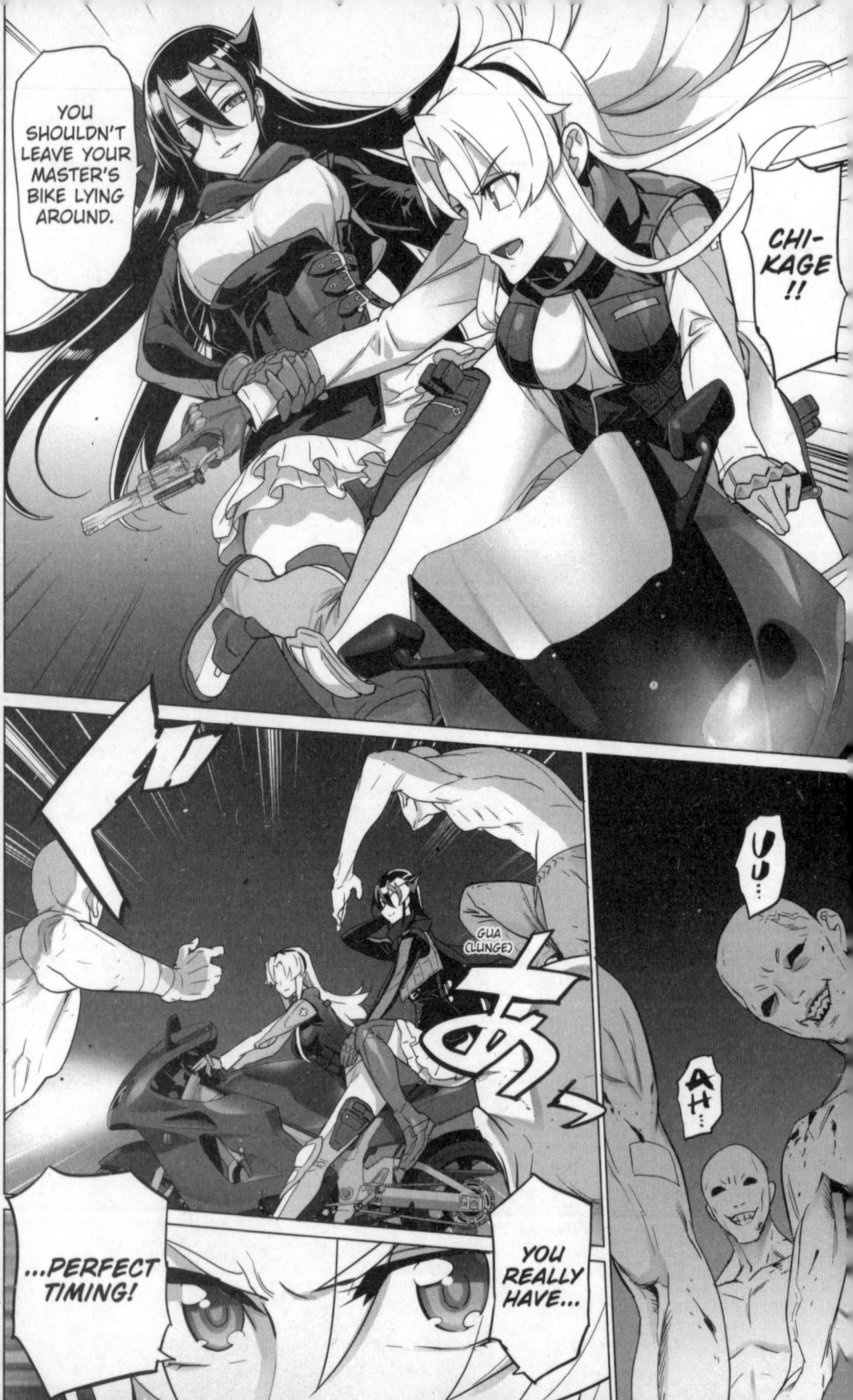
CHI-KAGE!!
YOU SHOULDN'T LEAVE YOUR MASTER'S BIKE LYING AROUND.
UU...
AH...
GUA (LUNGE)
YOU REALLY HAVE...
...PERFECT TIMING!

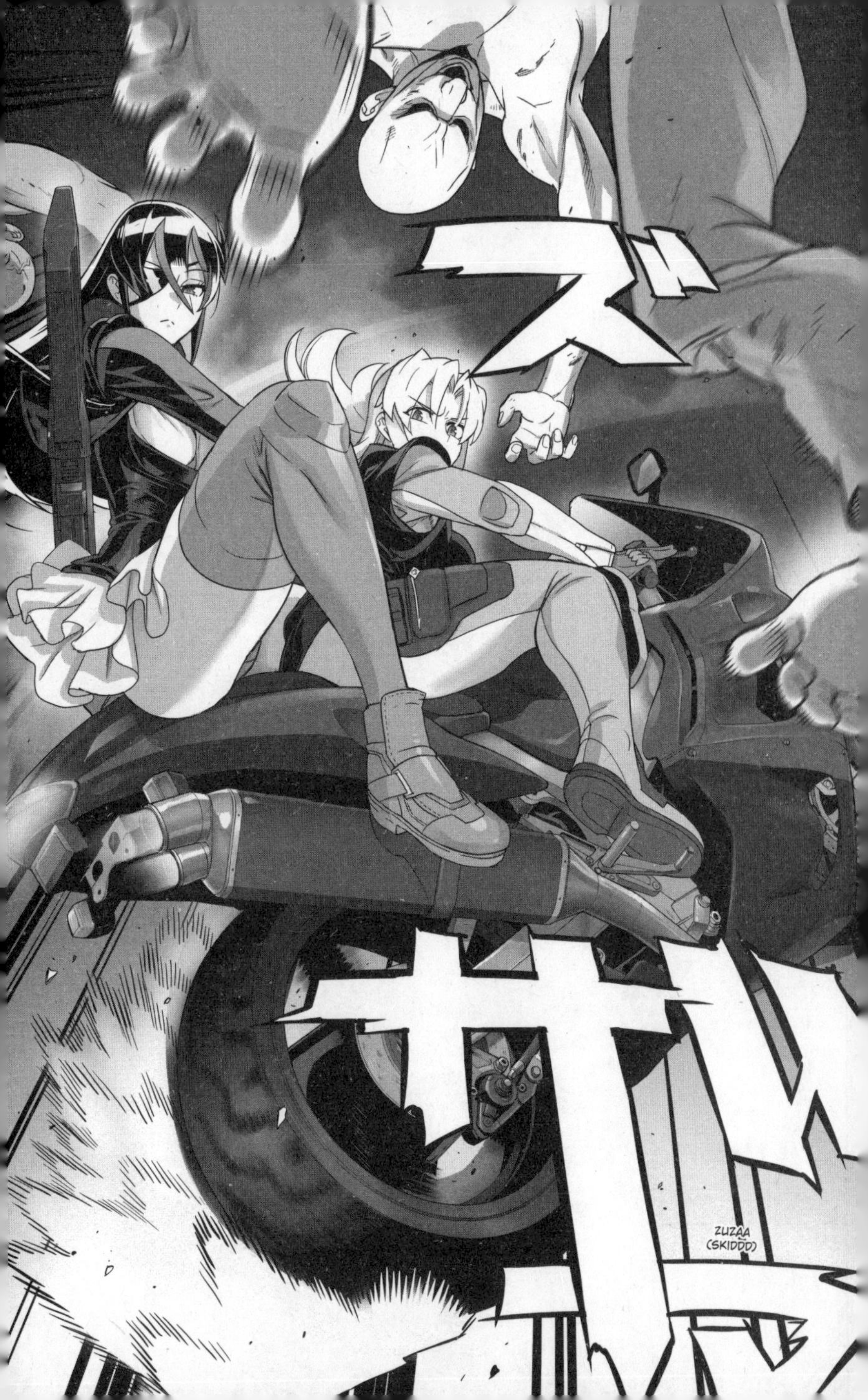
ZUZAA
(SKIDDD)

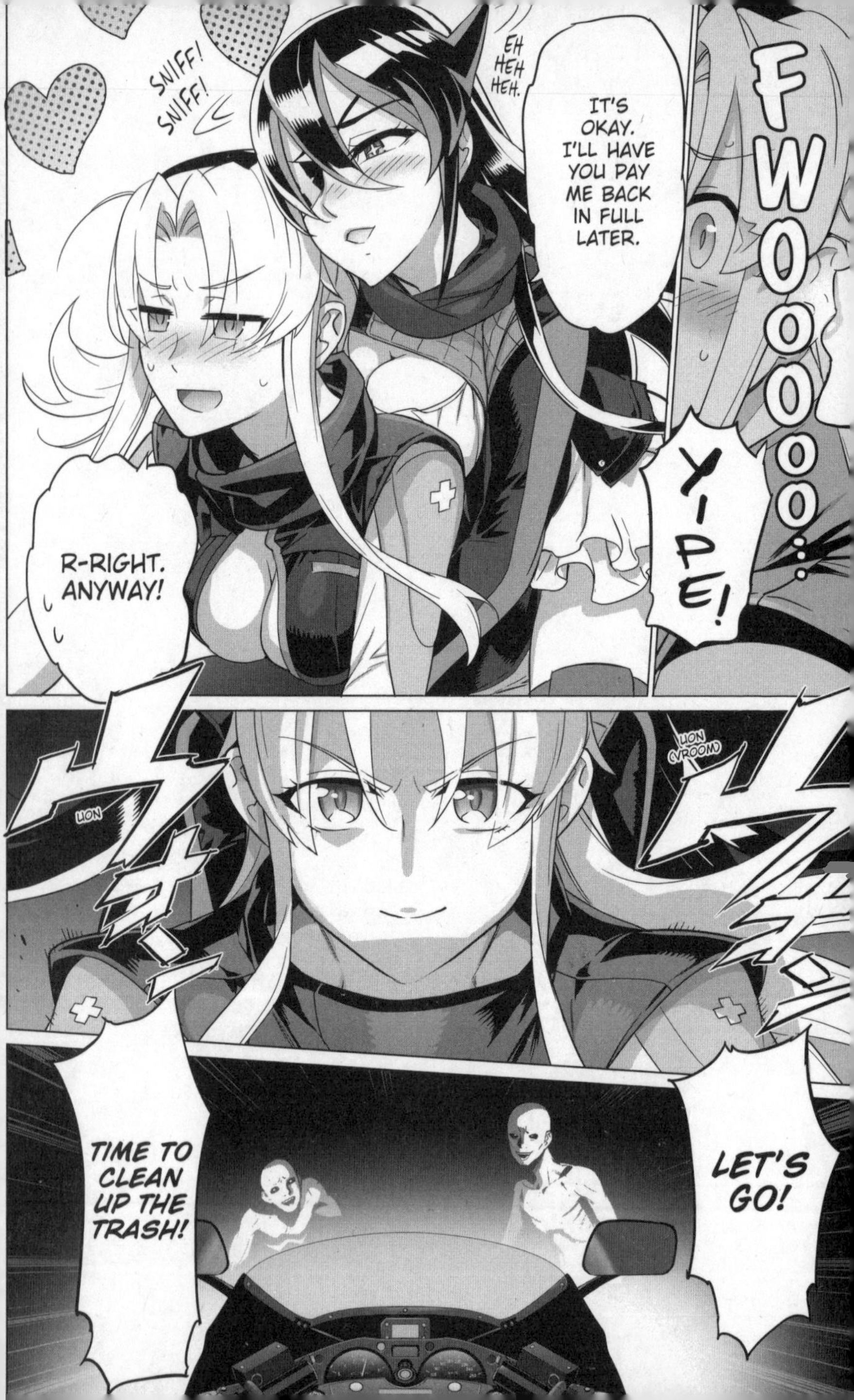
FWOOOOO...!
YIPE!
EH HEH HEH.
IT'S OKAY. I'LL HAVE YOU PAY ME BACK IN FULL LATER.
SNIFF! SNIFF!
R-RIGHT. ANYWAY!
UON (VROOM)
UON
LET'S GO!
TIME TO CLEAN UP THE TRASH!

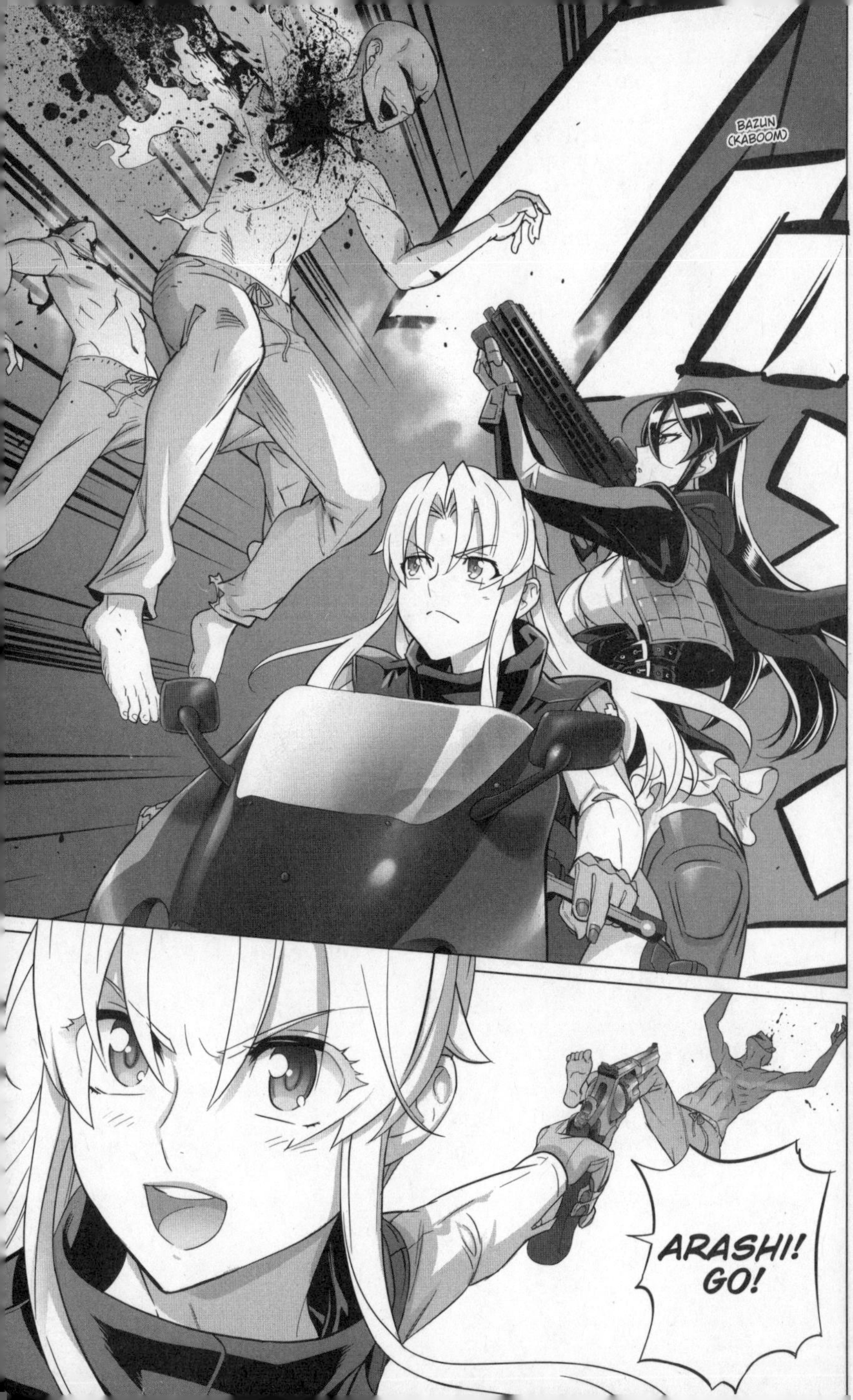
BAZUN
(KABOOM)
ARASHI! GO!

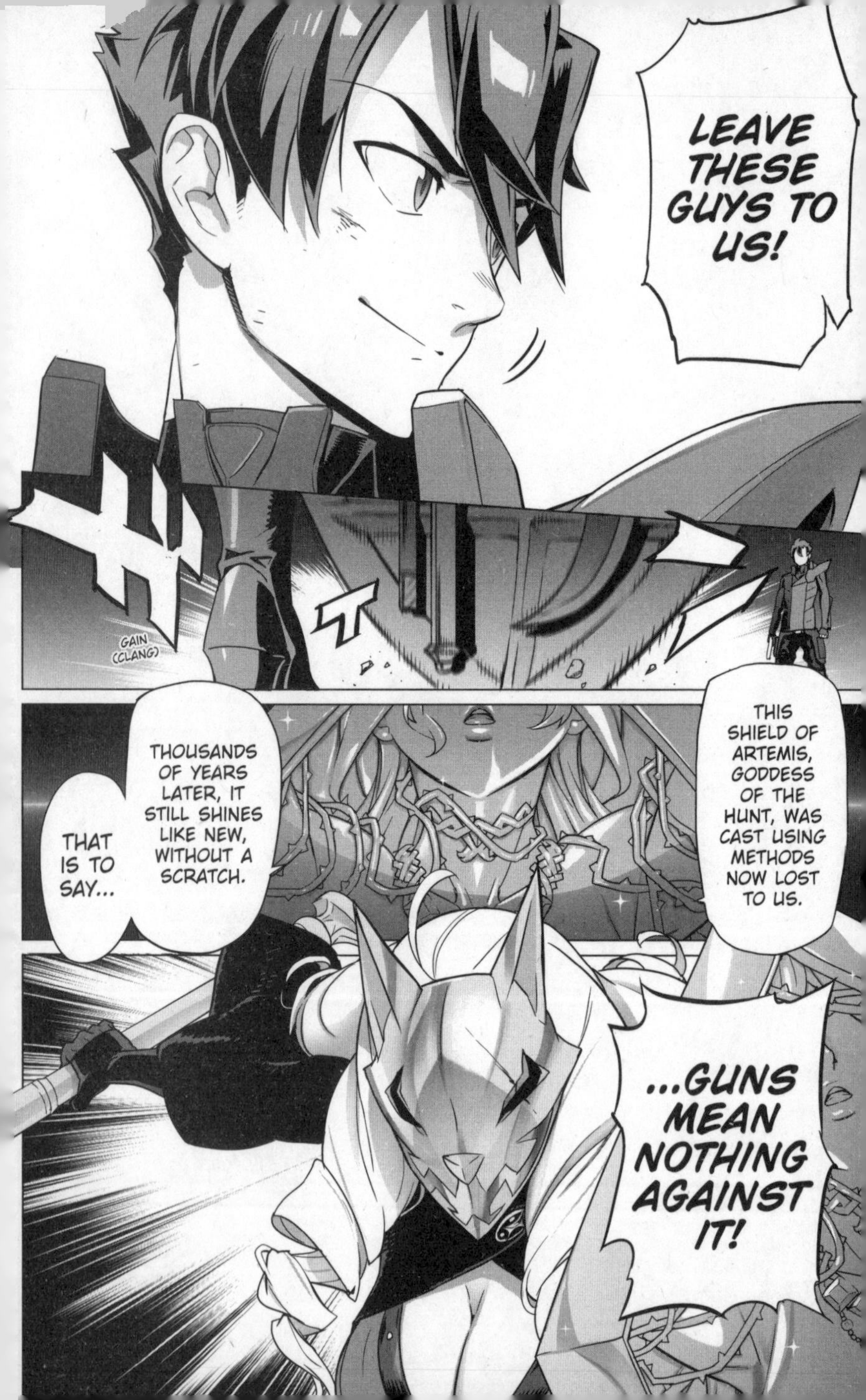
LEAVE THESE GUYS TO US!
GAIN (CLANG)
THIS SHIELD OF ARTEMIS, GODDESS OF THE HUNT, WAS CAST USING METHODS NOW LOST TO US.
THOUSANDS OF YEARS LATER, IT STILL SHINES LIKE NEW, WITHOUT A SCRATCH.
THAT IS TO SAY...
...GUNS MEAN NOTHING AGAINST IT!

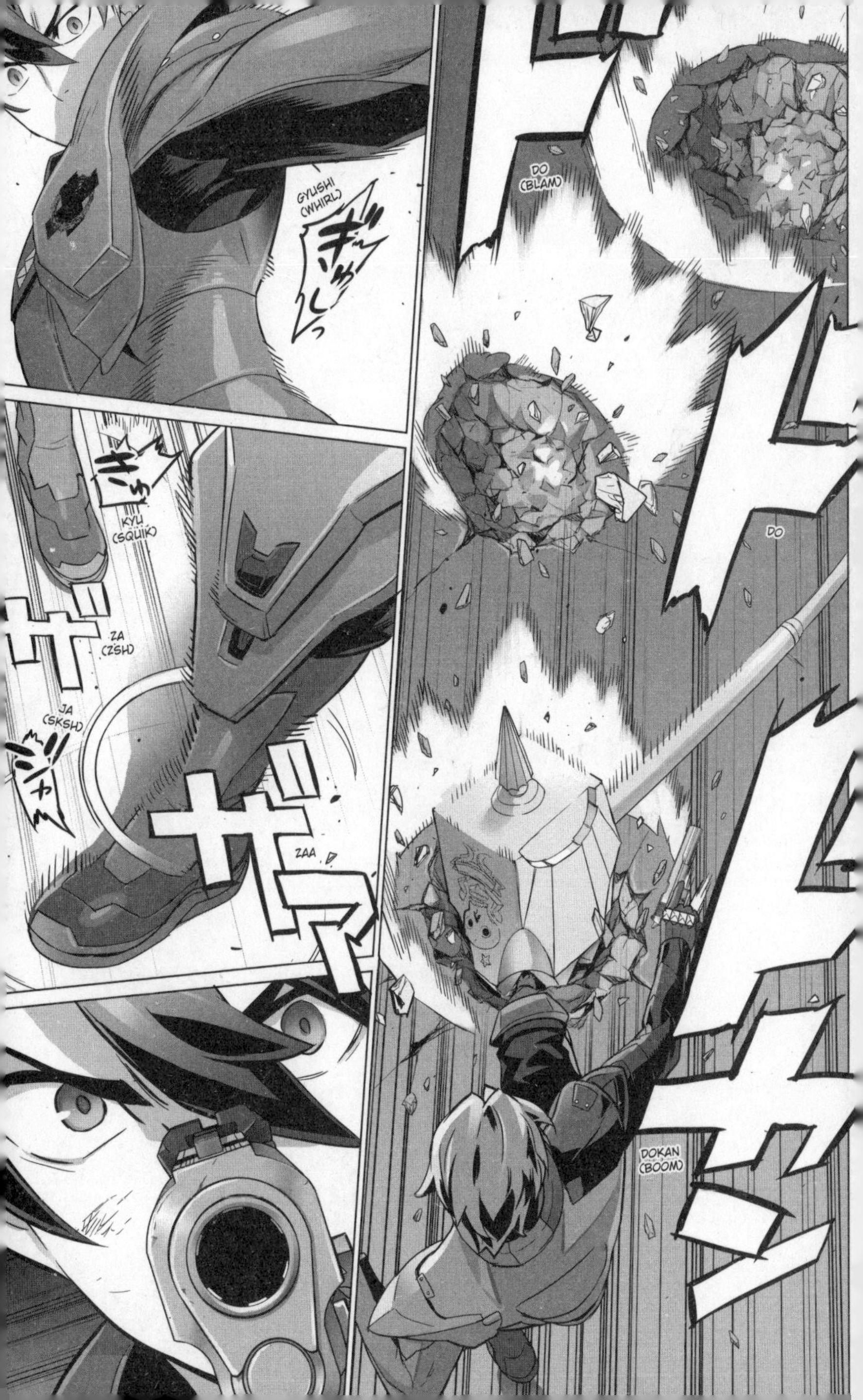
DO (BLAM)
DO
DOKAN (BOOM)
GYUSHI (WHIRL)
KYU (SQUIK)
ZA (ZSH)
JA (SKSH)
ZAA

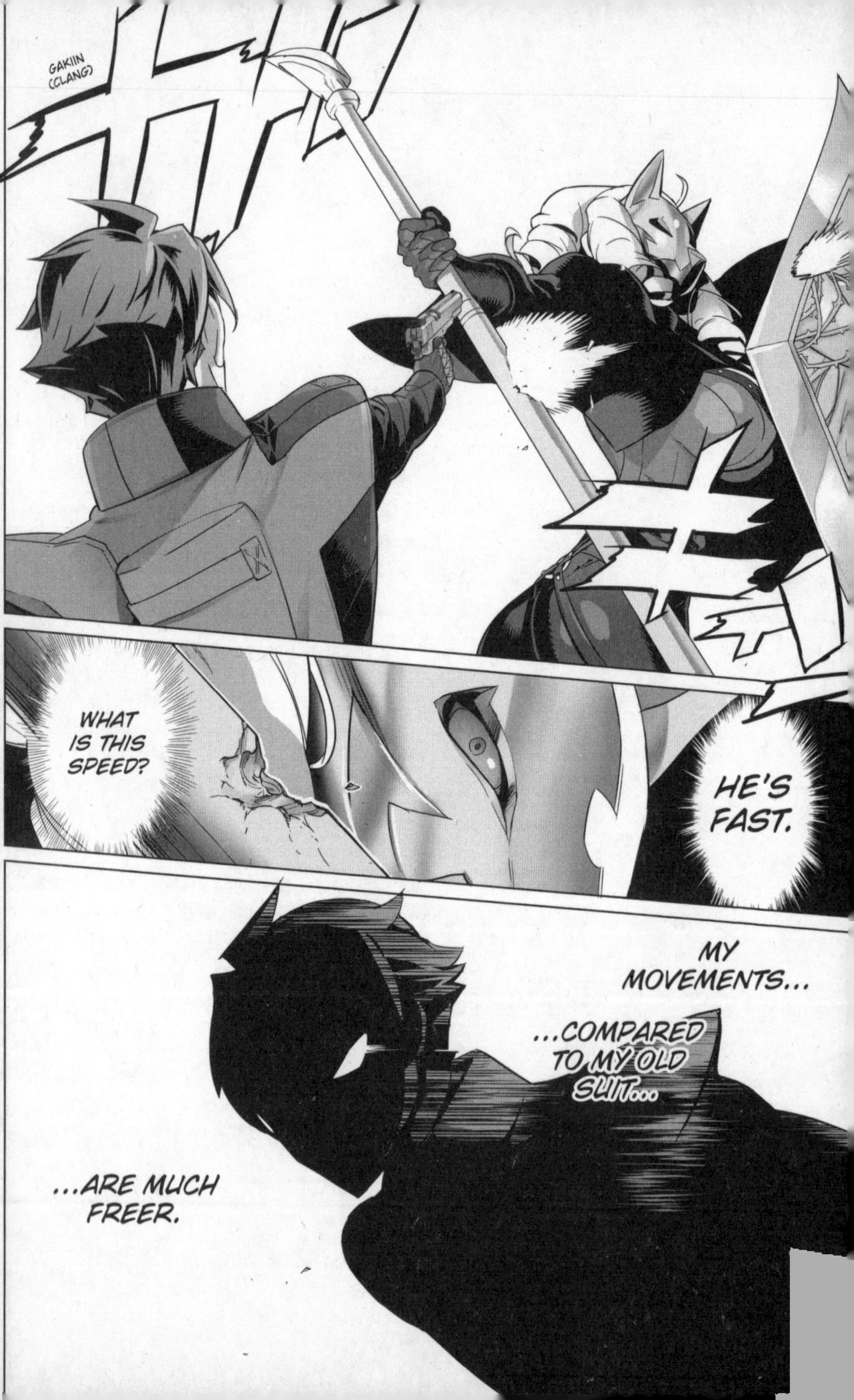
GAKIIN (CLANG)
HE'S FAST.
WHAT IS THIS SPEED?
MY MOVEMENTS...
...COMPARED TO MY OLD SUIT...
...ARE MUCH FREER.

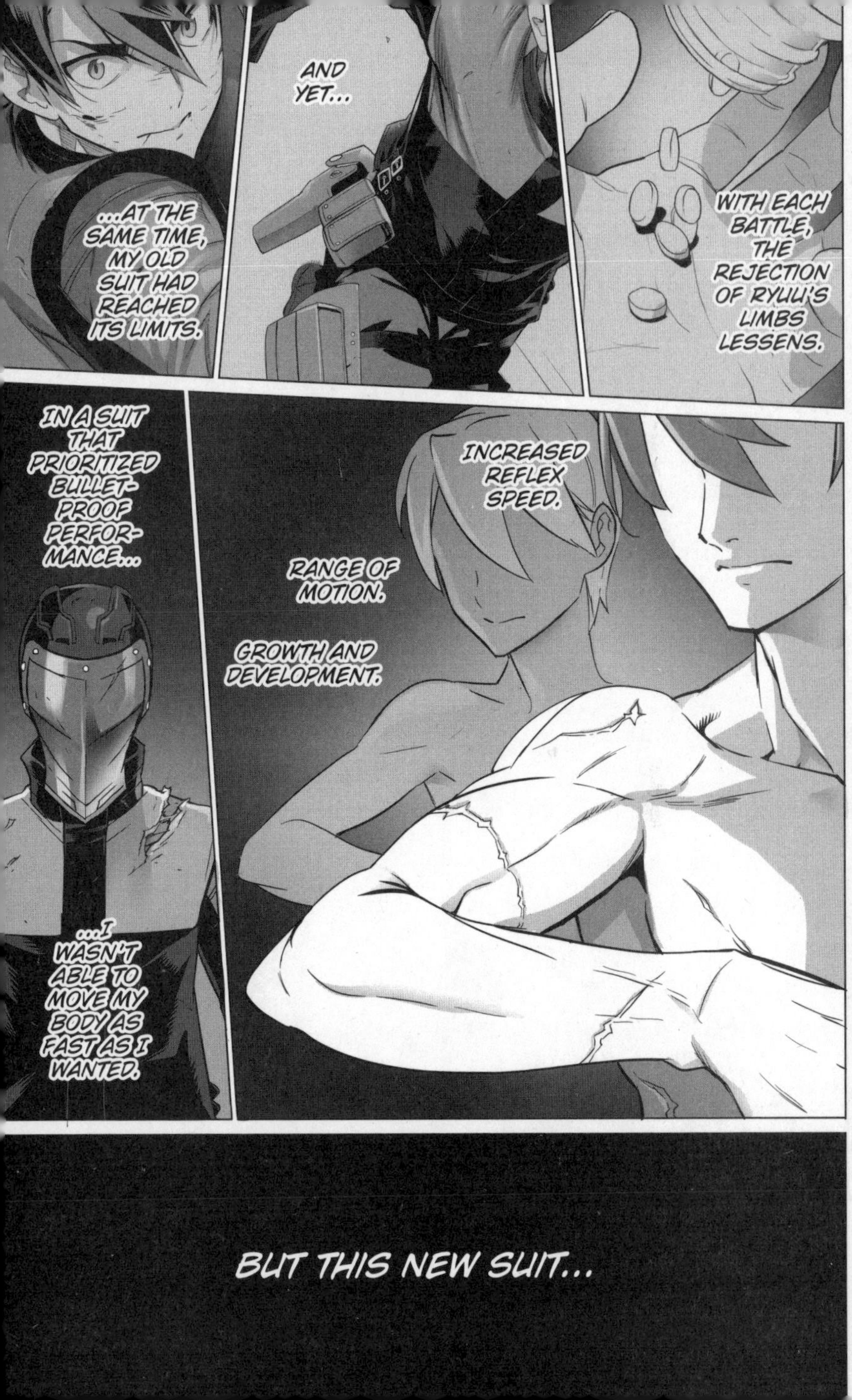
WITH EACH BATTLE, THE REJECTION OF RYUU'S LIMBS LESSENS.
AND YET...
...AT THE SAME TIME, MY OLD SUIT HAD REACHED ITS LIMITS.
INCREASED REFLEX SPEED.
RANGE OF MOTION.
GROWTH AND DEVELOPMENT.
IN A SUIT THAT PRIORITIZED BULLET-PROOF PERFORMANCE...
...I WASN'T ABLE TO MOVE MY BODY AS FAST AS I WANTED.
BUT THIS NEW SUIT...

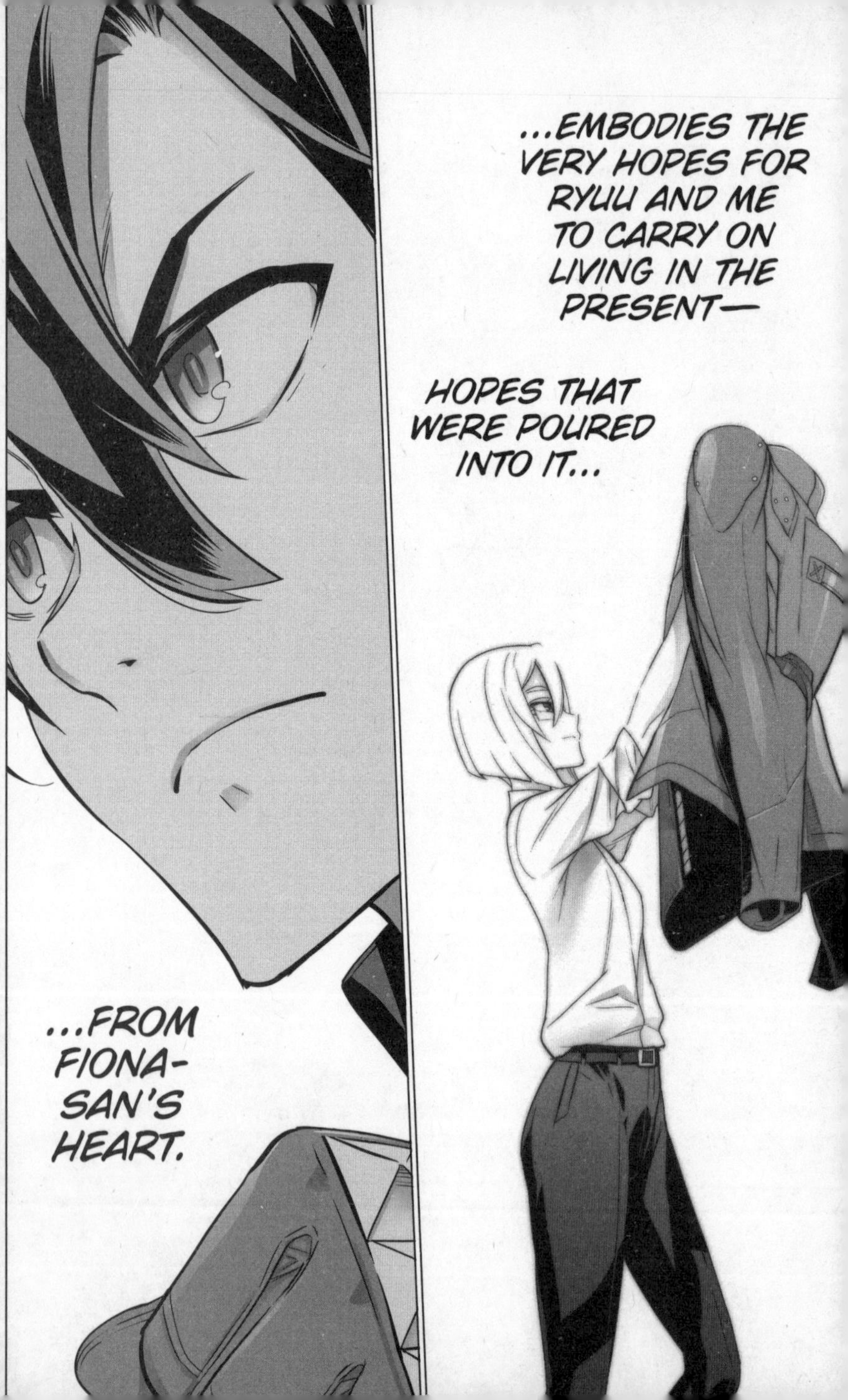
...EMBODIES THE VERY HOPES FOR RYUU AND ME TO CARRY ON LIVING IN THE PRESENT—
HOPES THAT WERE POURED INTO IT...
...FROM FIONA-SAN'S HEART.

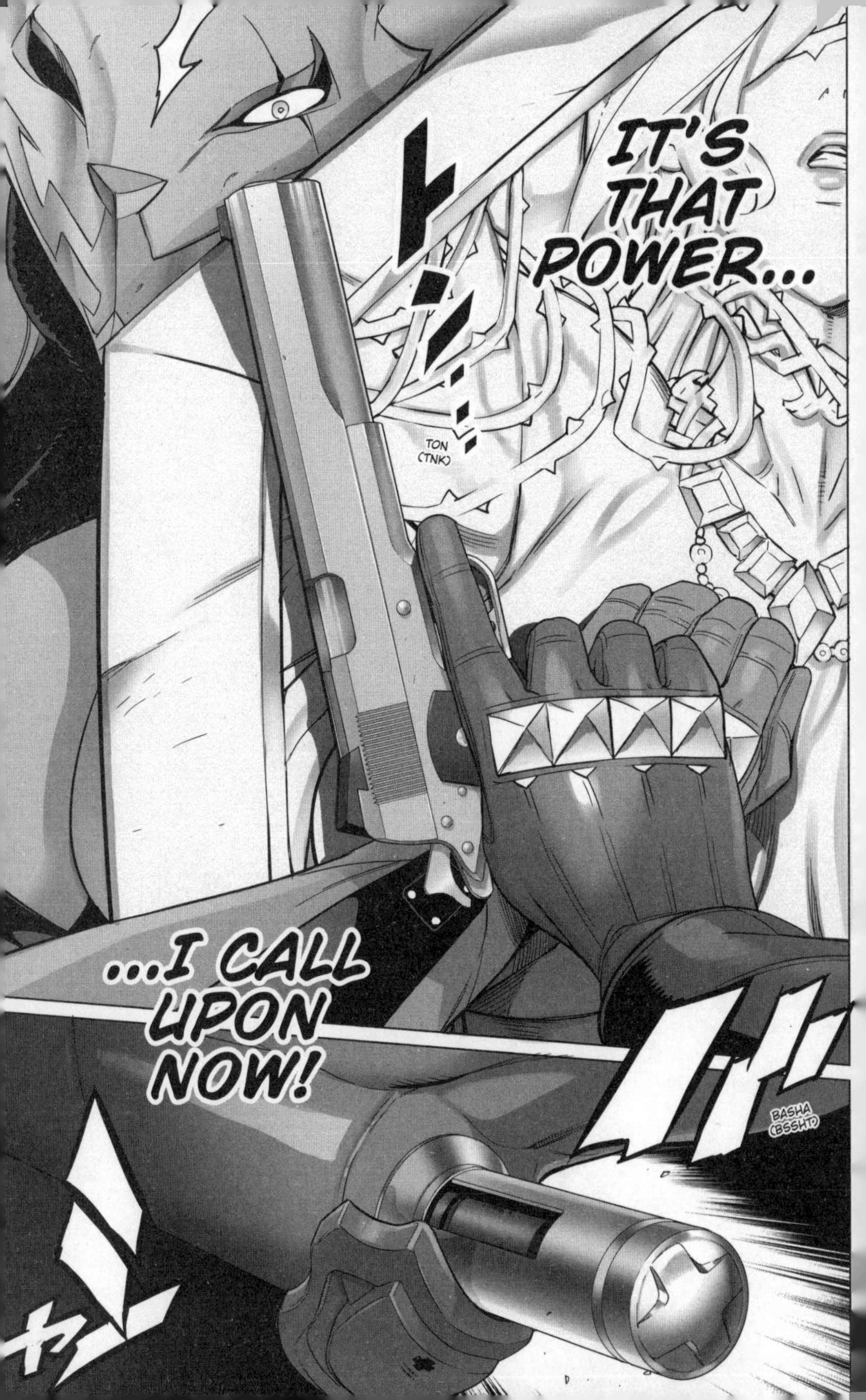
IT'S THAT POWER...
TON (TNK)
...I CALL UPON NOW!
BASHA (BSSHT)

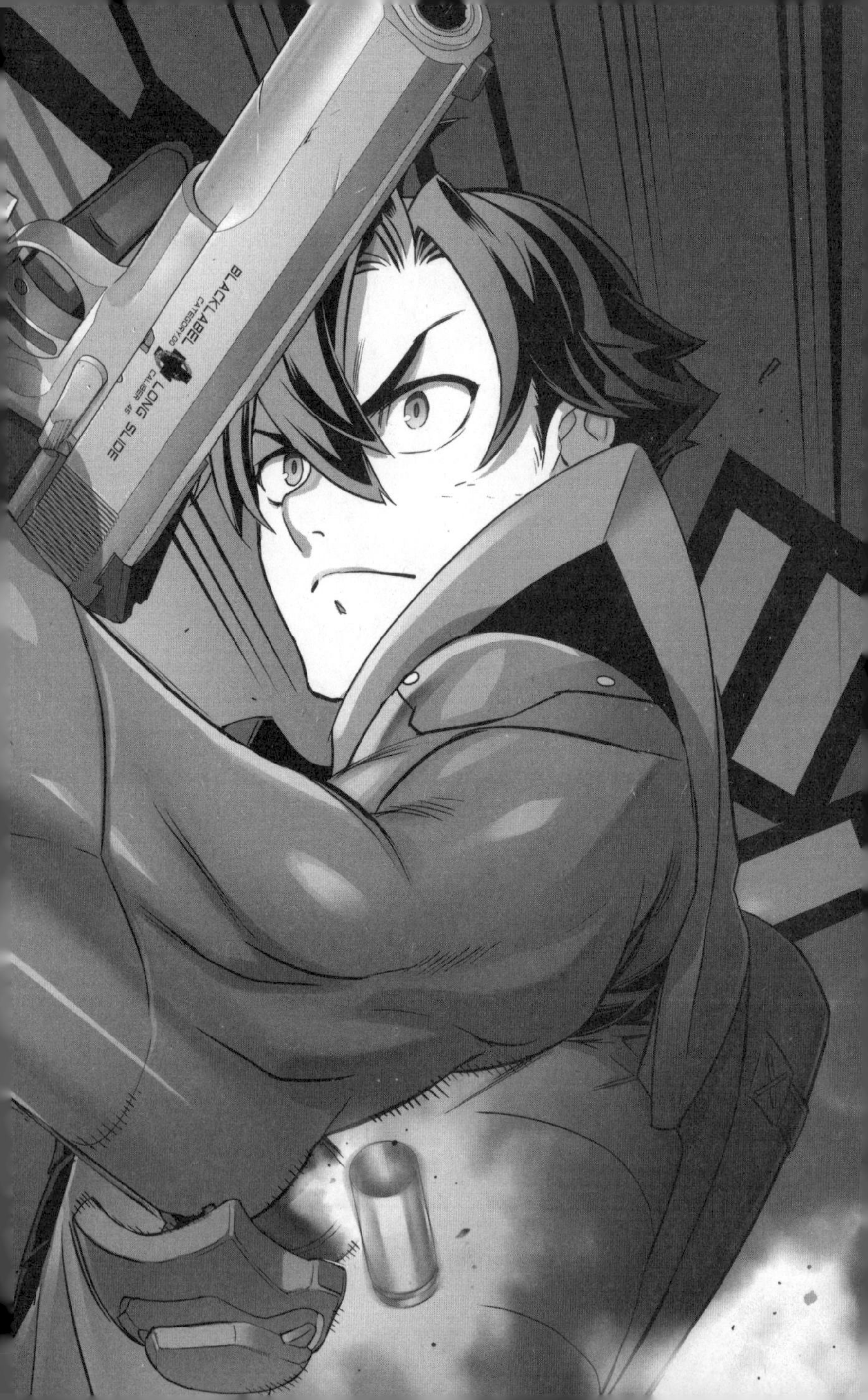
BLACKLABEL
CATEGORY:00
LONG SLIDE
CALIBER 45

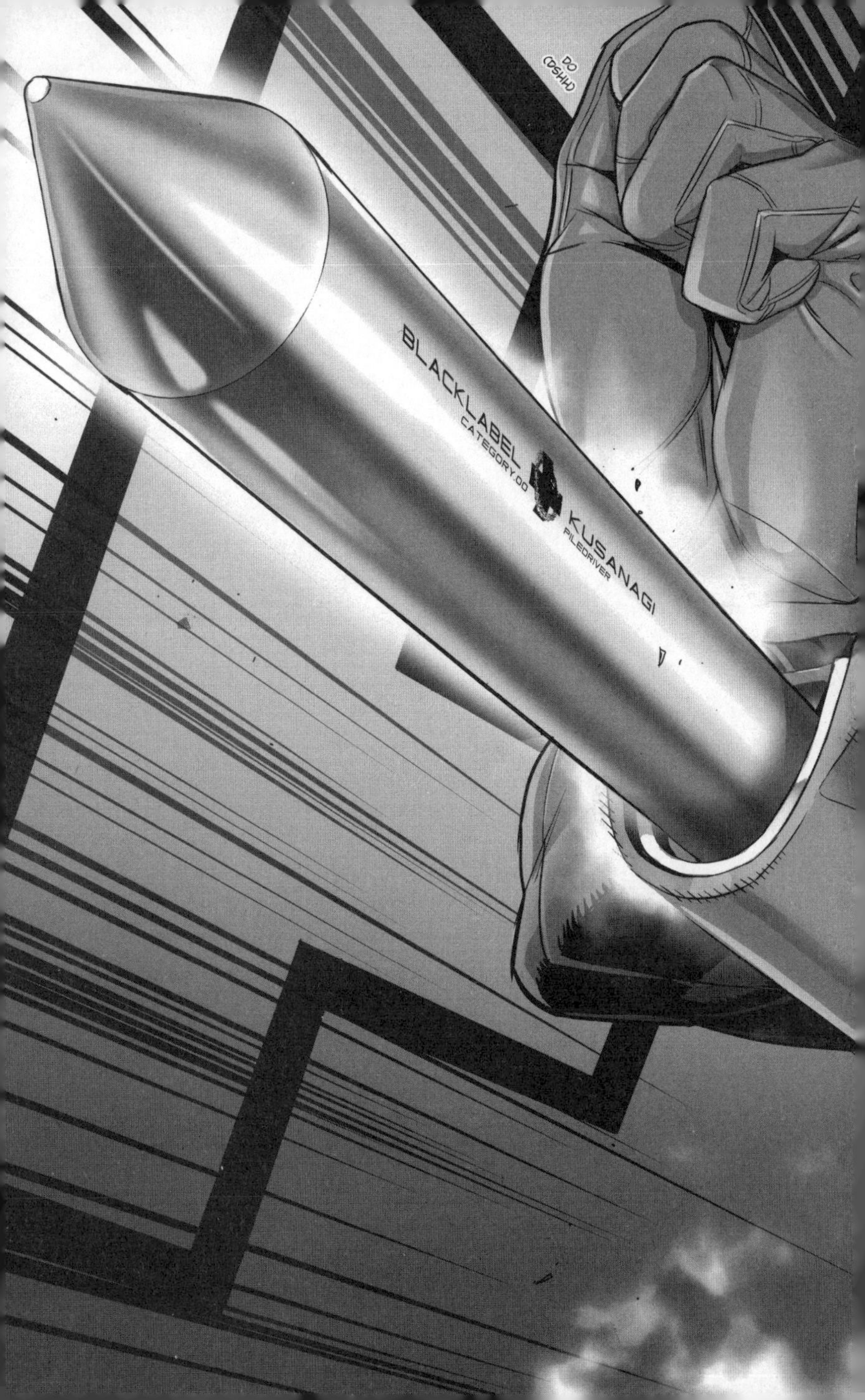
DO
(DSHH)
BLACKLABEL KUSANAGI
CATEGORY.00 PILEDRIVER

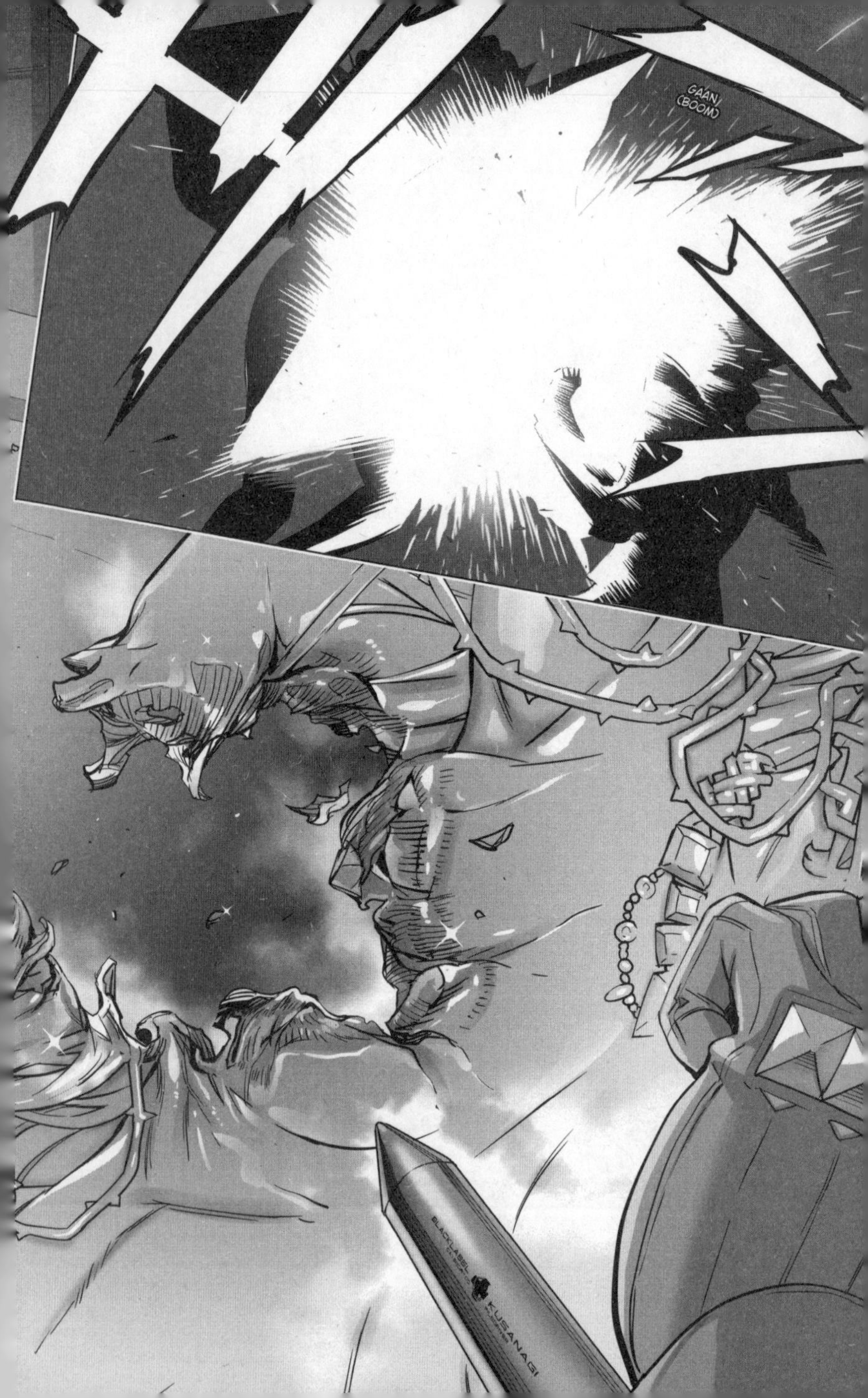
GAAN
(BOOM)
BLACKLABEL
KUSANAGI

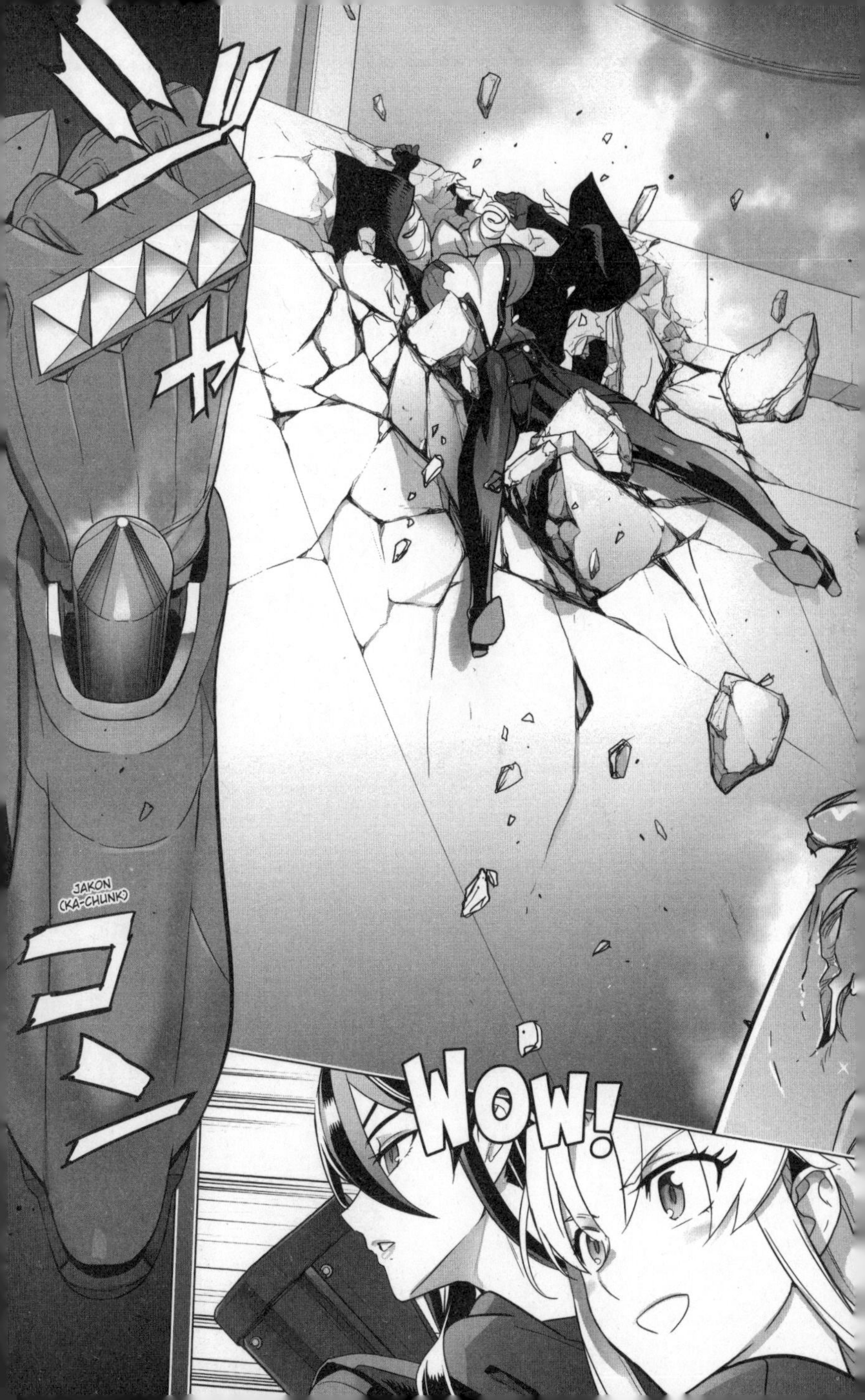
ジャコン
JAKON (KA-CHUNK)
WOW!

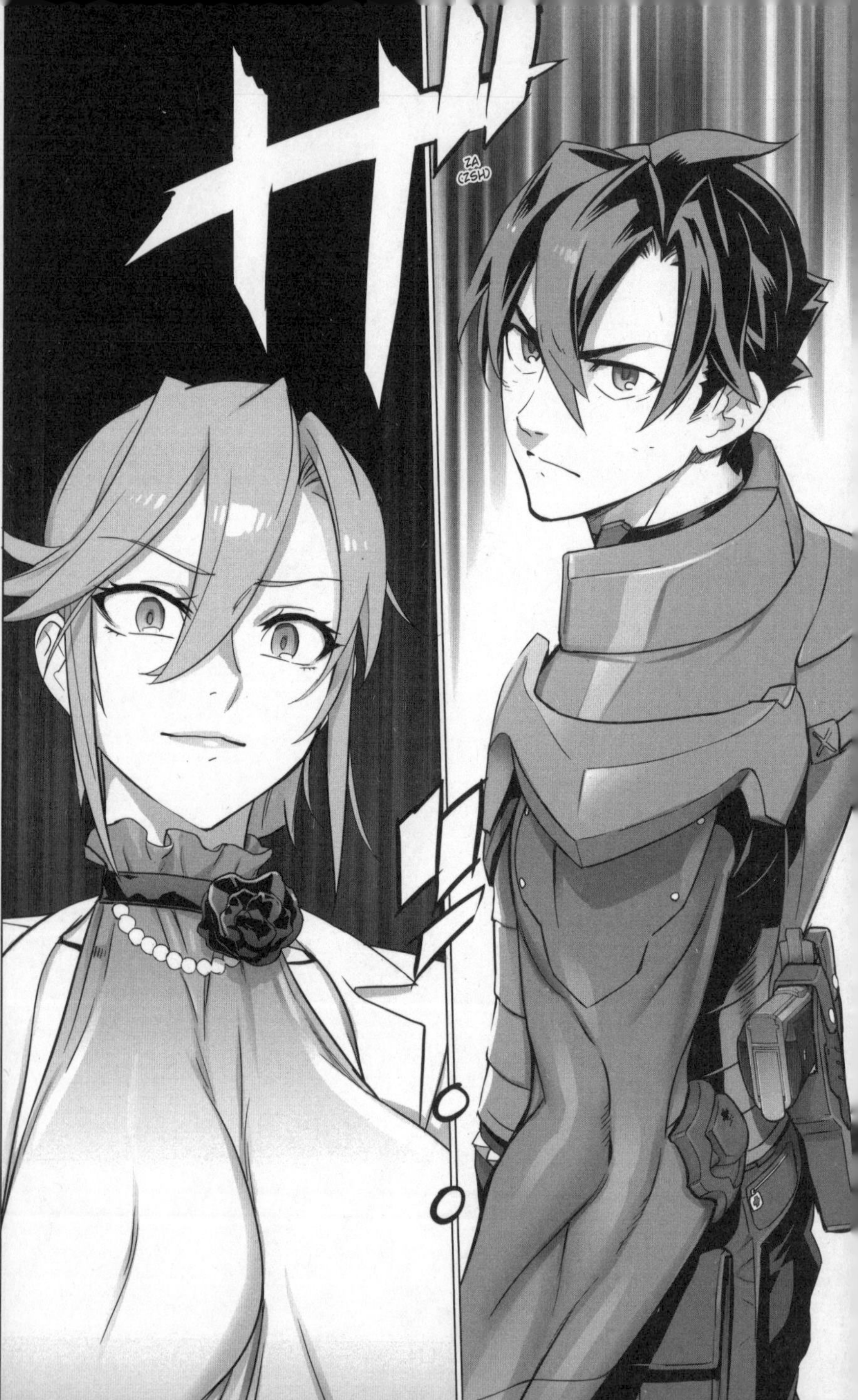
ZA
(ZSH)

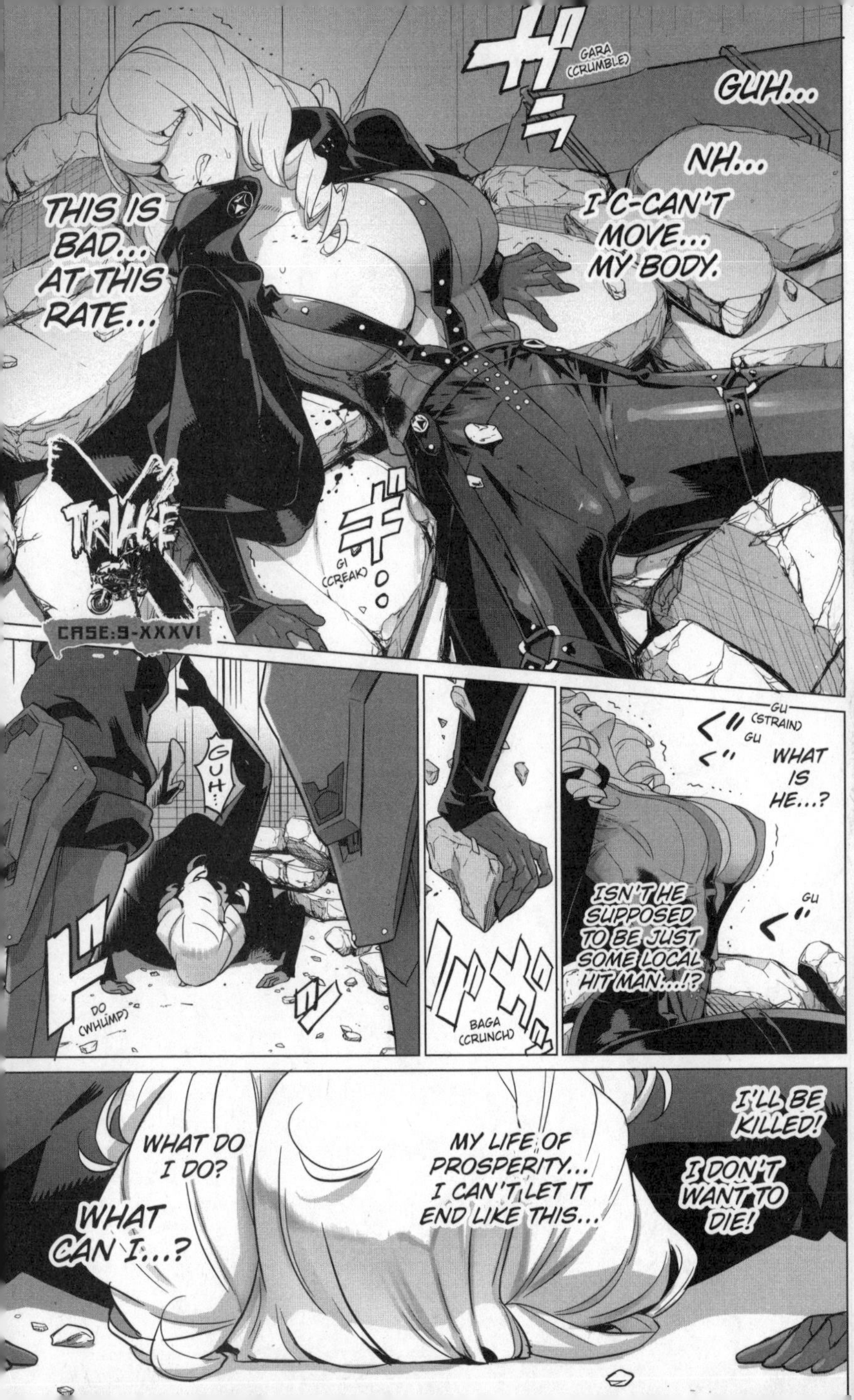
GARA (CRUMBLE)
GUH...
NH...
I C-CAN'T MOVE... MY BODY.
THIS IS BAD... AT THIS RATE...
GI (CREAK)
CASE:9-XXXVI
GU (STRAIN) GU
WHAT IS HE...?
ISN'T HE SUPPOSED TO BE JUST SOME LOCAL HIT MAN...!?
GU
BAGA (CRUNCH)
GUH...
DO (WHUMP)
I'LL BE KILLED!
I DON'T WANT TO DIE!
MY LIFE OF PROSPERITY... I CAN'T LET IT END LIKE THIS...
WHAT DO I DO?
WHAT CAN I...?

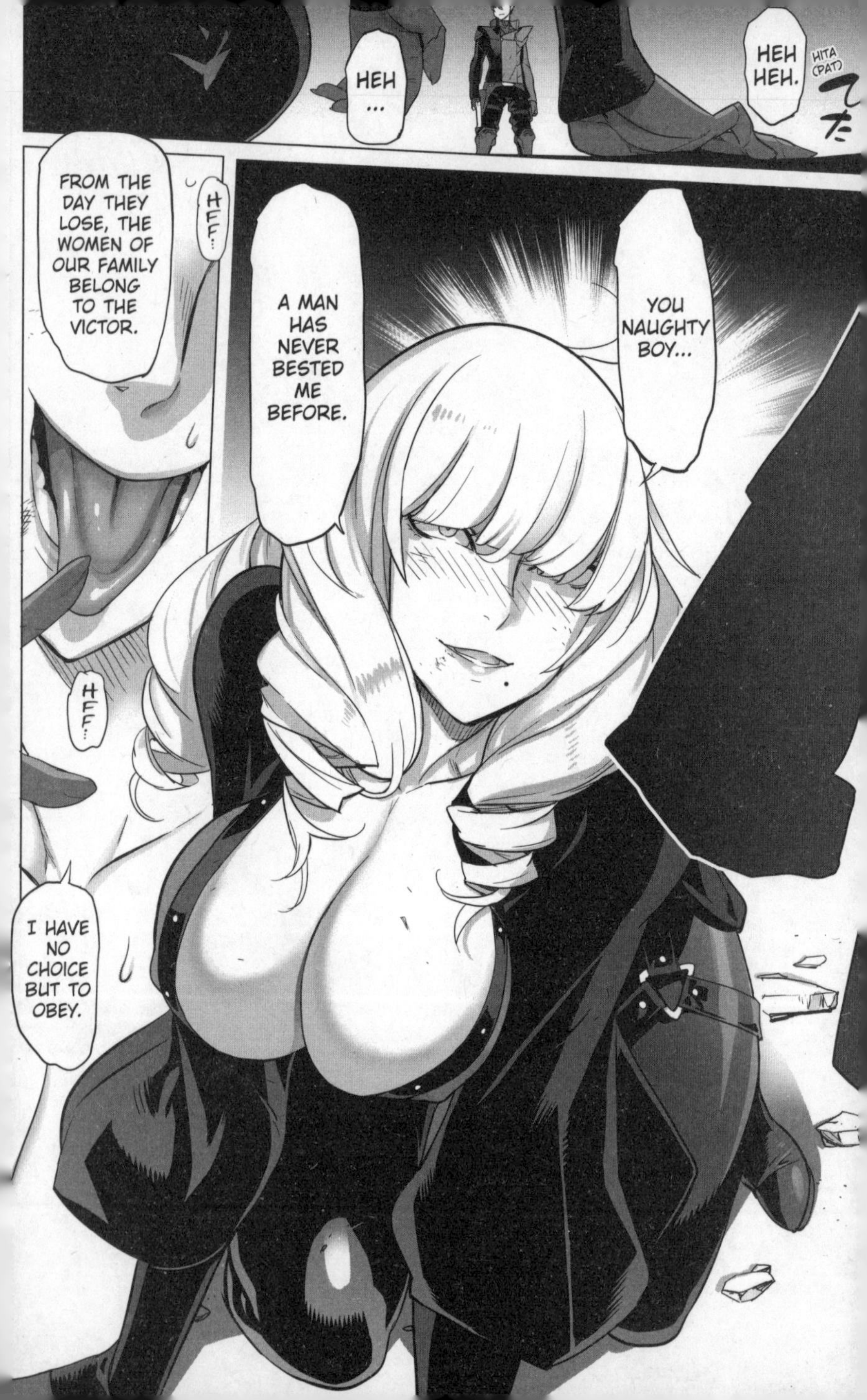
HEH HEH.
HITA (PAT)
てた
HEH ...
YOU NAUGHTY BOY...
A MAN HAS NEVER BESTED ME BEFORE.
HFF...
FROM THE DAY THEY LOSE, THE WOMEN OF OUR FAMILY BELONG TO THE VICTOR.
HFF...
I HAVE NO CHOICE BUT TO OBEY.

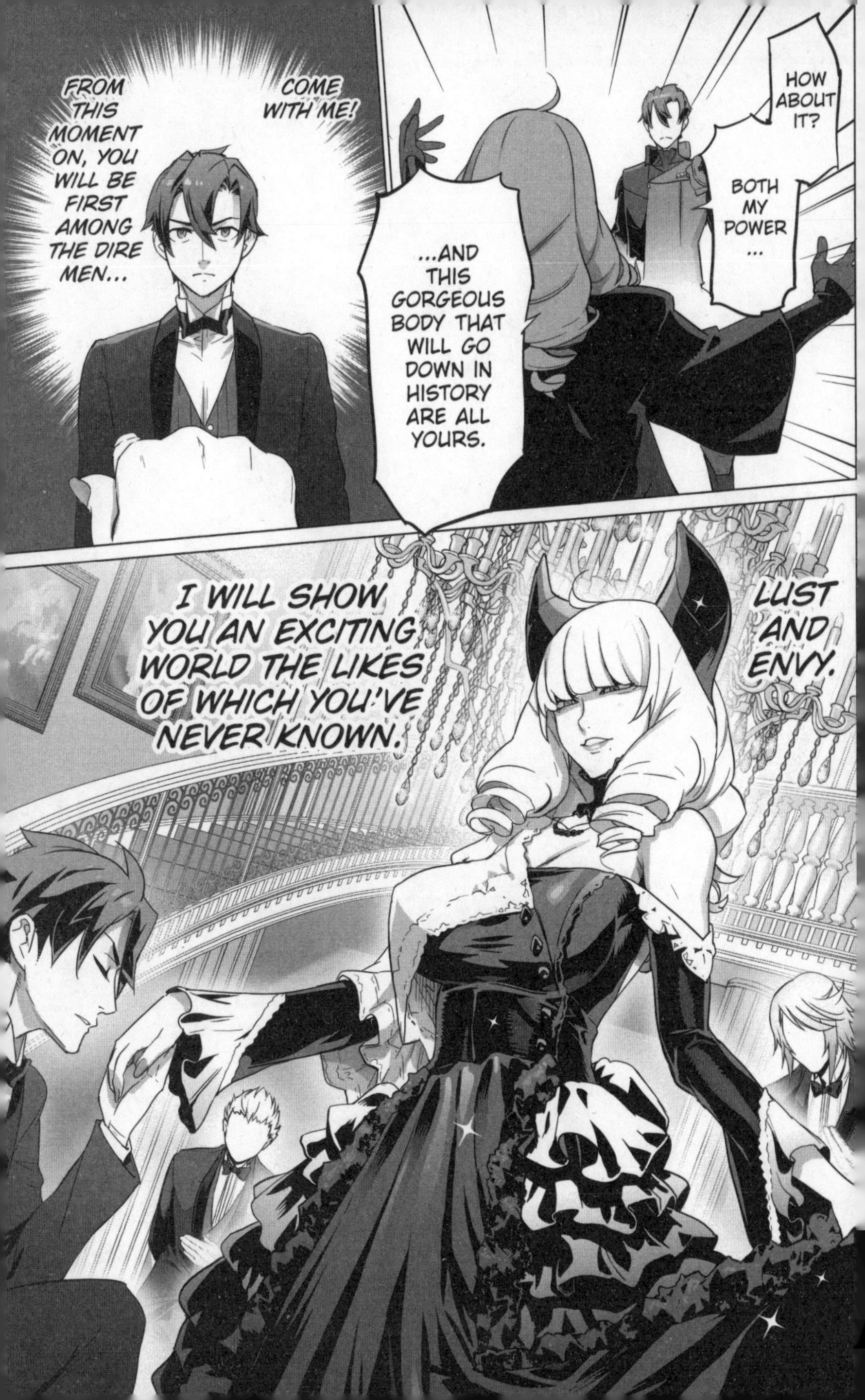
HOW ABOUT IT?
BOTH MY POWER...
...AND THIS GORGEOUS BODY THAT WILL GO DOWN IN HISTORY ARE ALL YOURS.
COME WITH ME!
FROM THIS MOMENT ON, YOU WILL BE FIRST AMONG THE DIRE MEN...
LUST AND ENVY.
I WILL SHOW YOU AN EXCITING WORLD THE LIKES OF WHICH YOU'VE NEVER KNOWN.

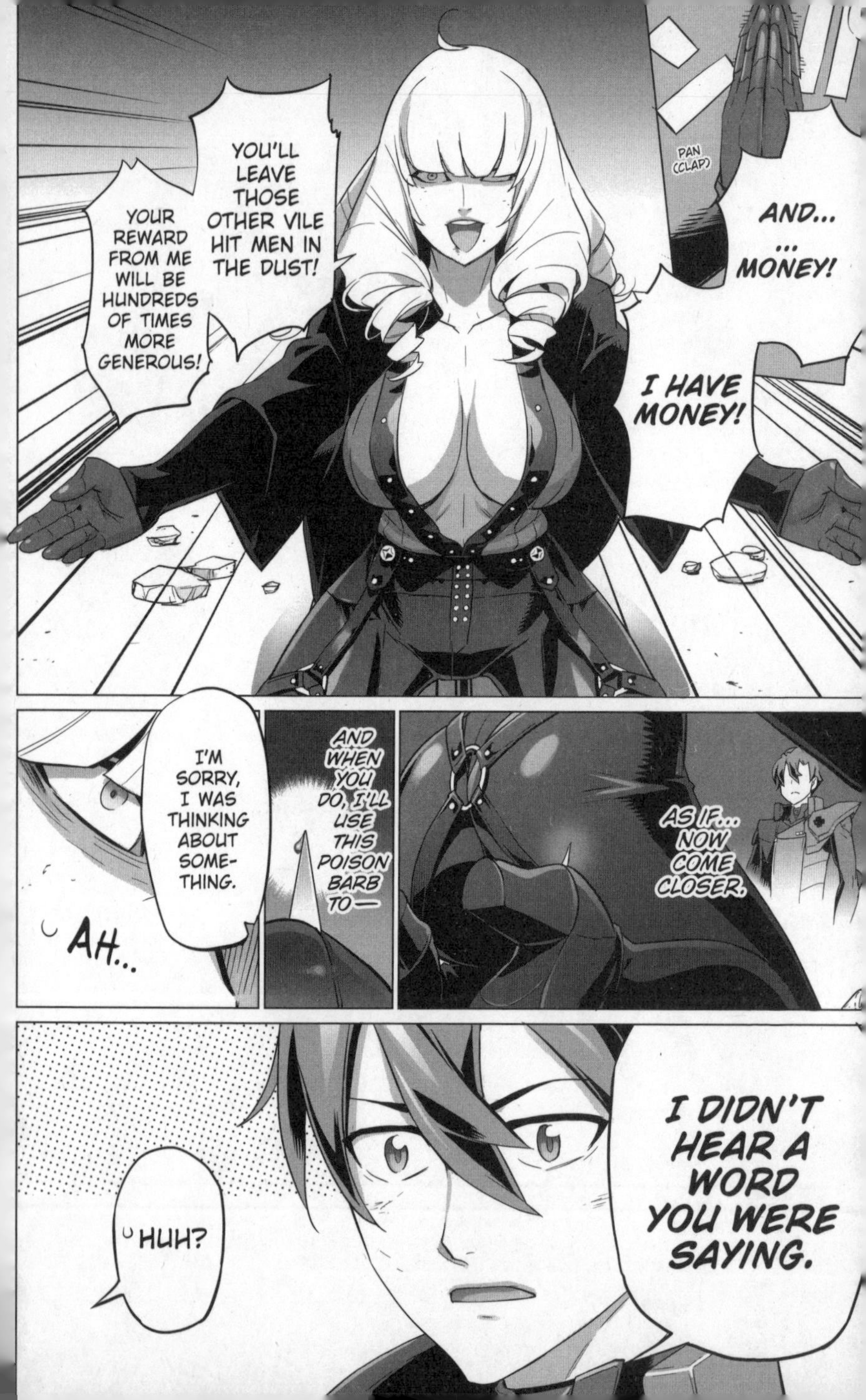
PAN (CLAP)
AND... ...MONEY!
I HAVE MONEY!
YOU'LL LEAVE THOSE OTHER VILE HIT MEN IN THE DUST!
YOUR REWARD FROM ME WILL BE HUNDREDS OF TIMES MORE GENEROUS!
AS IF... NOW COME CLOSER.
AND WHEN YOU DO, I'LL USE THIS POISON BARB TO—
I'M SORRY, I WAS THINKING ABOUT SOME-THING.
AH...
I DIDN'T HEAR A WORD YOU WERE SAYING.
HUH?

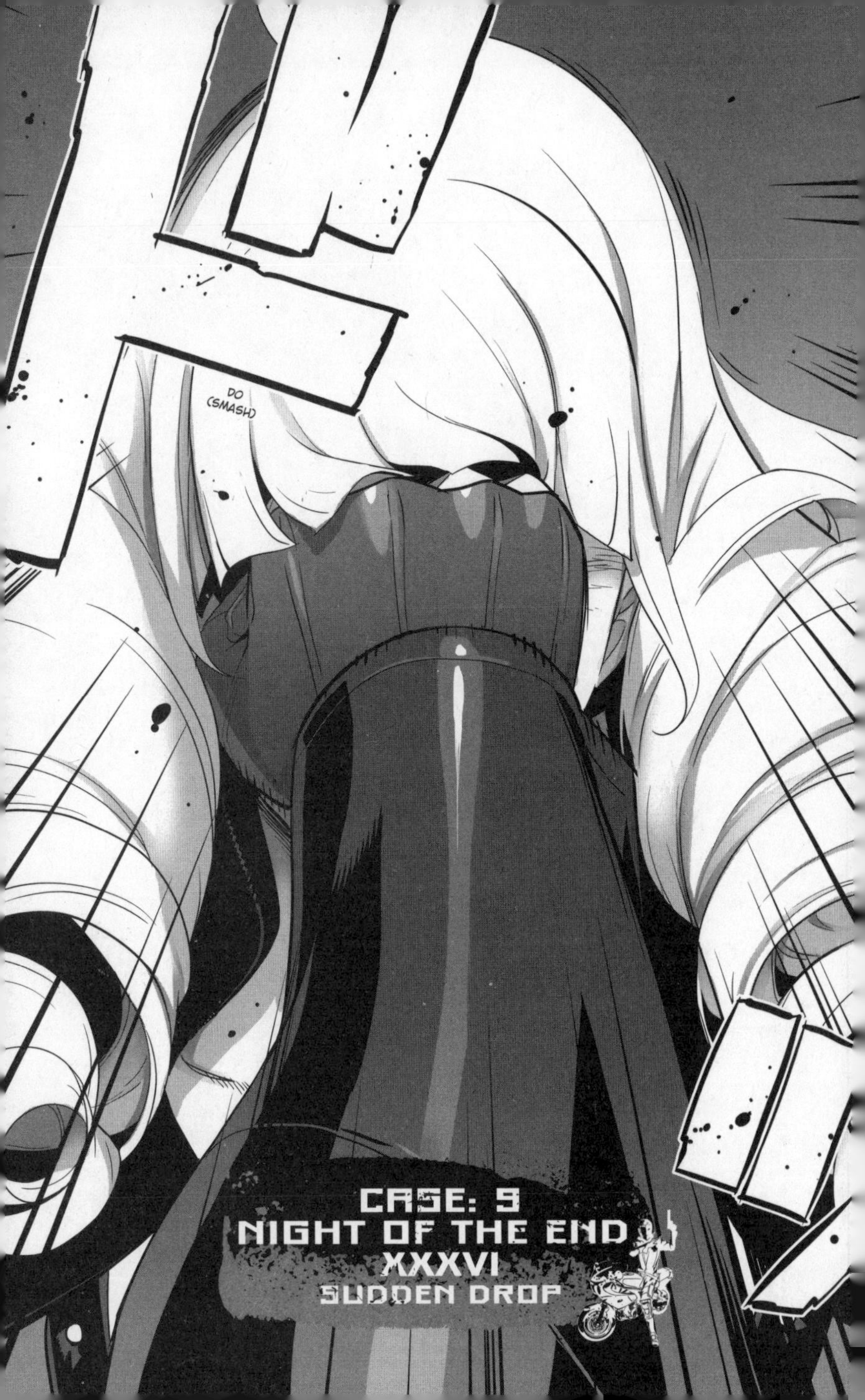
DO
(SMASH)
CASE: 9
NIGHT OF THE END
XXXVI
SUDDEN DROP

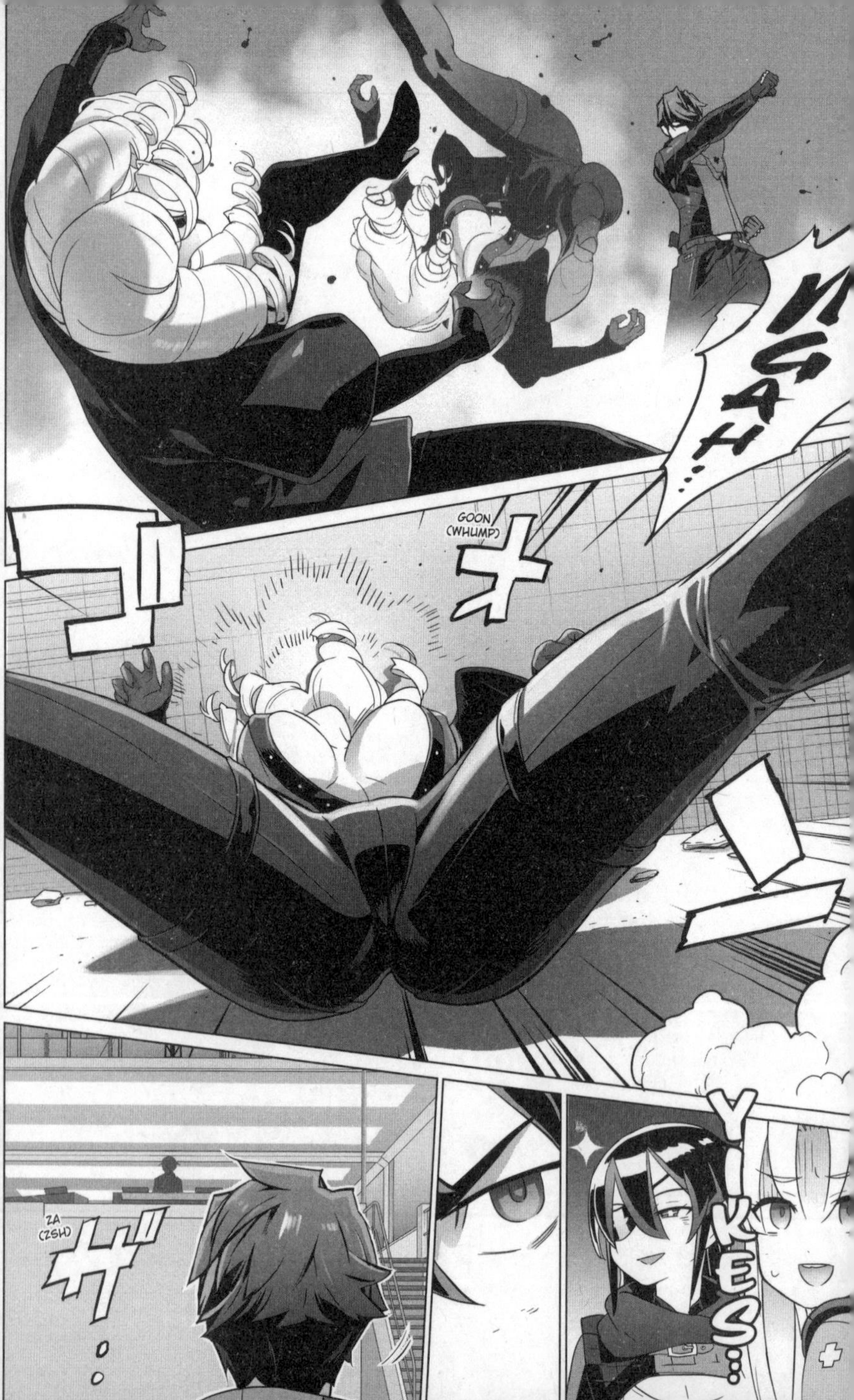
NGAH...!
GOON
(WHUMP)
YIKES...
ZA
(ZSH)

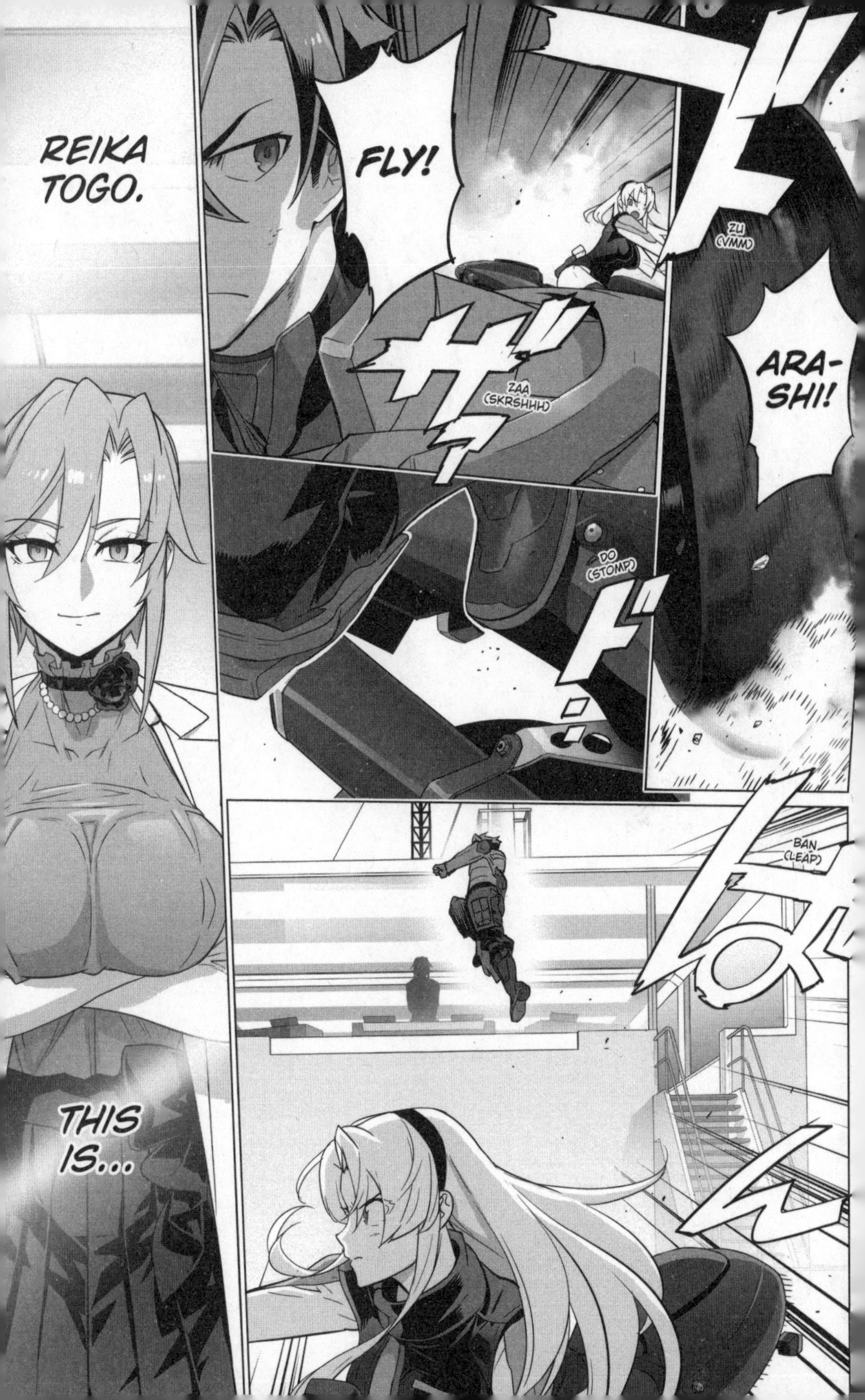
ZU (VMM)
ARA-SHI!
FLY!
ZAA (SKRSHHH)
DO (STOMP)
BAN (LEAP)
REIKA TOGO.
THIS IS...

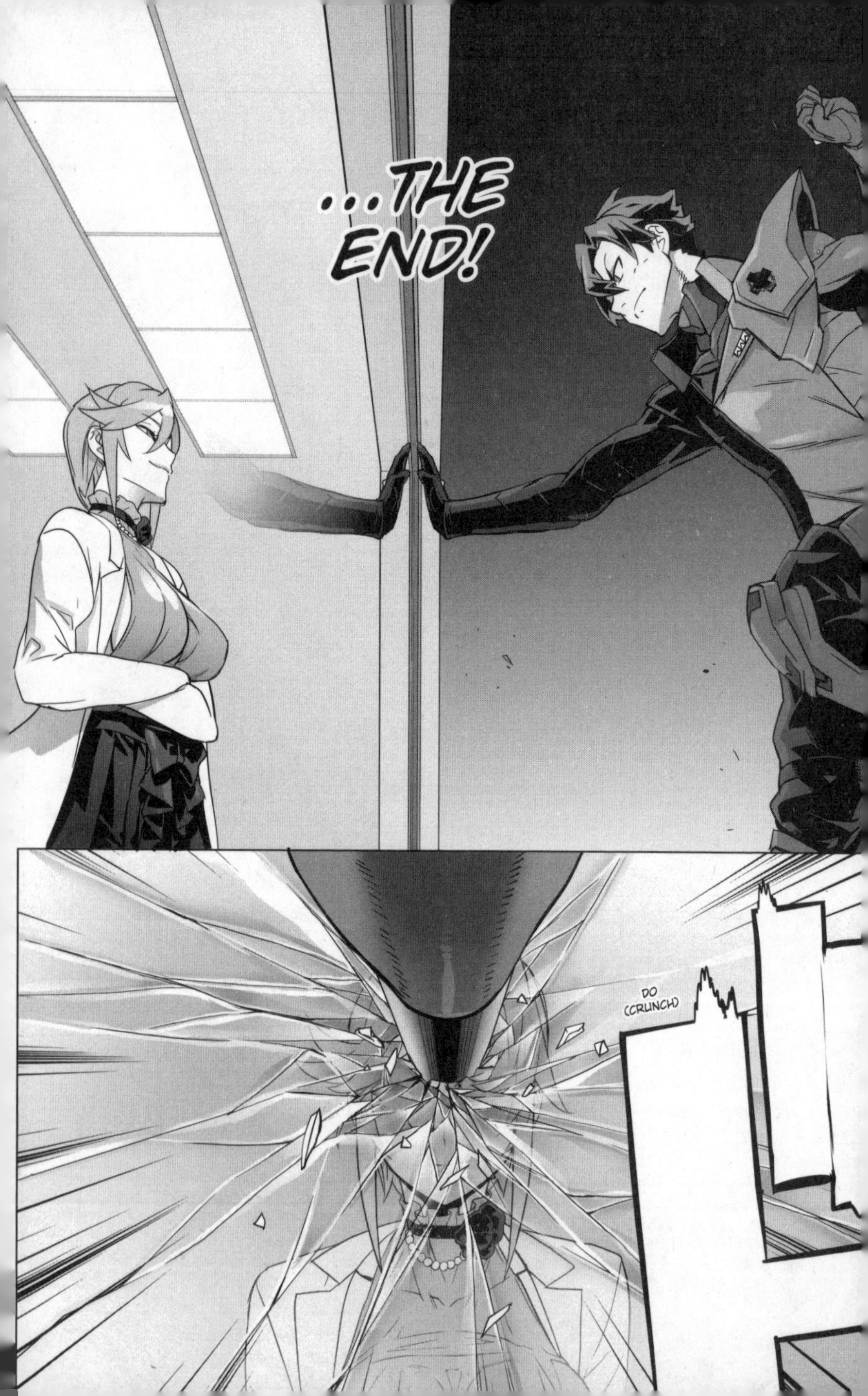
...THE END!
DO (CRUNCH)

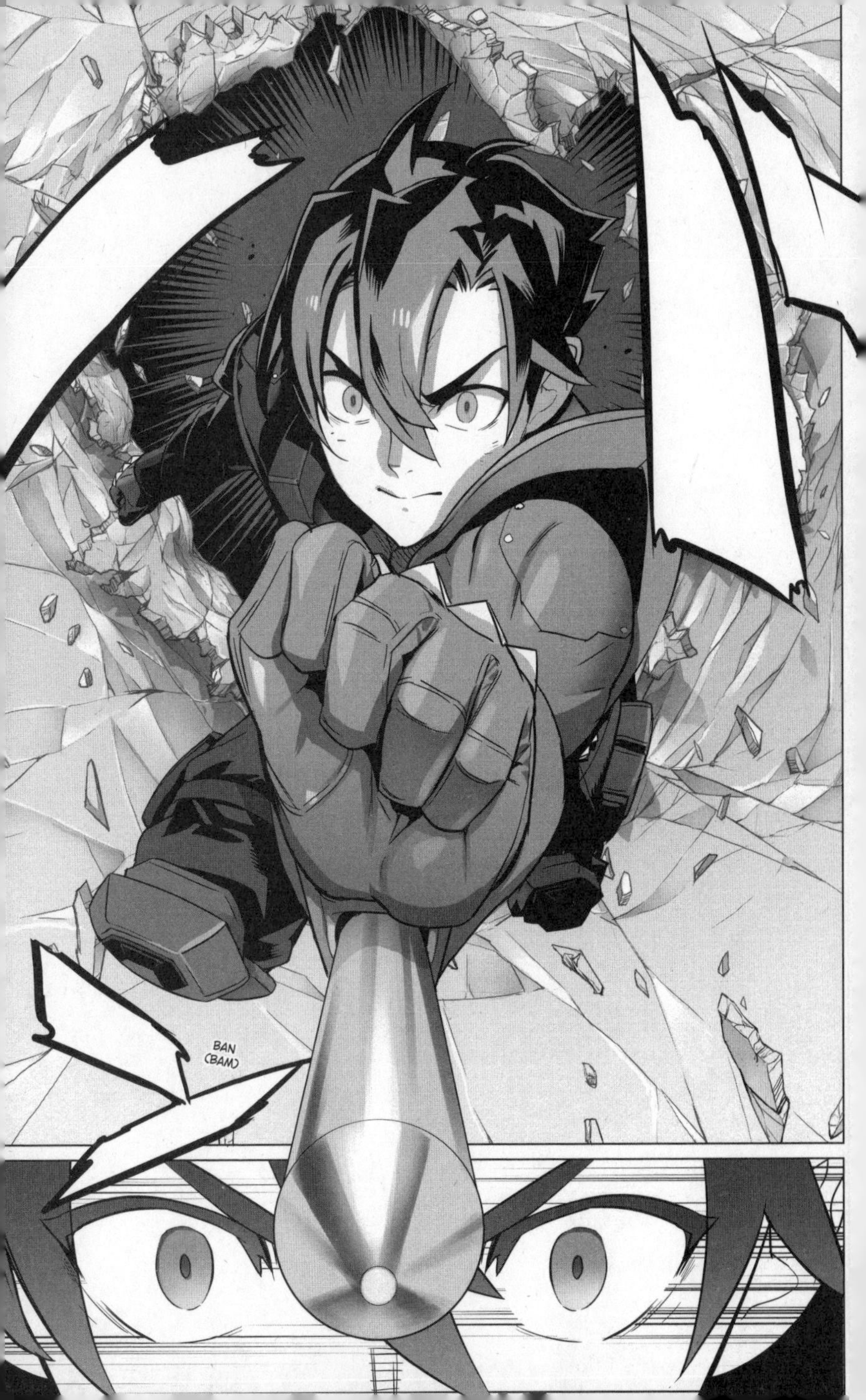
BAN
(BAM)

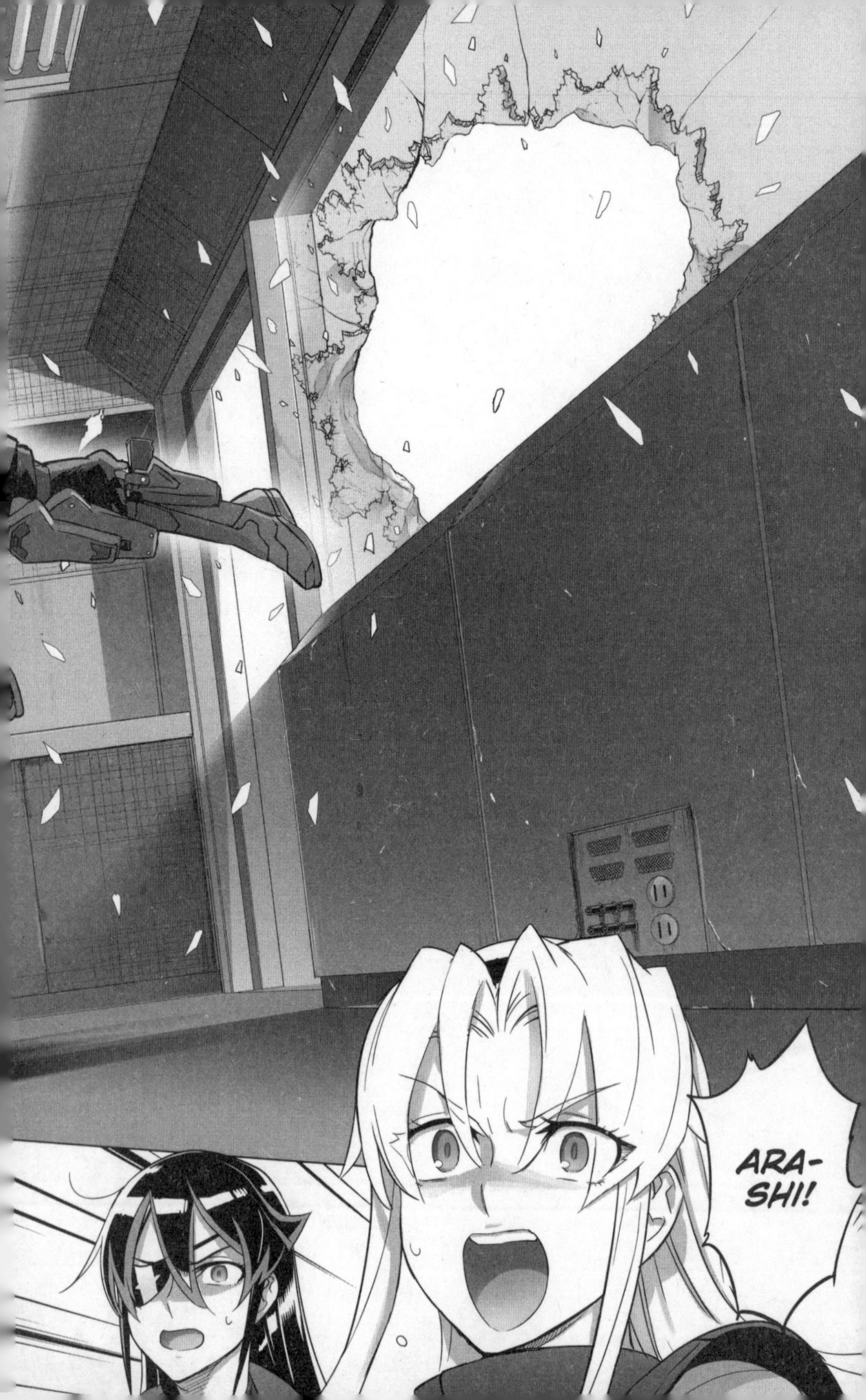
ARA-
SHI!

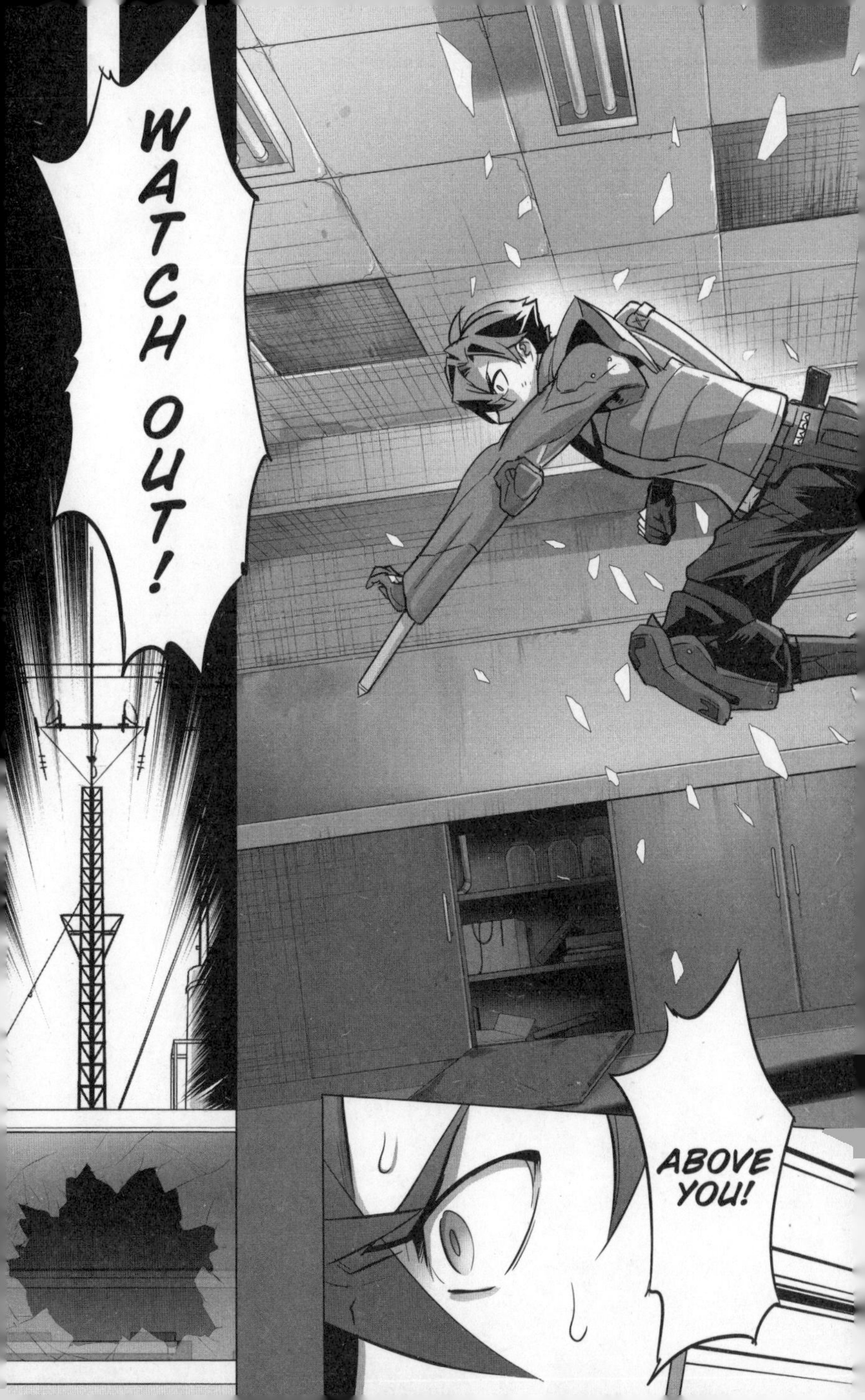
WATCH OUT!
ABOVE YOU!

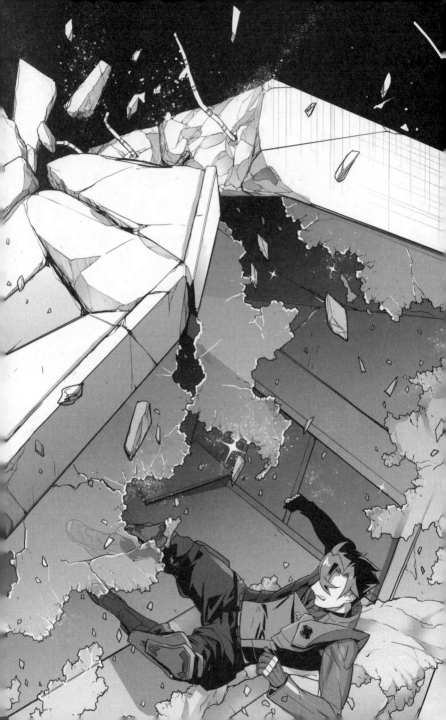

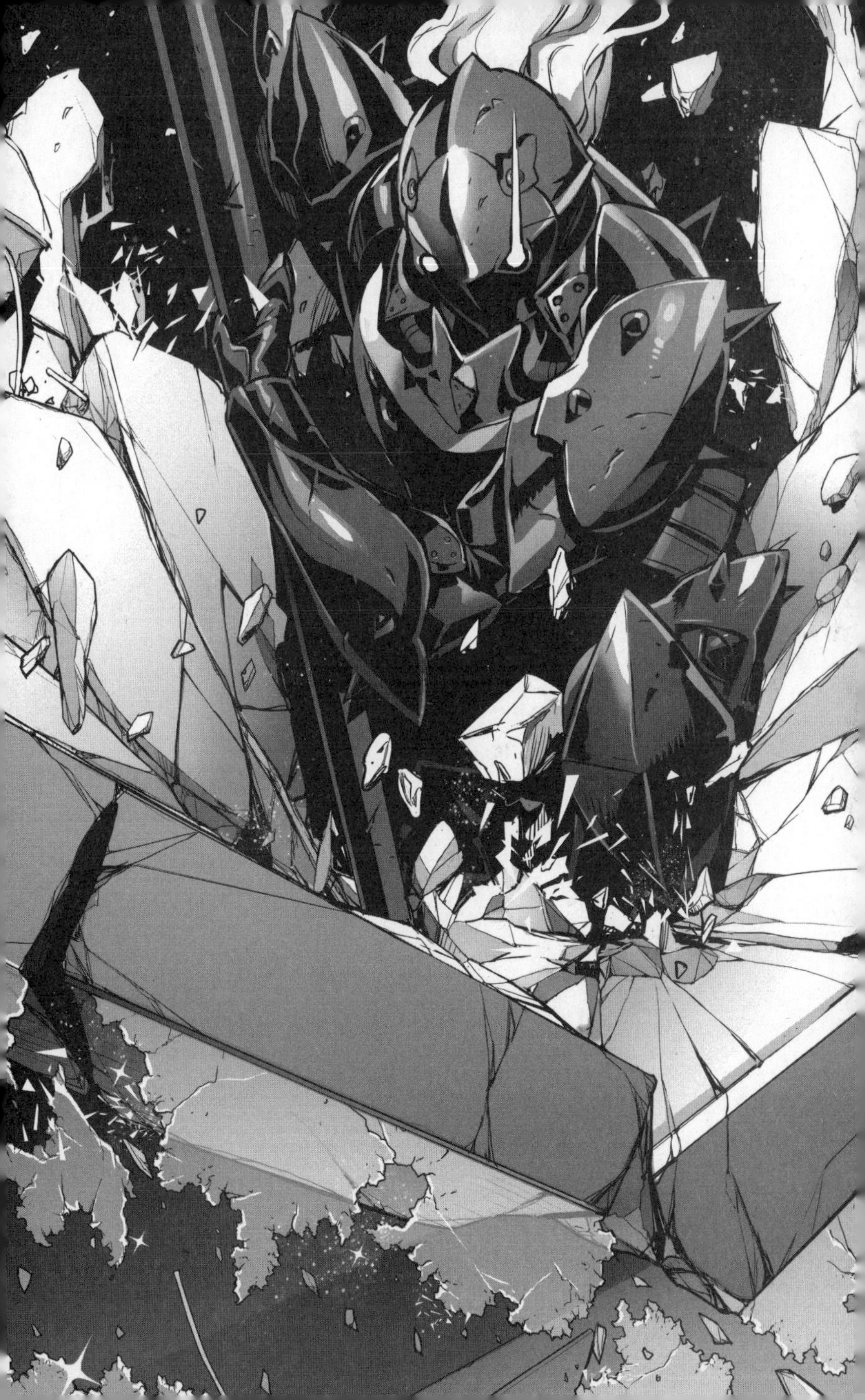

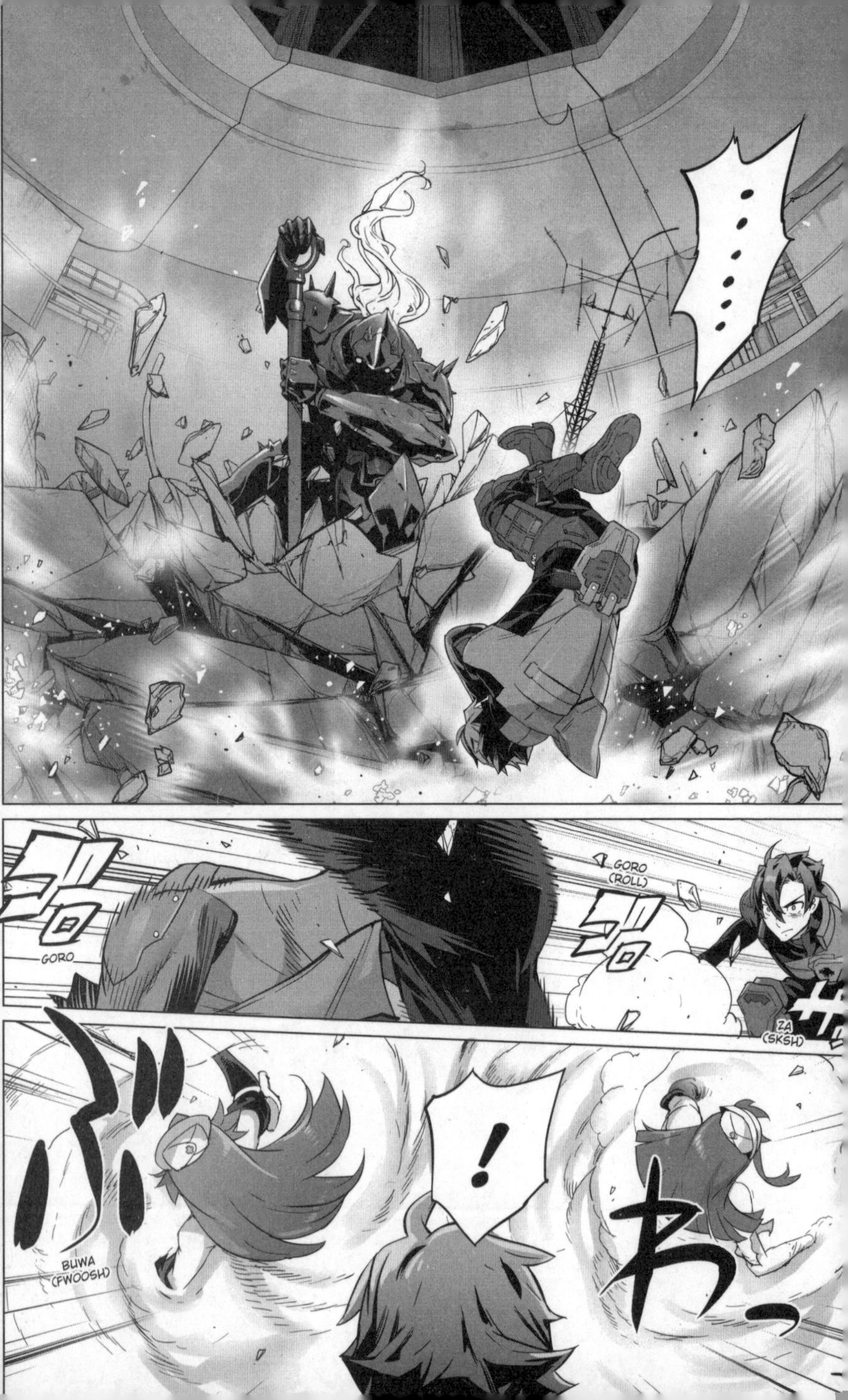
......
GORO (ROLL)
ZA (SKSH)
GORO
!
BUWA (FWOOSH)

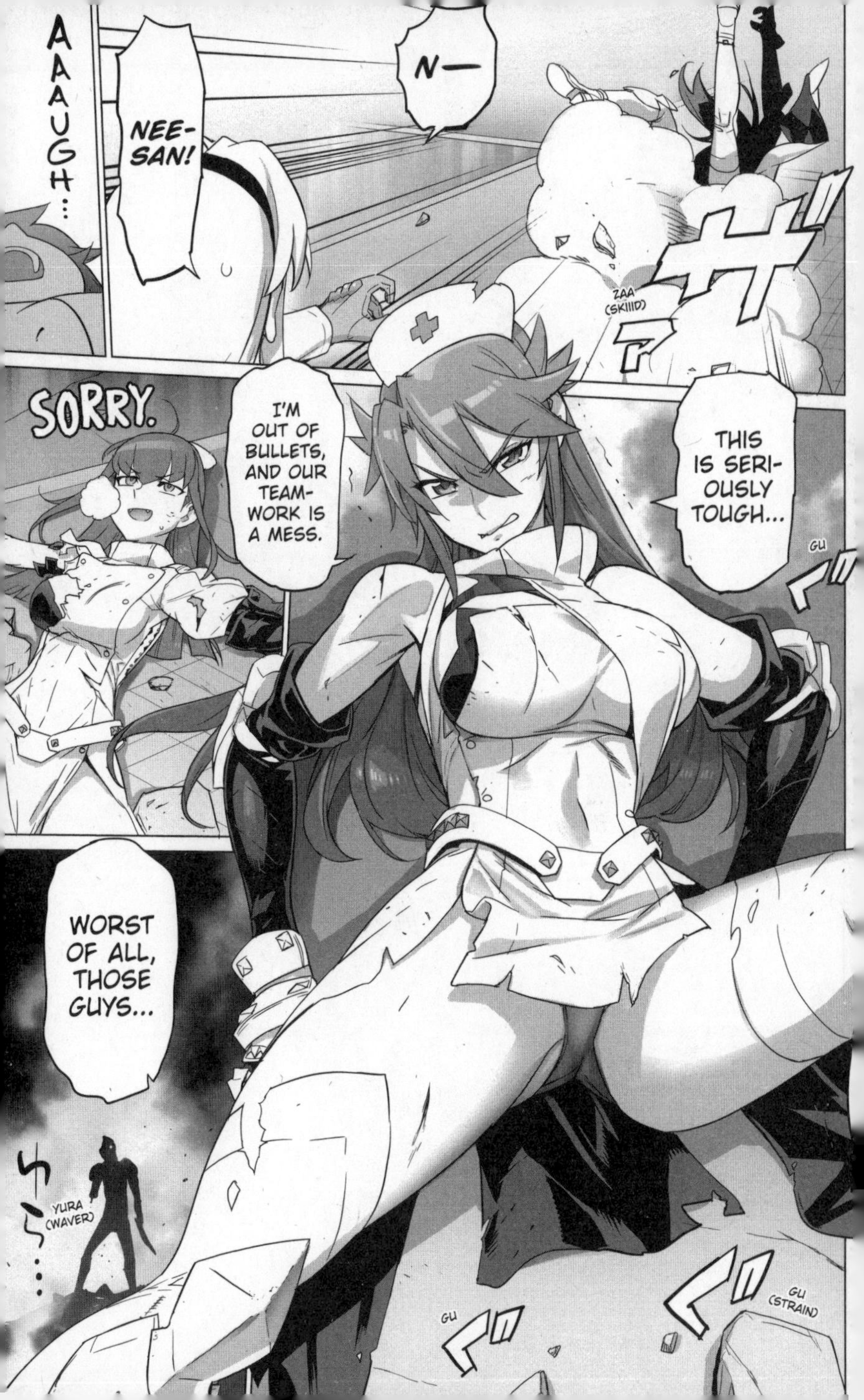
ZAA
(SKIIID)
N—
NEE-SAN!
AAAUGH...
THIS IS SERI-OUSLY TOUGH...
GU
I'M OUT OF BULLETS, AND OUR TEAM-WORK IS A MESS.
SORRY.
WORST OF ALL, THOSE GUYS...
GU
(STRAIN)
GU
YURA
(WAVER)

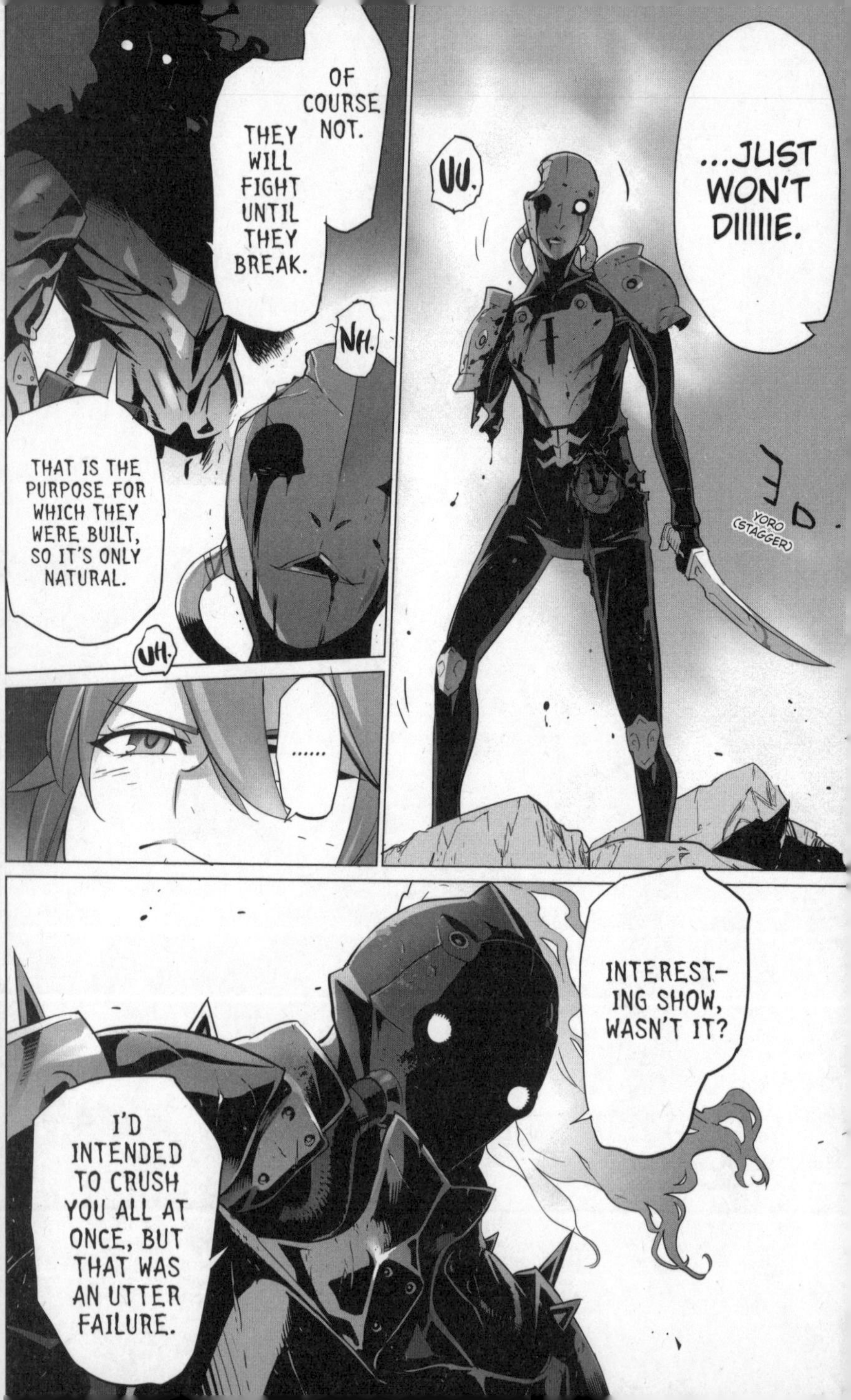
...JUST WON'T DIIIIE.
UU.
YORO (STAGGER)
OF COURSE NOT.
THEY WILL FIGHT UNTIL THEY BREAK.
NH.
THAT IS THE PURPOSE FOR WHICH THEY WERE BUILT, SO IT'S ONLY NATURAL.
UH.
......
INTEREST-ING SHOW, WASN'T IT?
I'D INTENDED TO CRUSH YOU ALL AT ONCE, BUT THAT WAS AN UTTER FAILURE.

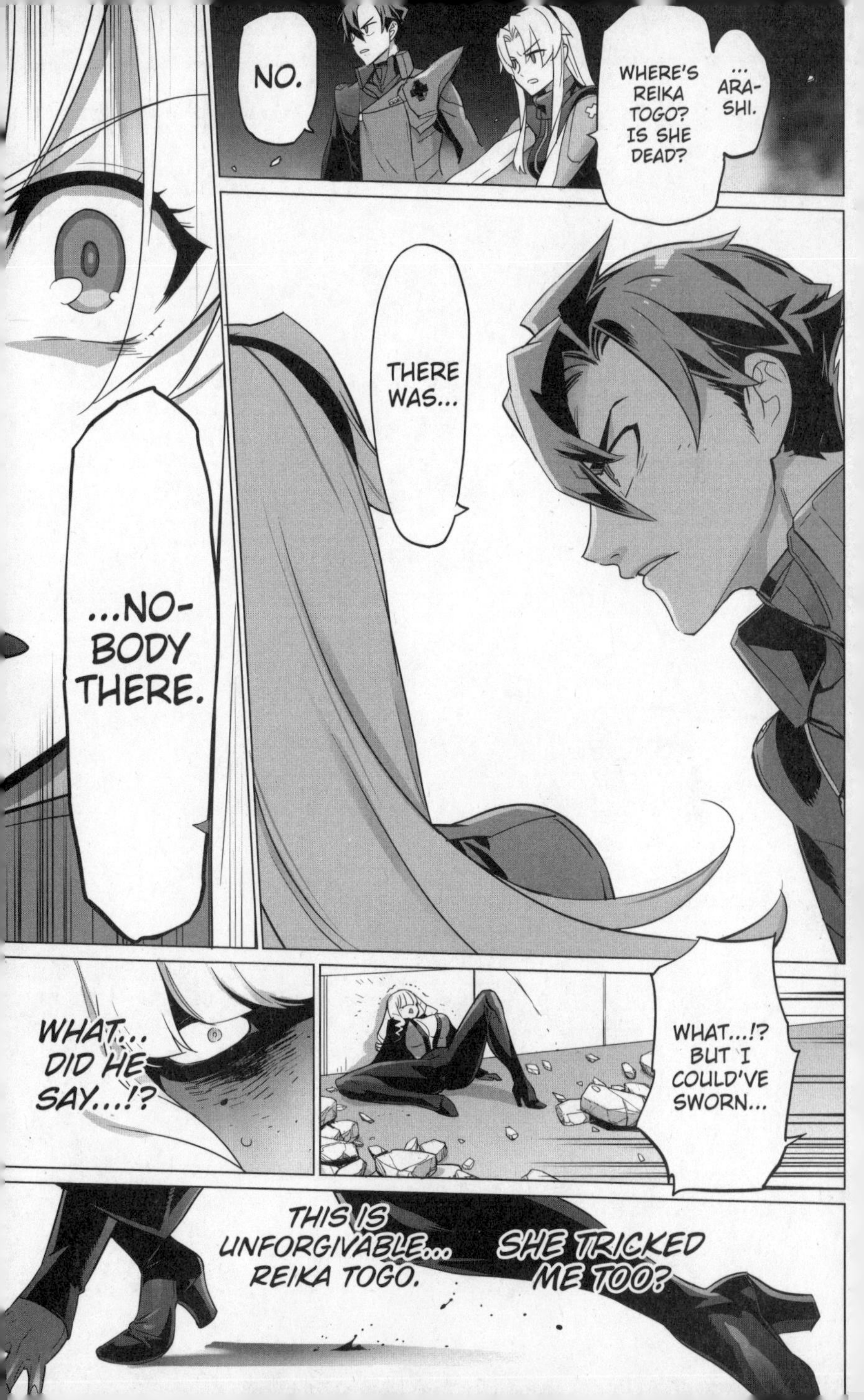
...ARA-SHI.
WHERE'S REIKA TOGO? IS SHE DEAD?
NO.
THERE WAS...
...NO-BODY THERE.
WHAT...!? BUT I COULD'VE SWORN...
WHAT... DID HE SAY...!?
SHE TRICKED ME TOO?
THIS IS UNFORGIVABLE... REIKA TOGO.

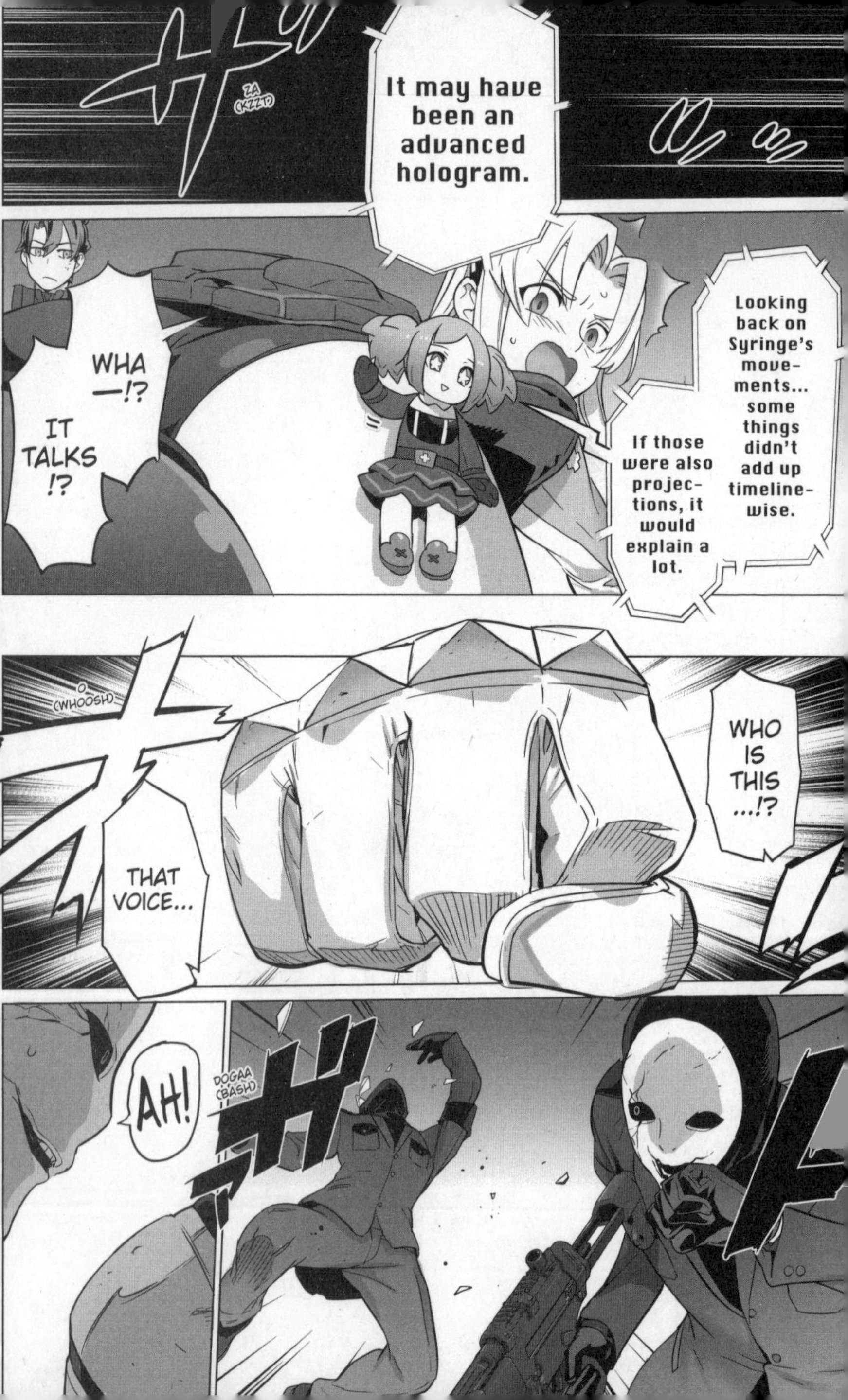
It may have been an advanced hologram.
ZA (KZZT)
Looking back on Syringe's movements... some things didn't add up timeline-wise.
If those were also projections, it would explain a lot.
WHA—!? IT TALKS!?
WHO IS THIS...!?
O (WHOOSH)
THAT VOICE...
DOGAA (BASH)
AH!

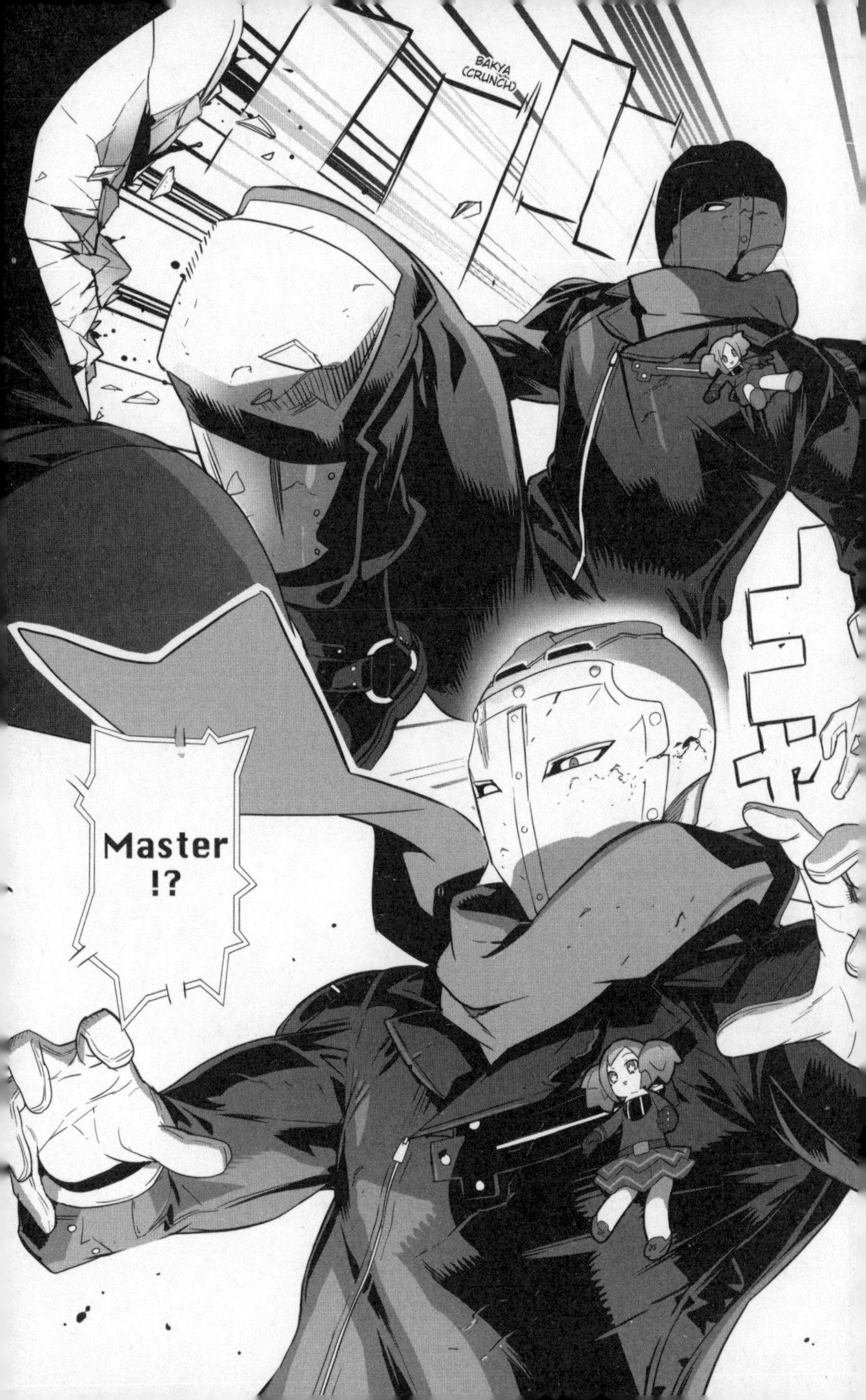
BAKYA (CRUNCH)
Master !?

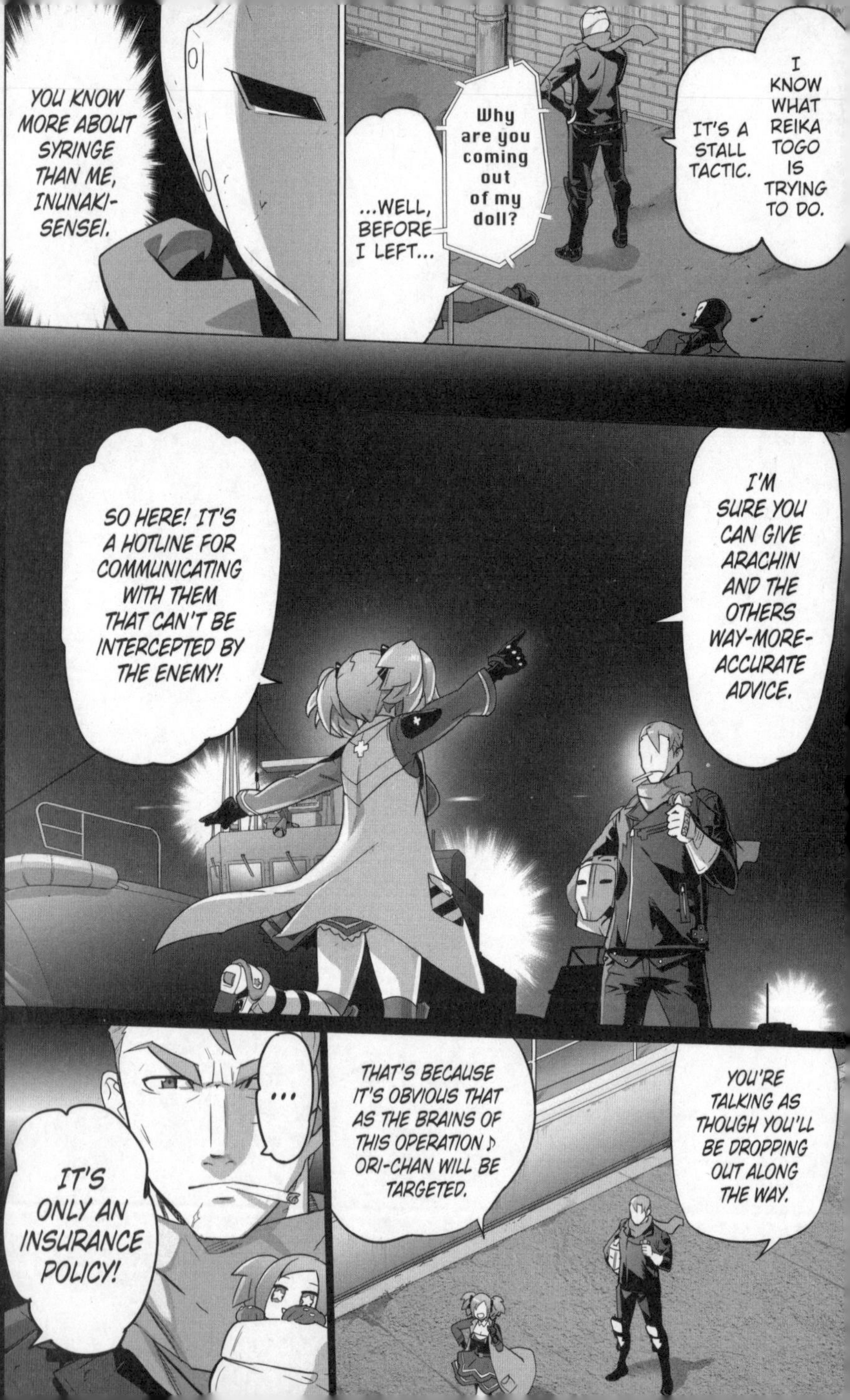
I KNOW WHAT REIKA TOGO IS TRYING TO DO.
IT'S A STALL TACTIC.
Why are you coming out of my doll?
...WELL, BEFORE I LEFT...
YOU KNOW MORE ABOUT SYRINGE THAN ME, INUNAKI-SENSEI.
I'M SURE YOU CAN GIVE ARACHIN AND THE OTHERS WAY-MORE-ACCURATE ADVICE.
SO HERE! IT'S A HOTLINE FOR COMMUNICATING WITH THEM THAT CAN'T BE INTERCEPTED BY THE ENEMY!
YOU'RE TALKING AS THOUGH YOU'LL BE DROPPING OUT ALONG THE WAY.
THAT'S BECAUSE IT'S OBVIOUS THAT AS THE BRAINS OF THIS OPERATION ♪ ORI-CHAN WILL BE TARGETED.
...
IT'S ONLY AN INSURANCE POLICY!

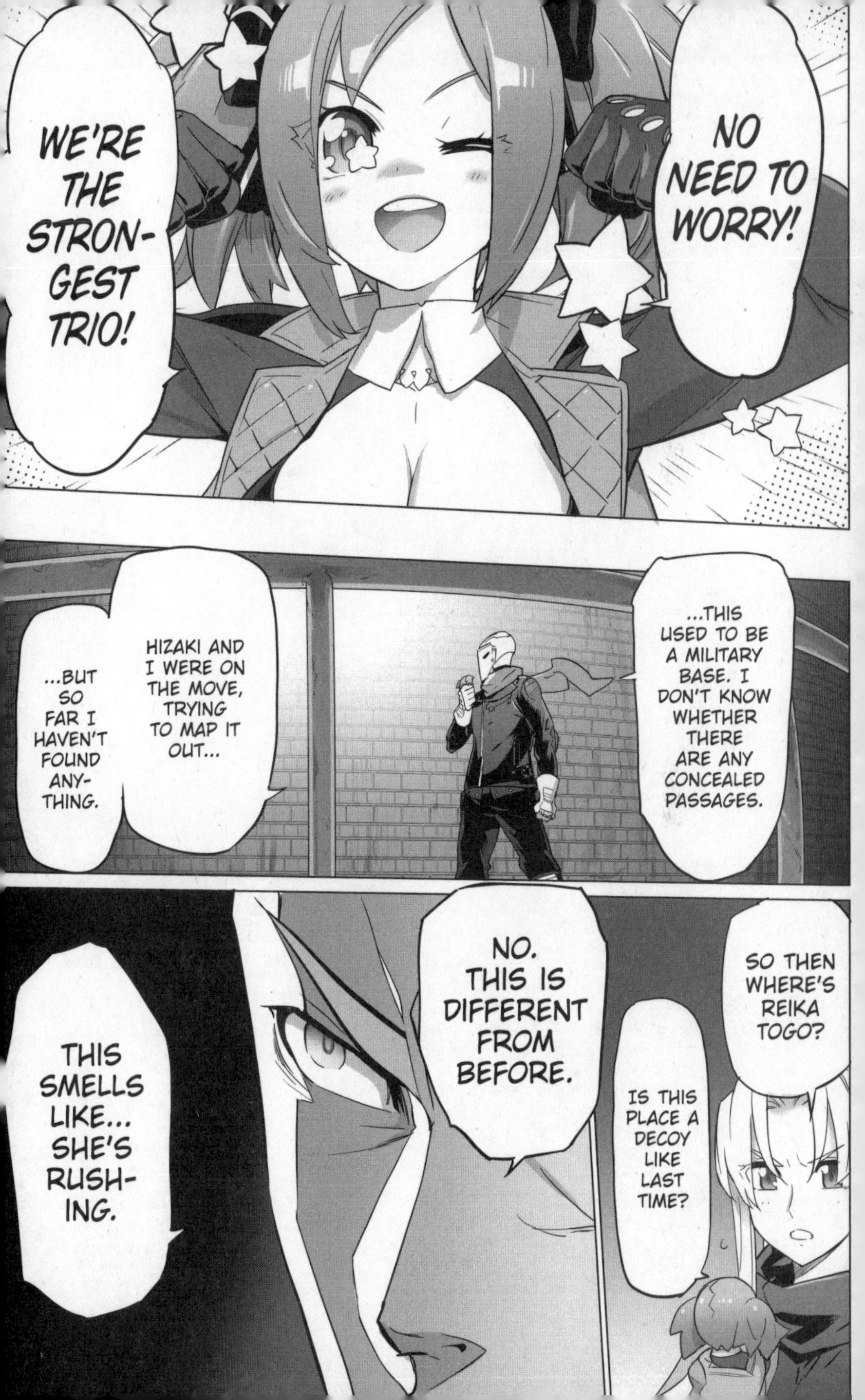
NO NEED TO WORRY!
WE'RE THE STRON-GEST TRIO!
...THIS USED TO BE A MILITARY BASE. I DON'T KNOW WHETHER THERE ARE ANY CONCEALED PASSAGES.
HIZAKI AND I WERE ON THE MOVE, TRYING TO MAP IT OUT...
...BUT SO FAR I HAVEN'T FOUND ANY-THING.
SO THEN WHERE'S REIKA TOGO?
IS THIS PLACE A DECOY LIKE LAST TIME?
NO. THIS IS DIFFERENT FROM BEFORE.
THIS SMELLS LIKE... SHE'S RUSH-ING.

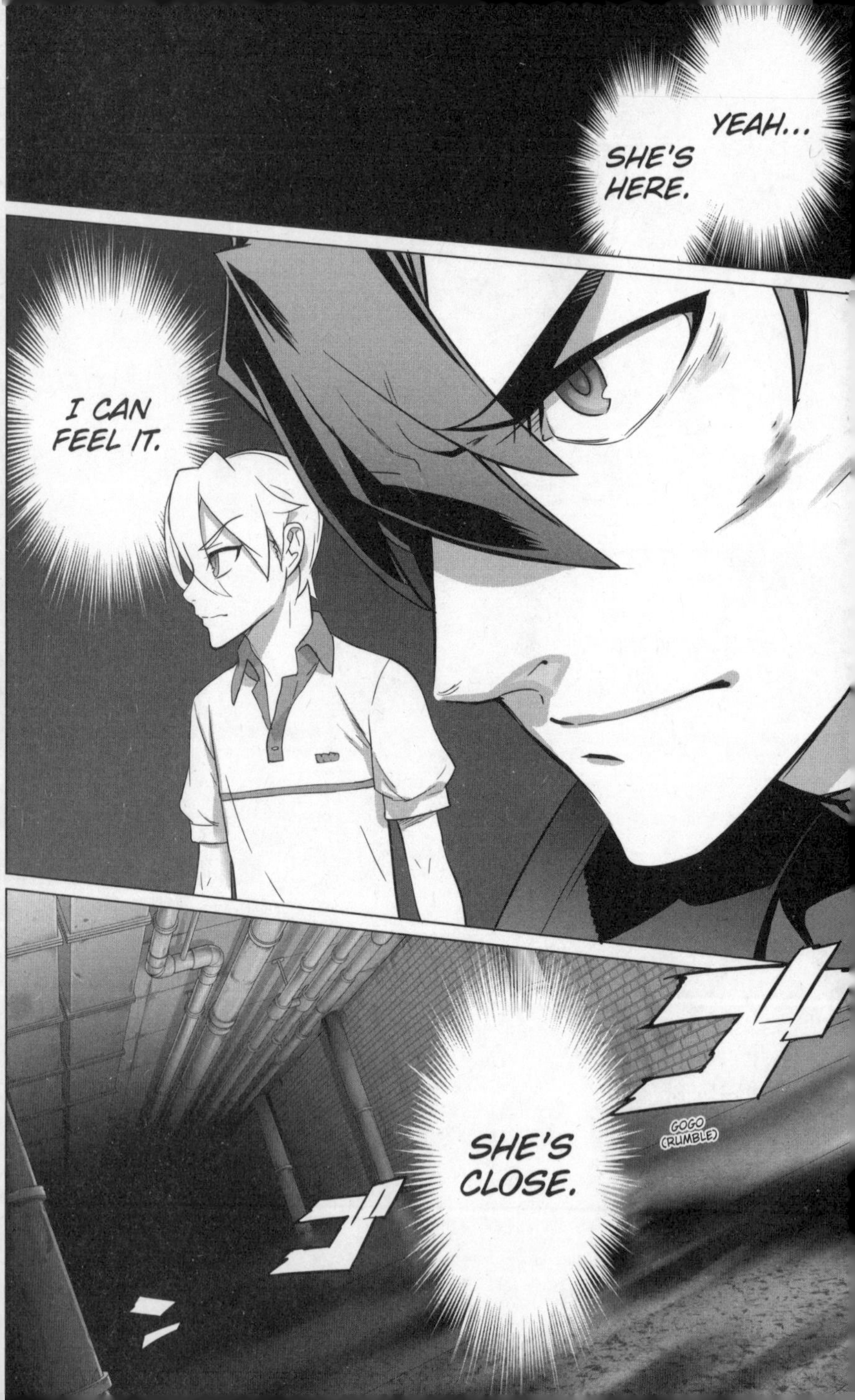
YEAH... SHE'S HERE.
I CAN FEEL IT.
GOGO (RUMBLE)
SHE'S CLOSE.

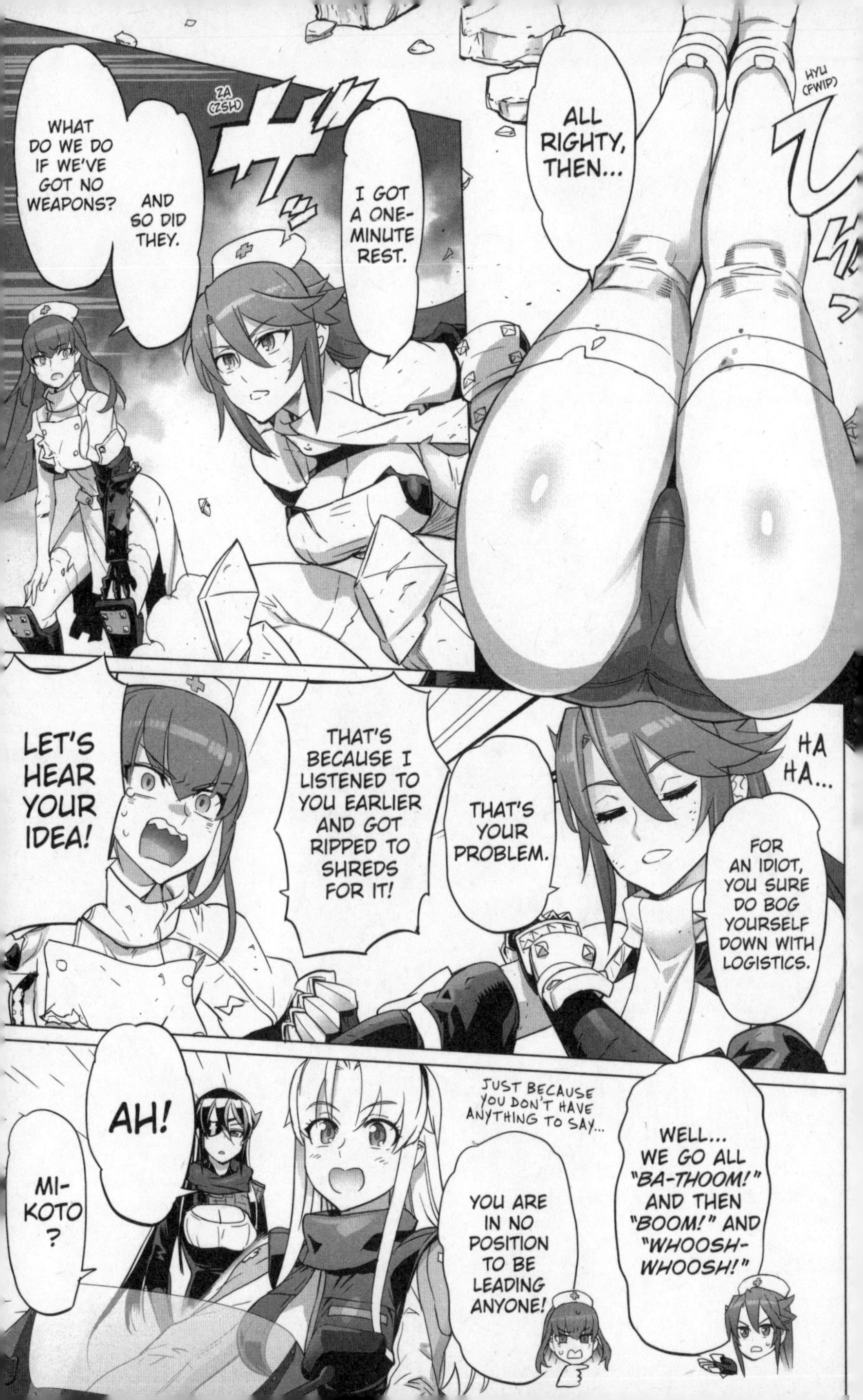
HYU (FWIP)
ALL RIGHTY, THEN...
ZA (ZSHH)
I GOT A ONE-MINUTE REST.
AND SO DID THEY.
WHAT DO WE DO IF WE'VE GOT NO WEAPONS?
HA HA...
FOR AN IDIOT, YOU SURE DO BOG YOURSELF DOWN WITH LOGISTICS.
THAT'S YOUR PROBLEM.
THAT'S BECAUSE I LISTENED TO YOU EARLIER AND GOT RIPPED TO SHREDS FOR IT!
LET'S HEAR YOUR IDEA!
WELL... WE GO ALL "BA-THOOM!" AND THEN "BOOM!" AND "WHOOSH-WHOOSH!"
JUST BECAUSE YOU DON'T HAVE ANYTHING TO SAY...
YOU ARE IN NO POSITION TO BE LEADING ANYONE!
AH!
MI-KOTO?

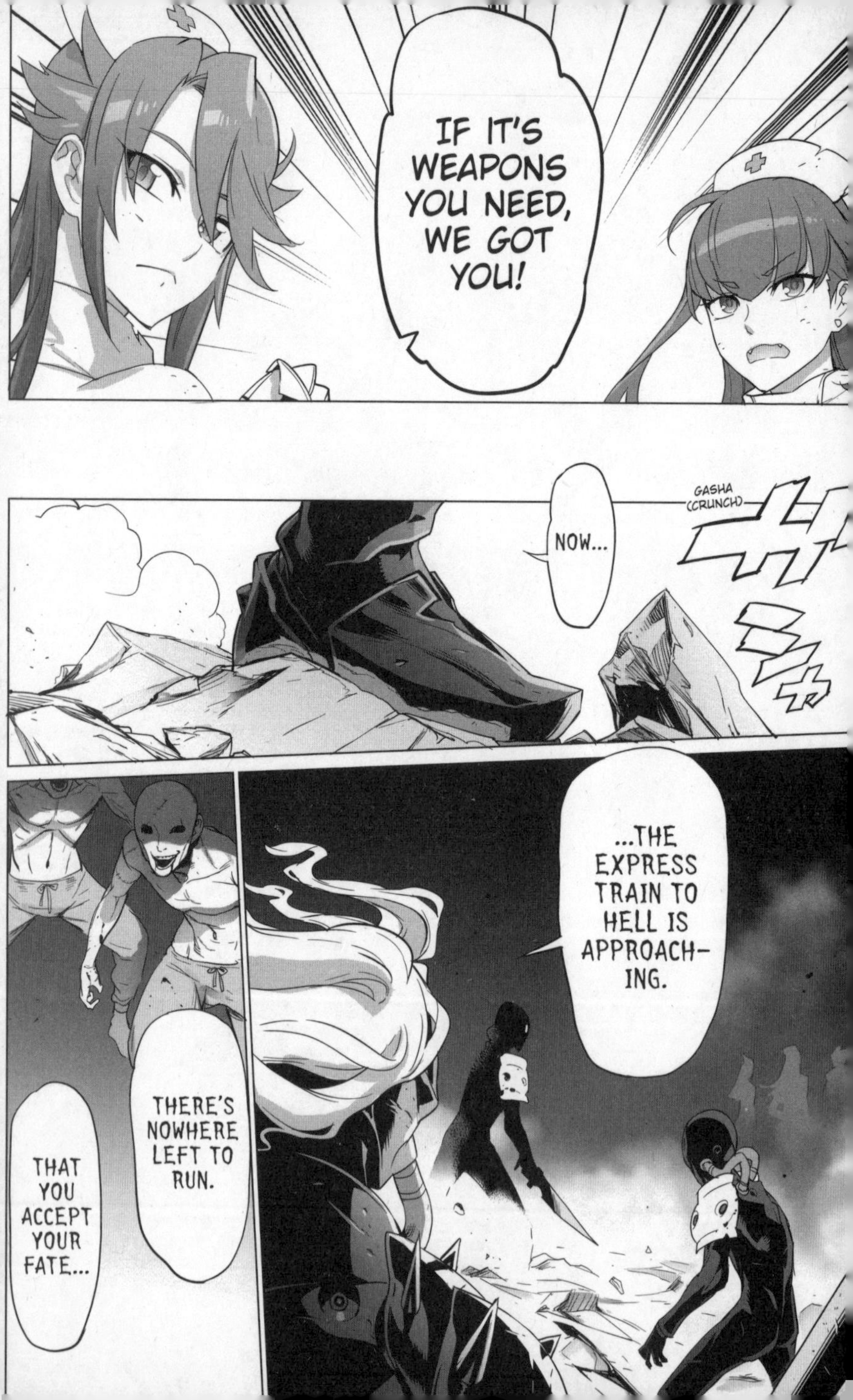
IF IT'S WEAPONS YOU NEED, WE GOT YOU!
GASHA (CRUNCH)
NOW...
...THE EXPRESS TRAIN TO HELL IS APPROACH-ING.
THERE'S NOWHERE LEFT TO RUN.
THAT YOU ACCEPT YOUR FATE...

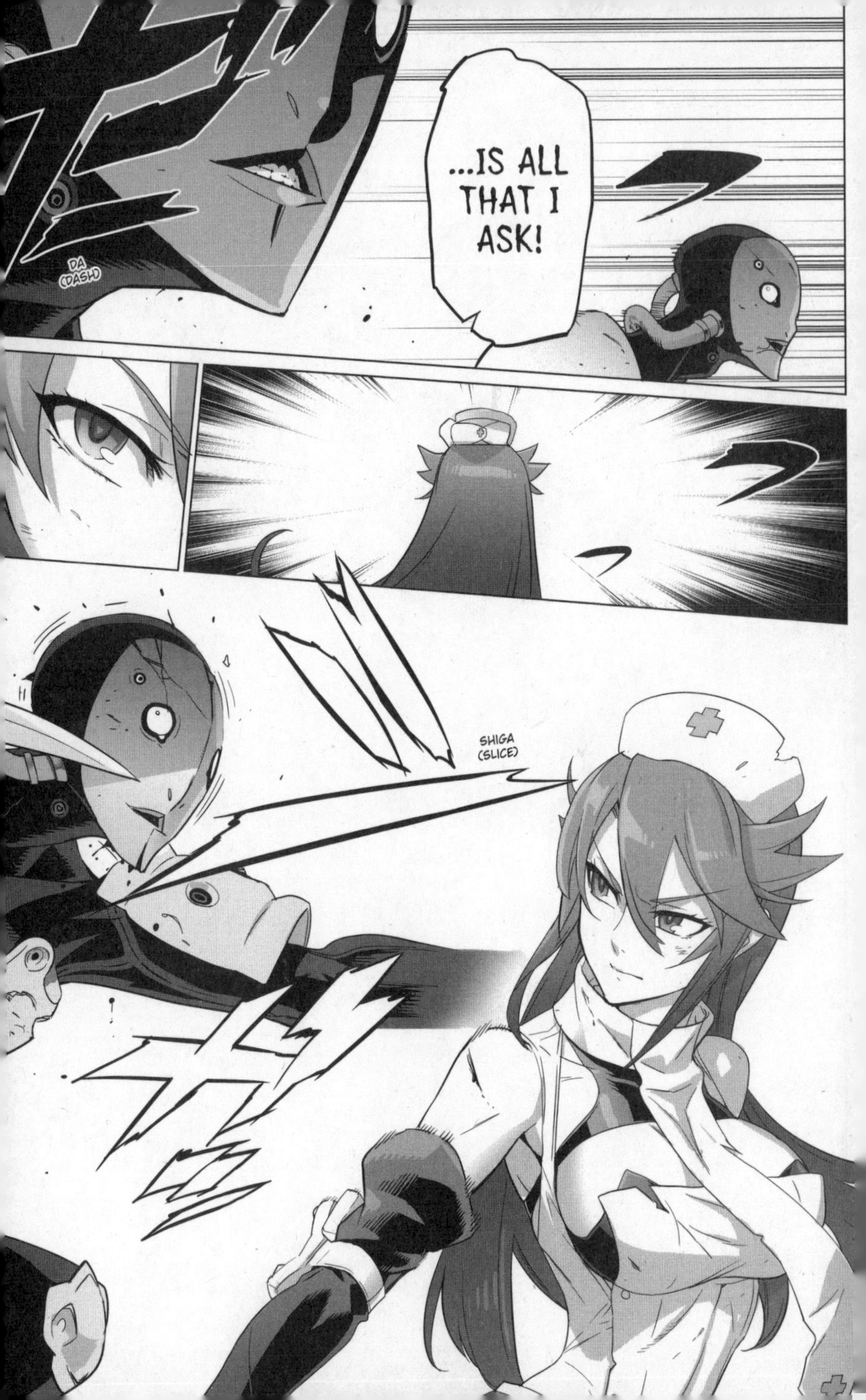
...IS ALL THAT I ASK!
DA (DASH)
SHIGA (SLICE)

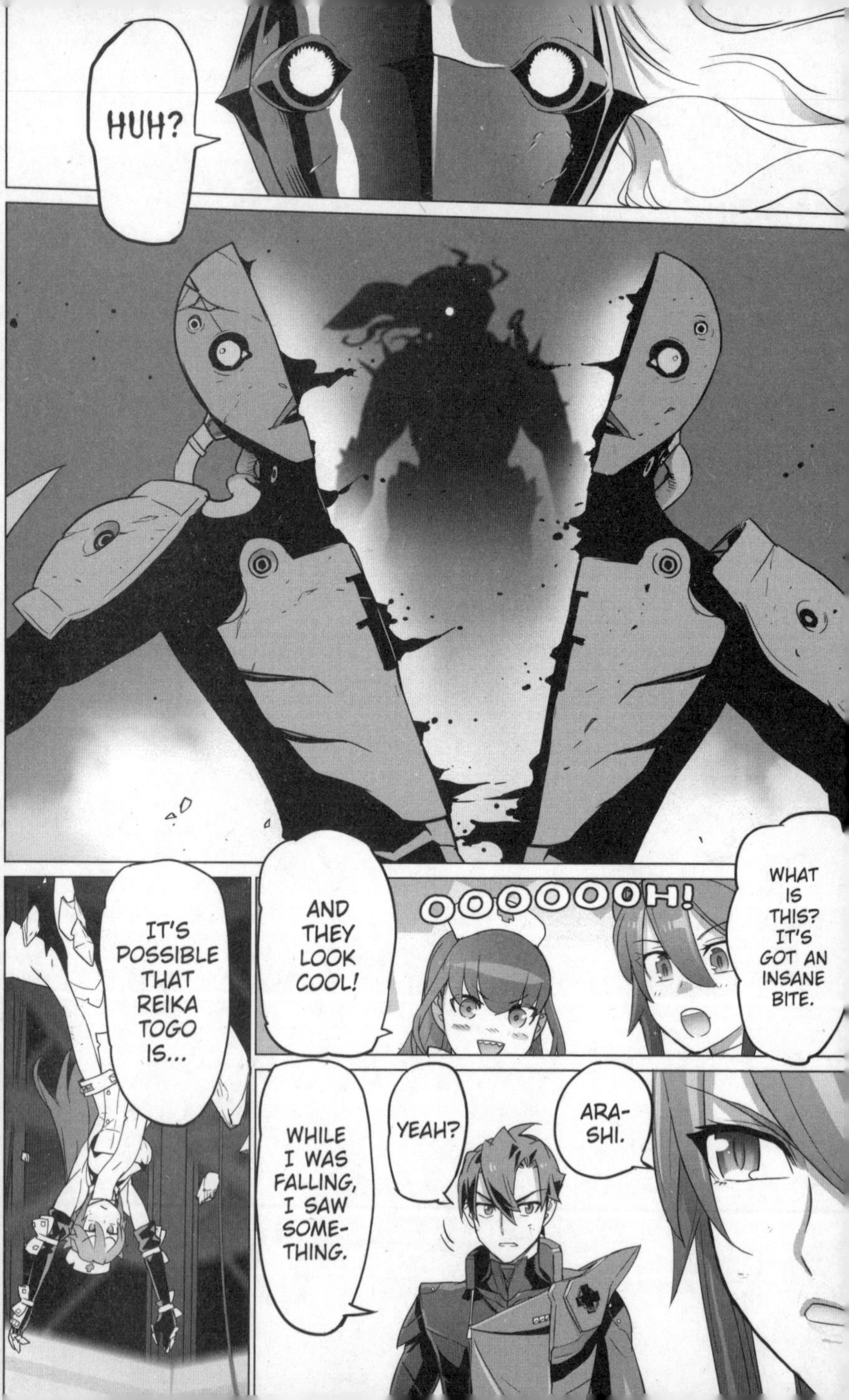
HUH?
WHAT IS THIS? IT'S GOT AN INSANE BITE.
OOOOOOOH!
AND THEY LOOK COOL!
ARA-SHI.
YEAH?
WHILE I WAS FALLING, I SAW SOME-THING.
IT'S POSSIBLE THAT REIKA TOGO IS...

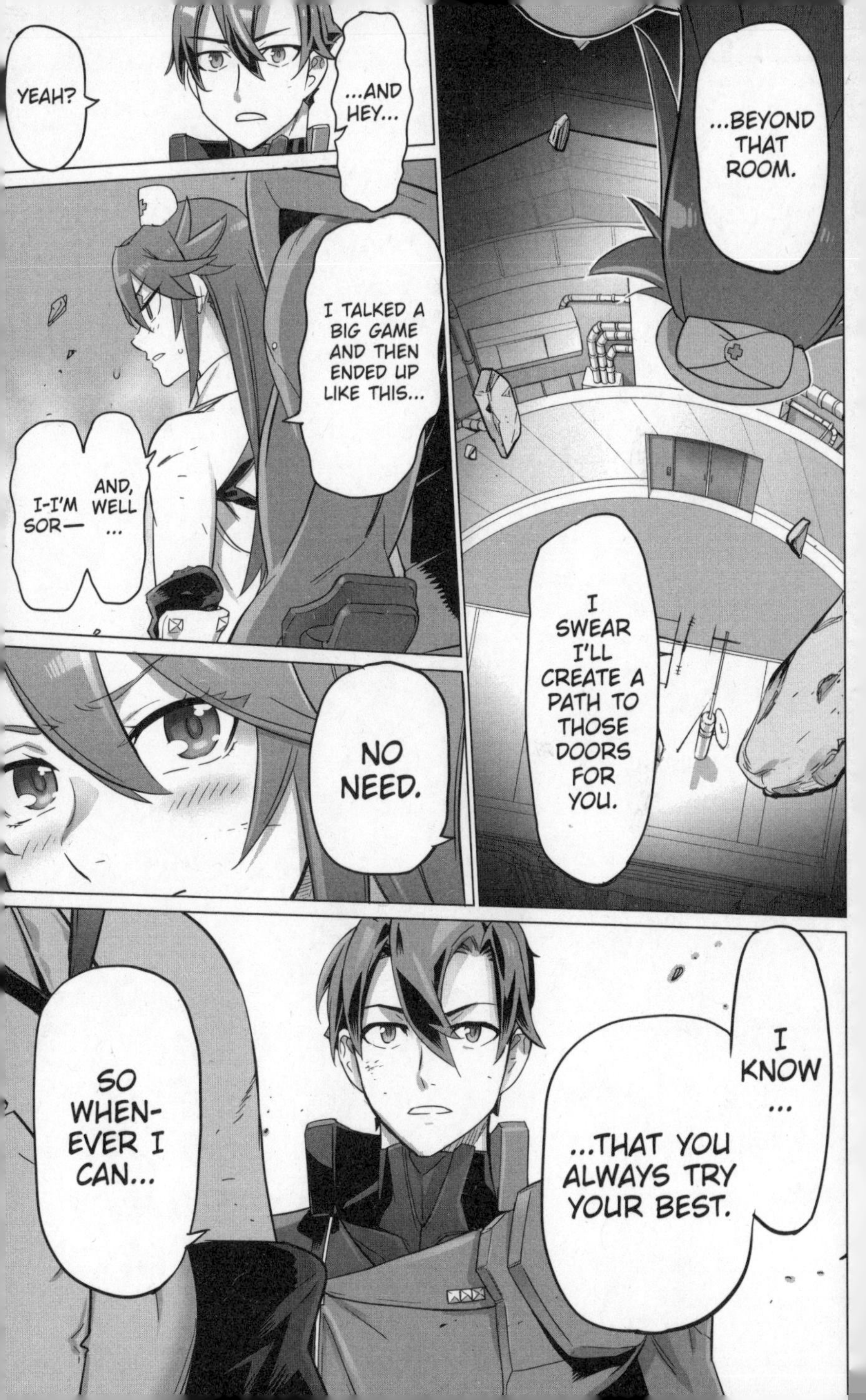
...BEYOND THAT ROOM.
I SWEAR I'LL CREATE A PATH TO THOSE DOORS FOR YOU.
...AND HEY...
YEAH?
I TALKED A BIG GAME AND THEN ENDED UP LIKE THIS...
AND, WELL...
I-I'M SOR—
NO NEED.
I KNOW...
...THAT YOU ALWAYS TRY YOUR BEST.
SO WHEN-EVER I CAN...

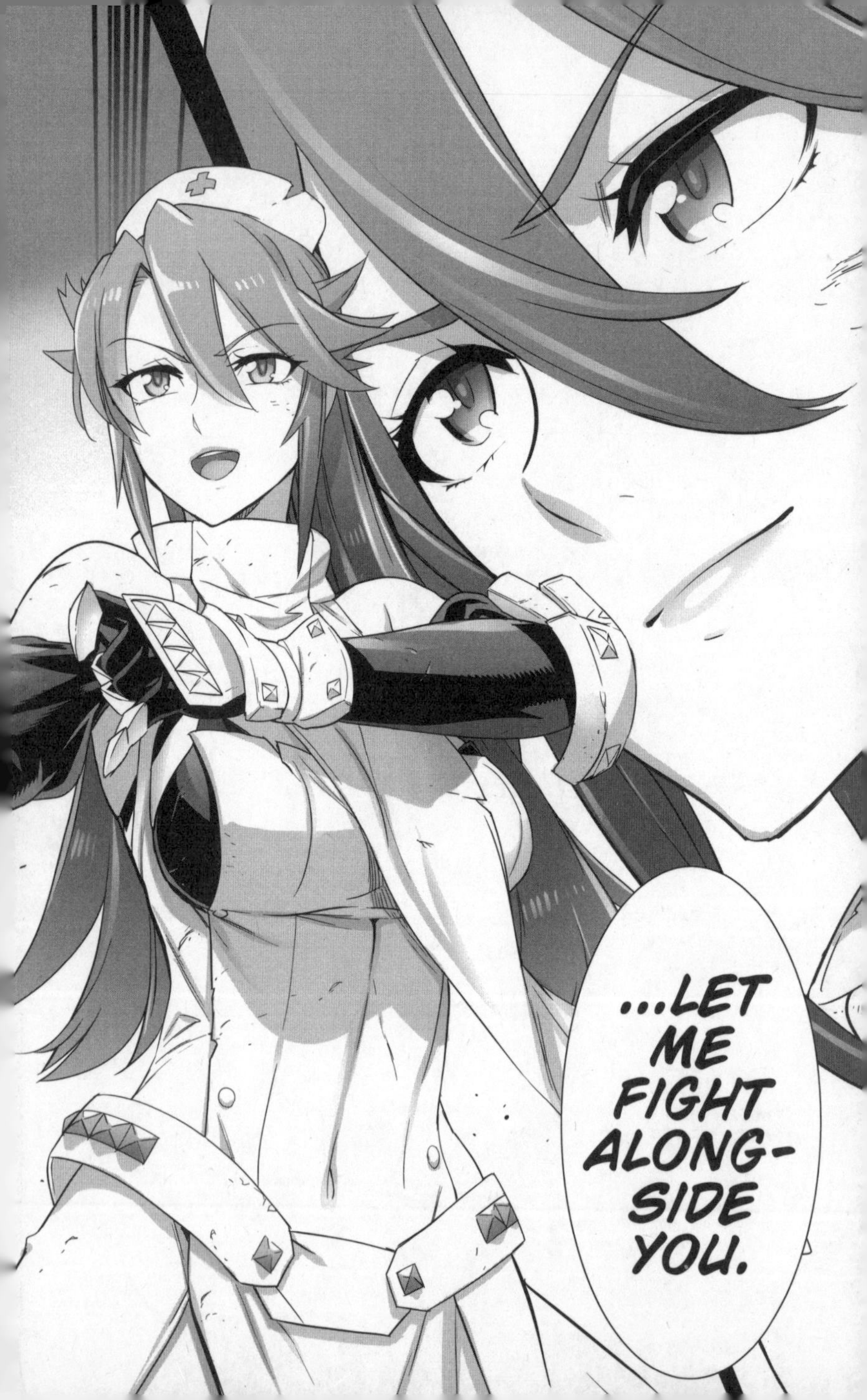
...LET ME FIGHT ALONG-SIDE YOU.

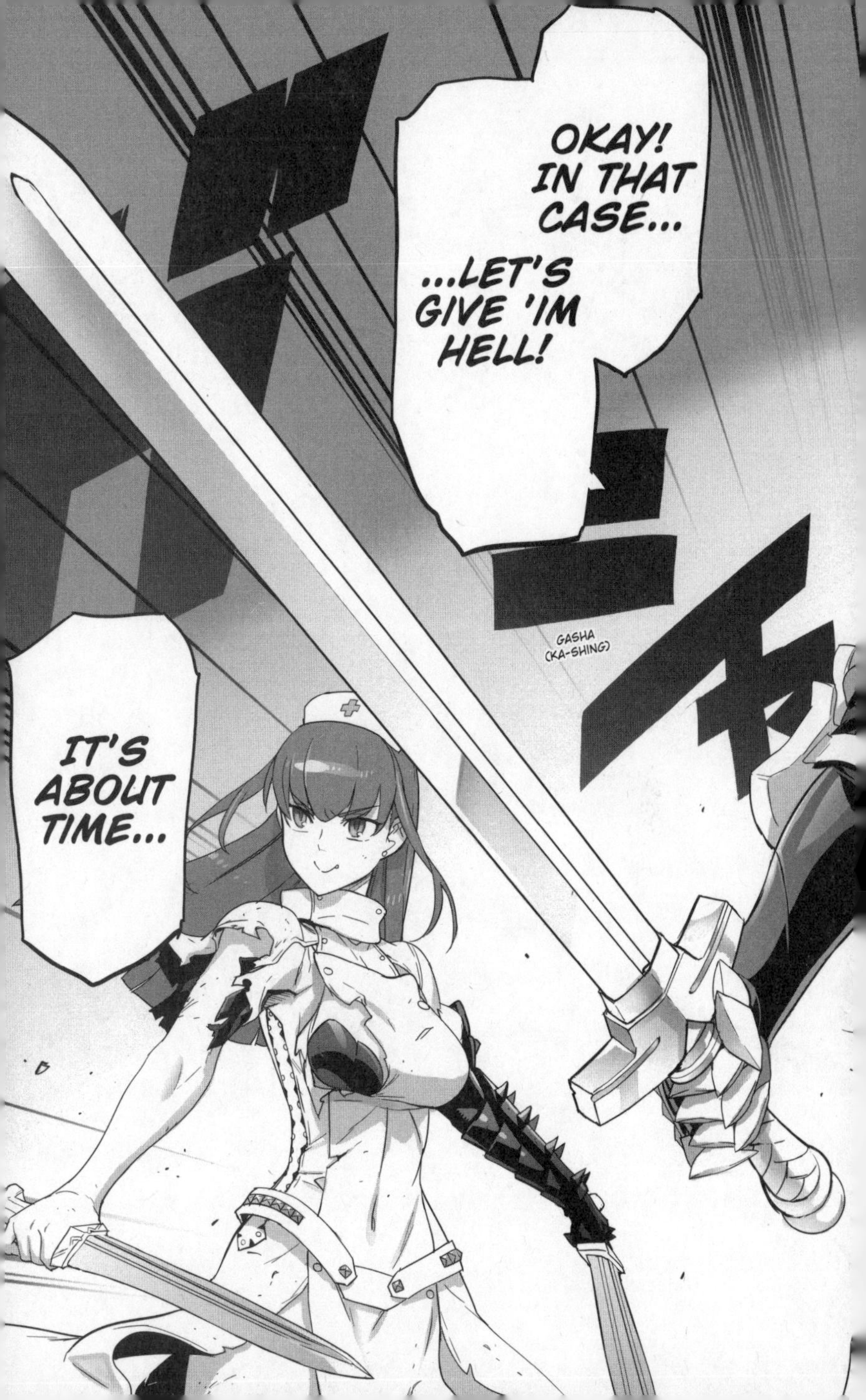
OKAY! IN THAT CASE...
...LET'S GIVE 'IM HELL!
GASHA (KA-SHING)
IT'S ABOUT TIME...

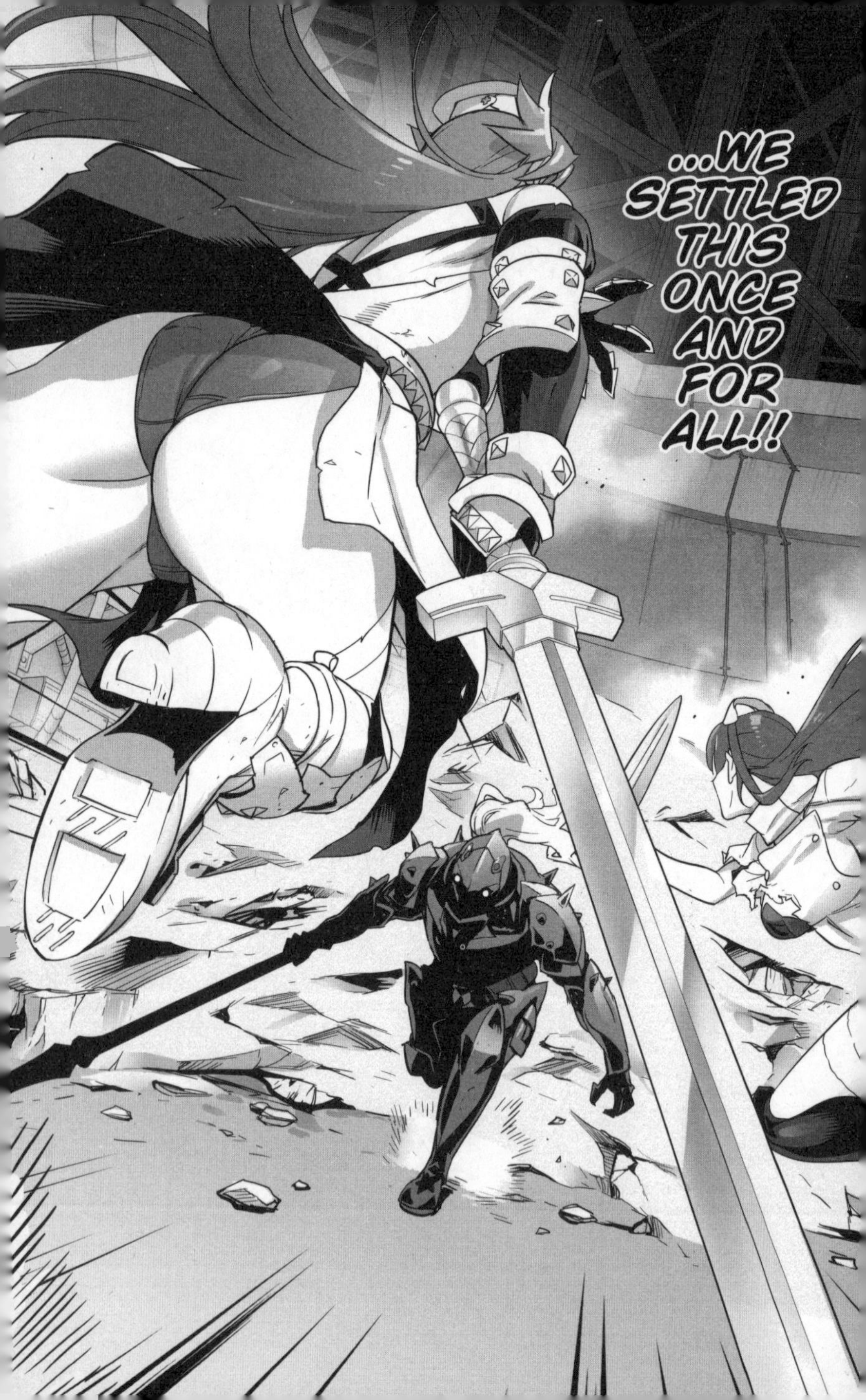
...WE SETTLED THIS ONCE AND FOR ALL!!

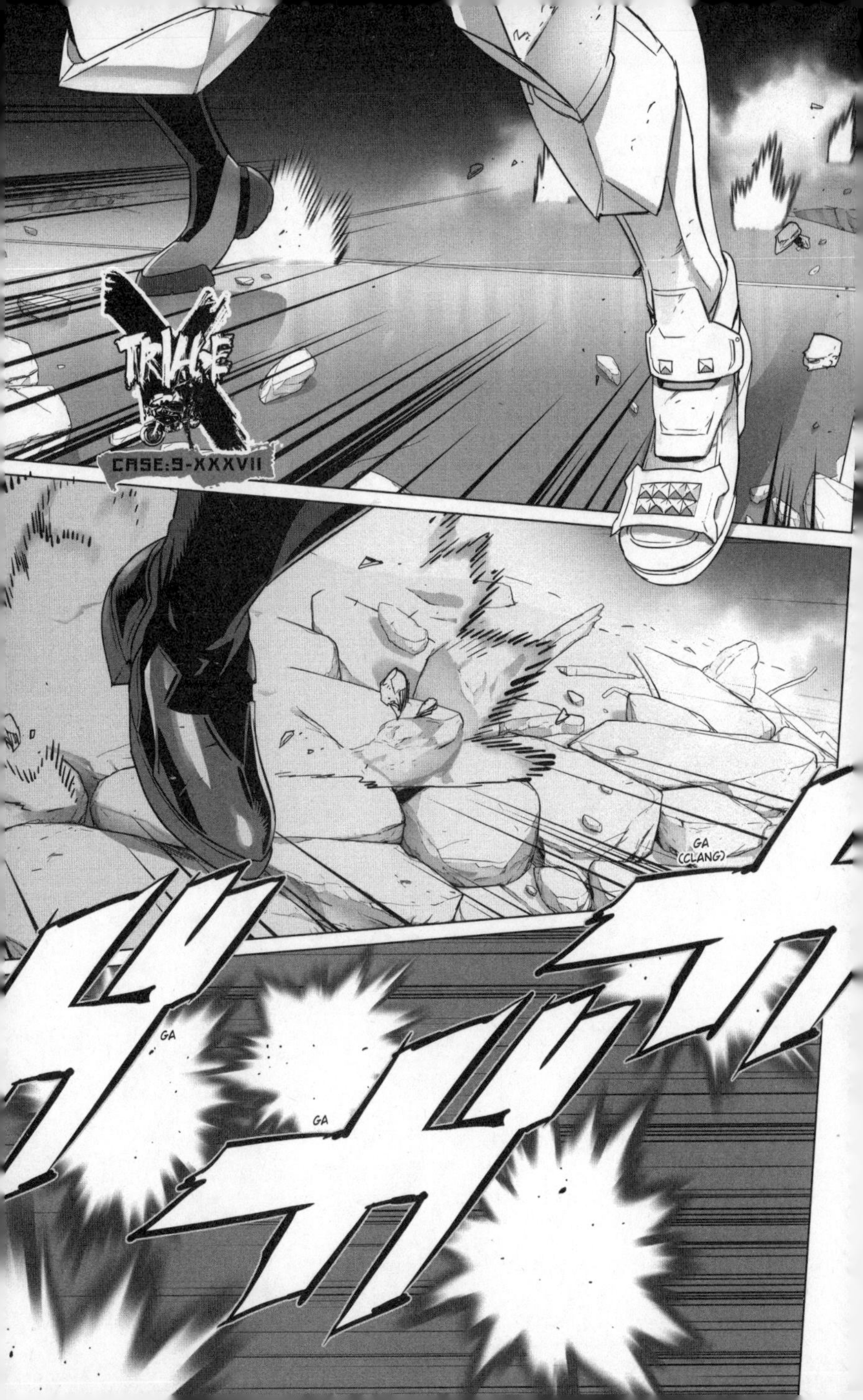
TRIAGE X
CASE:9-XXXVII
GA
(CLANG)
GA
GA

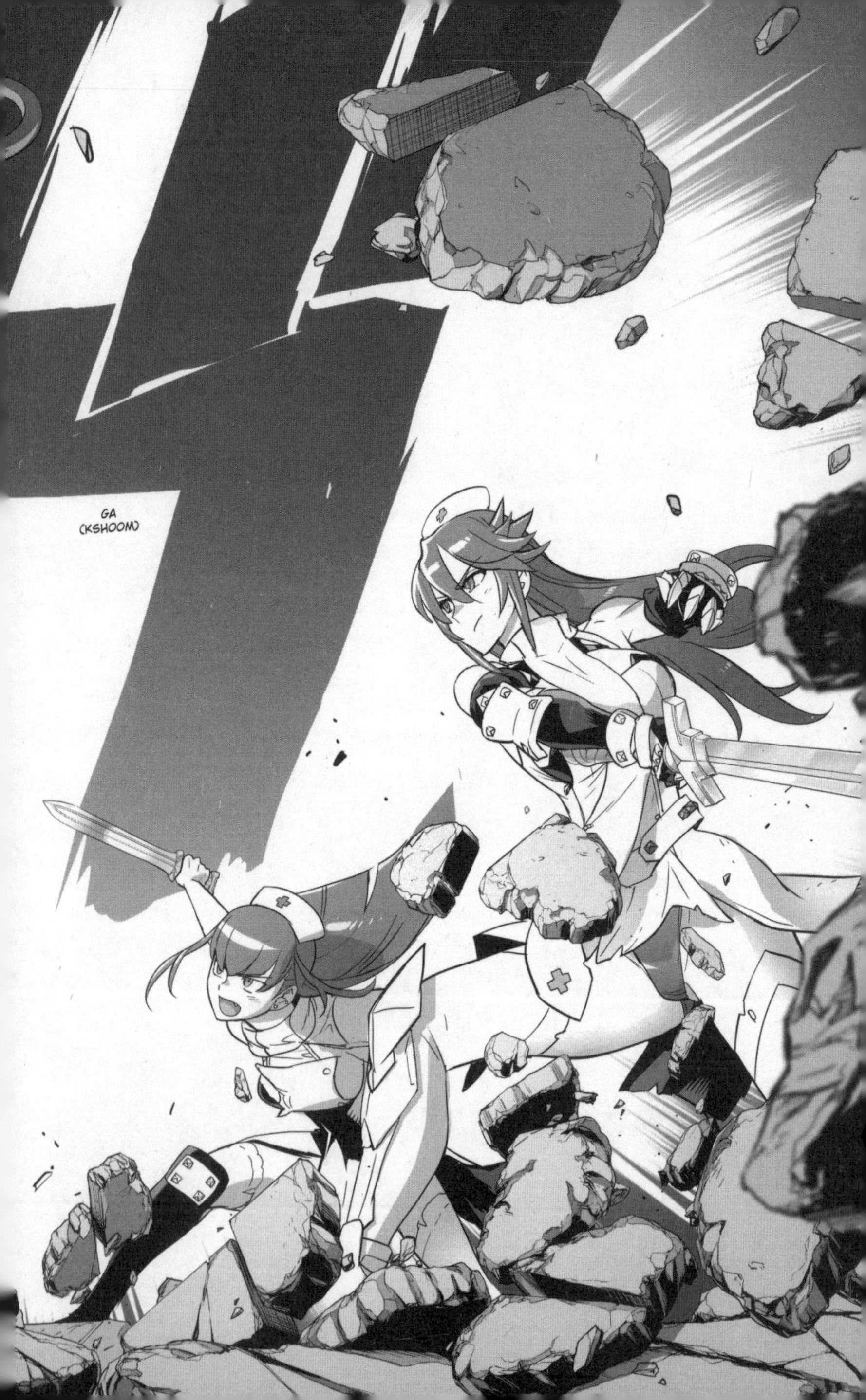
GA
(KSHOOM)

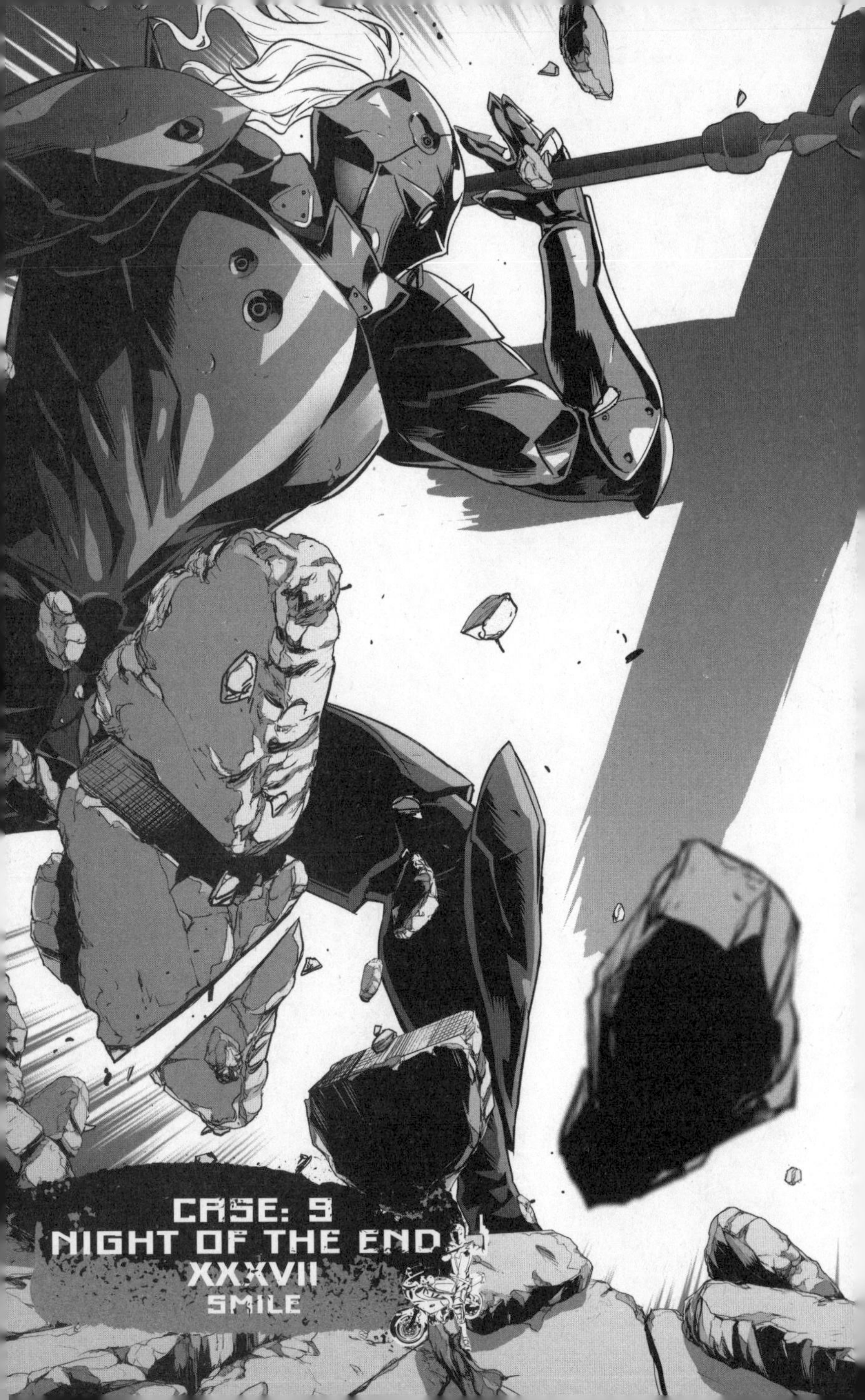
CASE: 9
NIGHT OF THE END
XXXVII
SMILE

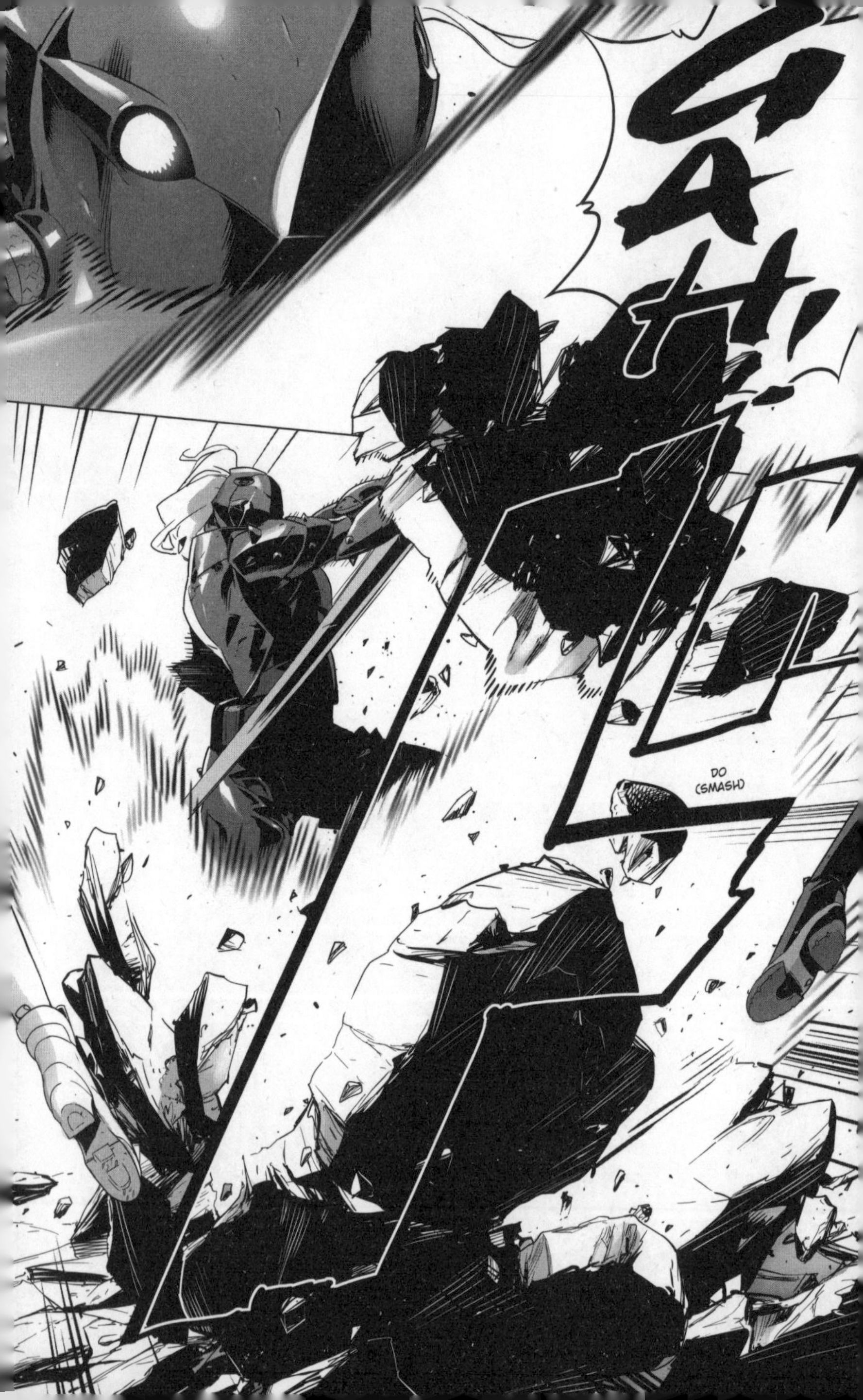
DO
(SMASH)

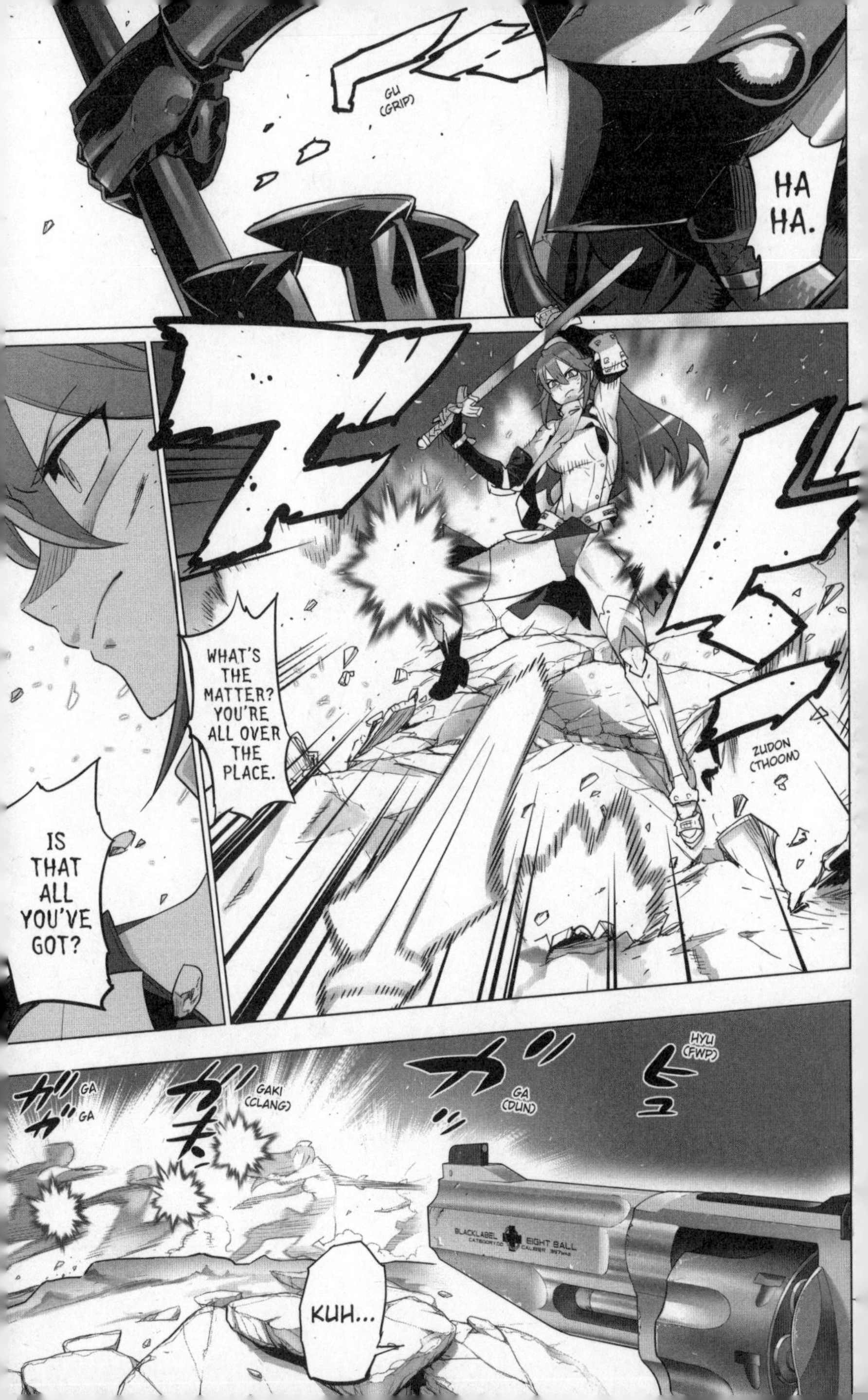
HA HA.
GU (GRIP)
ZUDON (THOOM)
WHAT'S THE MATTER? YOU'RE ALL OVER THE PLACE.
IS THAT ALL YOU'VE GOT?
HYU (FWP)
GA (DUN)
GAKI (CLANG)
GA GA
BLACKLABEL
EIGHT BALL
KUH...

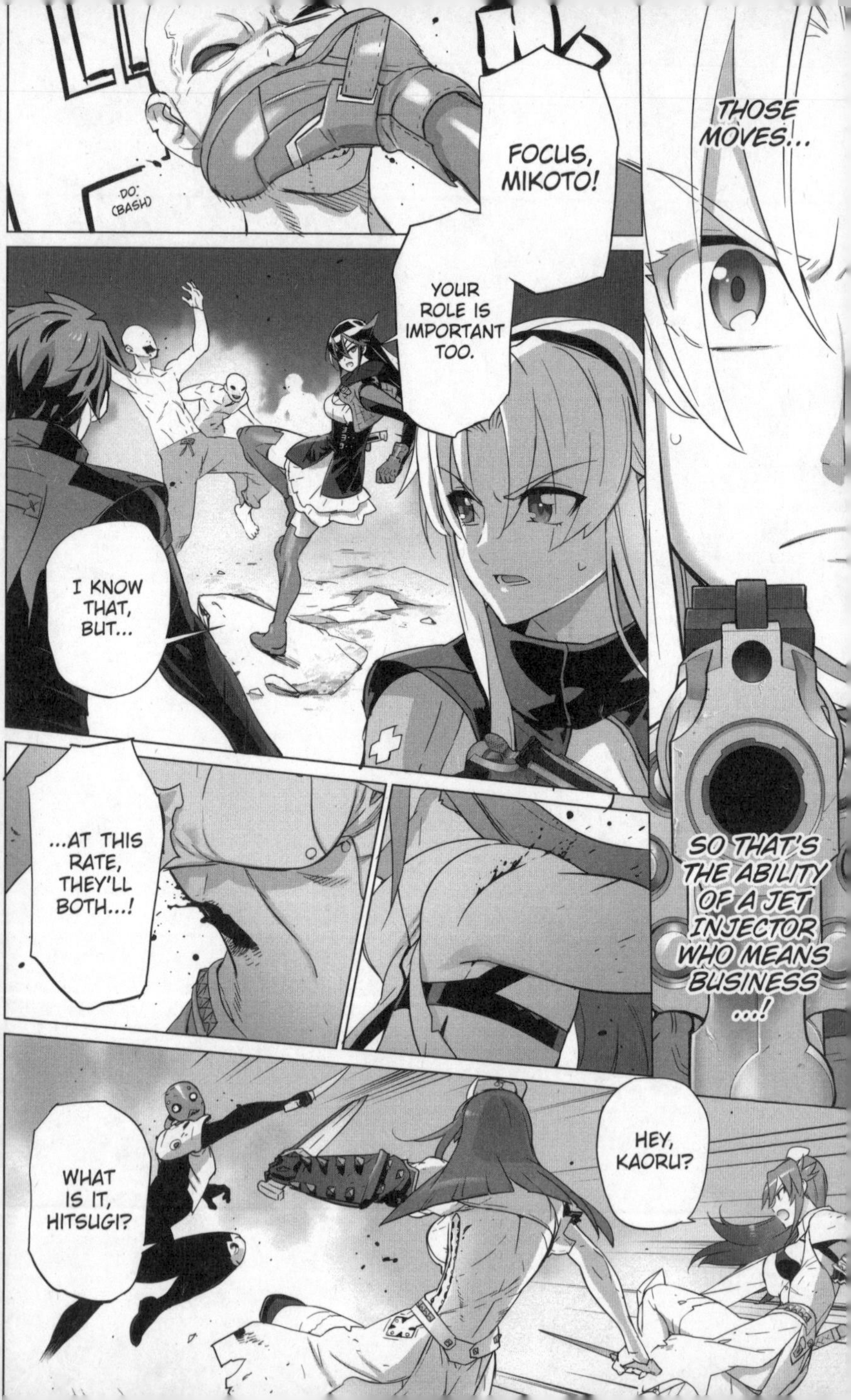
THOSE MOVES...
SO THAT'S THE ABILITY OF A JET INJECTOR WHO MEANS BUSINESS...!
DO (BASH)
FOCUS, MIKOTO!
YOUR ROLE IS IMPORTANT TOO.
I KNOW THAT, BUT...
...AT THIS RATE, THEY'LL BOTH...!
HEY, KAORU?
WHAT IS IT, HITSUGI?

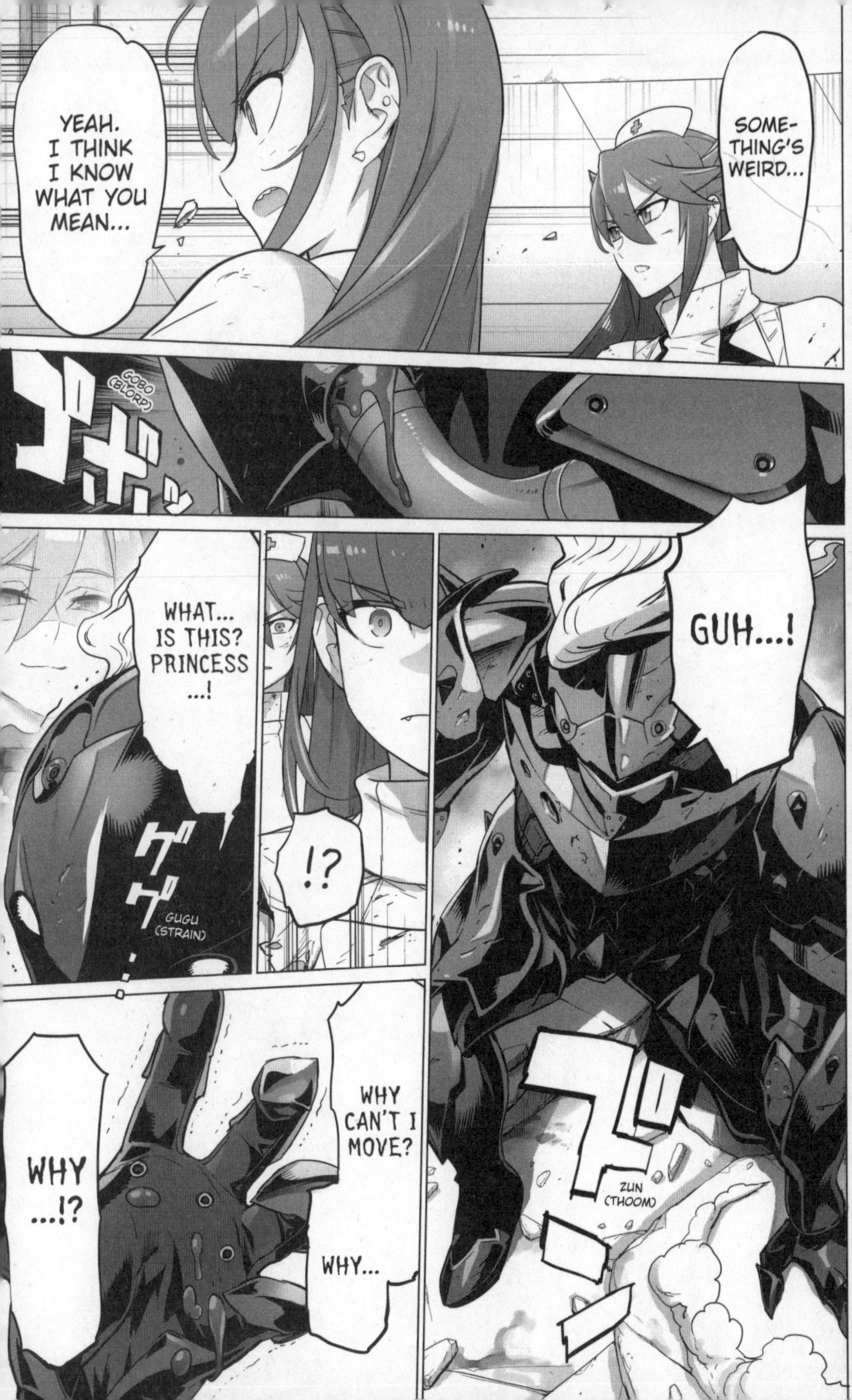
SOME-THING'S WEIRD...
YEAH. I THINK I KNOW WHAT YOU MEAN...
GOBO (BLORP)
GUH...!
ZUN (THOOM)
!?
WHAT... IS THIS? PRINCESS ...!
GUGU (STRAIN)
WHY CAN'T I MOVE?
WHY...
WHY ...!?

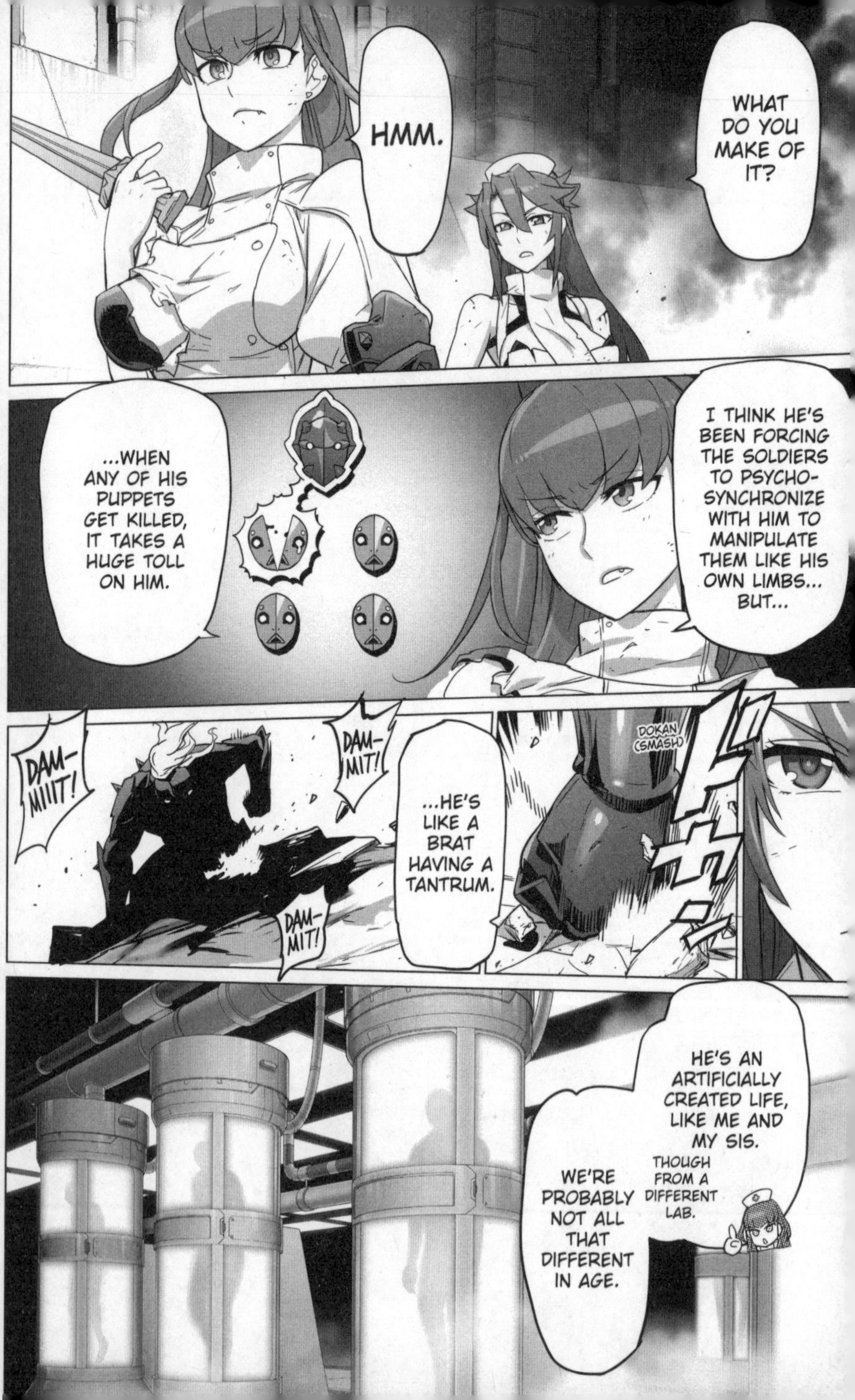
WHAT DO YOU MAKE OF IT?
HMM.
I THINK HE'S BEEN FORCING THE SOLDIERS TO PSYCHO-SYNCHRONIZE WITH HIM TO MANIPULATE THEM LIKE HIS OWN LIMBS... BUT...
...WHEN ANY OF HIS PUPPETS GET KILLED, IT TAKES A HUGE TOLL ON HIM.
DOKAN (SMASH)
...HE'S LIKE A BRAT HAVING A TANTRUM.
DAM-MIT!
DAM-MIIIT!
DAM-MIT!
HE'S AN ARTIFICIALLY CREATED LIFE, LIKE ME AND MY SIS.
THOUGH FROM A DIFFERENT LAB.
WE'RE PROBABLY NOT ALL THAT DIFFERENT IN AGE.

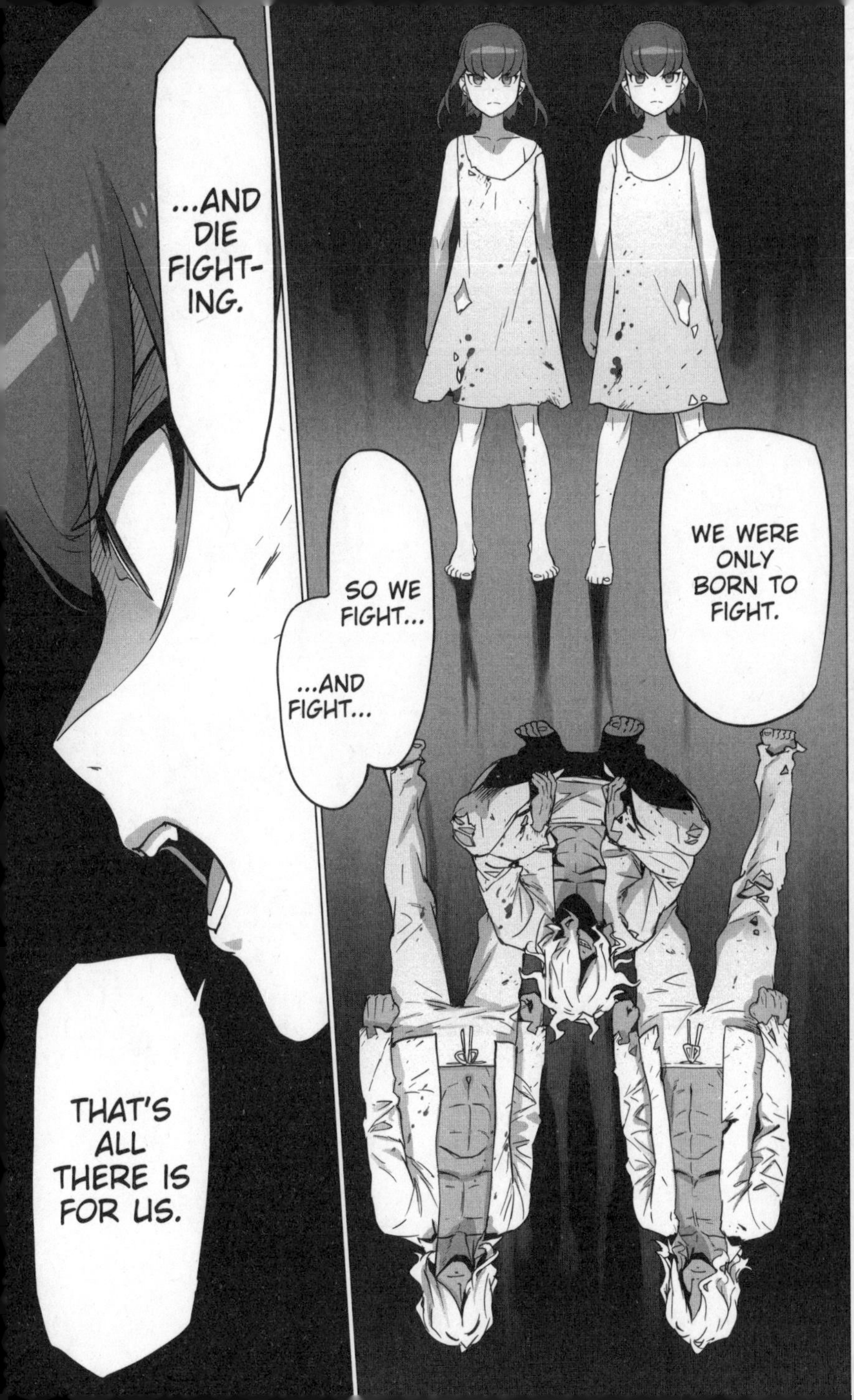
WE WERE ONLY BORN TO FIGHT.
SO WE FIGHT...
...AND FIGHT...
...AND DIE FIGHTING.
THAT'S ALL THERE IS FOR US.

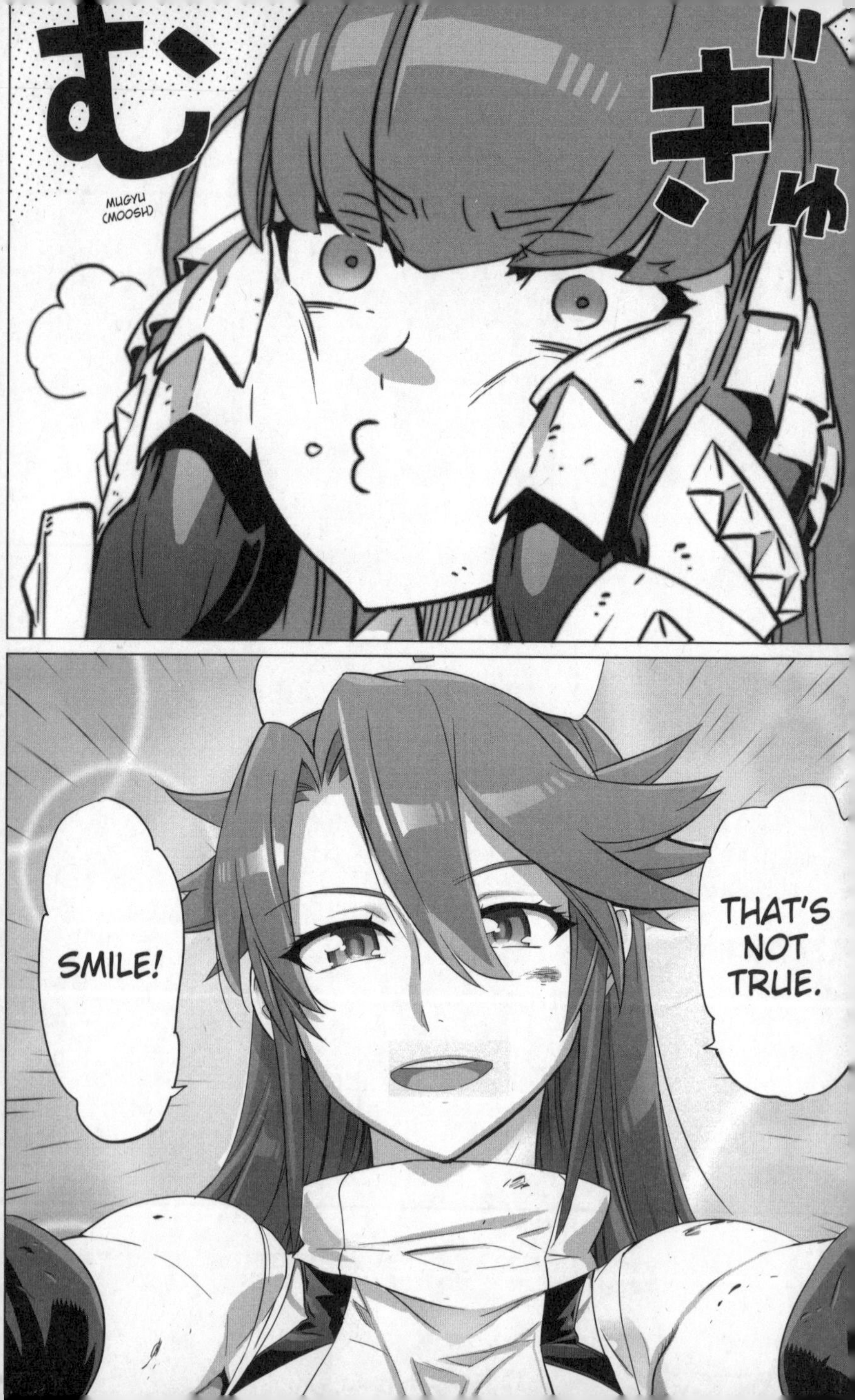
むぎゅ
MUGYU
(MOOSH)
THAT'S NOT TRUE.
SMILE!

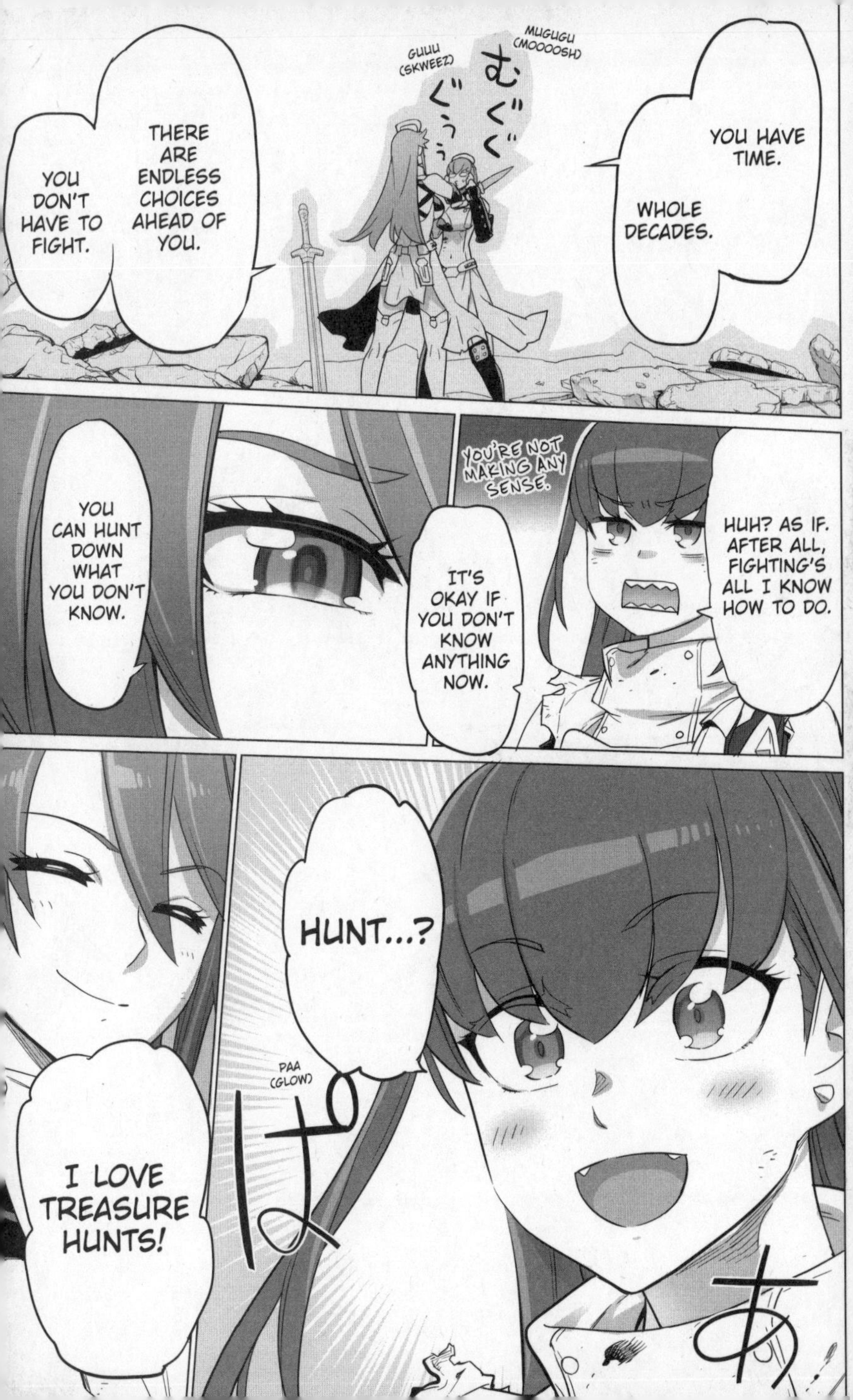
YOU HAVE TIME.
WHOLE DECADES.
MUGUGU (MOOOOSH)
GUUU (SKWEEZ)
THERE ARE ENDLESS CHOICES AHEAD OF YOU.
YOU DON'T HAVE TO FIGHT.
HUH? AS IF. AFTER ALL, FIGHTING'S ALL I KNOW HOW TO DO.
YOU'RE NOT MAKING ANY SENSE.
IT'S OKAY IF YOU DON'T KNOW ANYTHING NOW.
YOU CAN HUNT DOWN WHAT YOU DON'T KNOW.
HUNT...?
PAA (GLOW)
I LOVE TREASURE HUNTS!

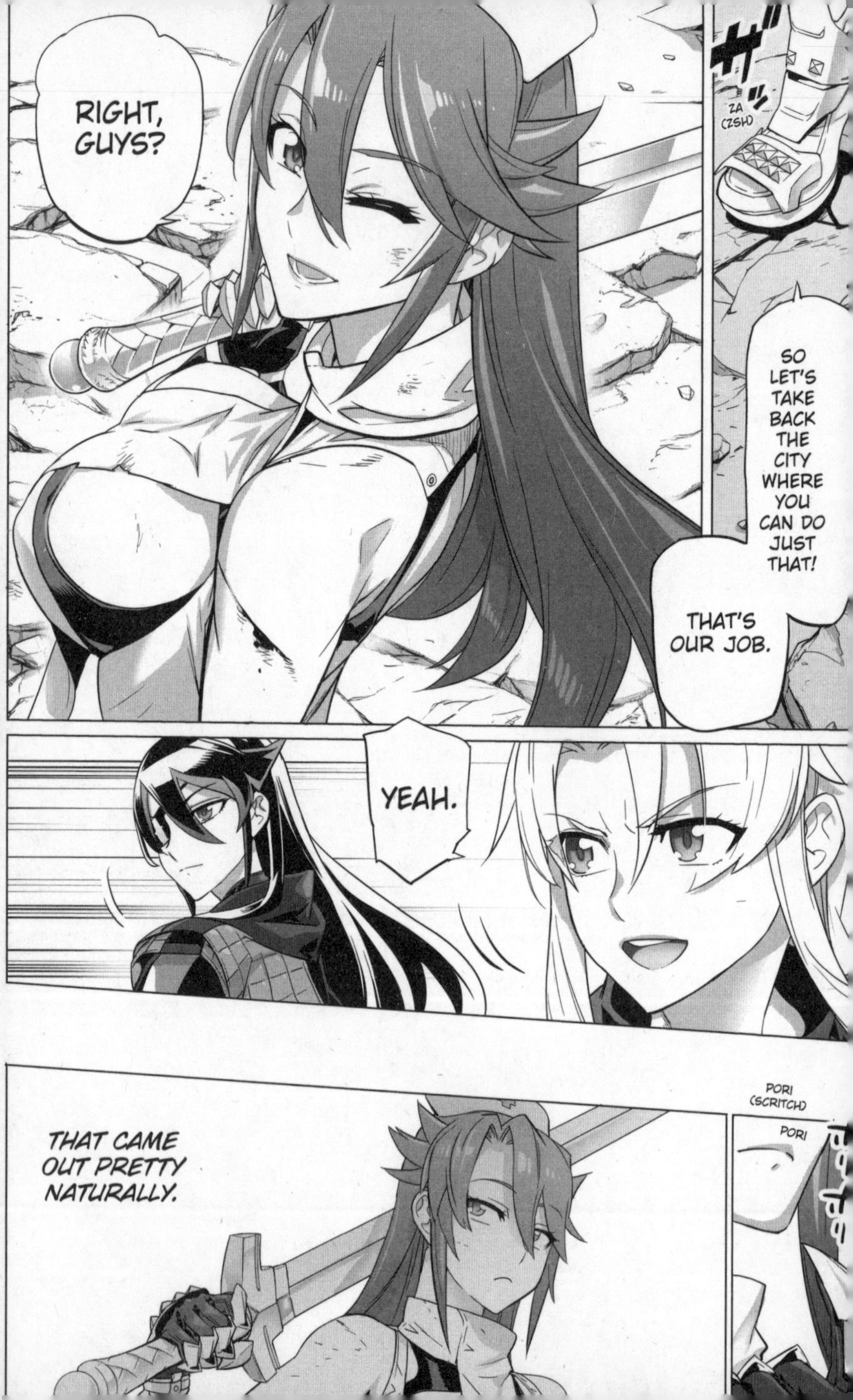
ZA
(ZSH)
SO LET'S TAKE BACK THE CITY WHERE YOU CAN DO JUST THAT!
THAT'S OUR JOB.
RIGHT, GUYS?
YEAH.
PORI
(SCRITCH)
PORI
THAT CAME OUT PRETTY NATURALLY.

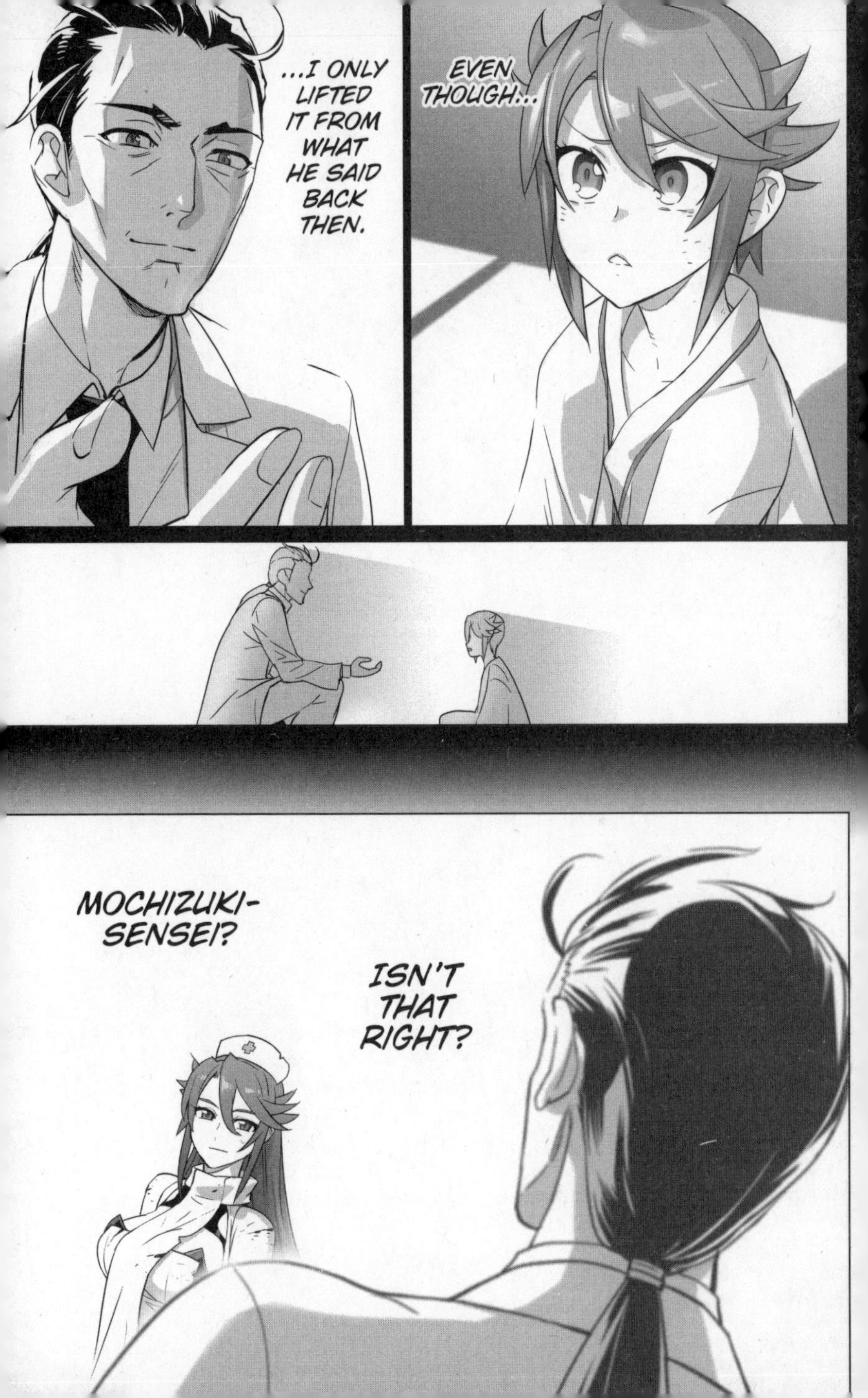
EVEN THOUGH...
...I ONLY LIFTED IT FROM WHAT HE SAID BACK THEN.
ISN'T THAT RIGHT?
MOCHIZUKI-SENSEI?

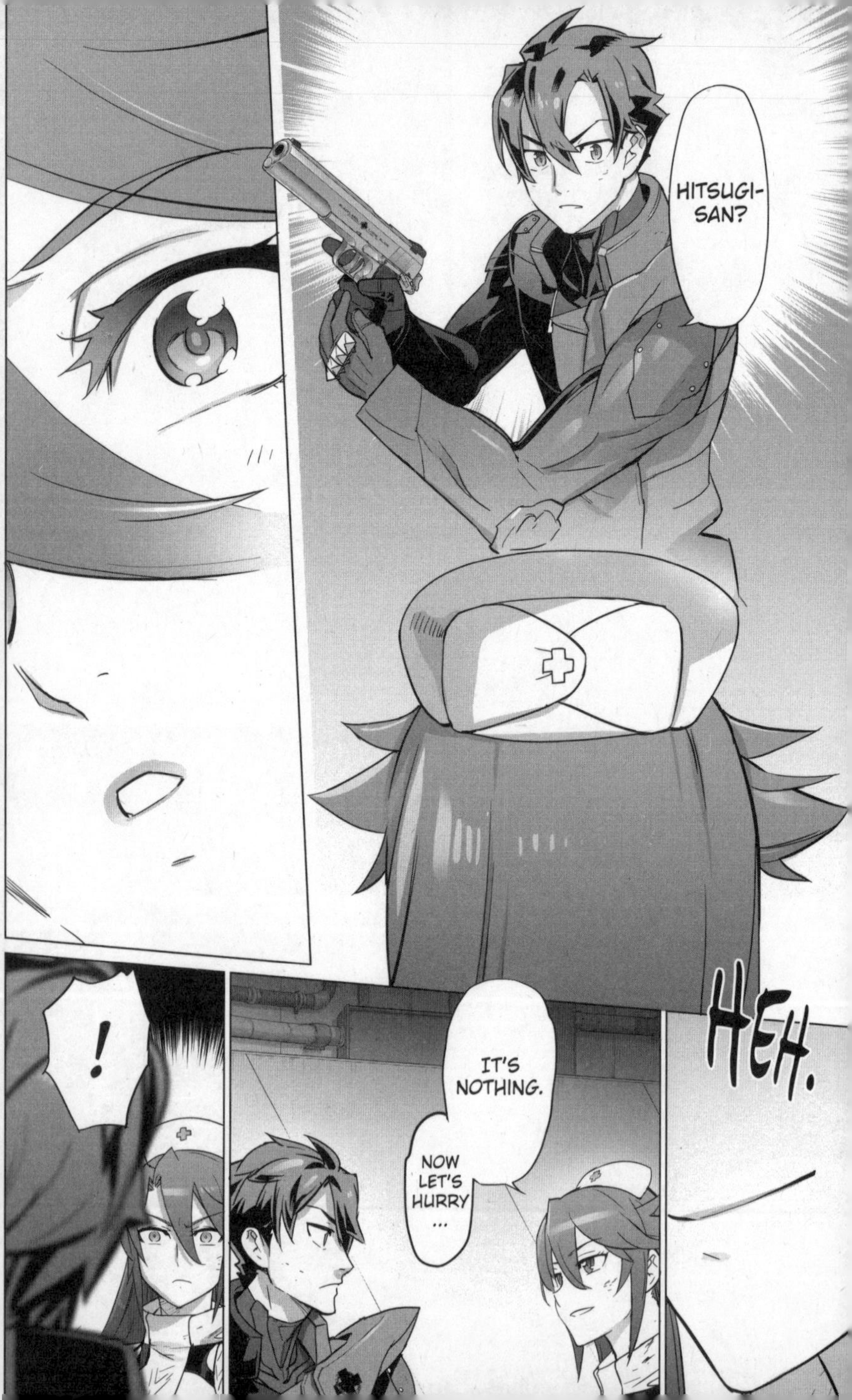
HITSUGI-SAN?
HEH.
IT'S NOTHING.
NOW LET'S HURRY ...
!

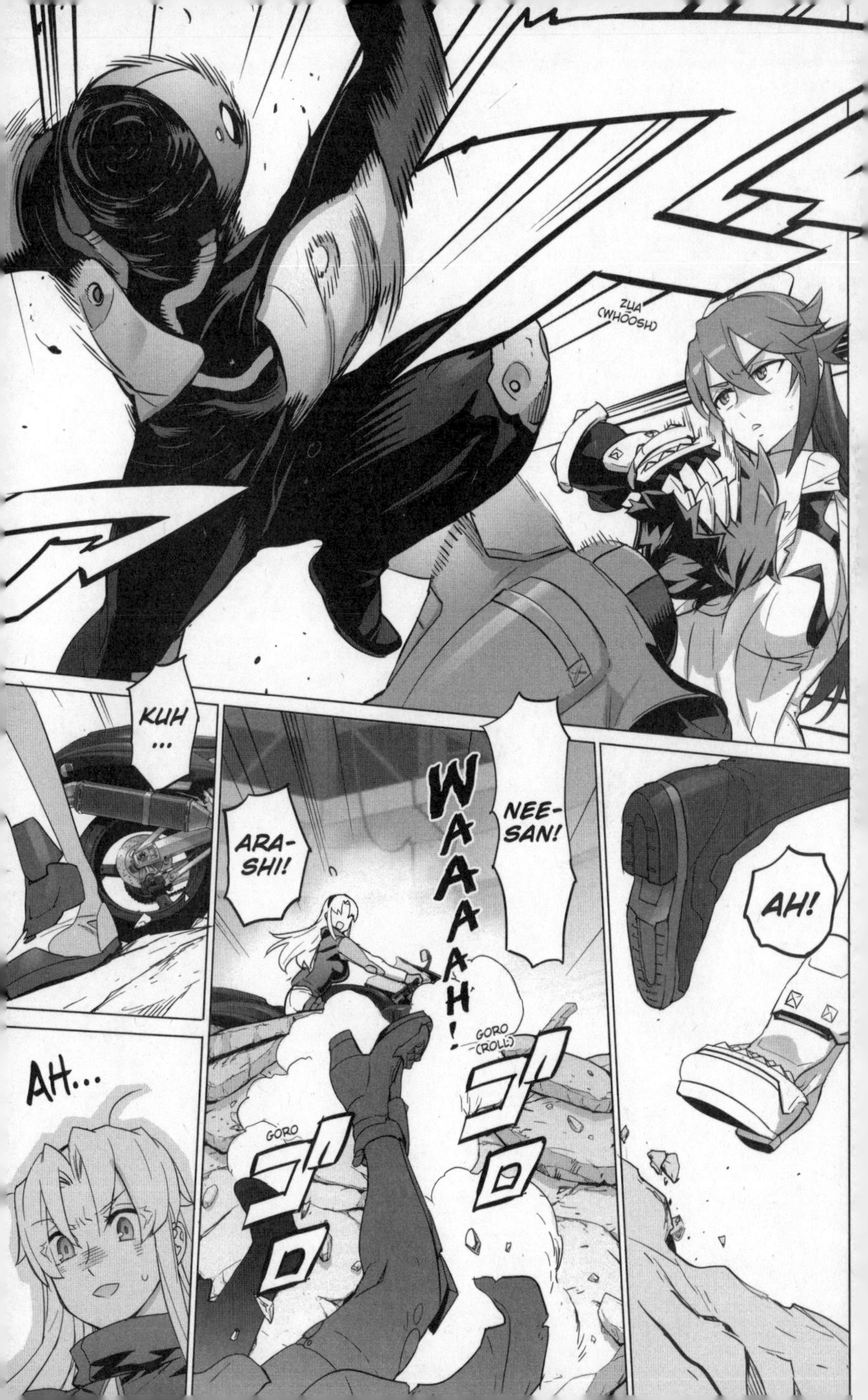
ZUA
(WHOOSH)
AH!
NEE-SAN!
WAAAAAH!
ARA-SHI!
GORO
(ROLL)
GORO
KUH ...
AH...

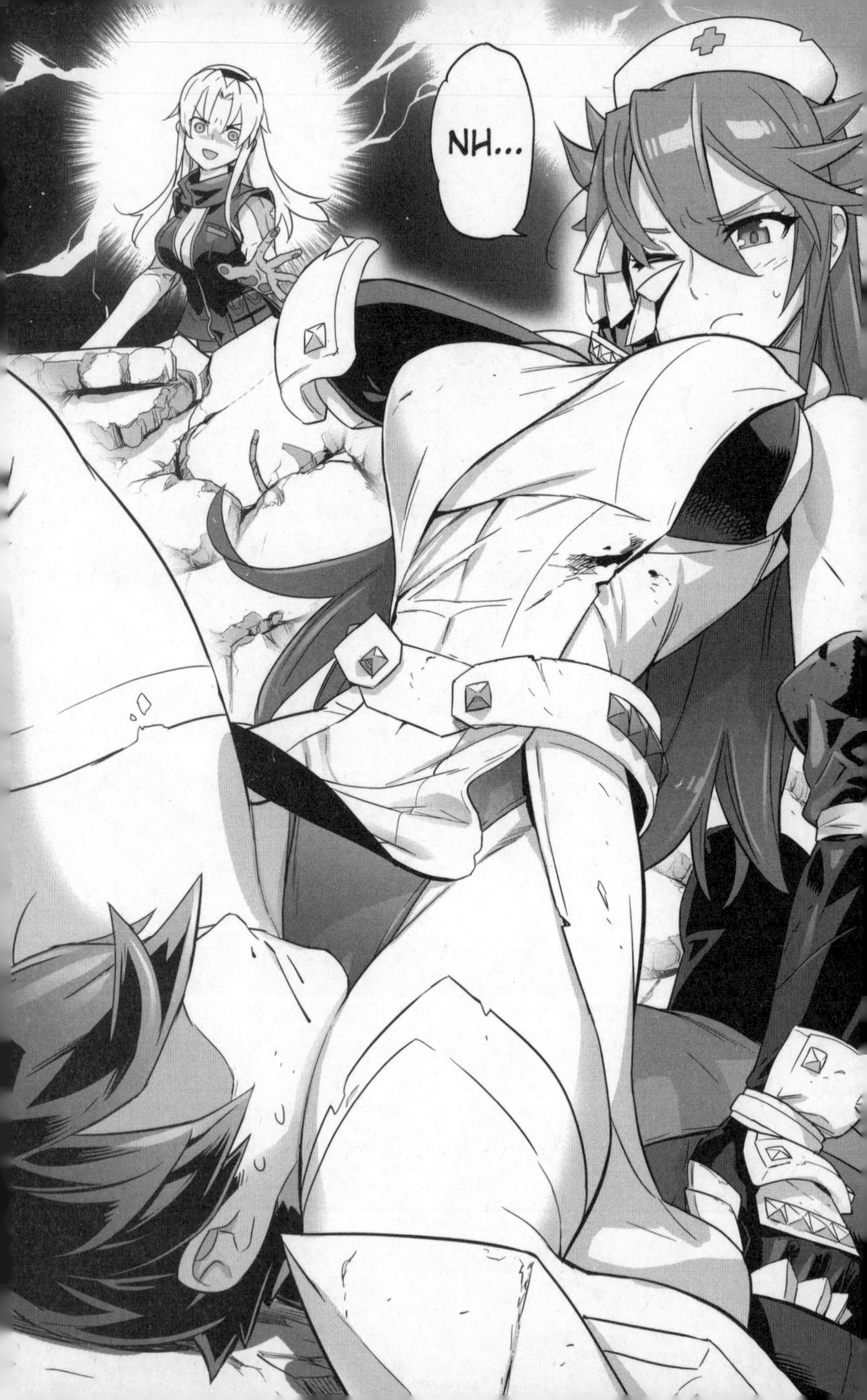
NH...

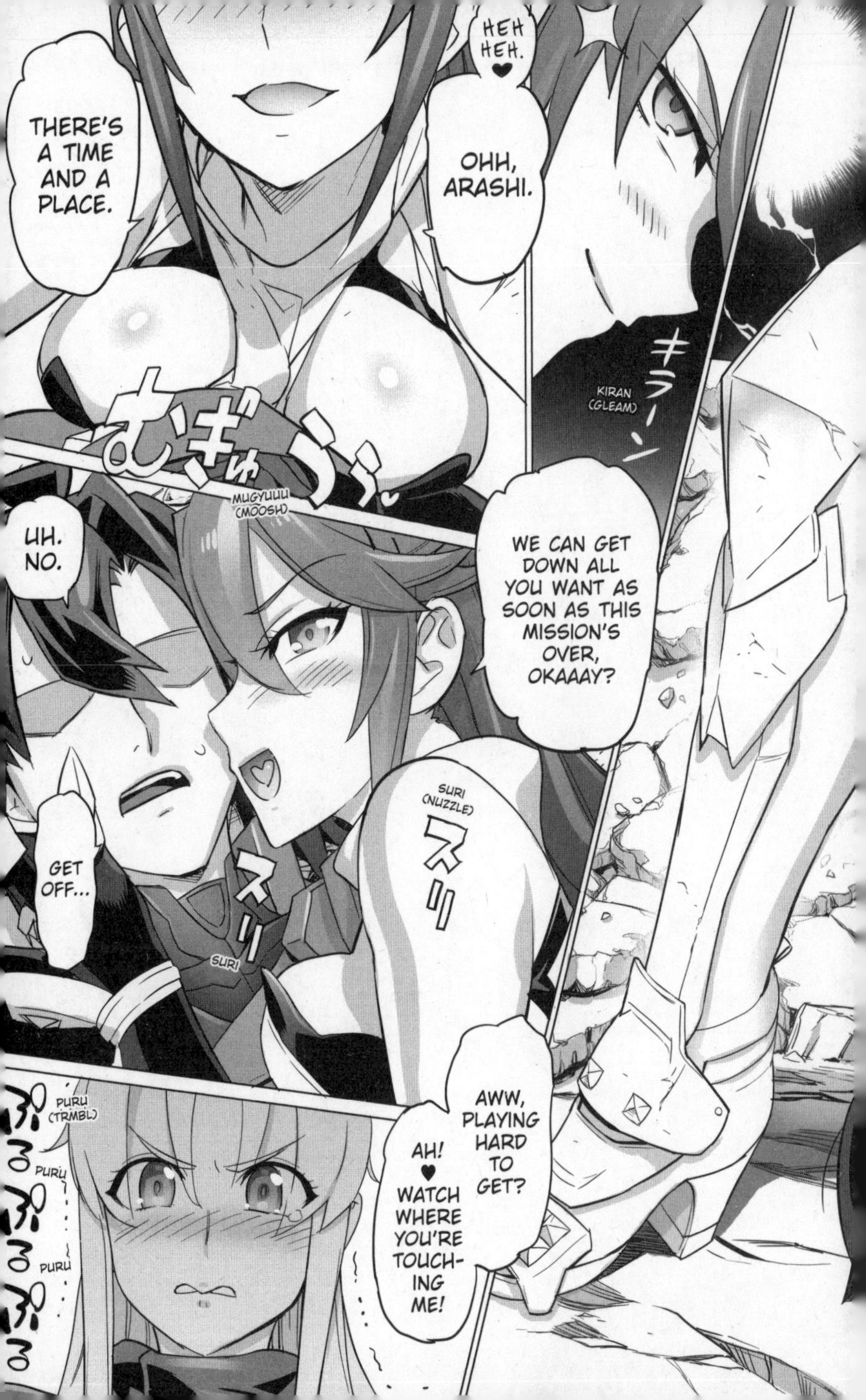
キラーン
KIRAN (GLEAM)
HEH HEH. ♥
OHH, ARASHI.
THERE'S A TIME AND A PLACE.
MUGYUUU (MOOSH)
WE CAN GET DOWN ALL YOU WANT AS SOON AS THIS MISSION'S OVER, OKAAAY?
UH. NO.
SURI (NUZZLE)
スリ
スリ
SURI
GET OFF...
AWW, PLAYING HARD TO GET?
AH! ♥ WATCH WHERE YOU'RE TOUCHING ME!
PURU (TRMBL)
PURU
PURU

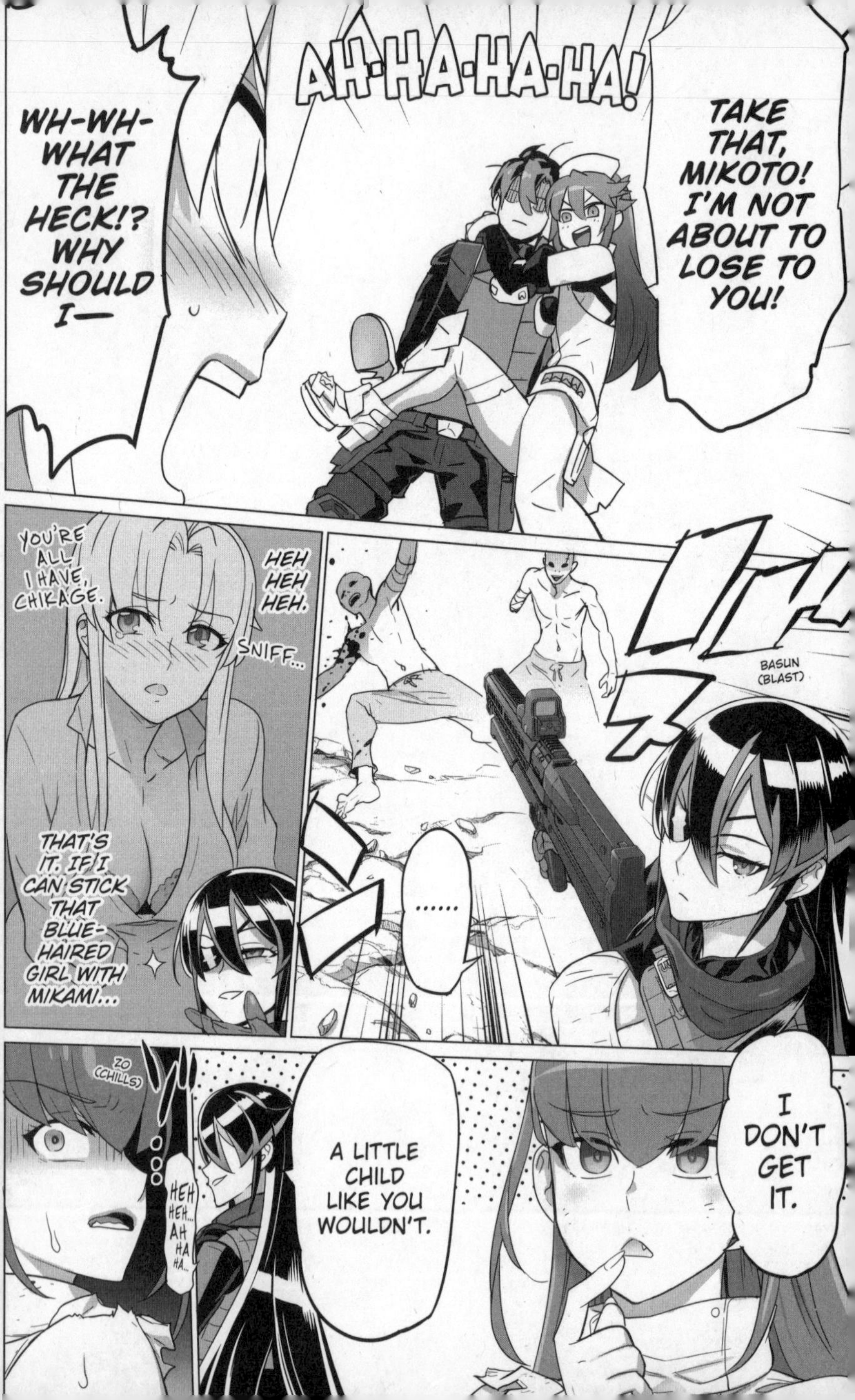
AH-HA-HA-HA!
TAKE THAT, MIKOTO! I'M NOT ABOUT TO LOSE TO YOU!
WH-WH-WHAT THE HECK!? WHY SHOULD I—
BASUN (BLAST)
......
HEH HEH HEH.
YOU'RE ALL I HAVE, CHIKAGE.
SNIFF...
THAT'S IT. IF I CAN STICK THAT BLUE-HAIRED GIRL WITH MIKAMI...
I DON'T GET IT.
A LITTLE CHILD LIKE YOU WOULDN'T.
ZO (CHILLS)
HEH HEH... AH HA HA...

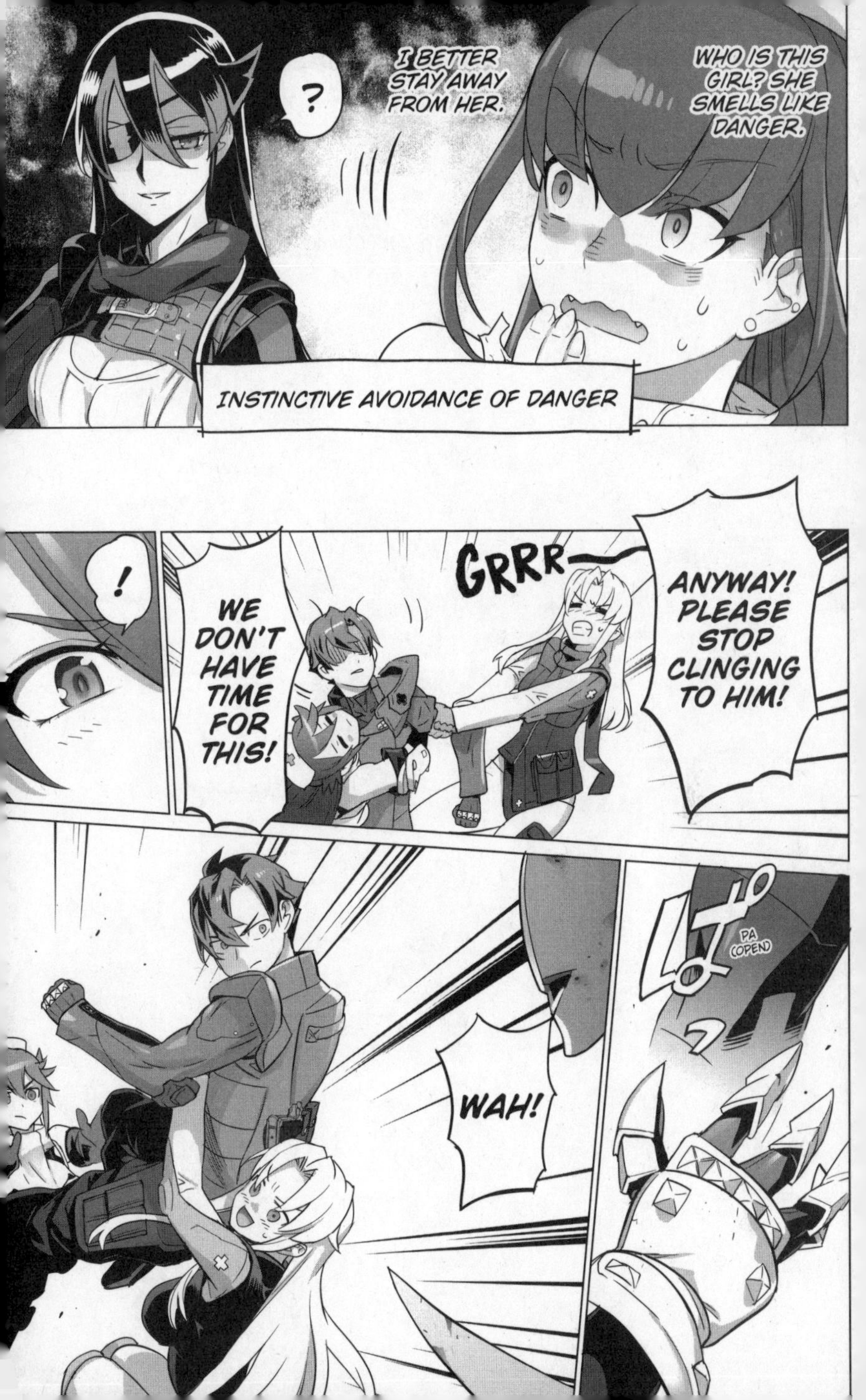
WHO IS THIS GIRL? SHE SMELLS LIKE DANGER.
I BETTER STAY AWAY FROM HER.
?
INSTINCTIVE AVOIDANCE OF DANGER
ANYWAY! PLEASE STOP CLINGING TO HIM!
GRRR—
WE DON'T HAVE TIME FOR THIS!
!
PA (OPEN)
WAH!

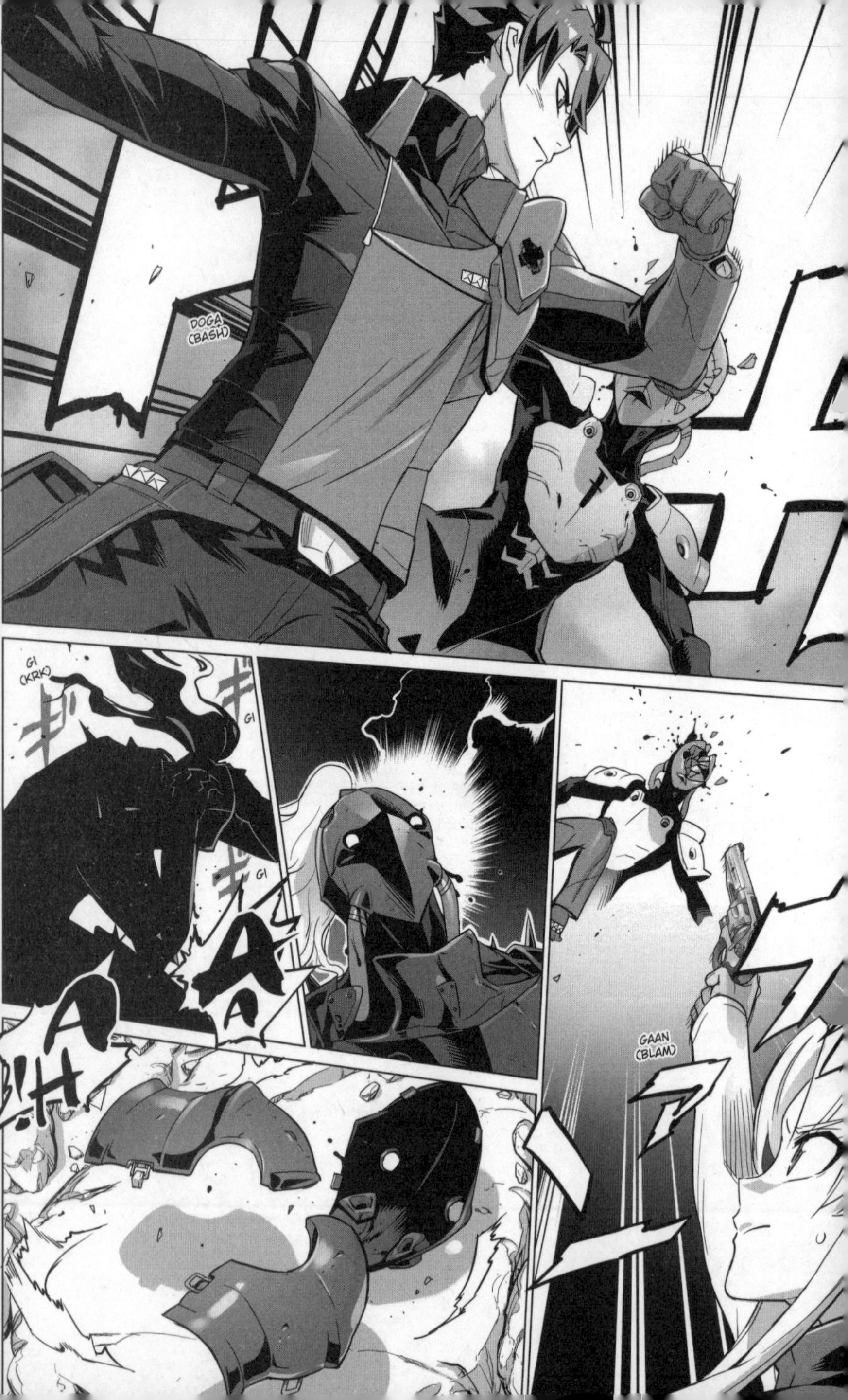
DOGA
(BASH)
GAAN
(BLAM)
GI
(KRK)
GI
GI

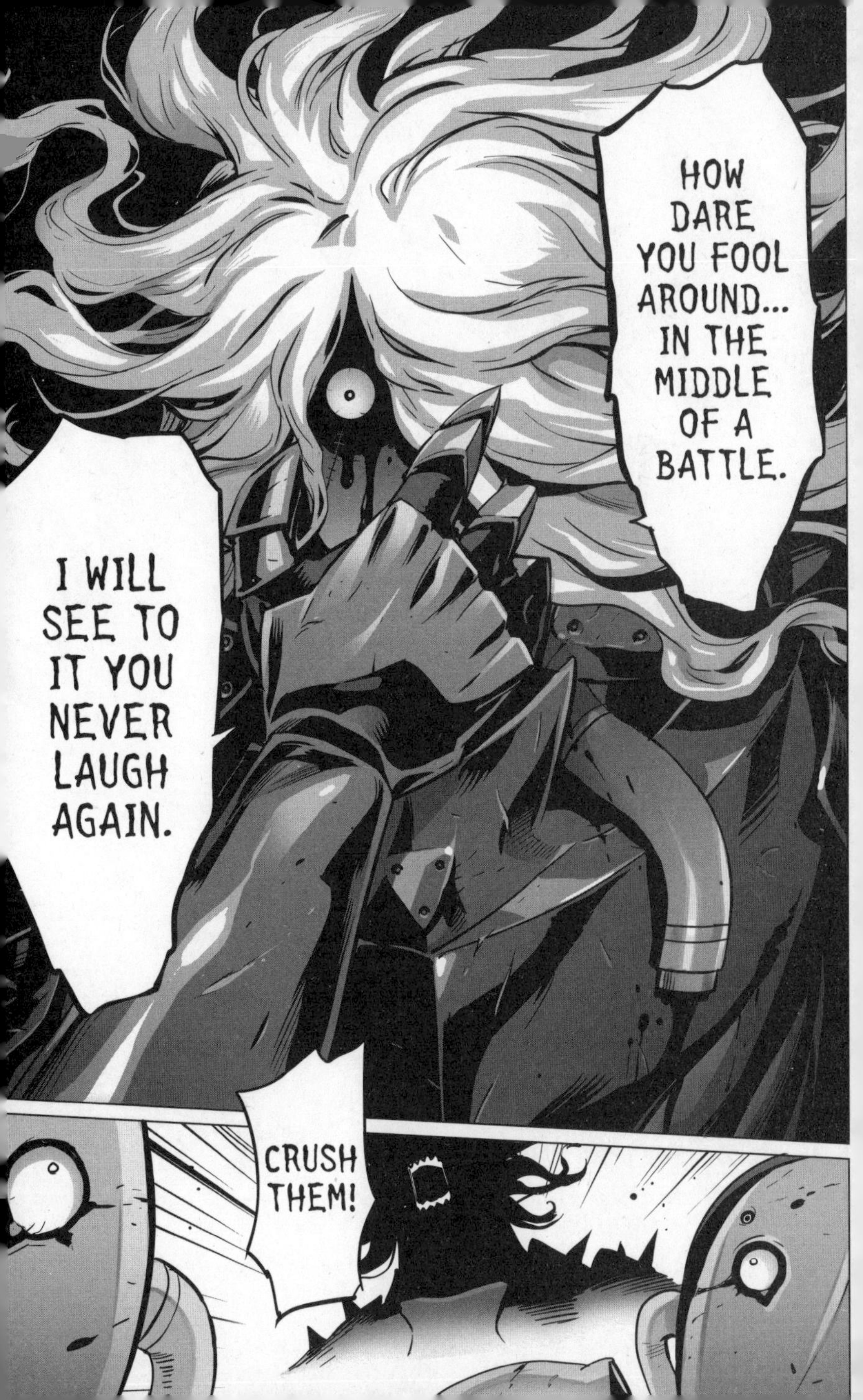
HOW DARE YOU FOOL AROUND... IN THE MIDDLE OF A BATTLE.
I WILL SEE TO IT YOU NEVER LAUGH AGAIN.
CRUSH THEM!

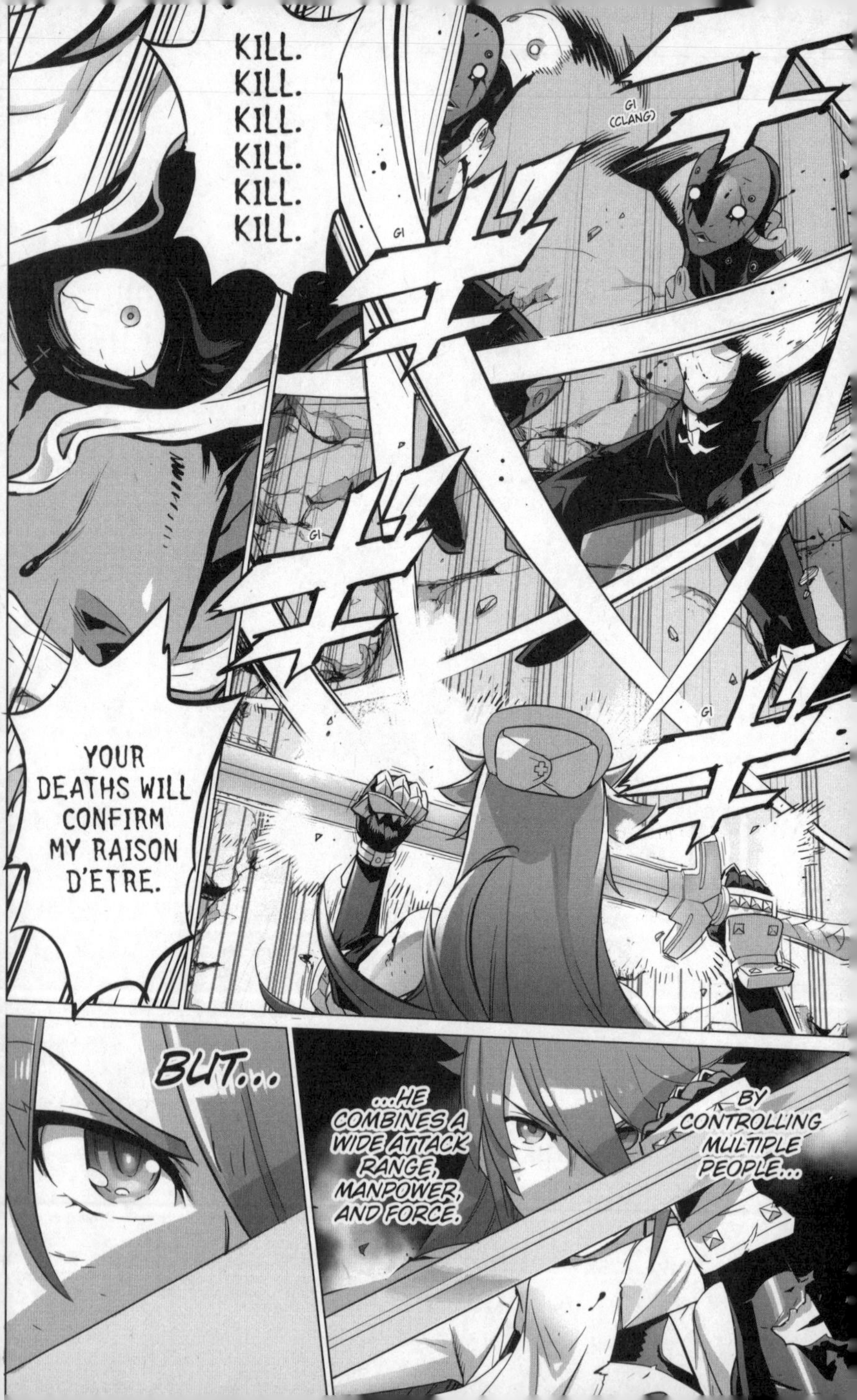
GI (CLANG)
KILL.
KILL.
KILL.
KILL.
KILL.
KILL.
GI
GI
GI
YOUR DEATHS WILL CONFIRM MY RAISON D'ETRE.
BY CONTROLLING MULTIPLE PEOPLE...
...HE COMBINES A WIDE ATTACK RANGE, MANPOWER, AND FORCE.
BUT...

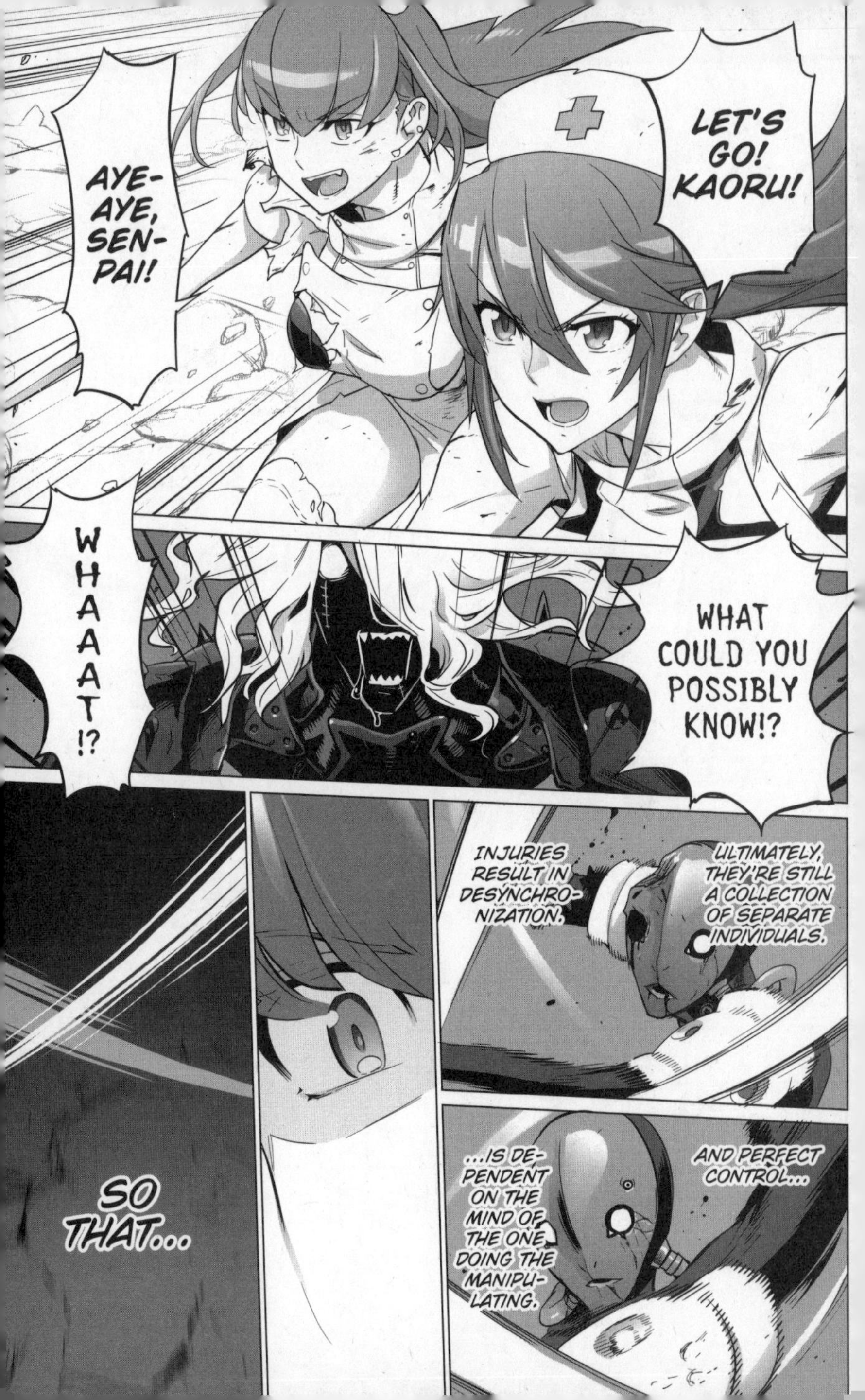

LET'S GO! KAORU!
AYE-AYE, SENPAI!
WHAT COULD YOU POSSIBLY KNOW!?
WHAAAAT!?
ULTIMATELY, THEY'RE STILL A COLLECTION OF SEPARATE INDIVIDUALS.
INJURIES RESULT IN DESYNCHRONIZATION.
AND PERFECT CONTROL...
...IS DEPENDENT ON THE MIND OF THE ONE DOING THE MANIPULATING.
SO THAT...

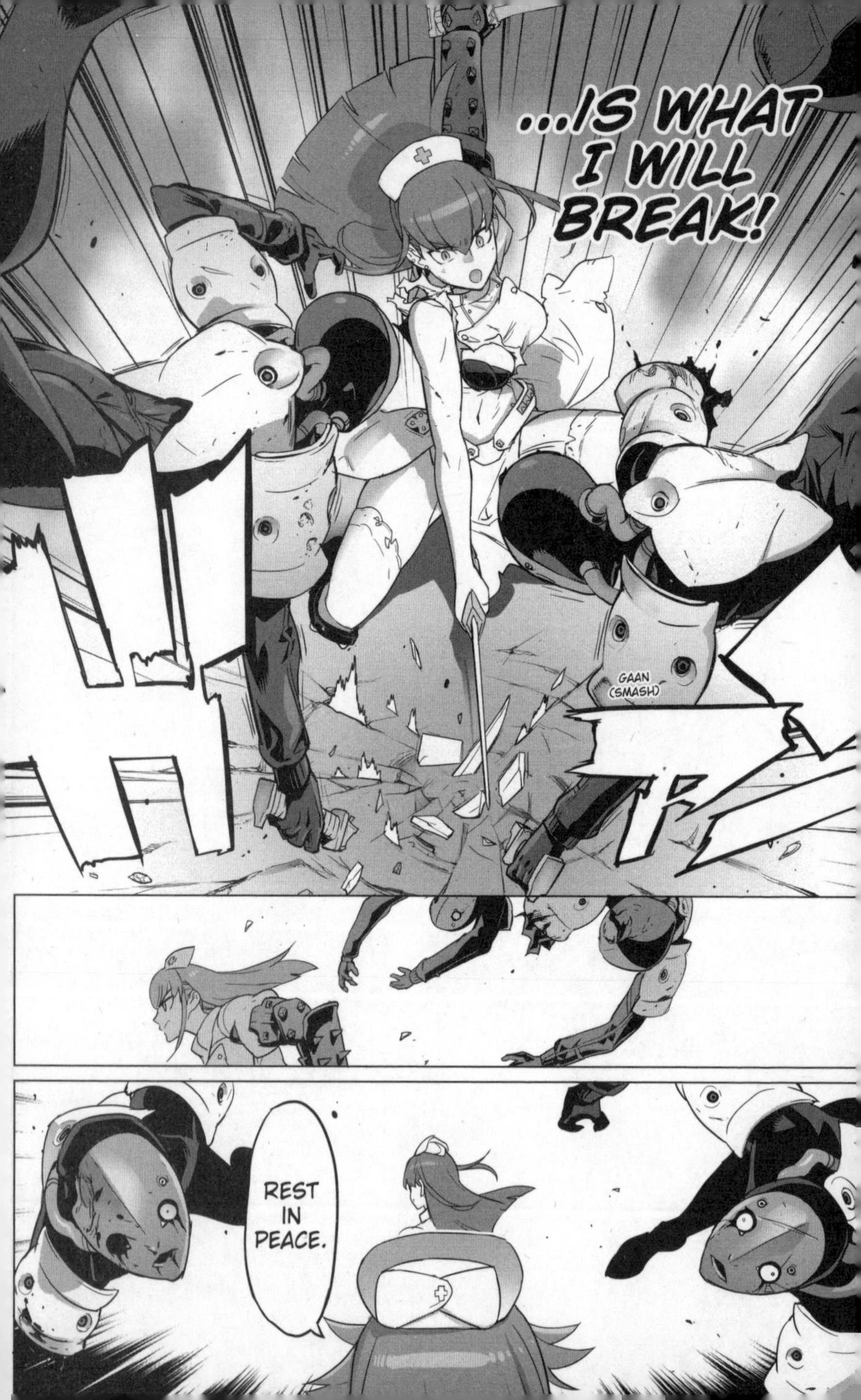
...IS WHAT I WILL BREAK!
GAAN (SMASH)
REST IN PEACE.

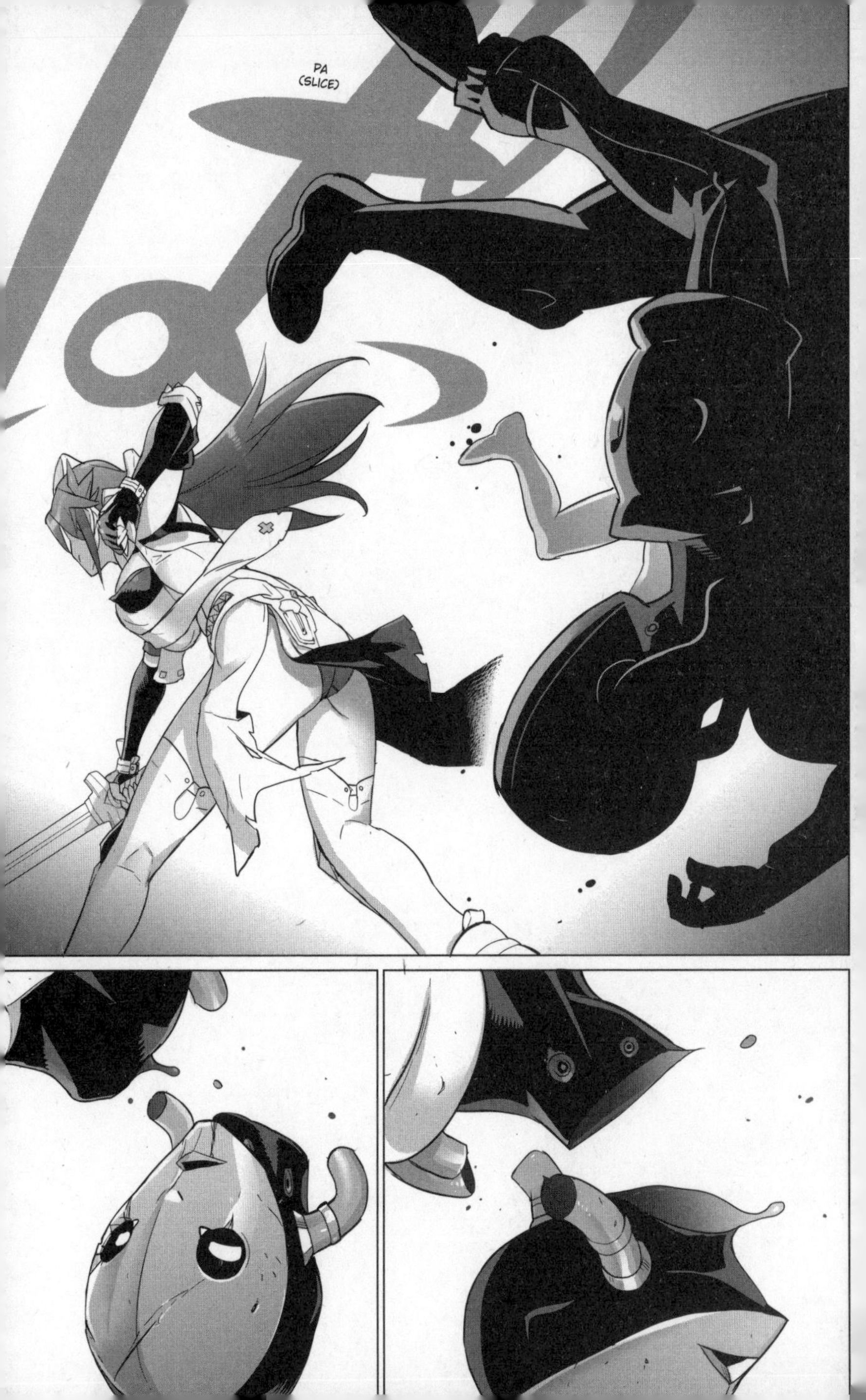
PA
(SLICE)

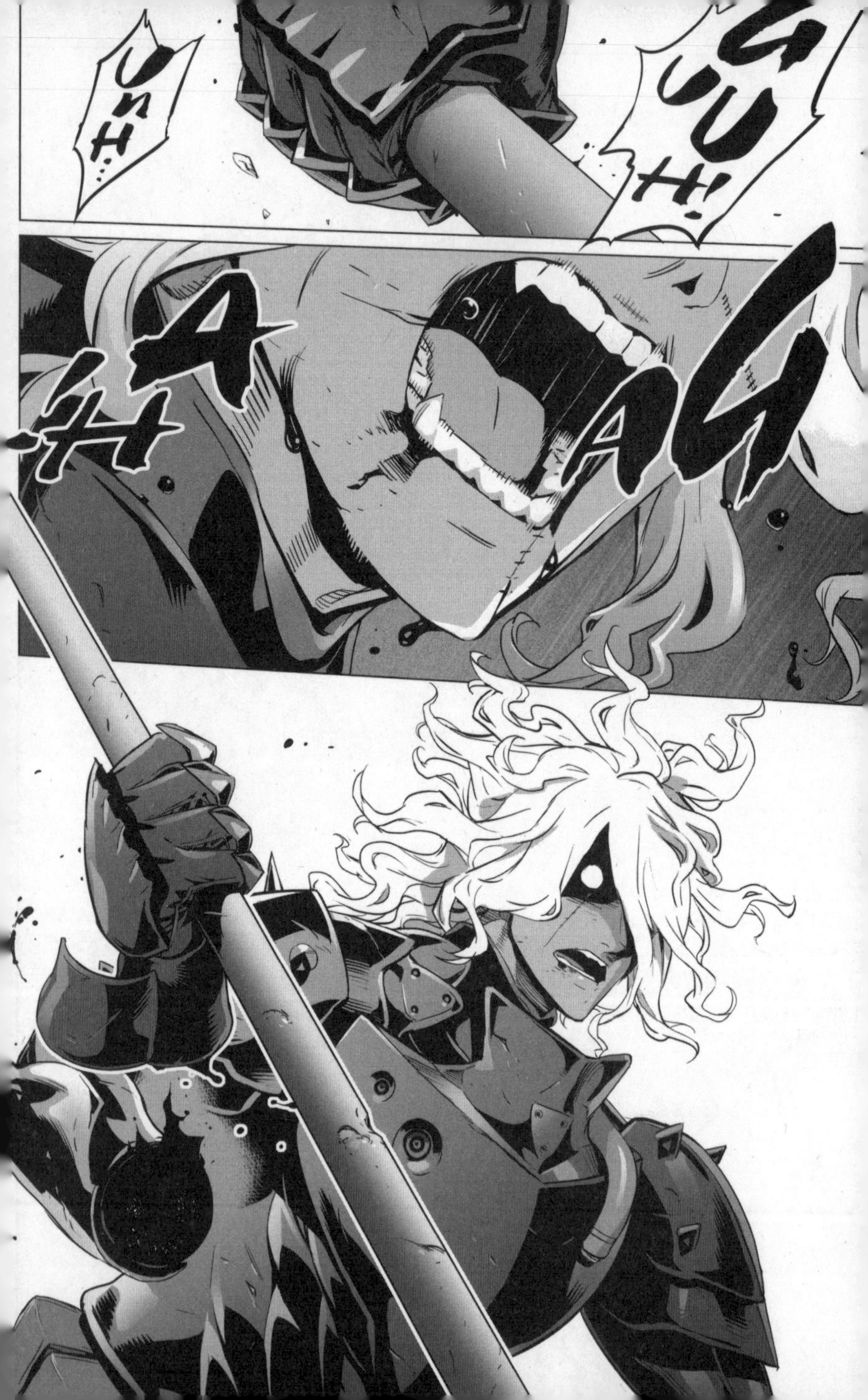
GUUH!
UNH...
AAAAH!

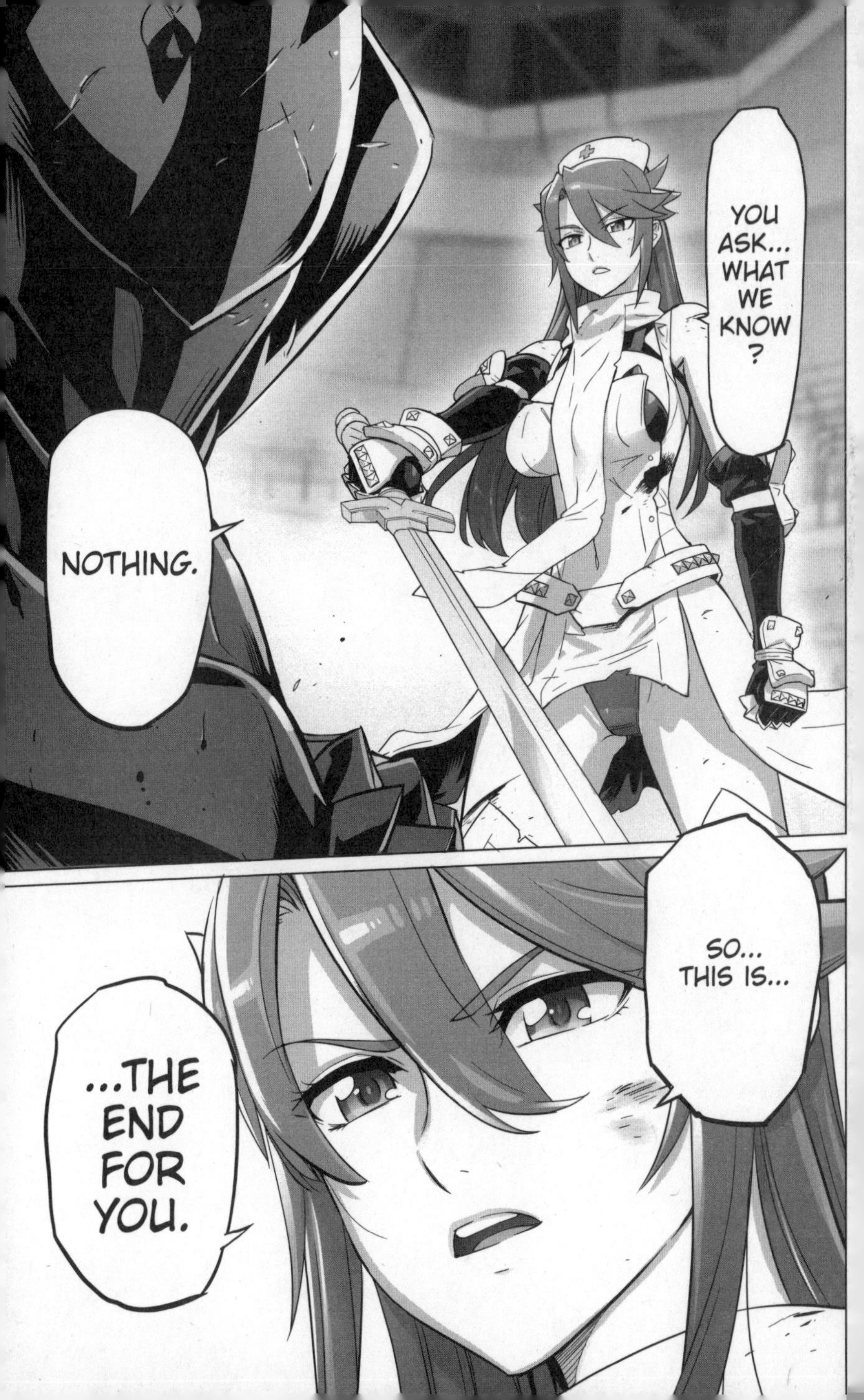
YOU ASK... WHAT WE KNOW?
NOTHING.
SO... THIS IS...
...THE END FOR YOU.

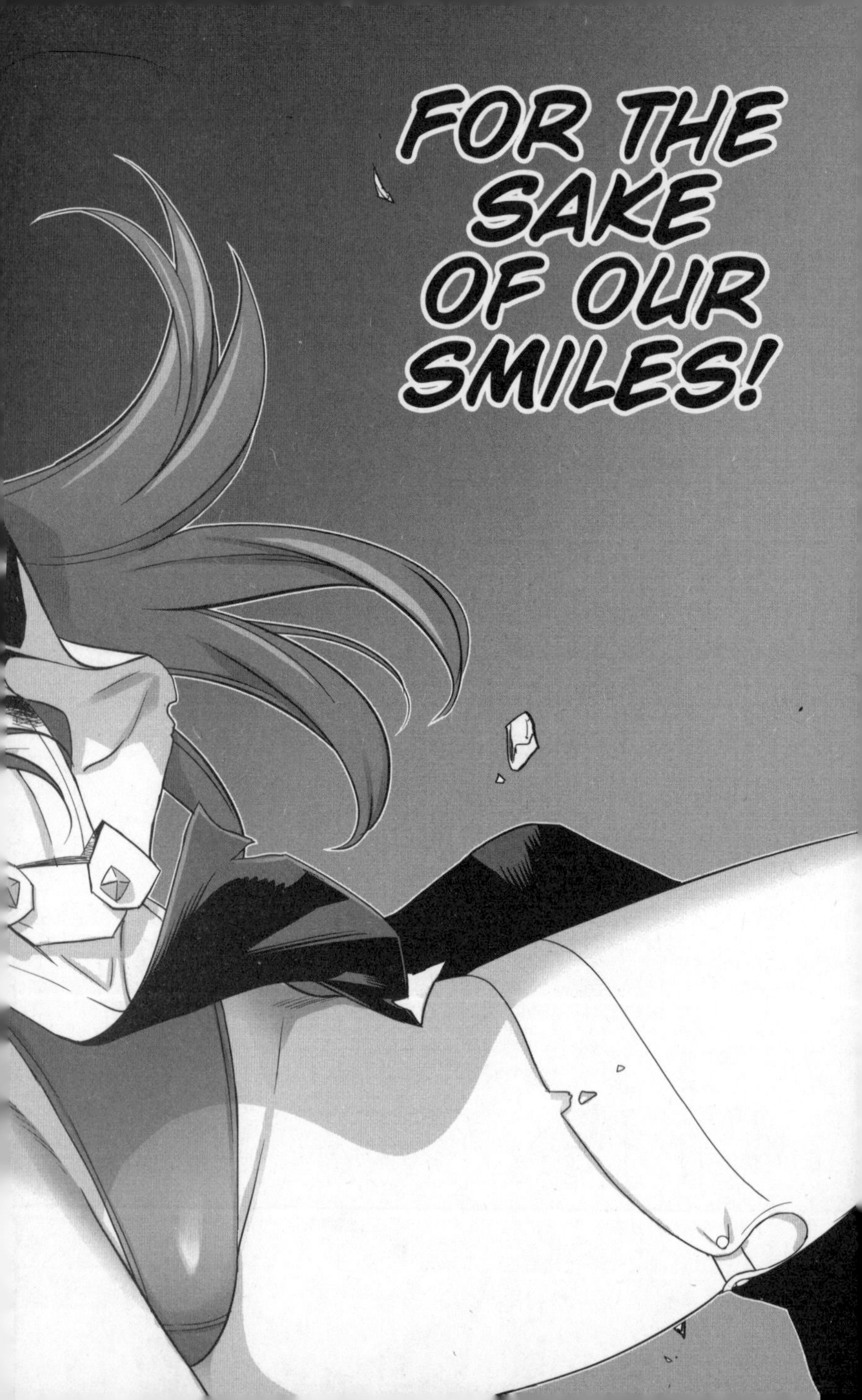
FOR THE SAKE OF OUR SMILES!

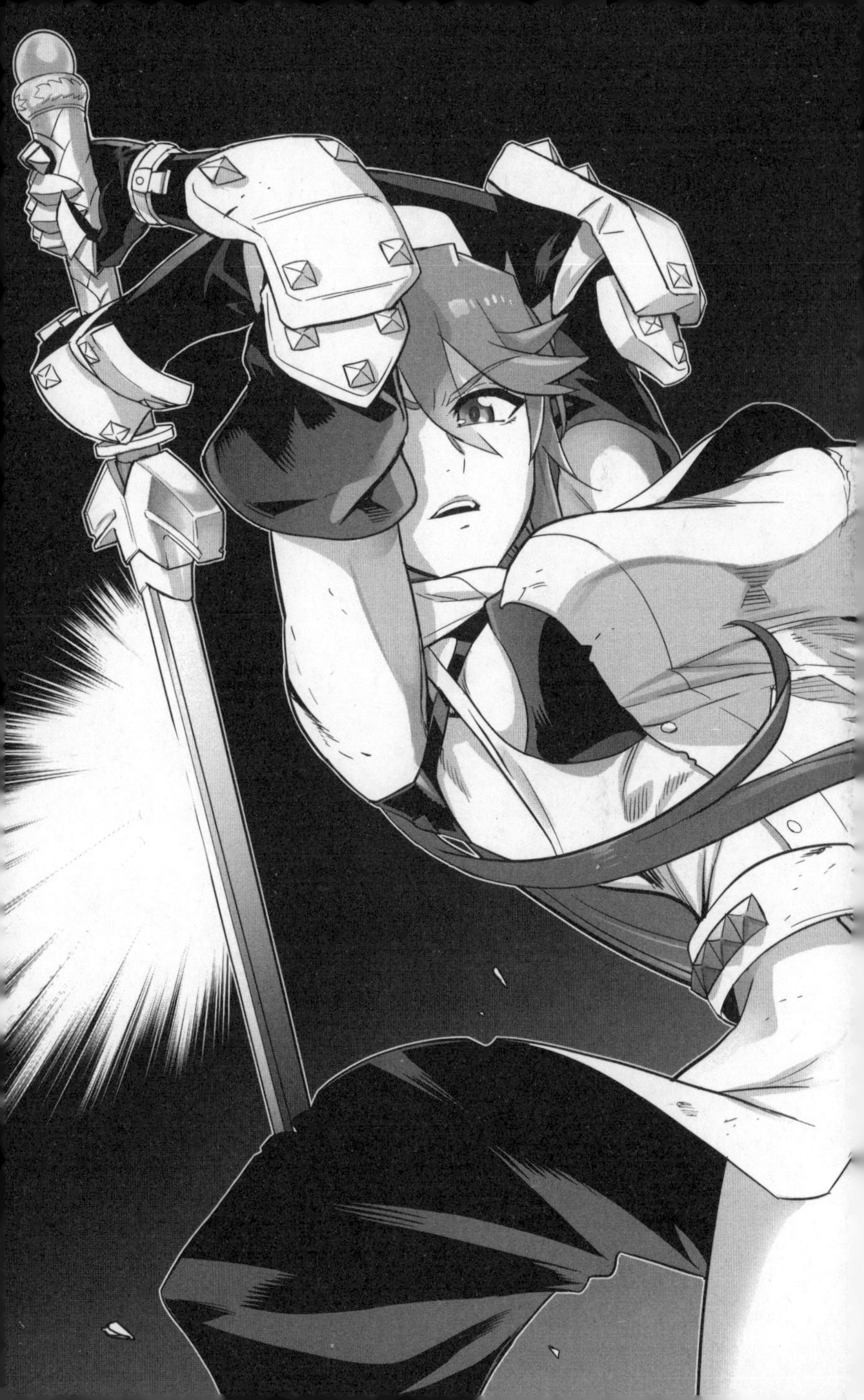

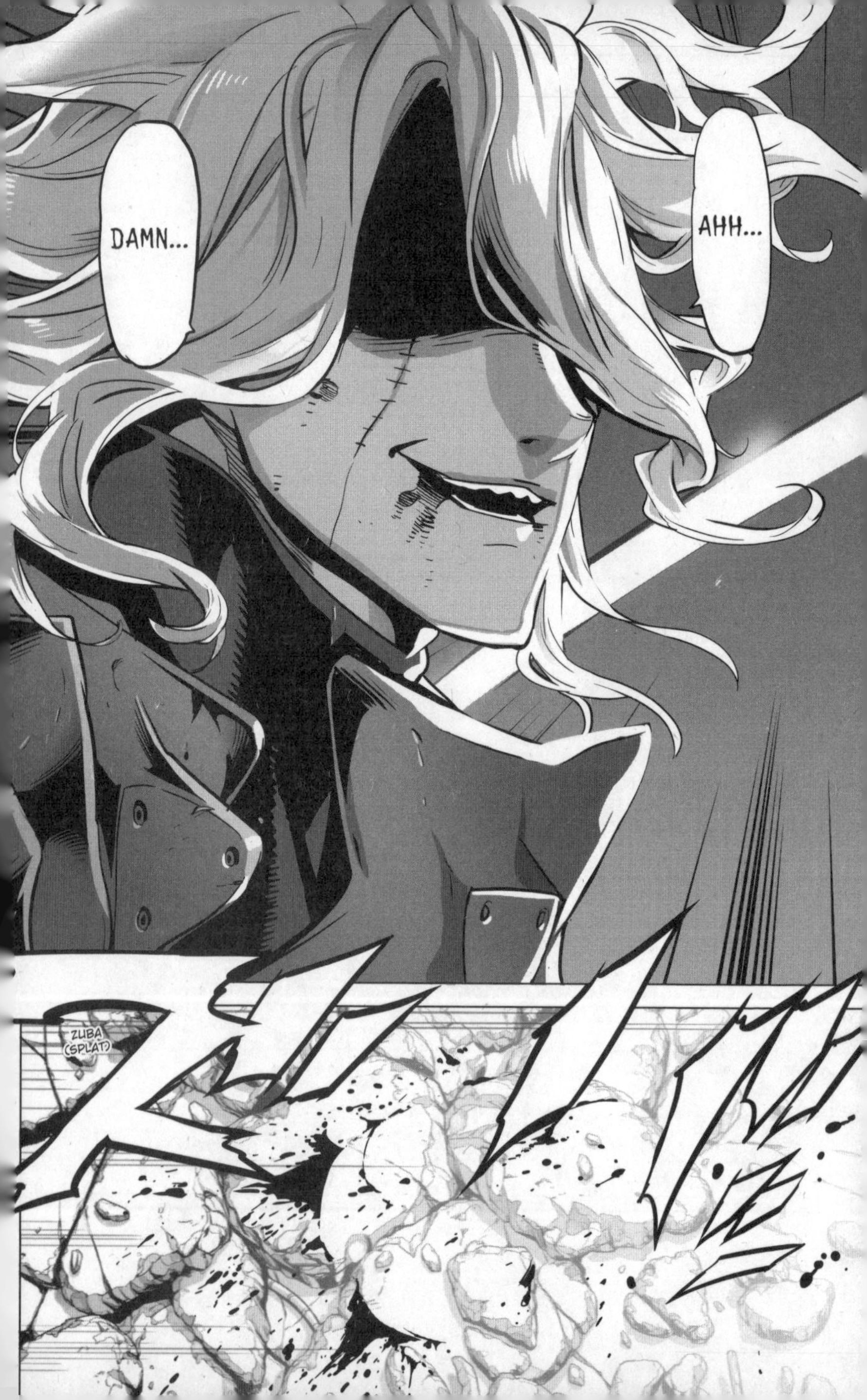
AHH...
DAMN...
ZUBA (SPLAT)

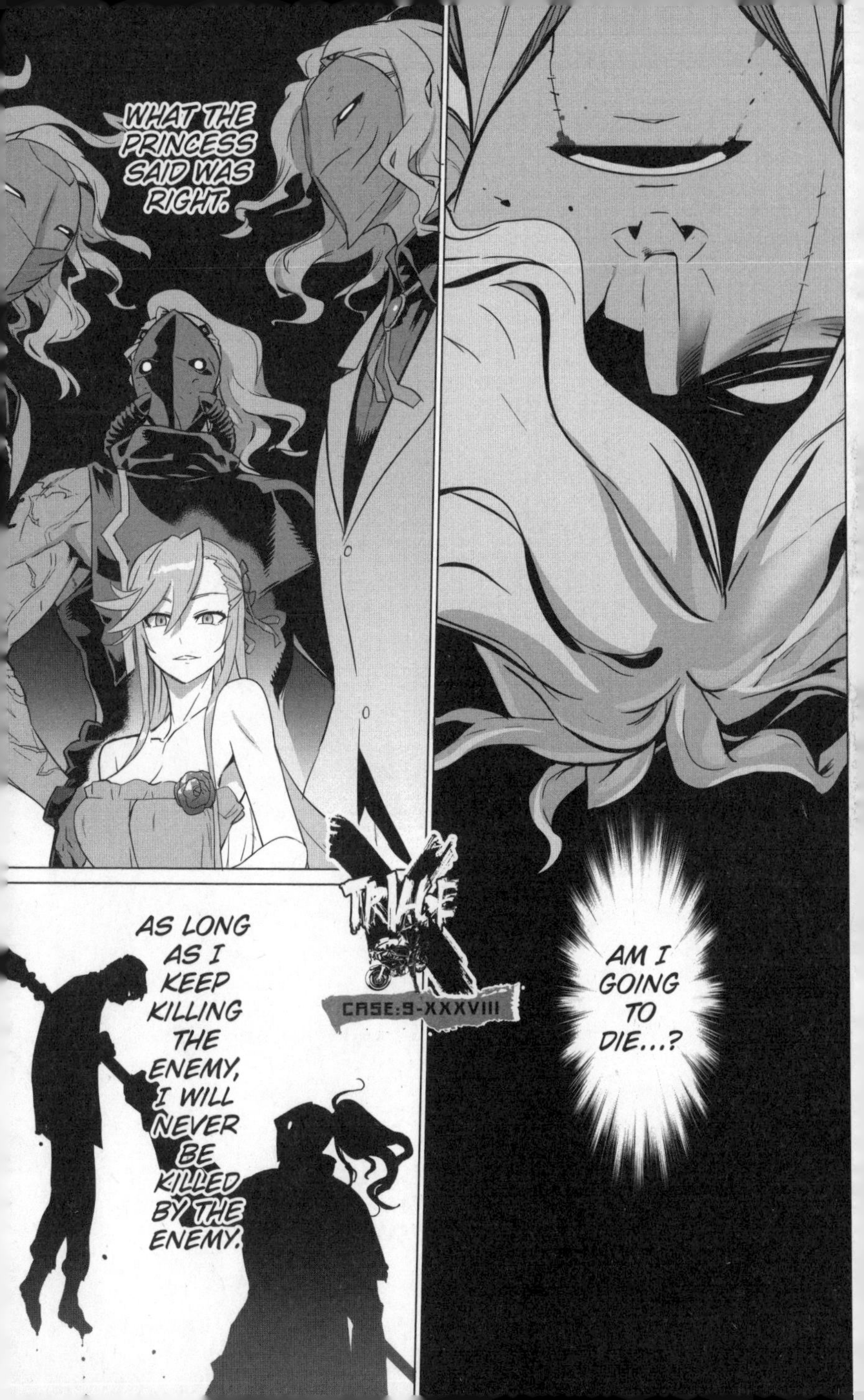
AM I GOING TO DIE...?
WHAT THE PRINCESS SAID WAS RIGHT.
TRIAGE X
CASE:9-XXXVIII
AS LONG AS I KEEP KILLING THE ENEMY, I WILL NEVER BE KILLED BY THE ENEMY.

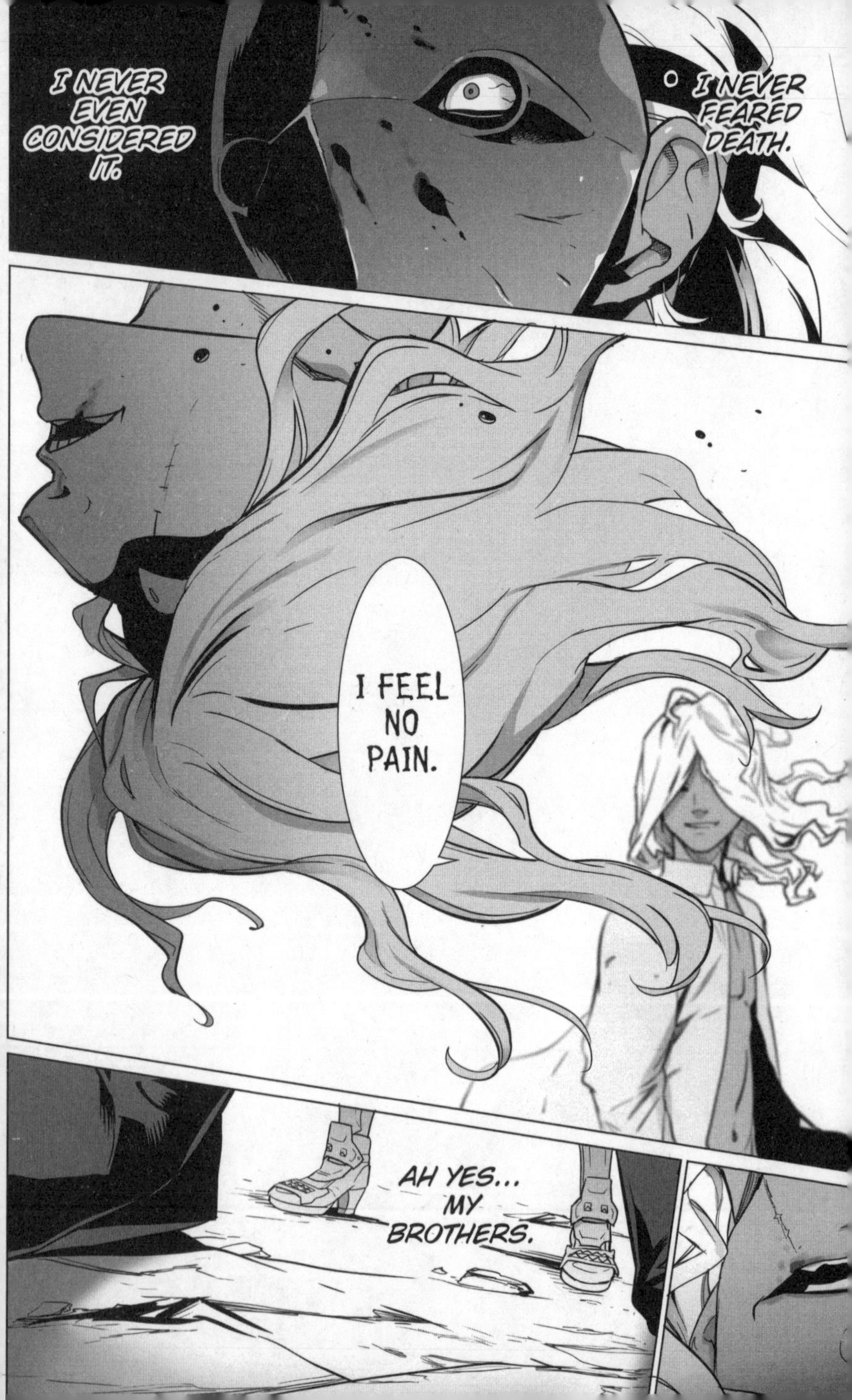
I NEVER FEARED DEATH.
I NEVER EVEN CONSIDERED IT.
I FEEL NO PAIN.
AH YES... MY BROTHERS.

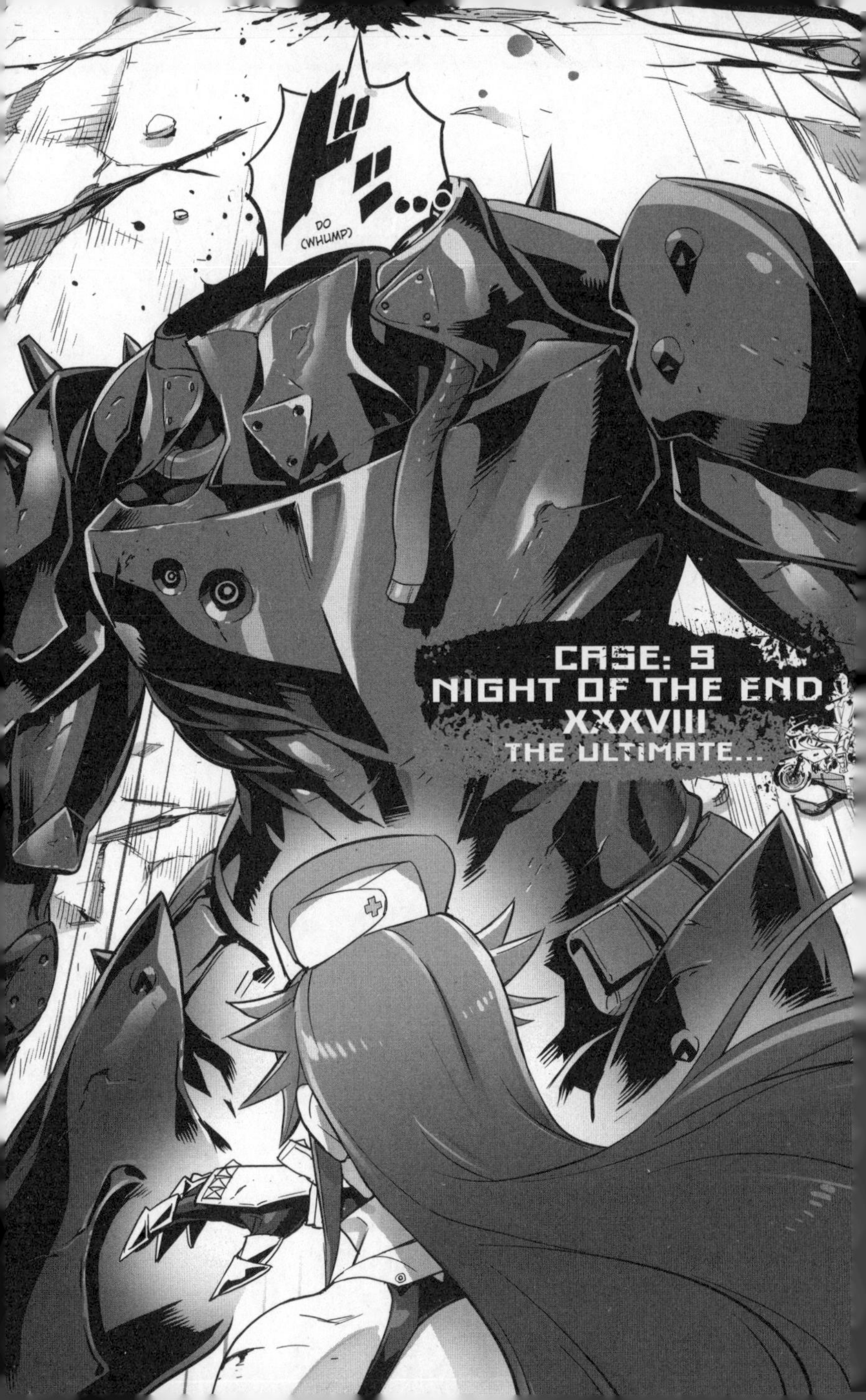
DO
(WHUMP)
CASE: 9
NIGHT OF THE END
XXXVIII
THE ULTIMATE...

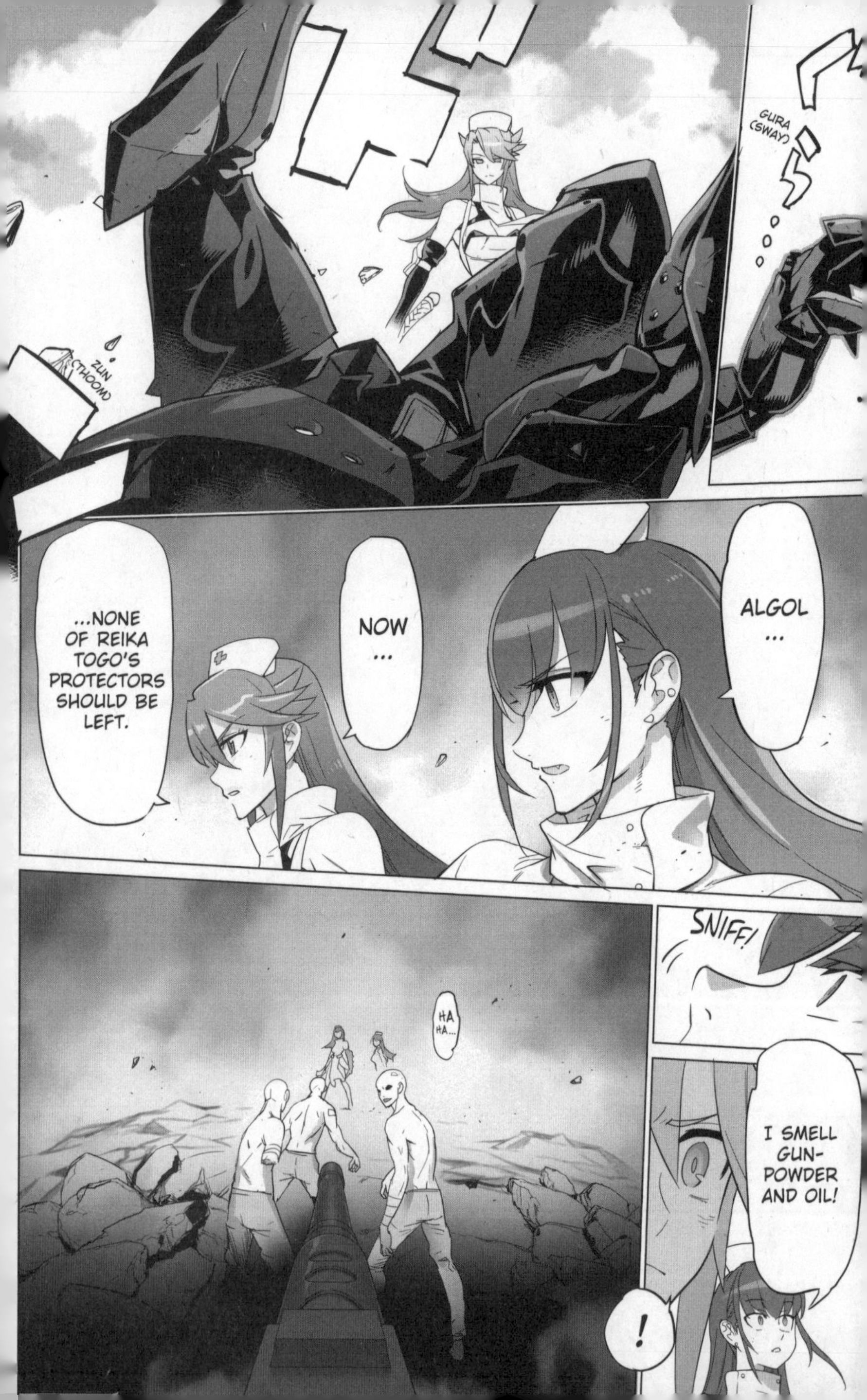
GURA (SWAY)
ZUN (THOOM)
ALGOL ...
NOW ...
...NONE OF REIKA TOGO'S PROTECTORS SHOULD BE LEFT.
SNIFF!
I SMELL GUN-POWDER AND OIL!
!
HA HA...

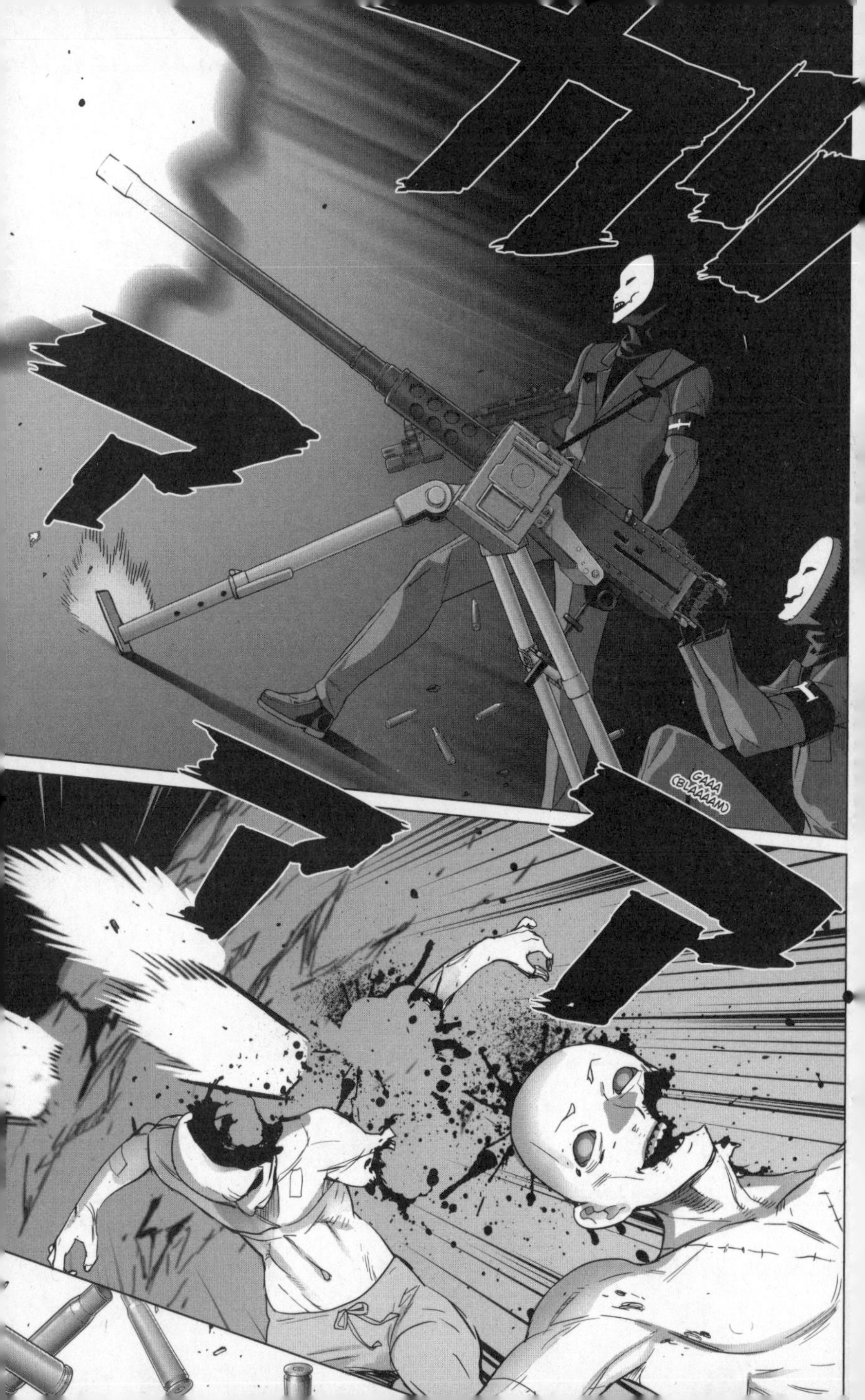
GAAA
(BLAAAAM)

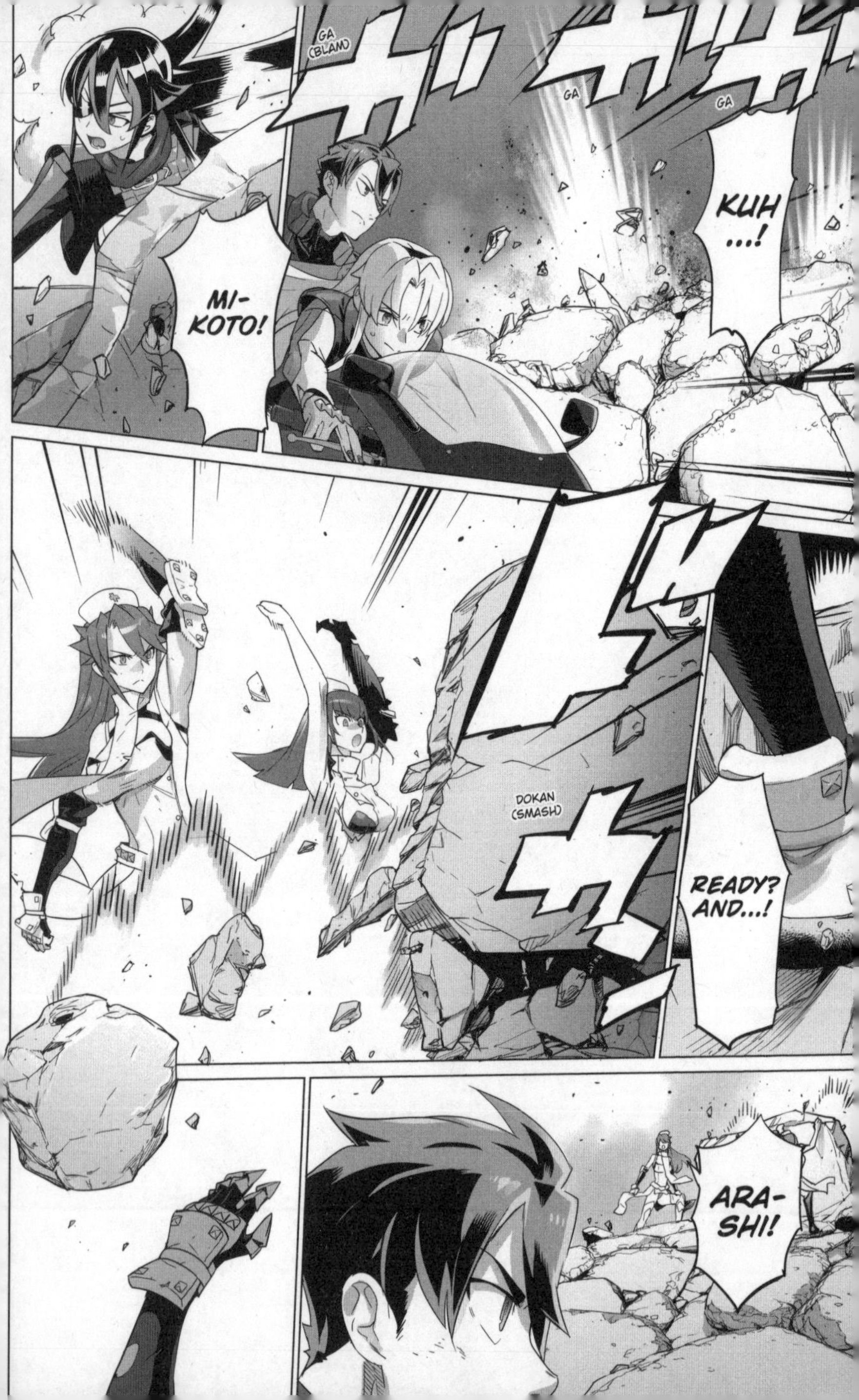
GA (BLAM)
GA
GA
KUH ...!
MI-KOTO!
READY? AND...!
DOKAN (SMASH)
ARA-SHI!

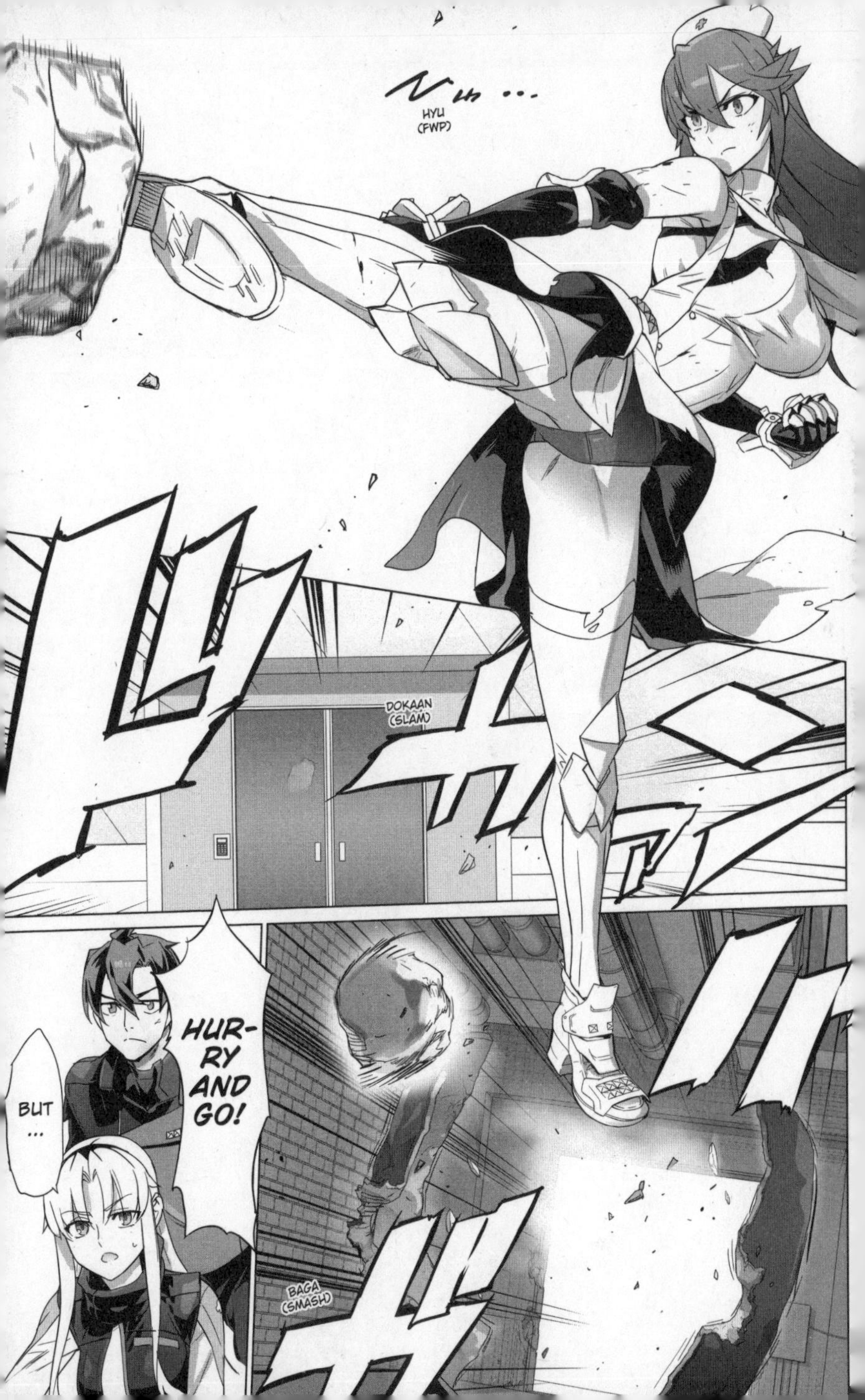
HYU (FWP)
DOKAAN (SLAM)
HUR-RY AND GO!
BUT...
BAGA (SMASH)

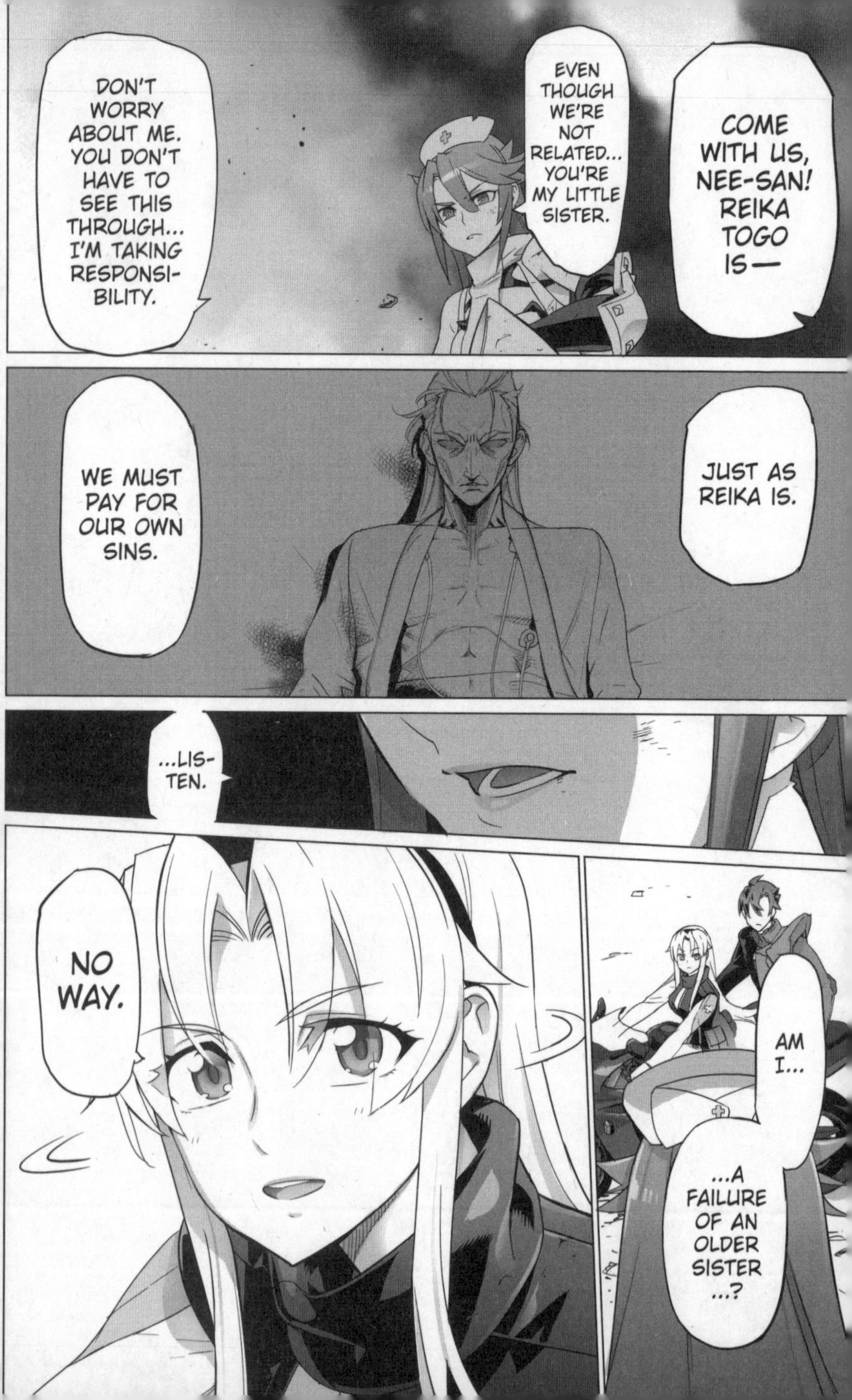
COME WITH US, NEE-SAN! REIKA TOGO IS—
EVEN THOUGH WE'RE NOT RELATED... YOU'RE MY LITTLE SISTER.
DON'T WORRY ABOUT ME. YOU DON'T HAVE TO SEE THIS THROUGH... I'M TAKING RESPONSI-BILITY.
JUST AS REIKA IS.
WE MUST PAY FOR OUR OWN SINS.
...LIS-TEN.
AM I...
...A FAILURE OF AN OLDER SISTER ...?
NO WAY.

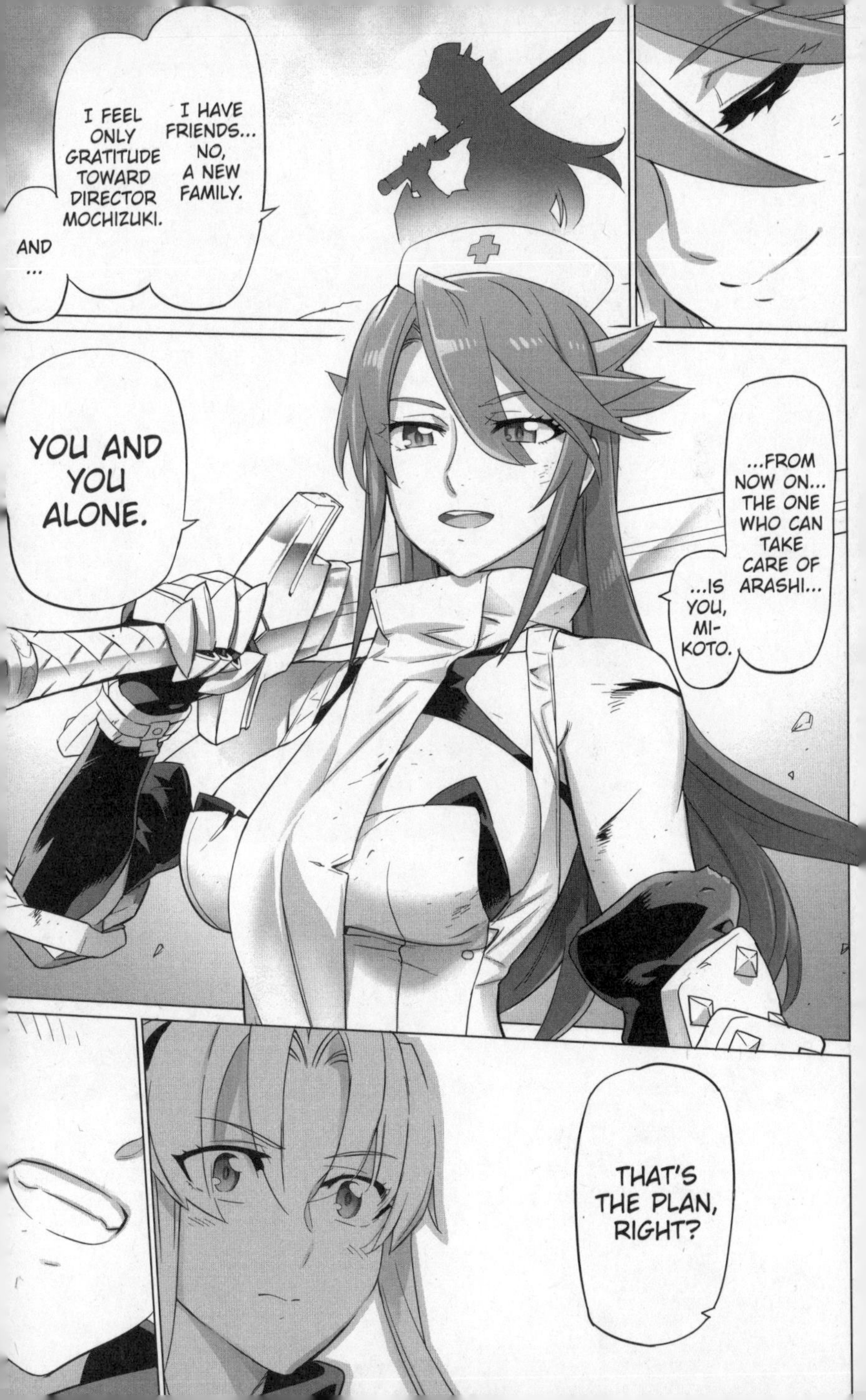
I HAVE FRIENDS... NO, A NEW FAMILY.
I FEEL ONLY GRATITUDE TOWARD DIRECTOR MOCHIZUKI.
AND ...
...FROM NOW ON... THE ONE WHO CAN TAKE CARE OF ARASHI...
...IS YOU, MI-KOTO.
YOU AND YOU ALONE.
THAT'S THE PLAN, RIGHT?

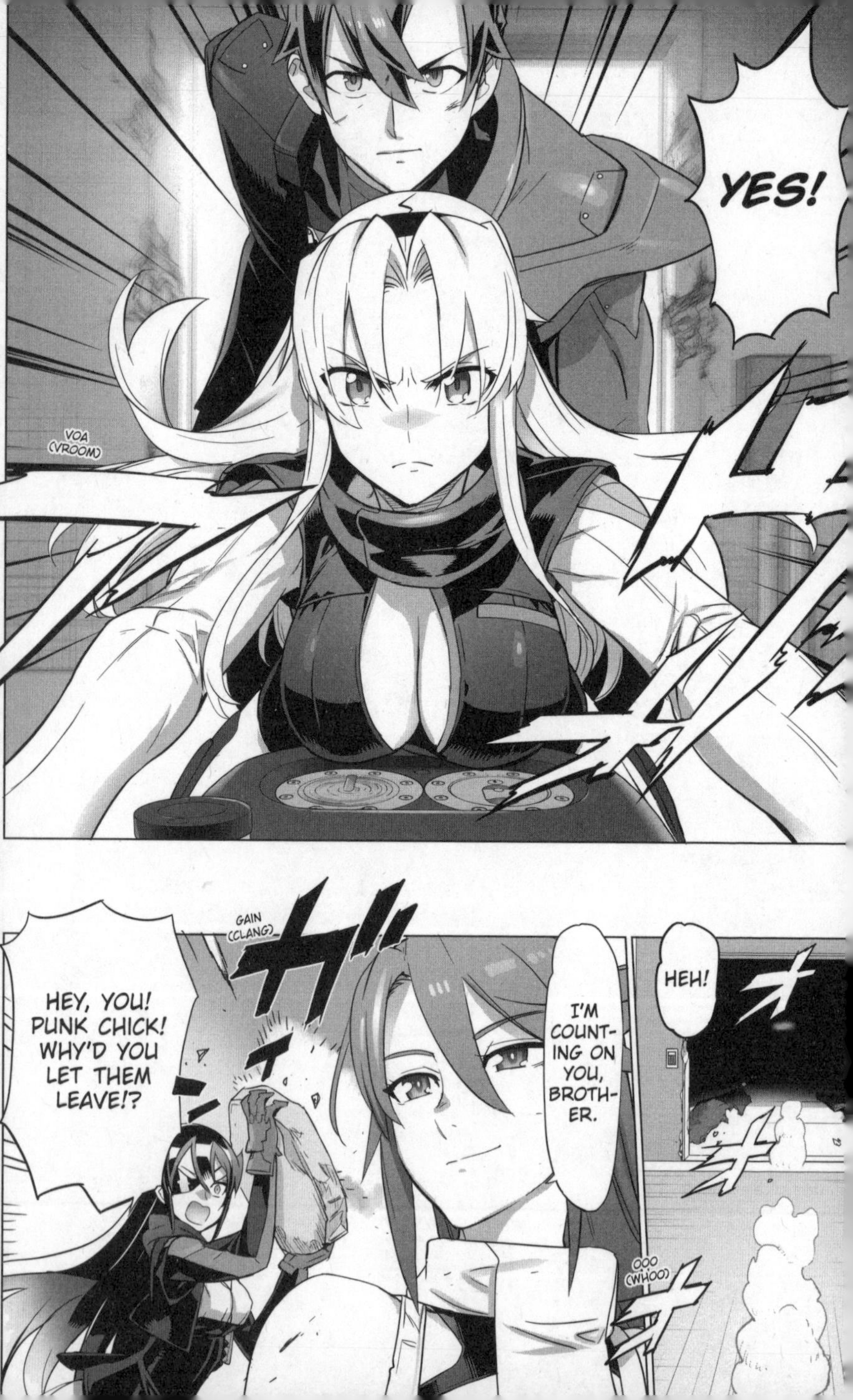
YES!
VOA (VROOM)
HEH!
I'M COUNT-ING ON YOU, BROTH-ER.
GAIN (CLANG)
HEY, YOU! PUNK CHICK! WHY'D YOU LET THEM LEAVE!?
OOO (WHOO)

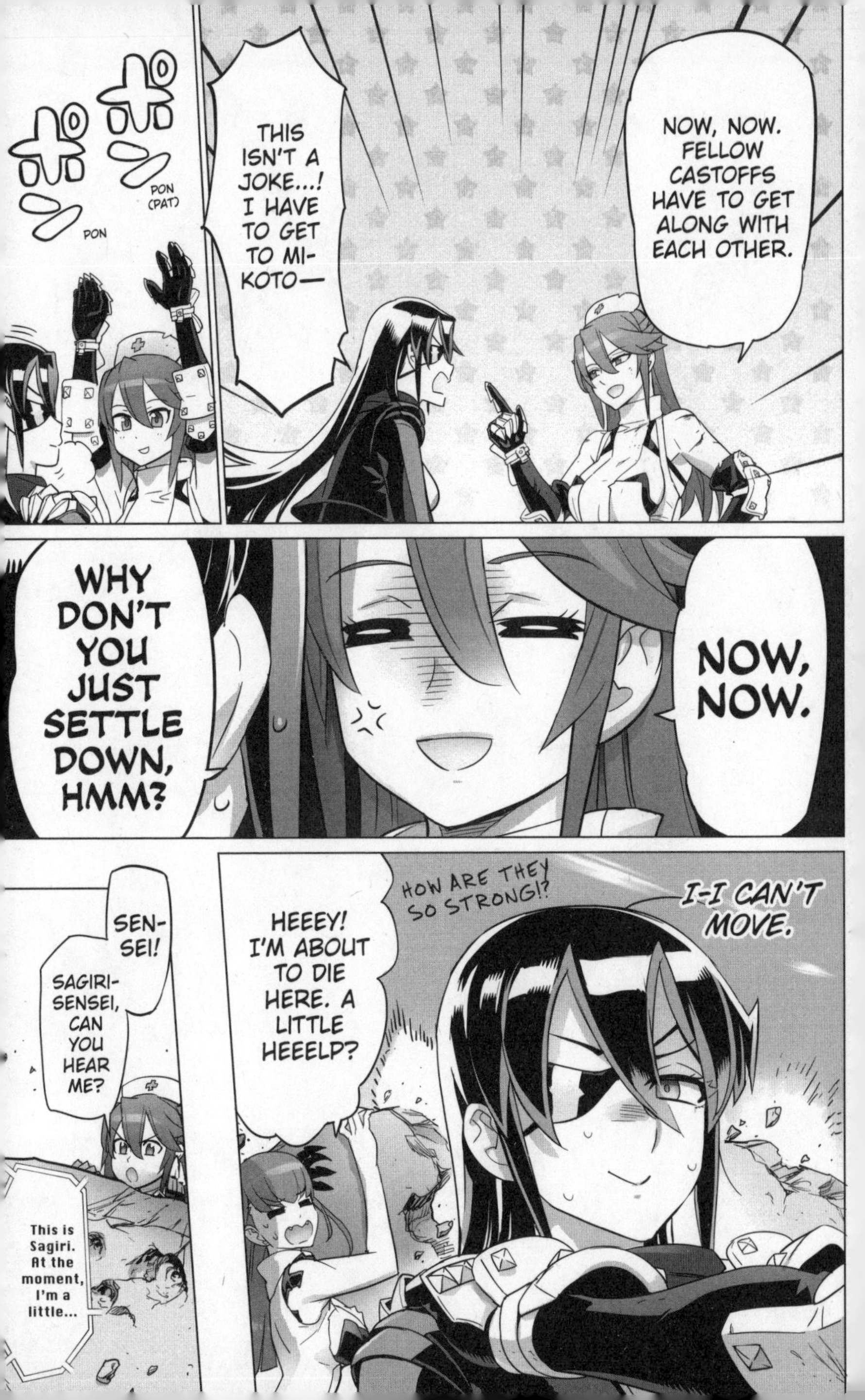
NOW, NOW. FELLOW CASTOFFS HAVE TO GET ALONG WITH EACH OTHER.
THIS ISN'T A JOKE...! I HAVE TO GET TO MI-KOTO—
PON (PAT)
PON
NOW, NOW.
WHY DON'T YOU JUST SETTLE DOWN, HMM?
I-I CAN'T MOVE.
HOW ARE THEY SO STRONG!?
HEEEY! I'M ABOUT TO DIE HERE. A LITTLE HEEELP?
SEN-SEI!
SAGIRI-SENSEI, CAN YOU HEAR ME?
This is Sagiri. At the moment, I'm a little...

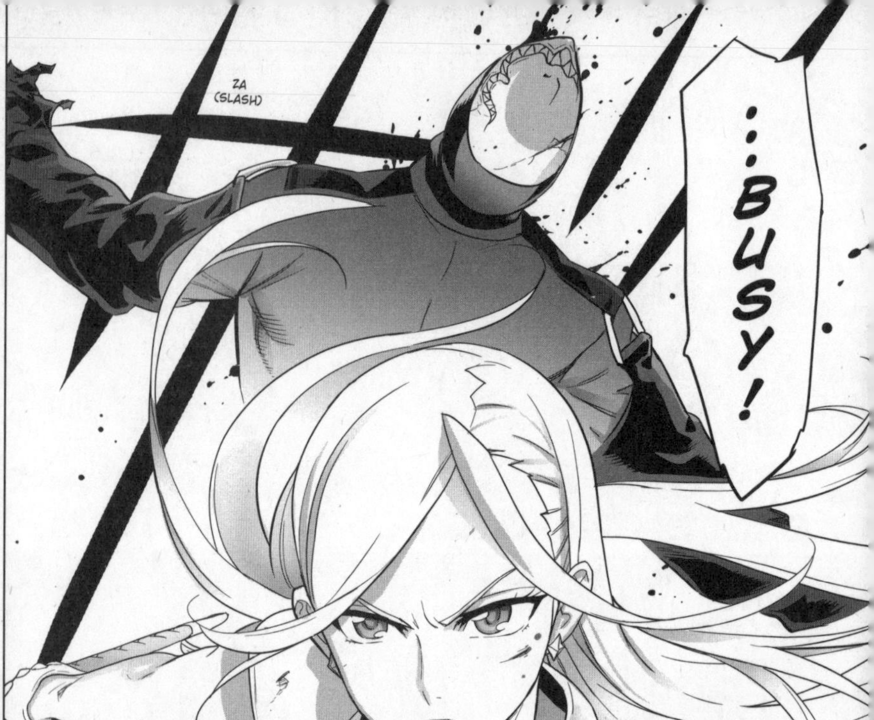
...BUSY!
ZA (SLASH)
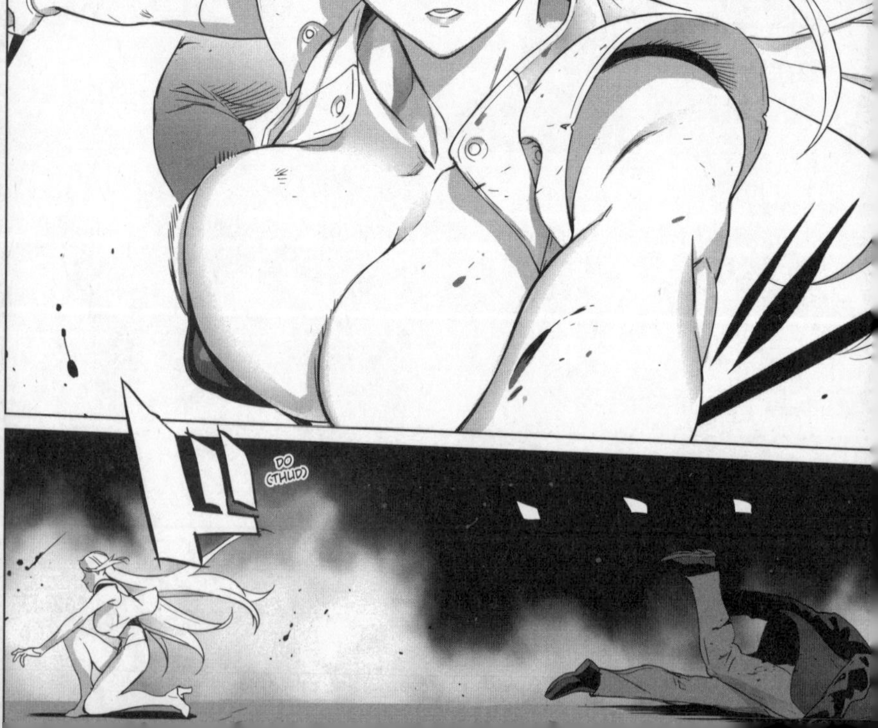
DO (THUD)

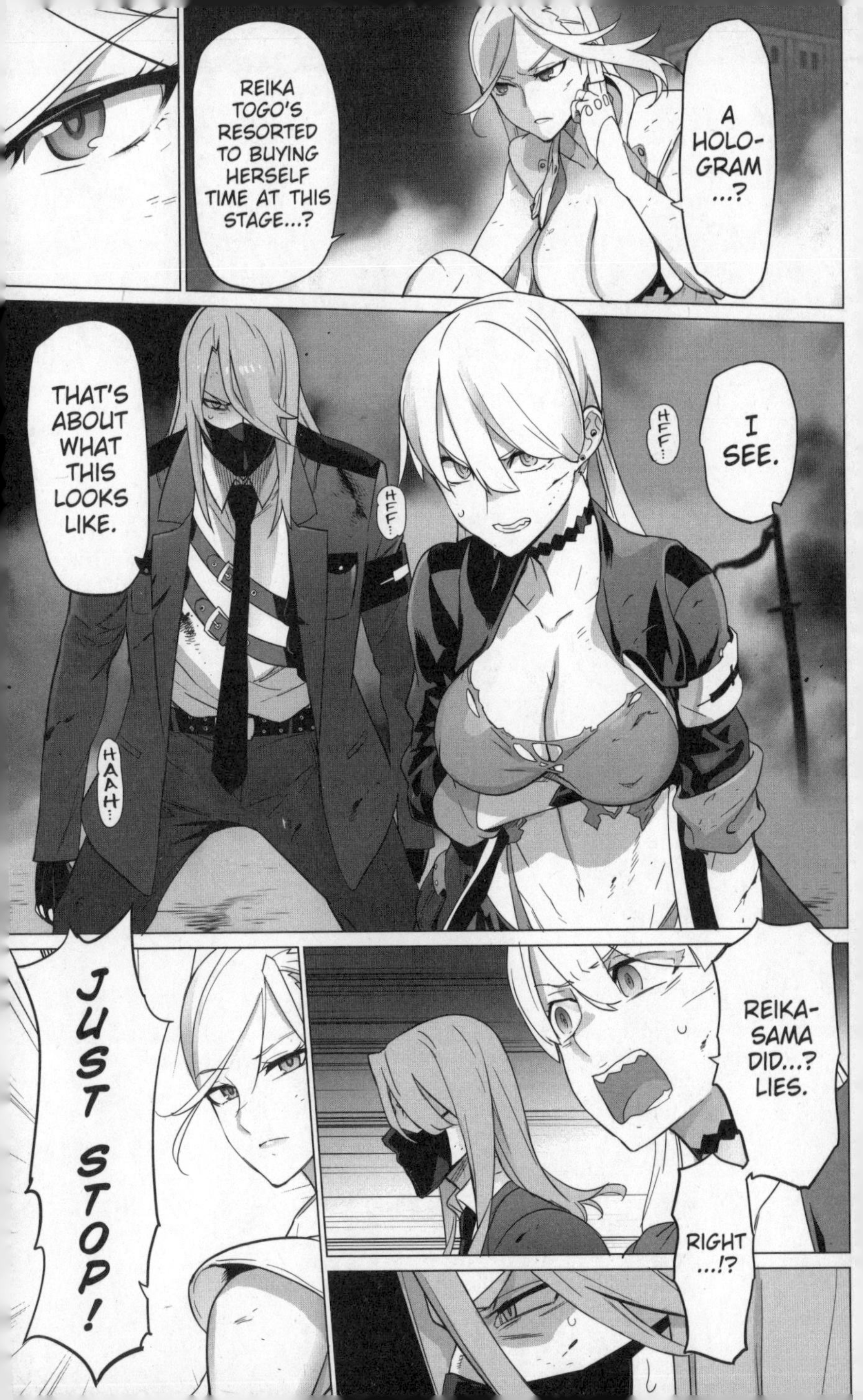
A HOLO-GRAM...?
REIKA TOGO'S RESORTED TO BUYING HERSELF TIME AT THIS STAGE...?
I SEE.
HFF...
HFF...
THAT'S ABOUT WHAT THIS LOOKS LIKE.
HAAH...
REIKA-SAMA DID...? LIES.
RIGHT...!?
JUST STOP!

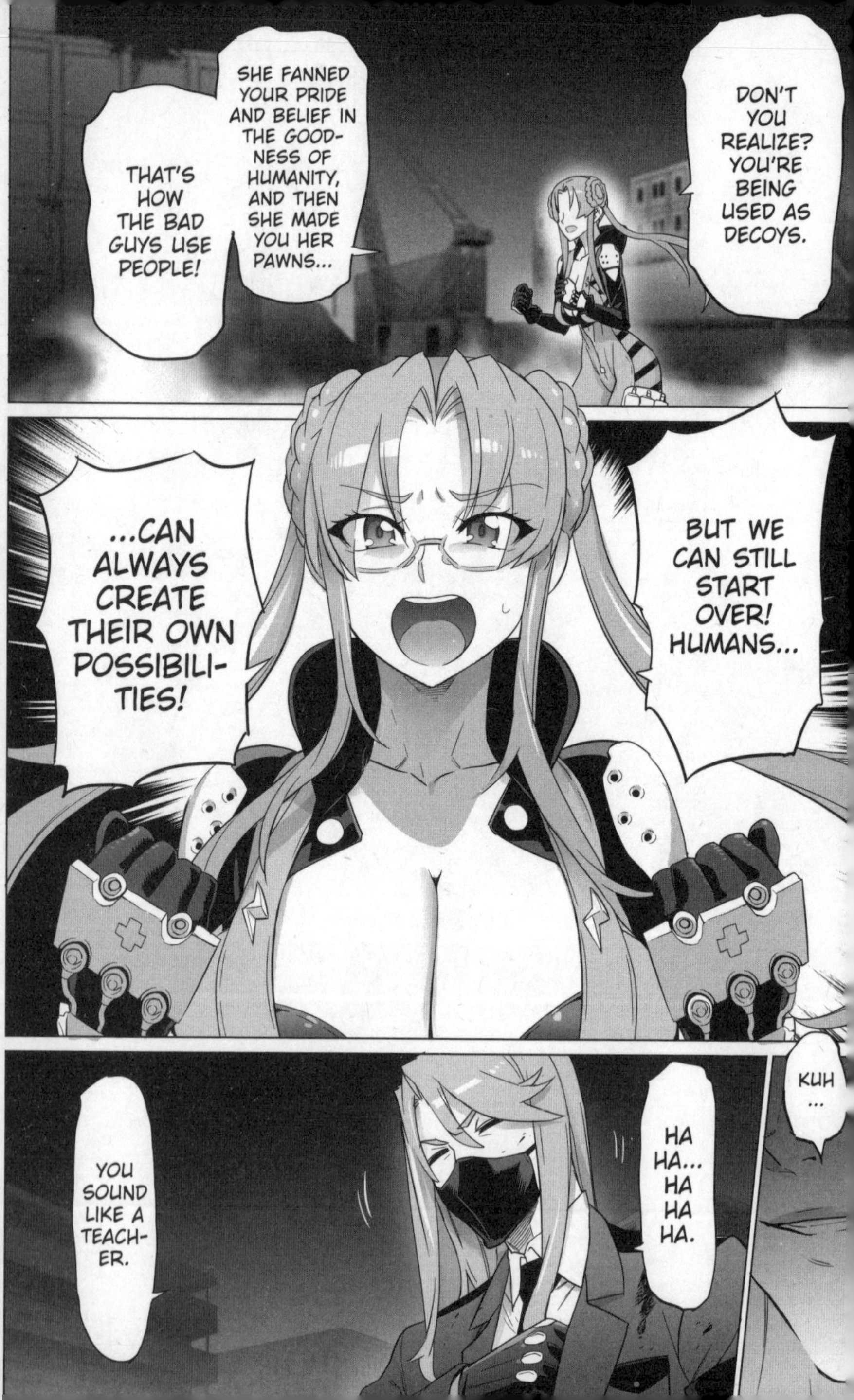
DON'T YOU REALIZE? YOU'RE BEING USED AS DECOYS.
SHE FANNED YOUR PRIDE AND BELIEF IN THE GOOD-NESS OF HUMANITY, AND THEN SHE MADE YOU HER PAWNS...
THAT'S HOW THE BAD GUYS USE PEOPLE!
BUT WE CAN STILL START OVER! HUMANS...
...CAN ALWAYS CREATE THEIR OWN POSSIBILI-TIES!
KUH ...
HA HA... HA HA HA HA.
YOU SOUND LIKE A TEACH-ER.

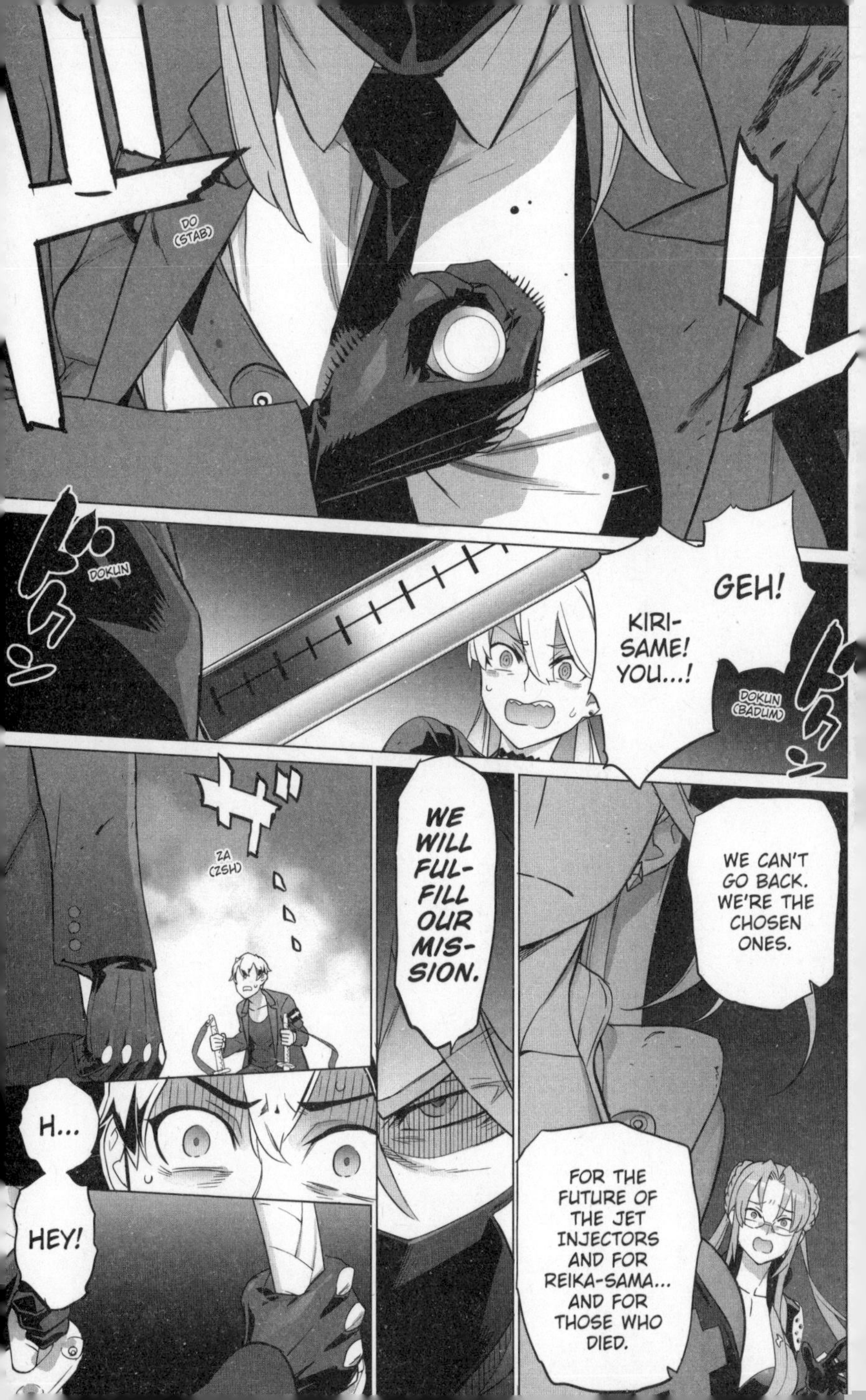
DO (STAB)
GEH!
DOKUN (BADUM)
KIRI-SAME! YOU...!
DOKUN
WE CAN'T GO BACK. WE'RE THE CHOSEN ONES.
FOR THE FUTURE OF THE JET INJECTORS AND FOR REIKA-SAMA... AND FOR THOSE WHO DIED.
WE WILL FUL-FILL OUR MIS-SION.
ZA (ZSH)
H...
HEY!

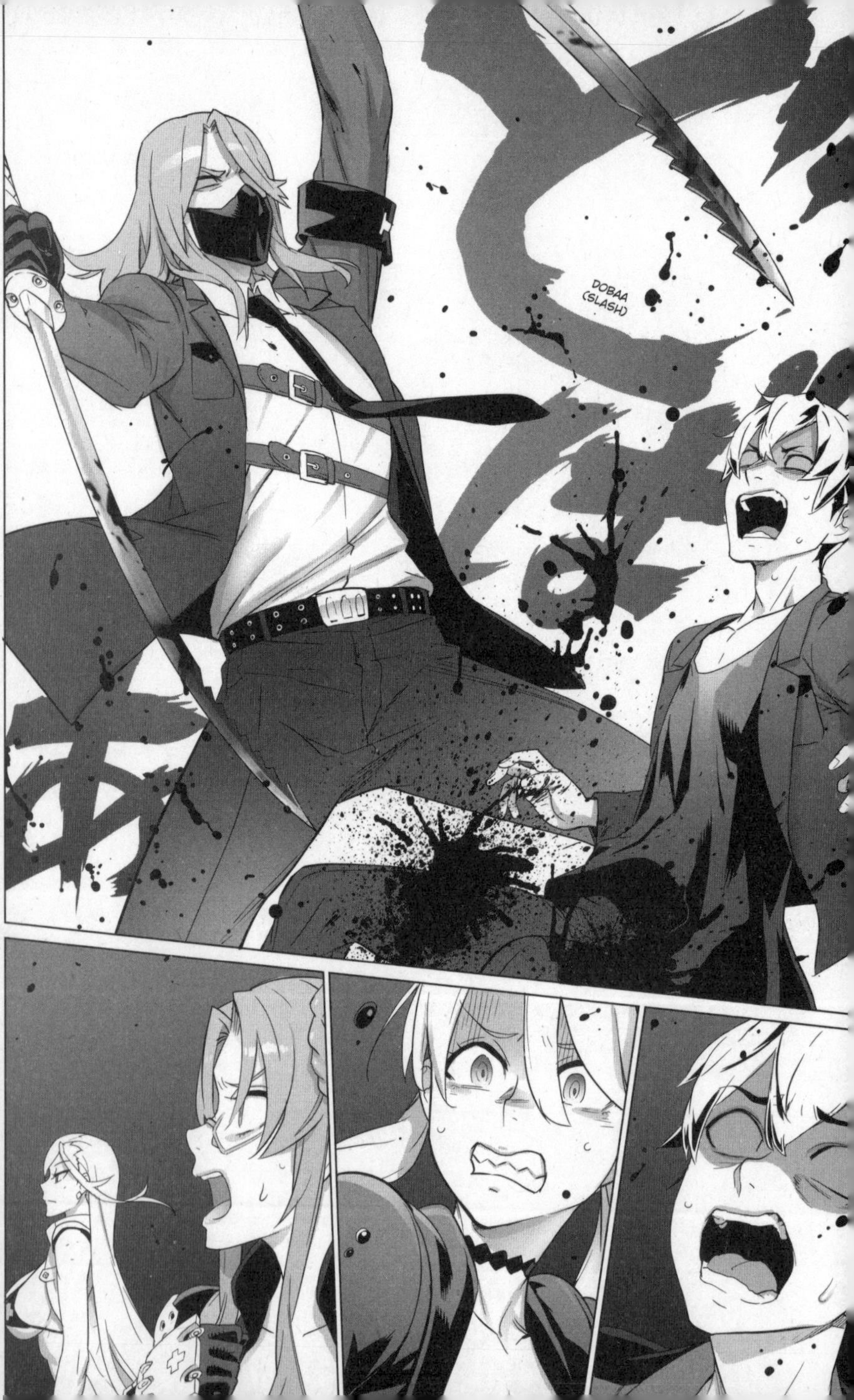
DOBAA
(SLASH)

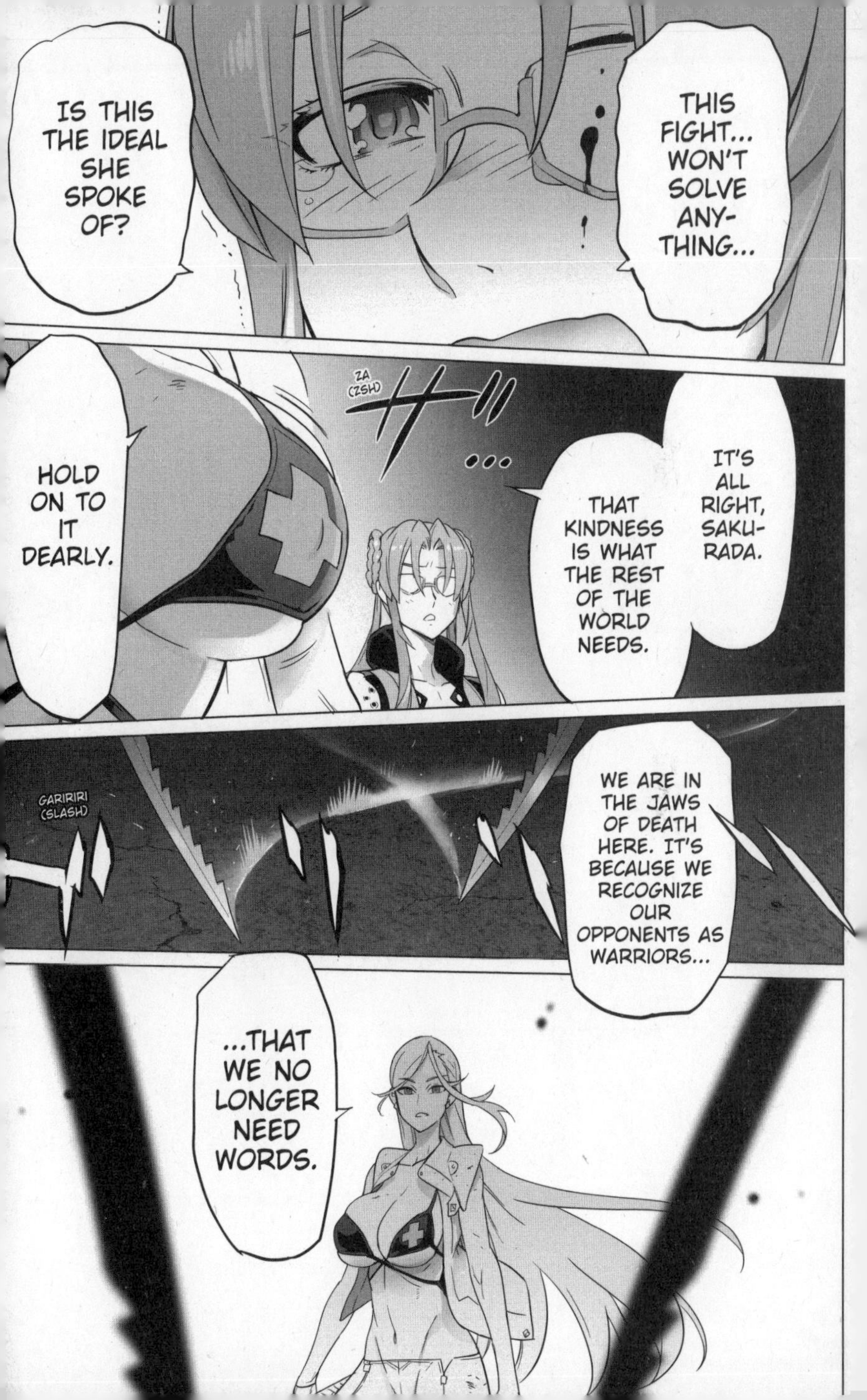
THIS FIGHT... WON'T SOLVE ANY-THING...
IS THIS THE IDEAL SHE SPOKE OF?
IT'S ALL RIGHT, SAKU-RADA.
THAT KINDNESS IS WHAT THE REST OF THE WORLD NEEDS.
...
ZA (ZSH)
HOLD ON TO IT DEARLY.
WE ARE IN THE JAWS OF DEATH HERE. IT'S BECAUSE WE RECOGNIZE OUR OPPONENTS AS WARRIORS...
GARIRIRI (SLASH)
...THAT WE NO LONGER NEED WORDS.

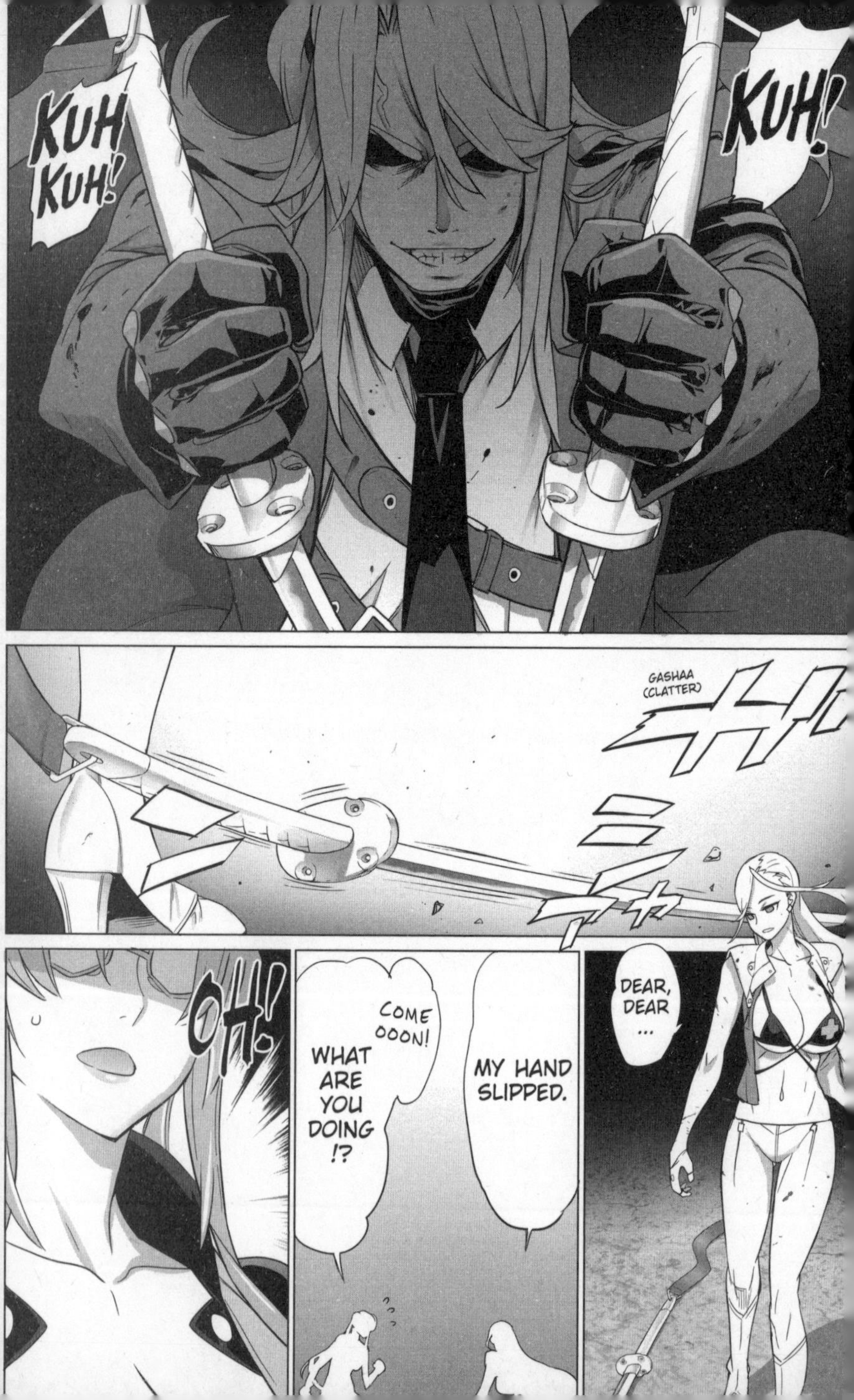
KUH!
KUH KUH!
GASHAA (CLATTER)
DEAR, DEAR ...
MY HAND SLIPPED.
COME OOON!
WHAT ARE YOU DOING !?
OH!

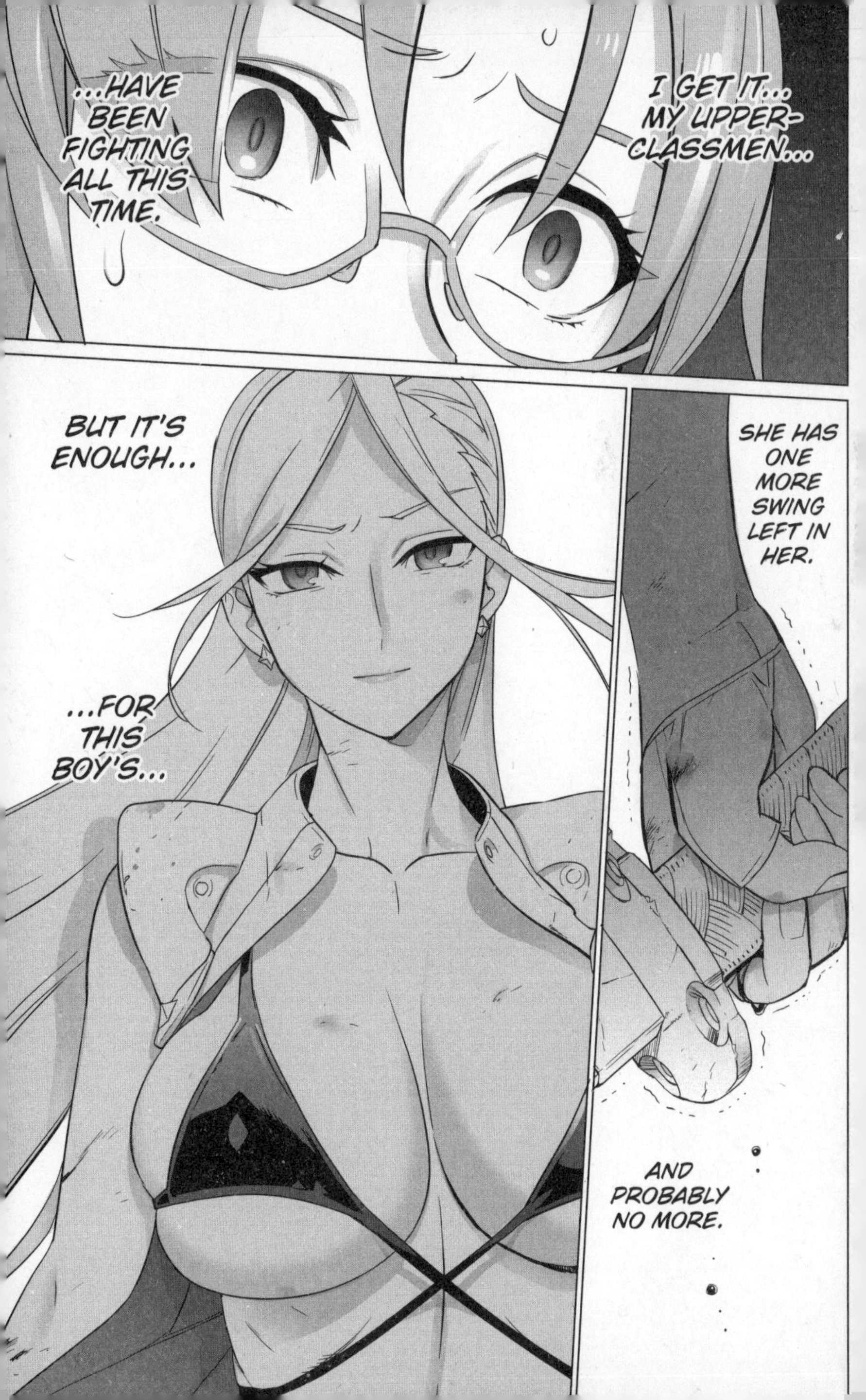
I GET IT... MY UPPER-CLASSMEN...
...HAVE BEEN FIGHTING ALL THIS TIME.
SHE HAS ONE MORE SWING LEFT IN HER.
AND PROBABLY NO MORE.
BUT IT'S ENOUGH...
...FOR THIS BOY'S...

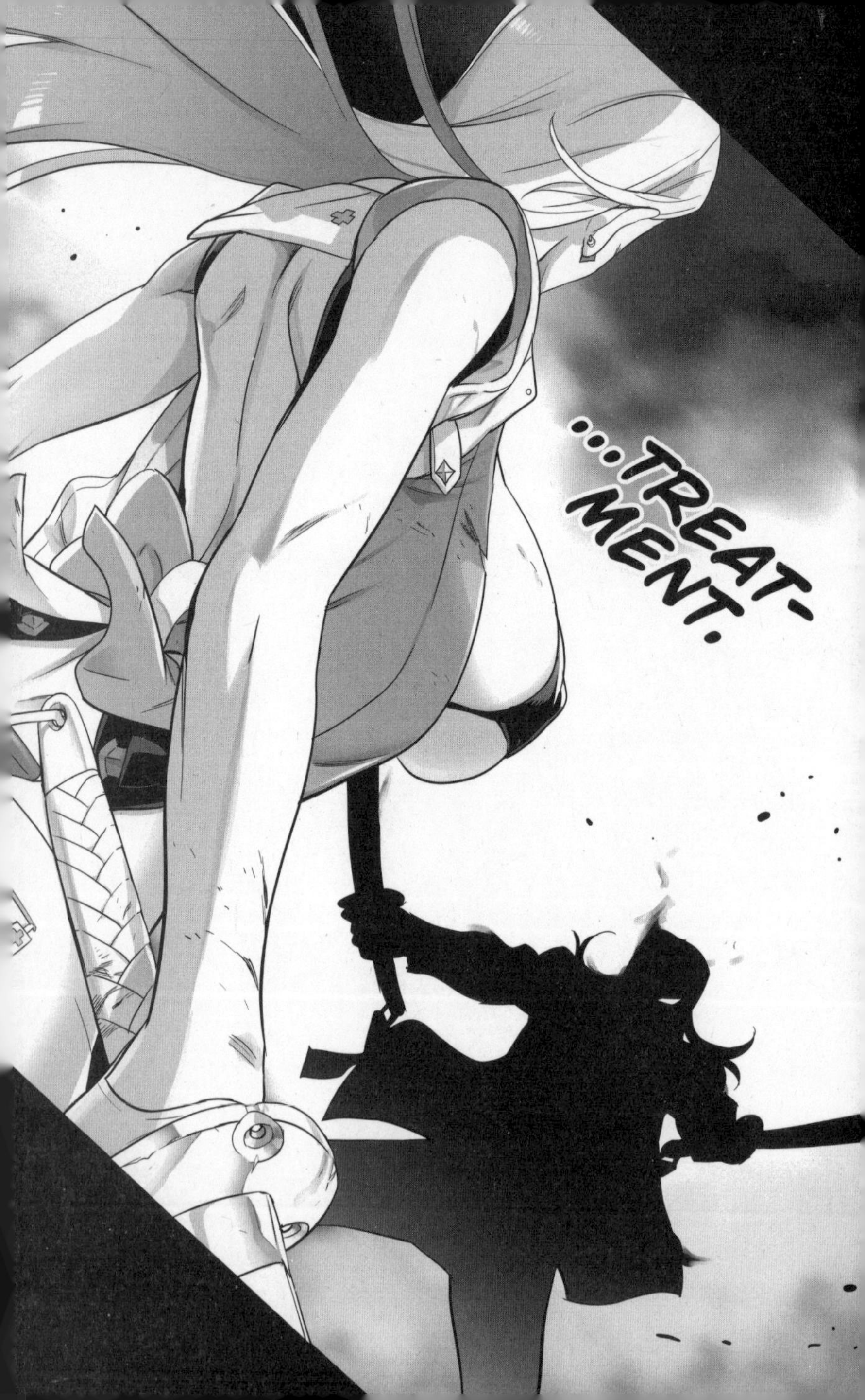
...TREAT-MENT.

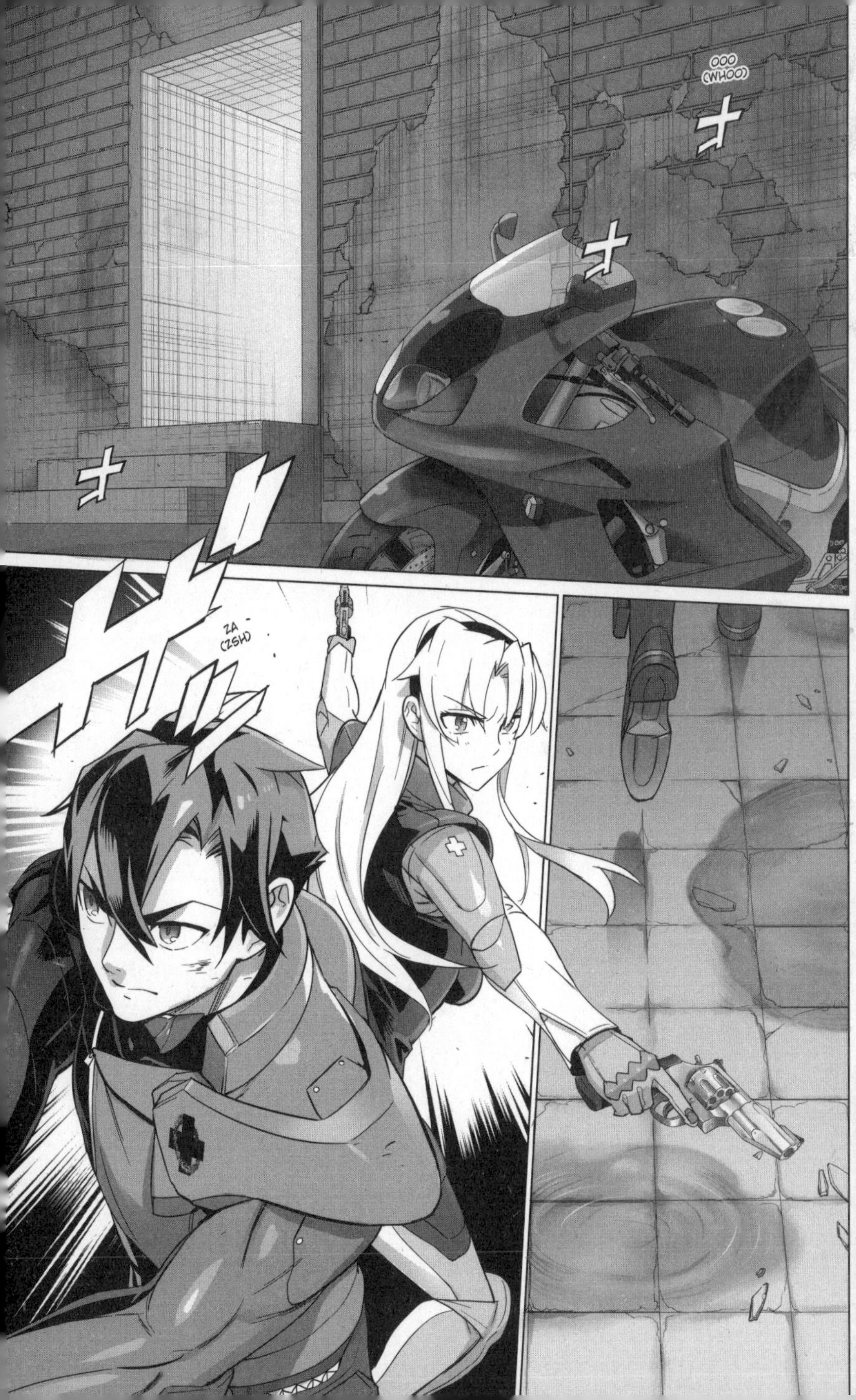
OOO
(WHOO)
ZA
(ZSH)

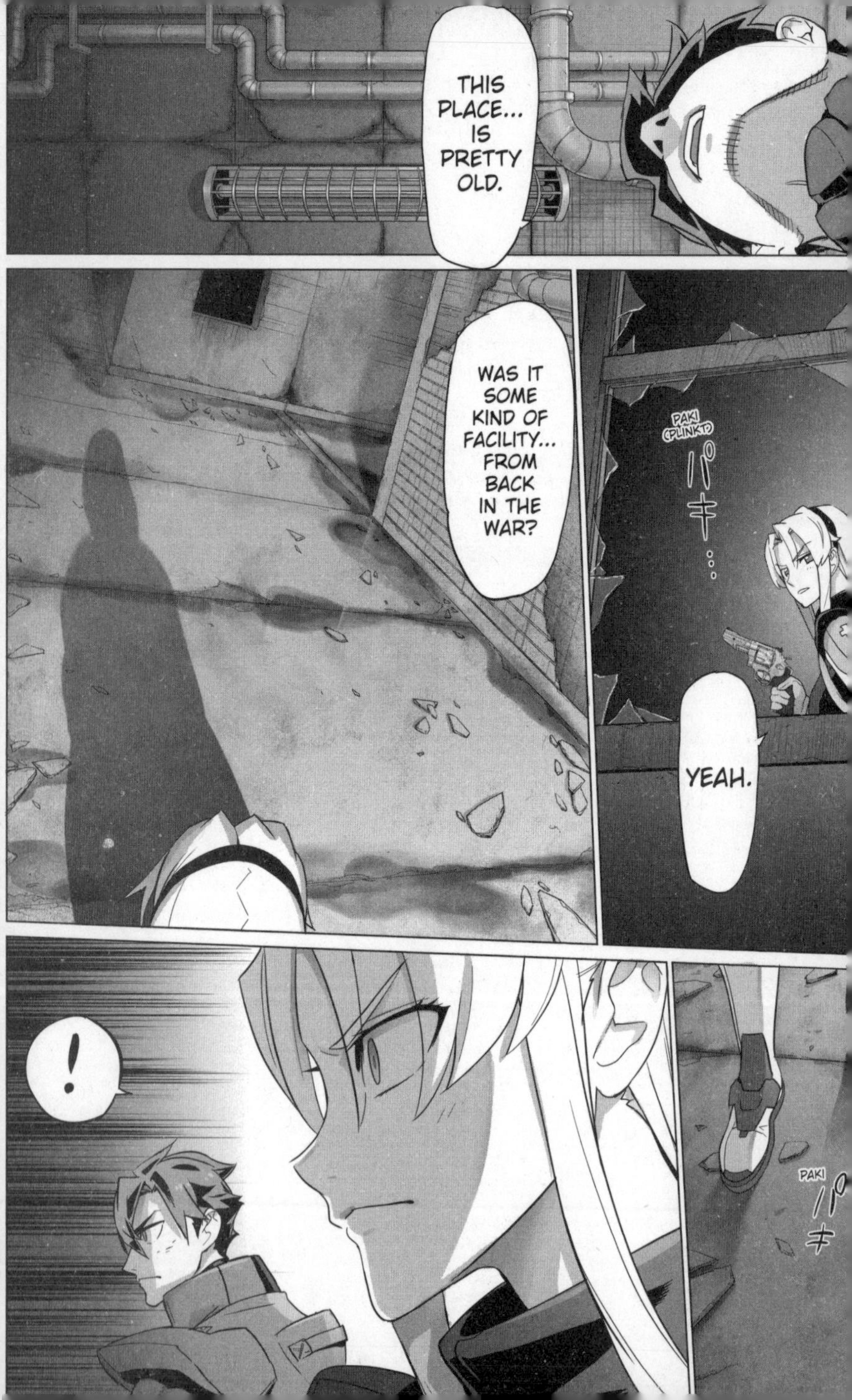
THIS PLACE... IS PRETTY OLD.
PAKI (PLINK?)
パキ…
YEAH.
WAS IT SOME KIND OF FACILITY... FROM BACK IN THE WAR?
PAKI
パキ
!

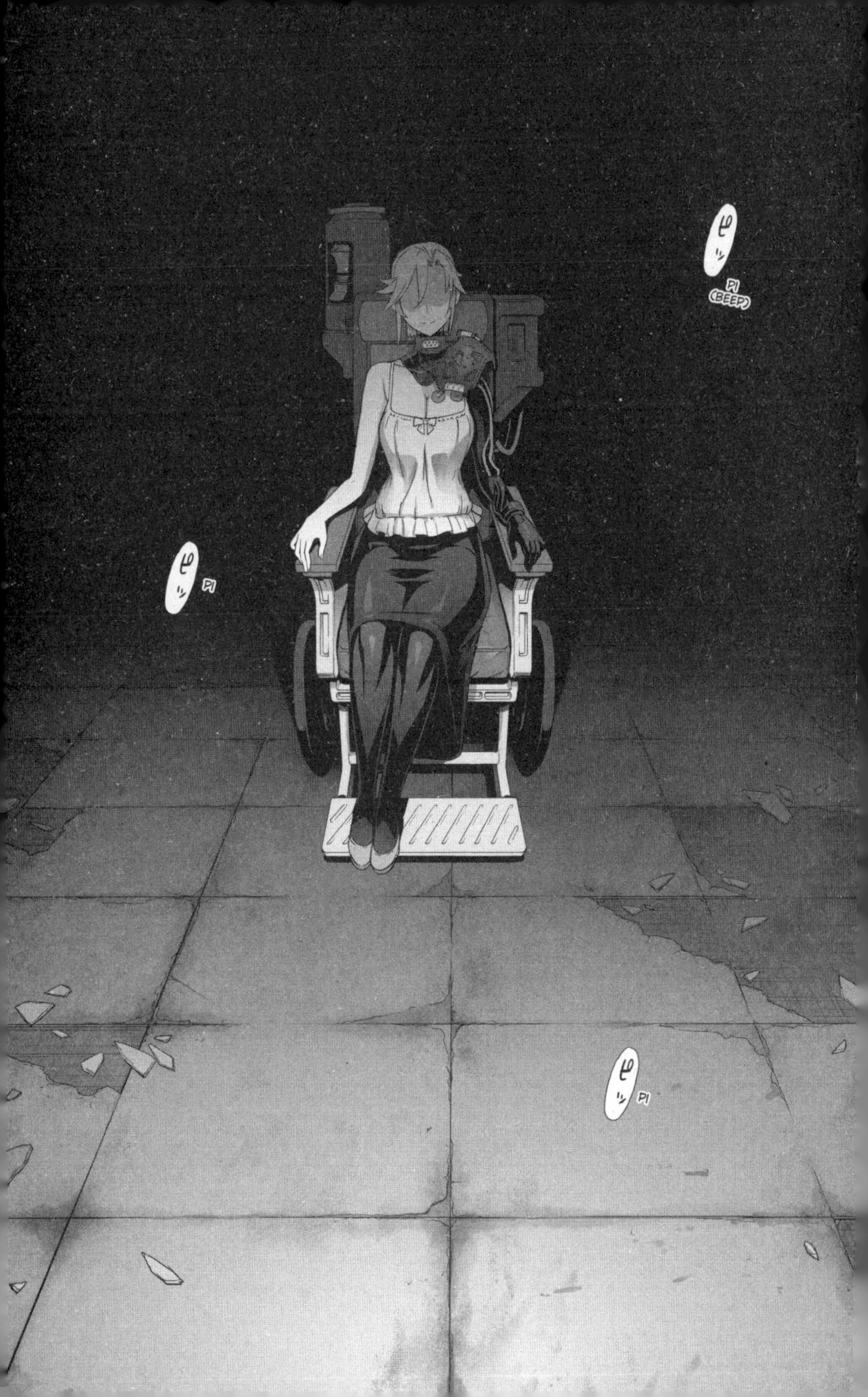
ピッ
PI (BEEP)
ピッ
PI
ピッ
PI

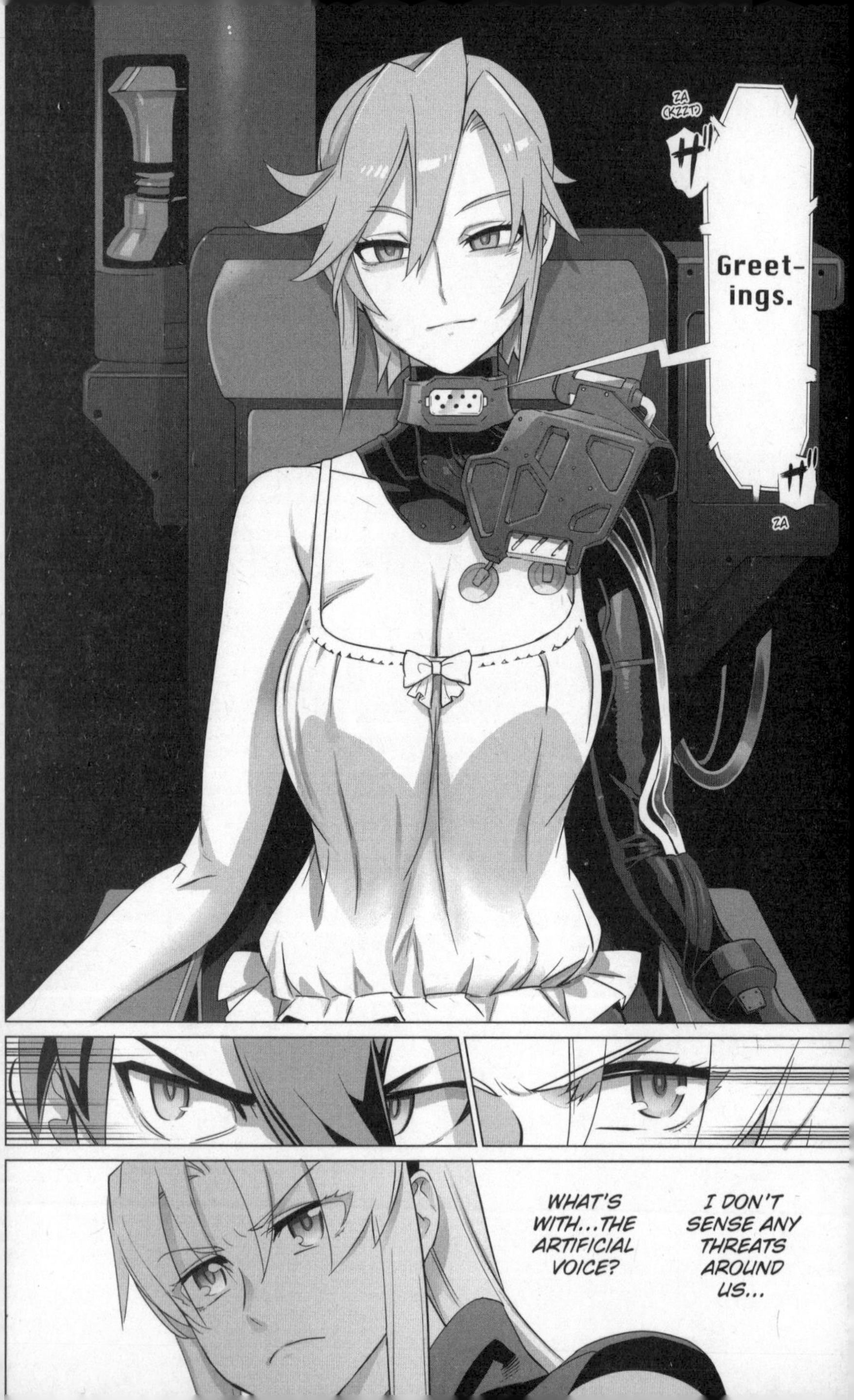
ZA (KZZT)
ザ
Greet-
ings.
ザ
ZA
I DON'T SENSE ANY THREATS AROUND US...
WHAT'S WITH...THE ARTIFICIAL VOICE?

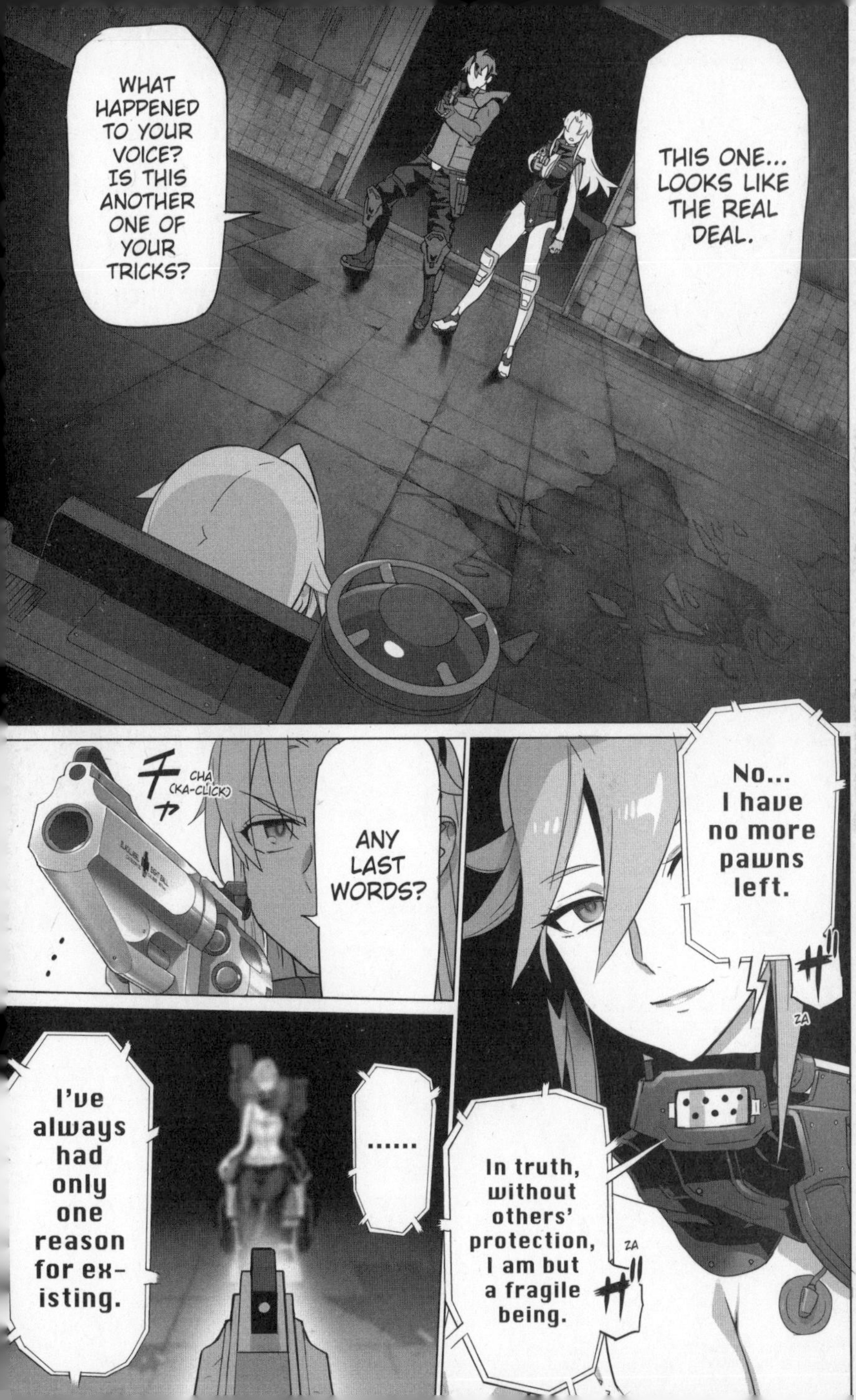
THIS ONE... LOOKS LIKE THE REAL DEAL.
WHAT HAPPENED TO YOUR VOICE? IS THIS ANOTHER ONE OF YOUR TRICKS?
No... I have no more pawns left.
ZA
In truth, without others' protection, I am but a fragile being.
ZA
チャ
CHA (KA-CLICK)
ANY LAST WORDS?
...
......
I've always had only one reason for existing.

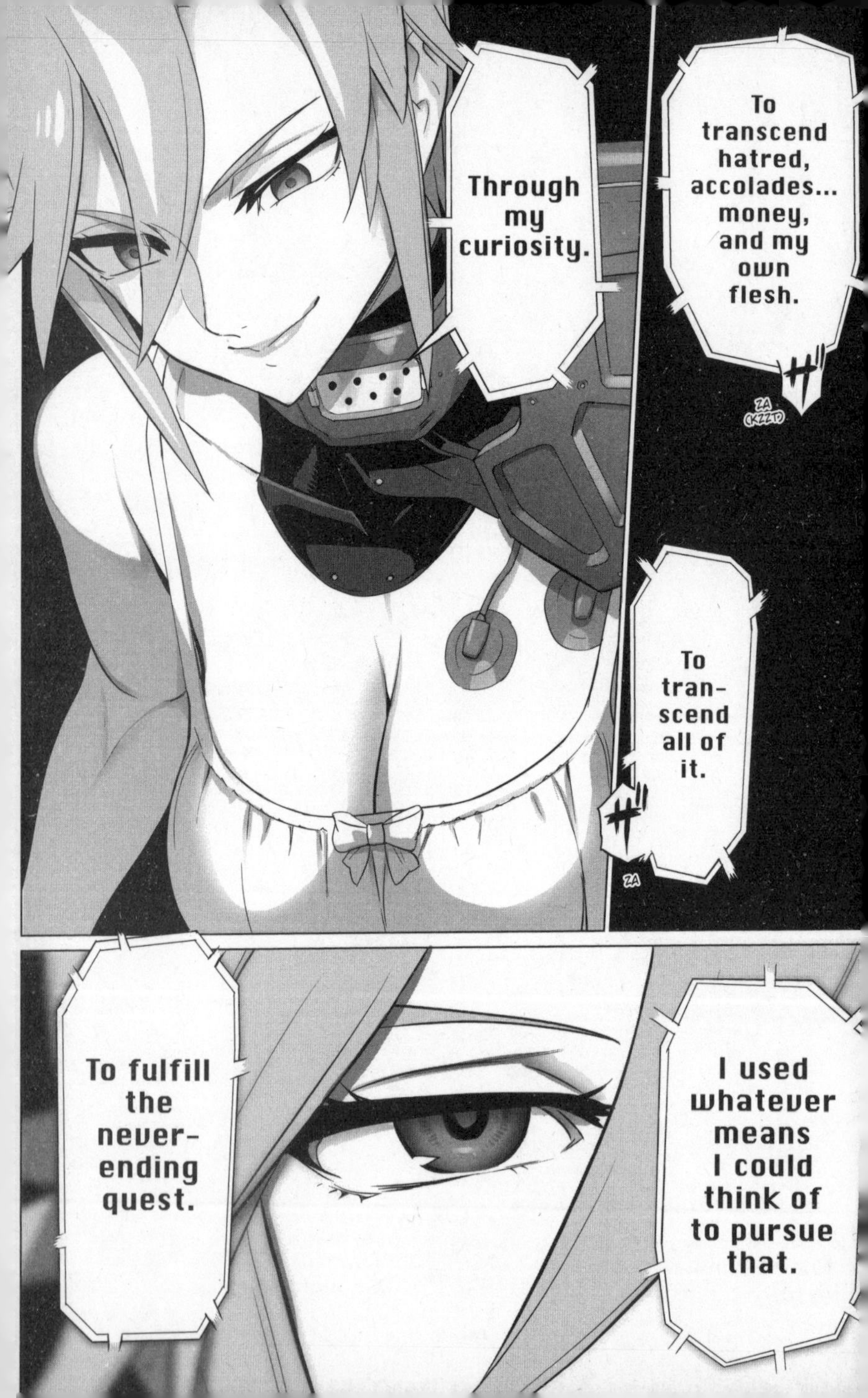
To transcend hatred, accolades... money, and my own flesh.
ZA (KZZT)
To tran-scend all of it.
ZA
Through my curiosity.
I used whatever means I could think of to pursue that.
To fulfill the never-ending quest.

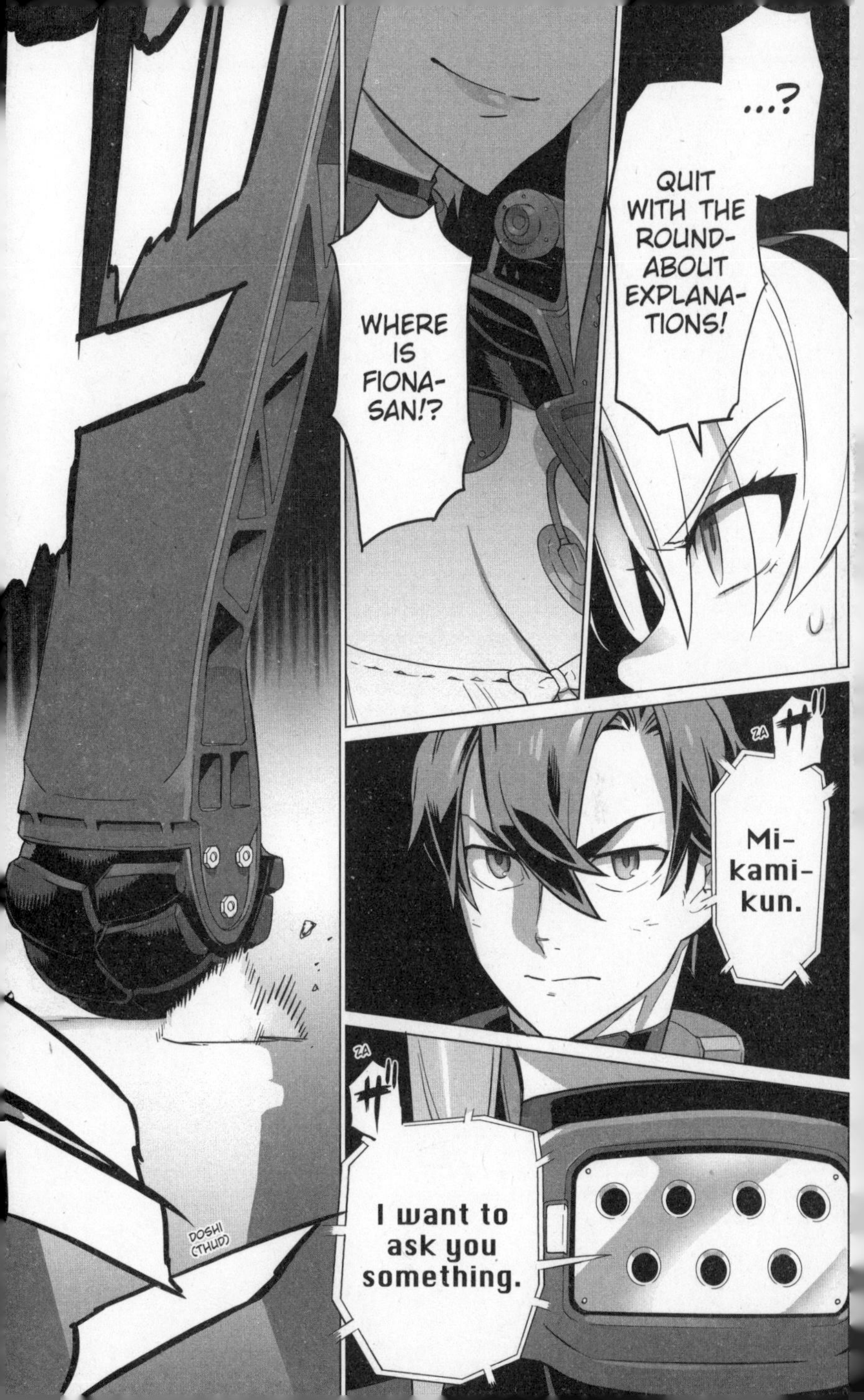
...?
QUIT WITH THE ROUND-ABOUT EXPLANA-TIONS!
WHERE IS FIONA-SAN!?
ZA
Mi-kami-kun.
ZA
I want to ask you something.
DOSHI (THUD)

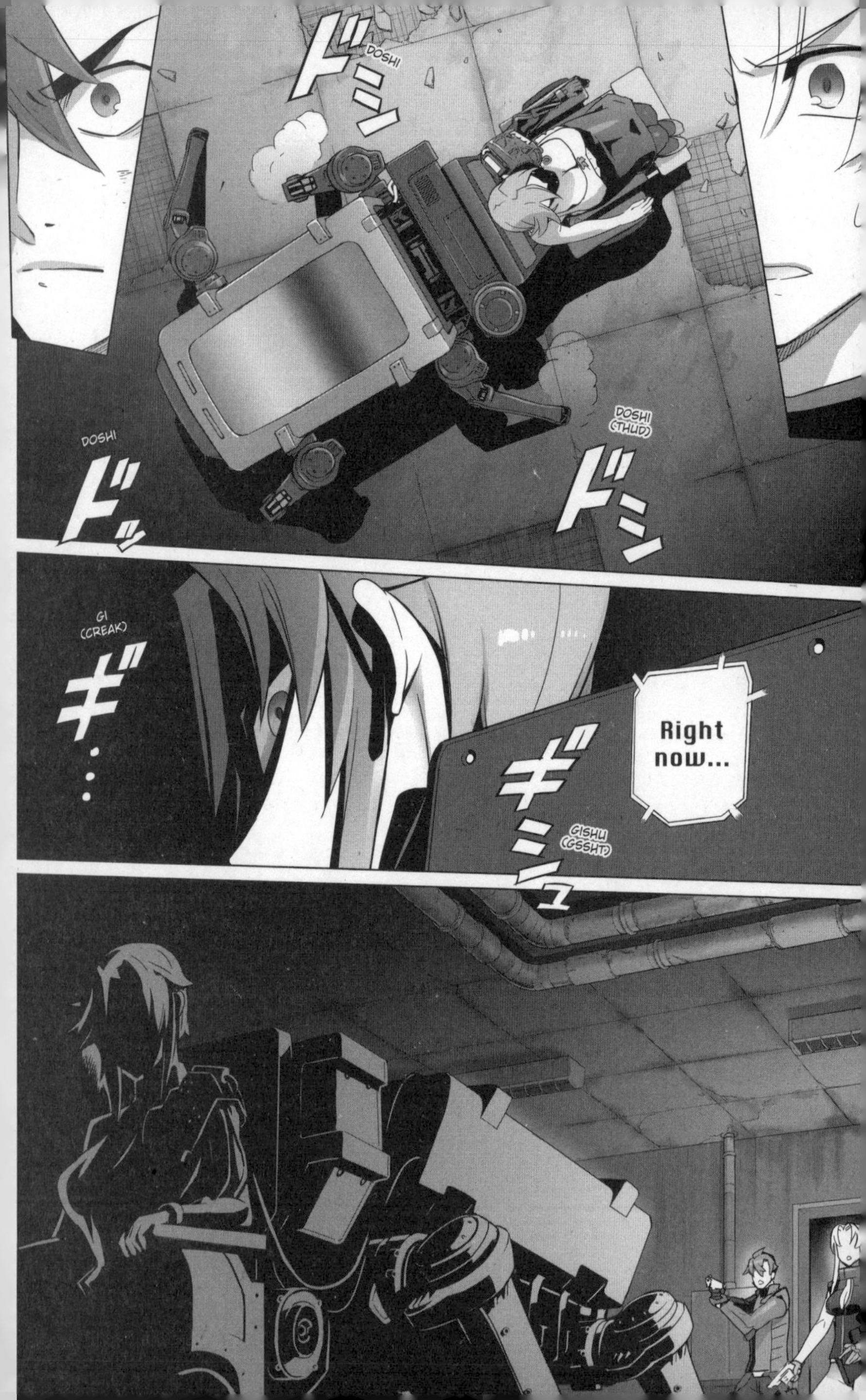
ドシン
DOSHI
ドシン
DOSHI (THUD)
ドッ
DOSHI
Right now...
ギシュ
GISHU (GSSHT)
ギ…
GI (CREAK)

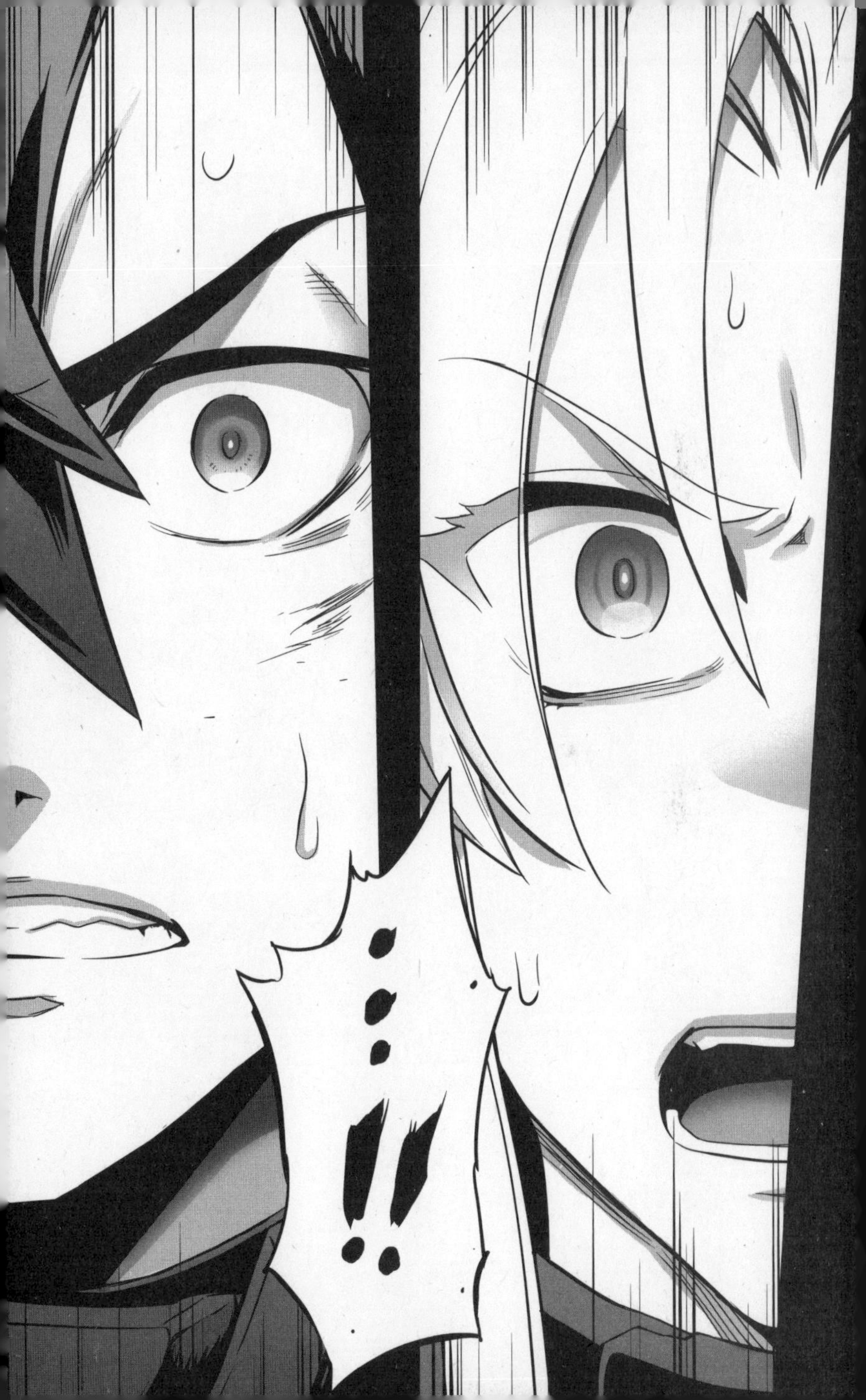
!!

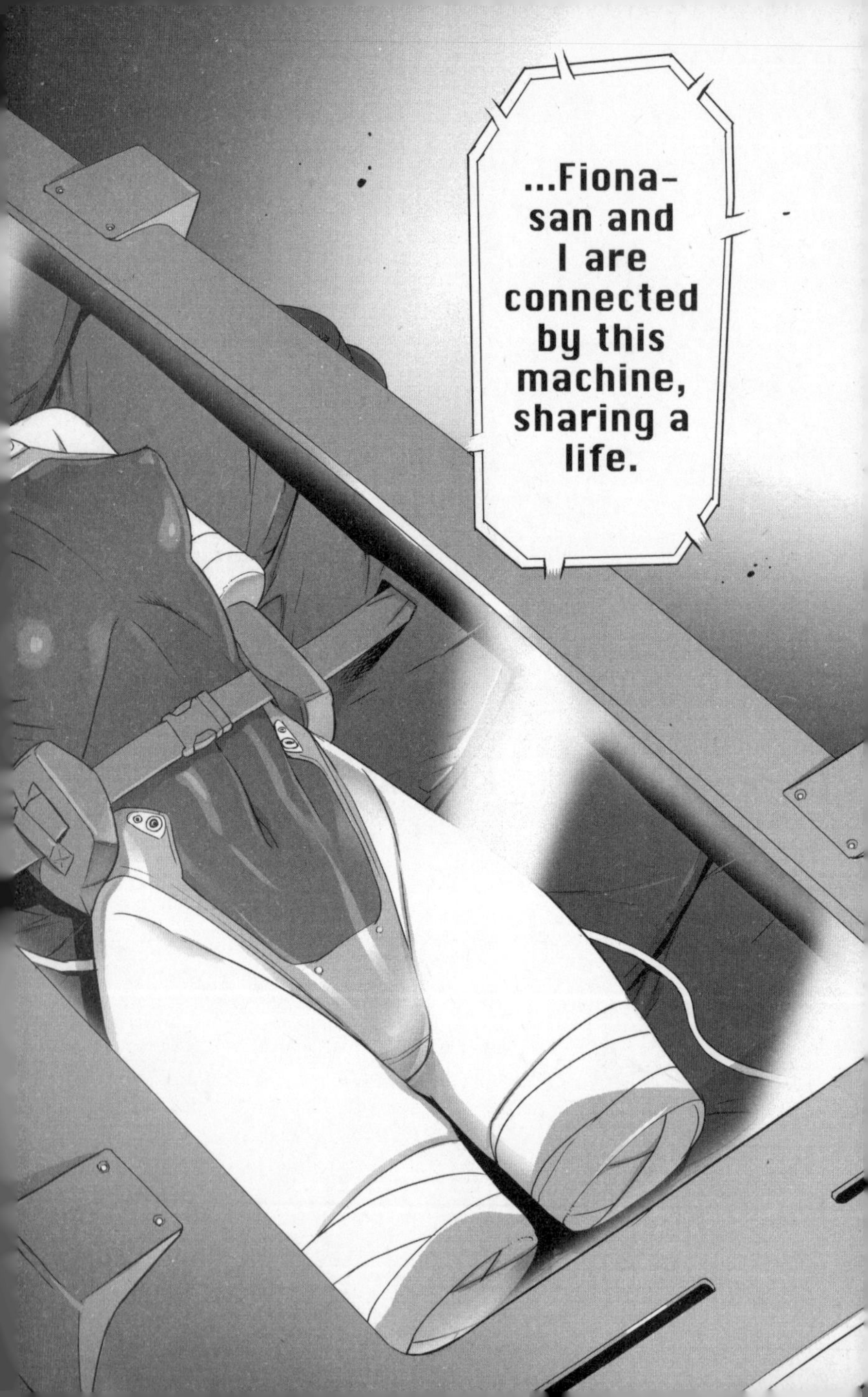
...Fiona-san and I are connected by this machine, sharing a life.

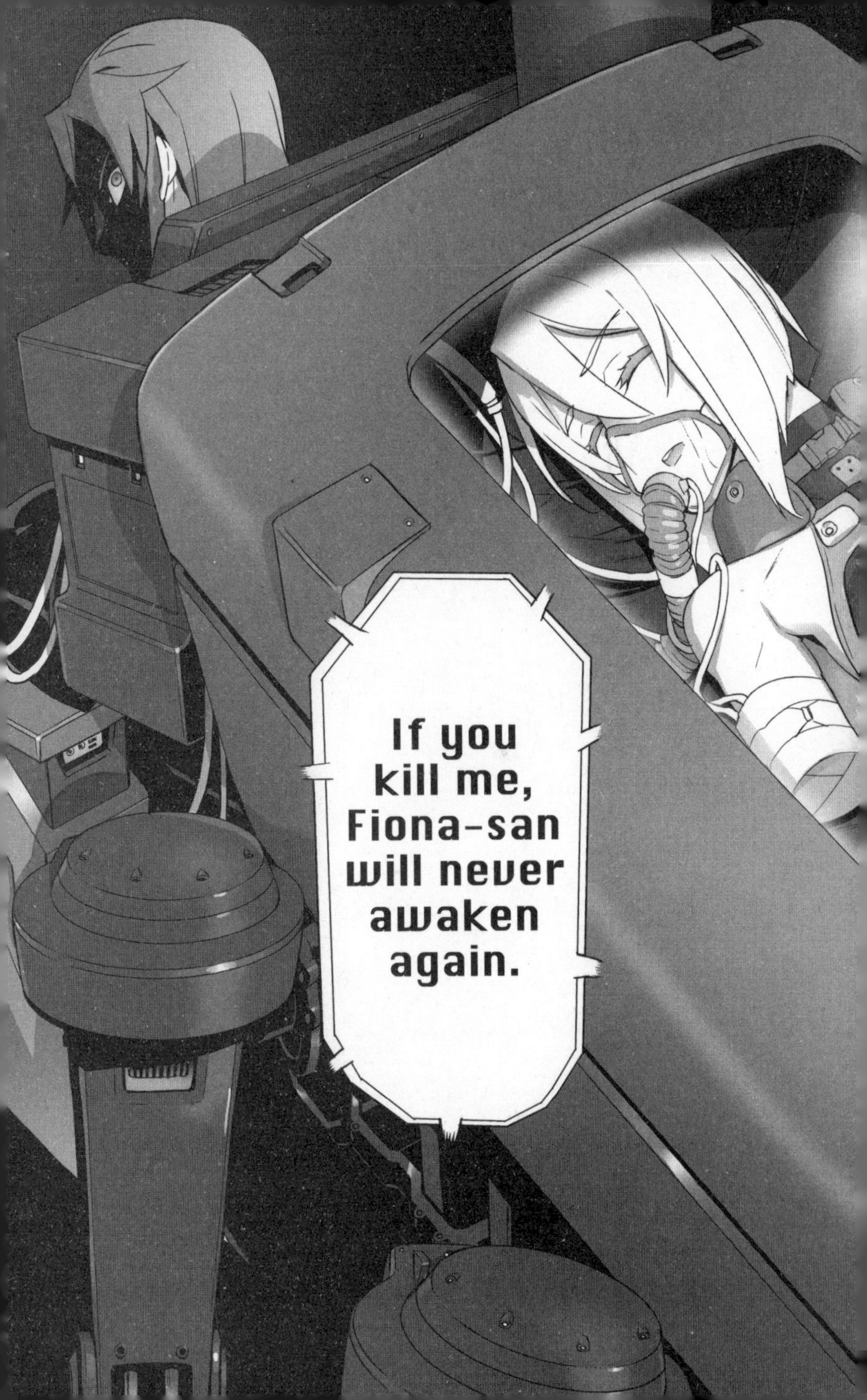
If you kill me, Fiona-san will never awaken again.

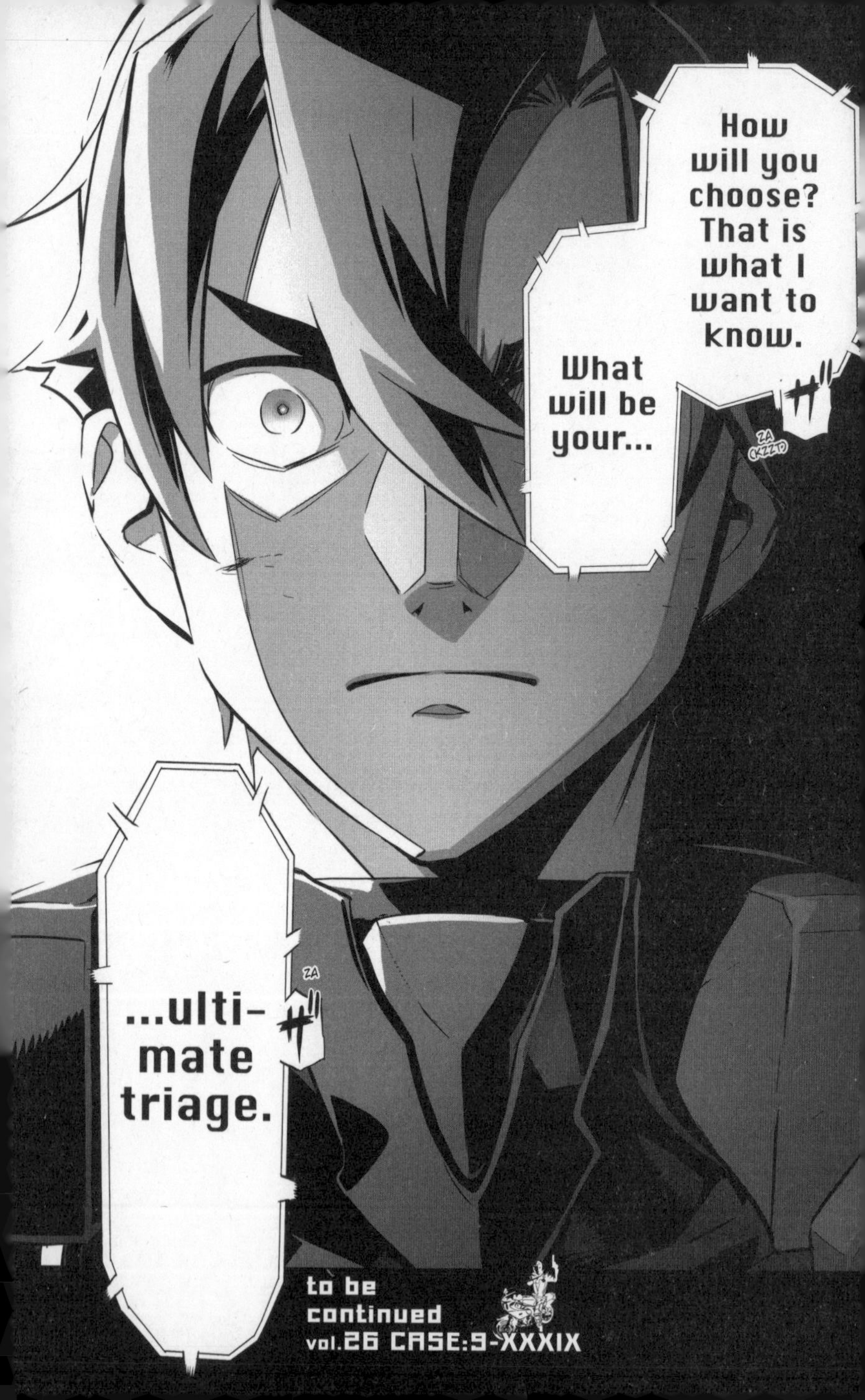
How will you choose? That is what I want to know.
ZA (KZZT)
What will be your...
ZA
...ulti-mate triage.
to be continued
vol.26 CASE:9-XXXIX

TRIAGE X

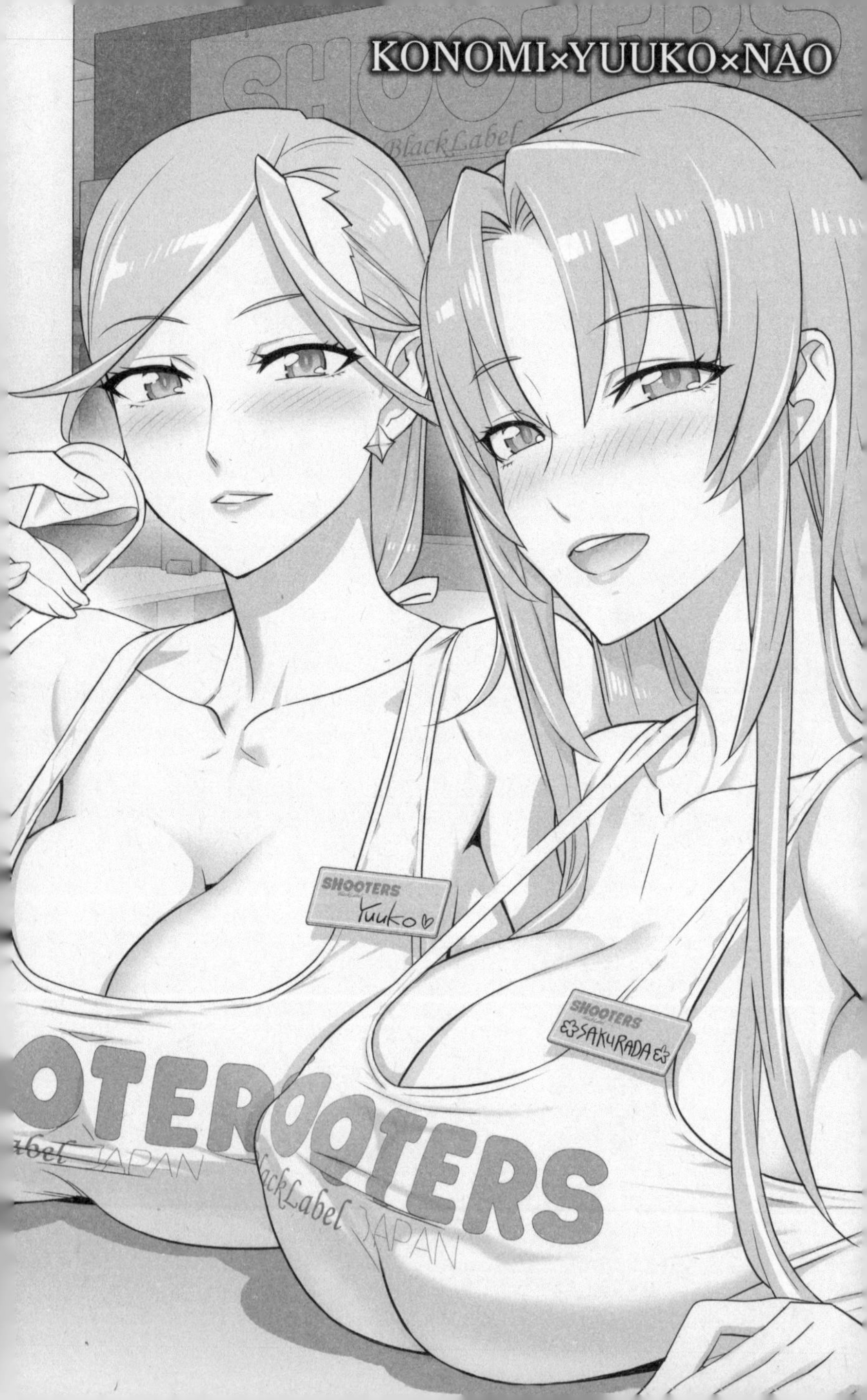
KONOMI×YUUKO×NAO
SHOOTERS
BlackLabel
SHOOTERS
Yuuko
SHOOTERS
SAKURADA
OTER
abel JAPAN
OOTERS
BlackLabel JAPAN

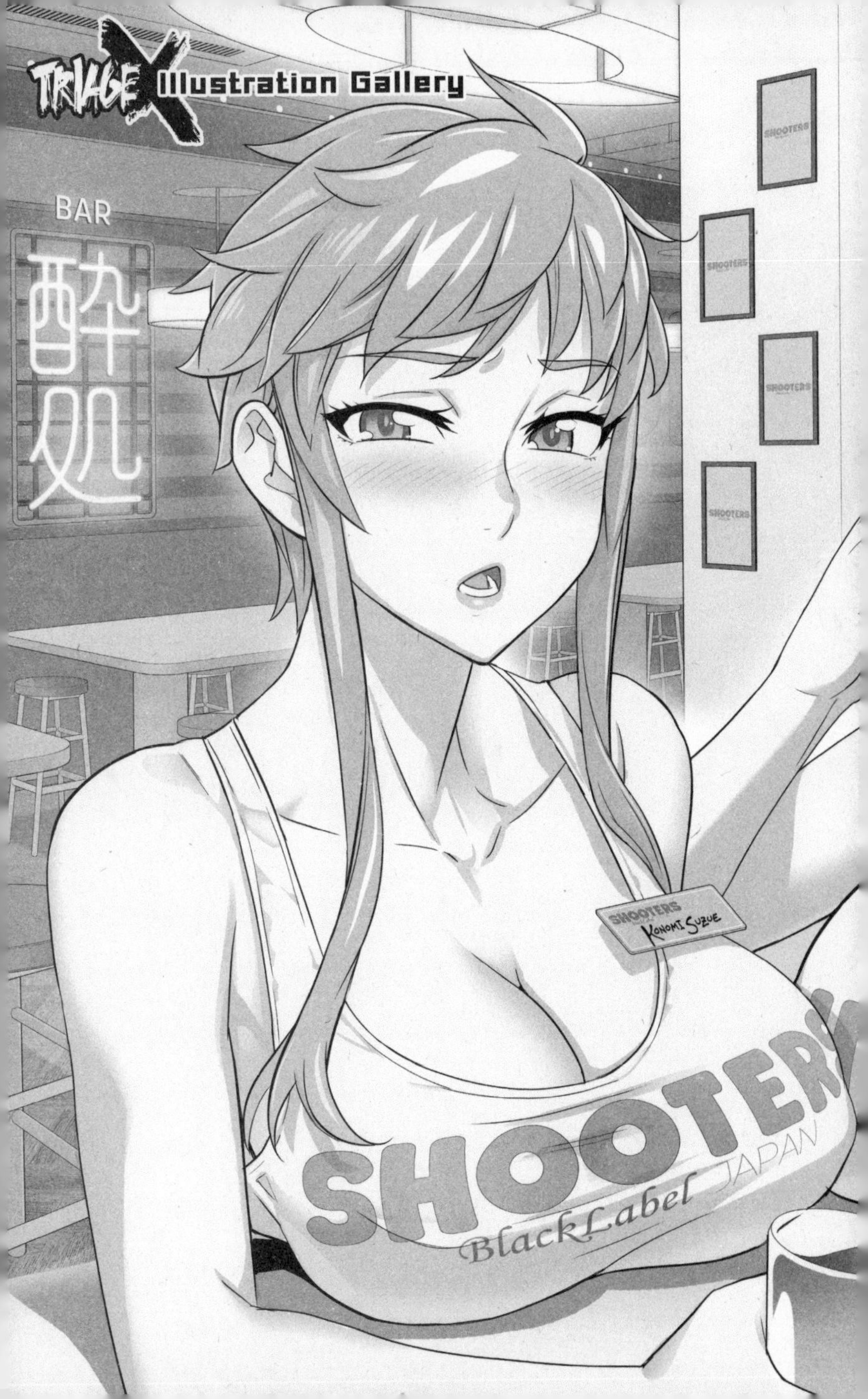
TRIAGE X Illustration Gallery
BAR
酔処
SHOOTERS
SHOOTERS
SHOOTERS
SHOOTERS
SHOOTERS
KONOMI SUZUE
SHOOTERS
BlackLabel JAPAN

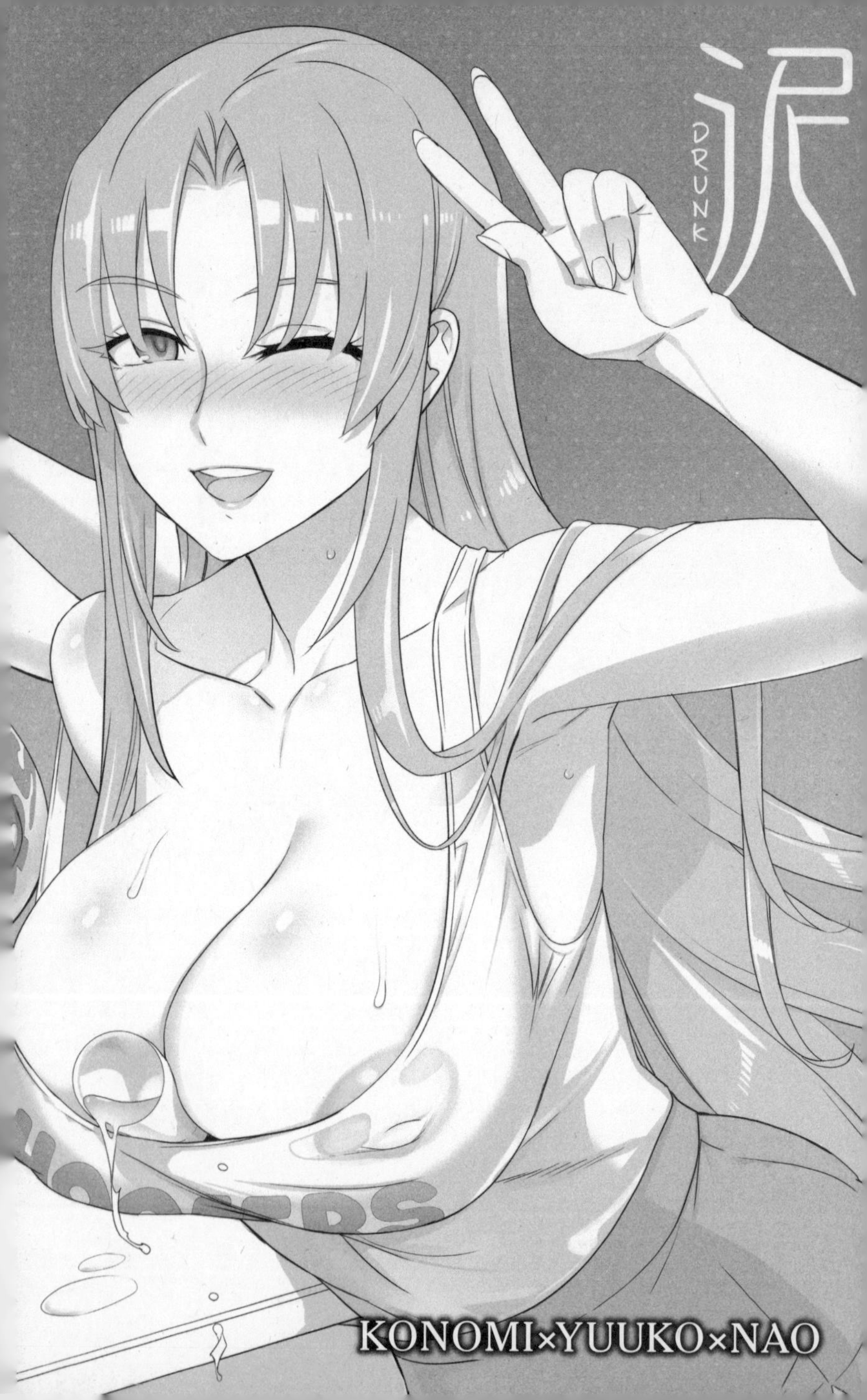
泥
DRUNK
KONOMI×YUUKO×NAO

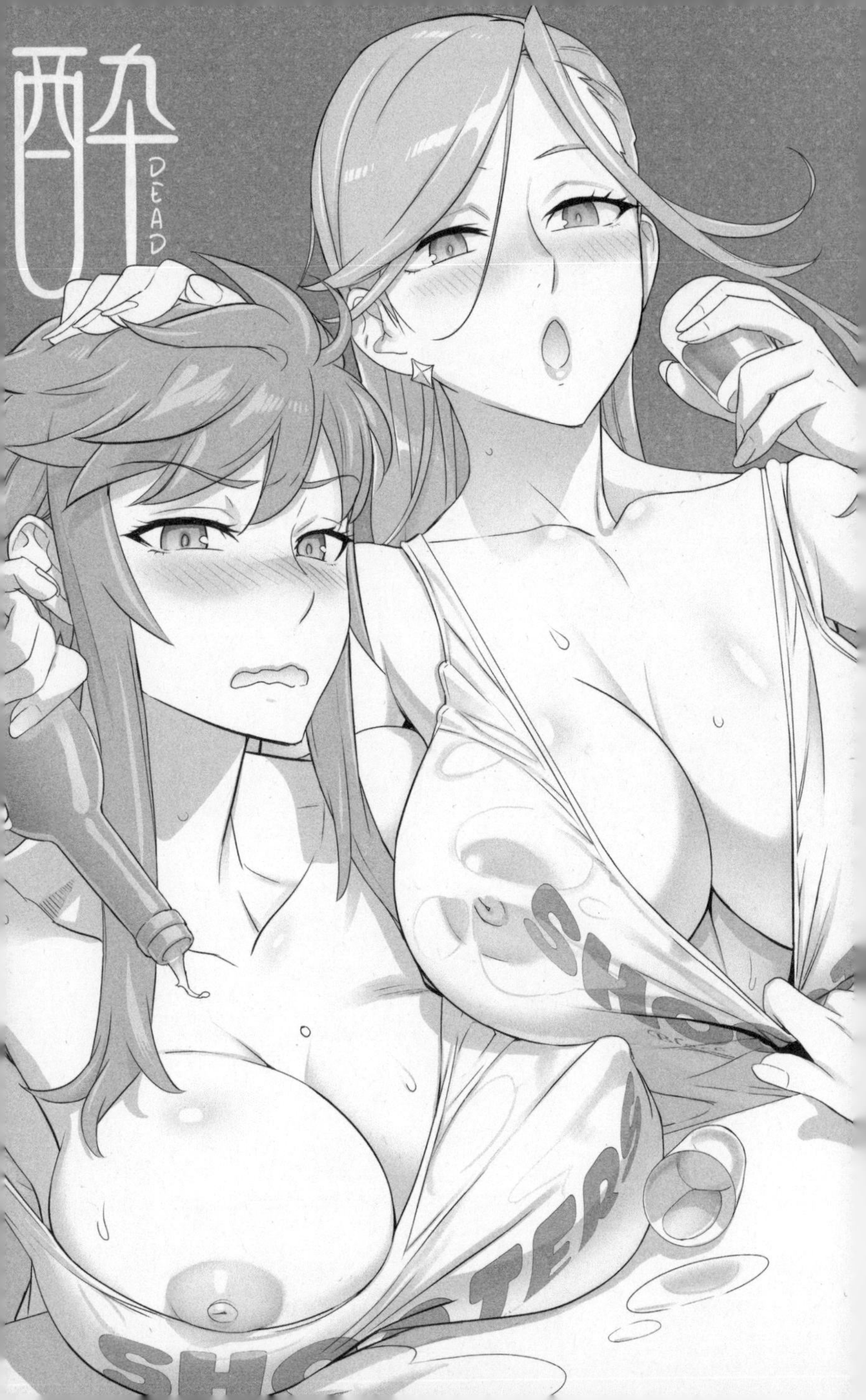
酔
DEAD

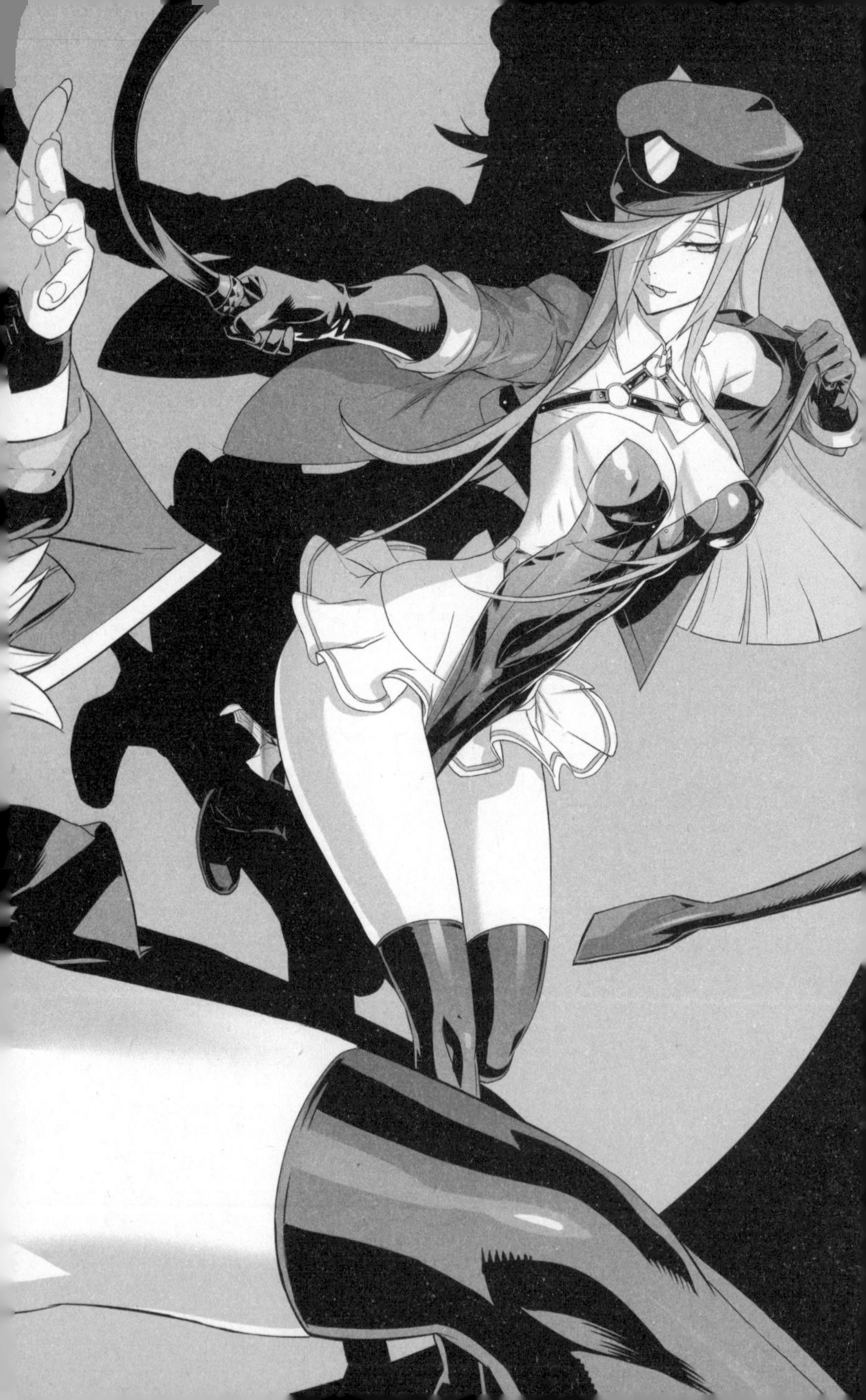

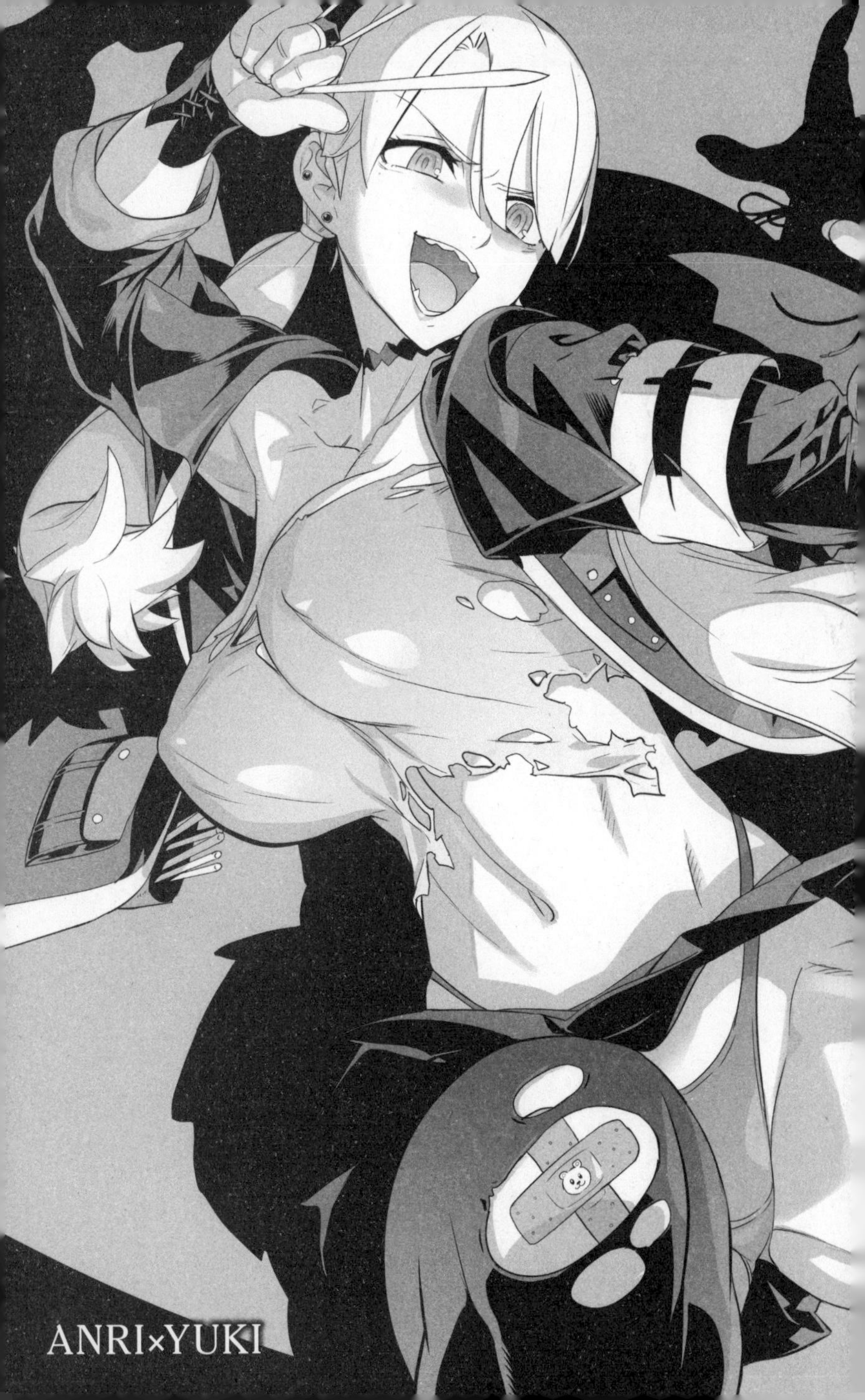
ANRI×YUKI

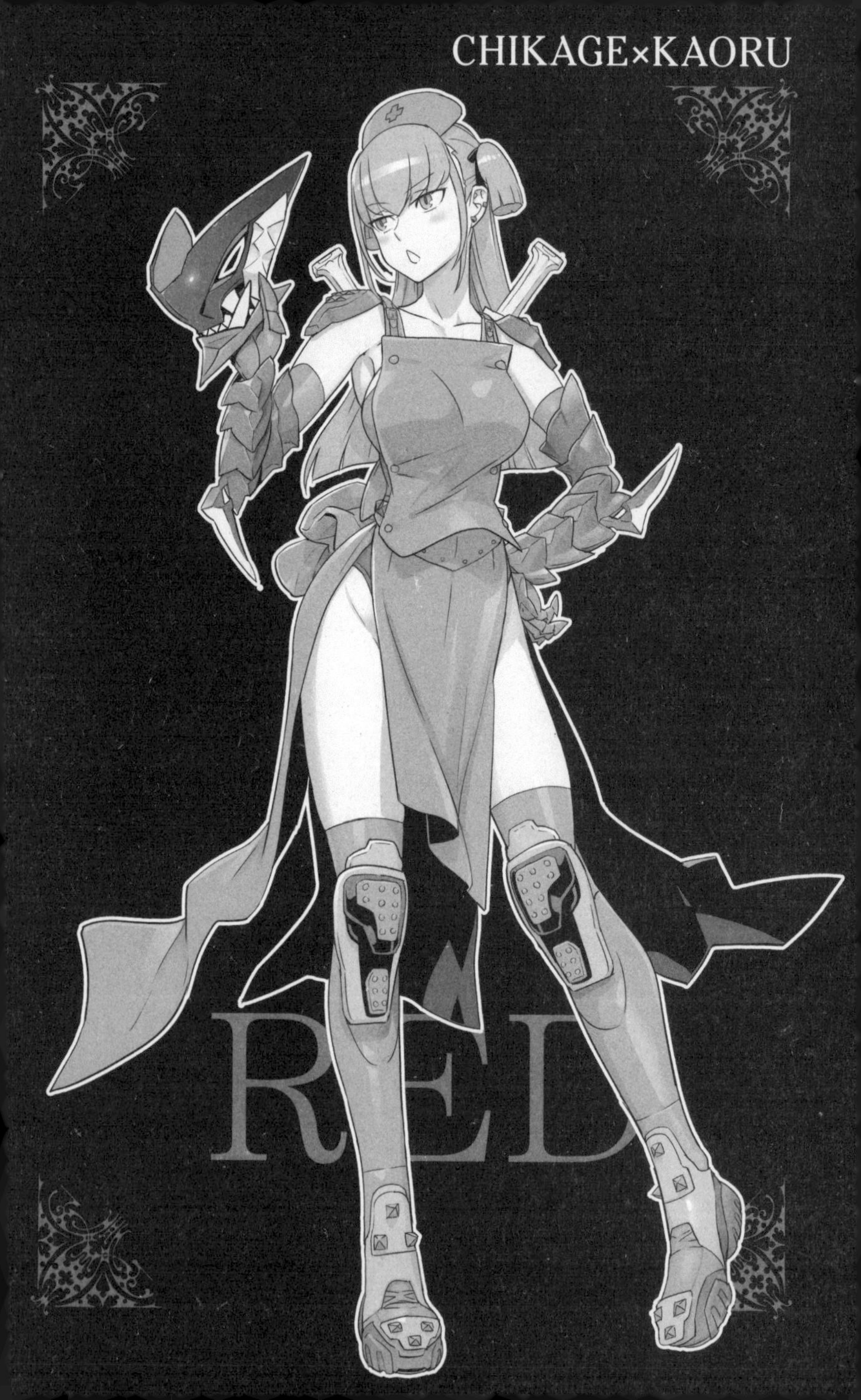
CHIKAGE×KAORU
RED

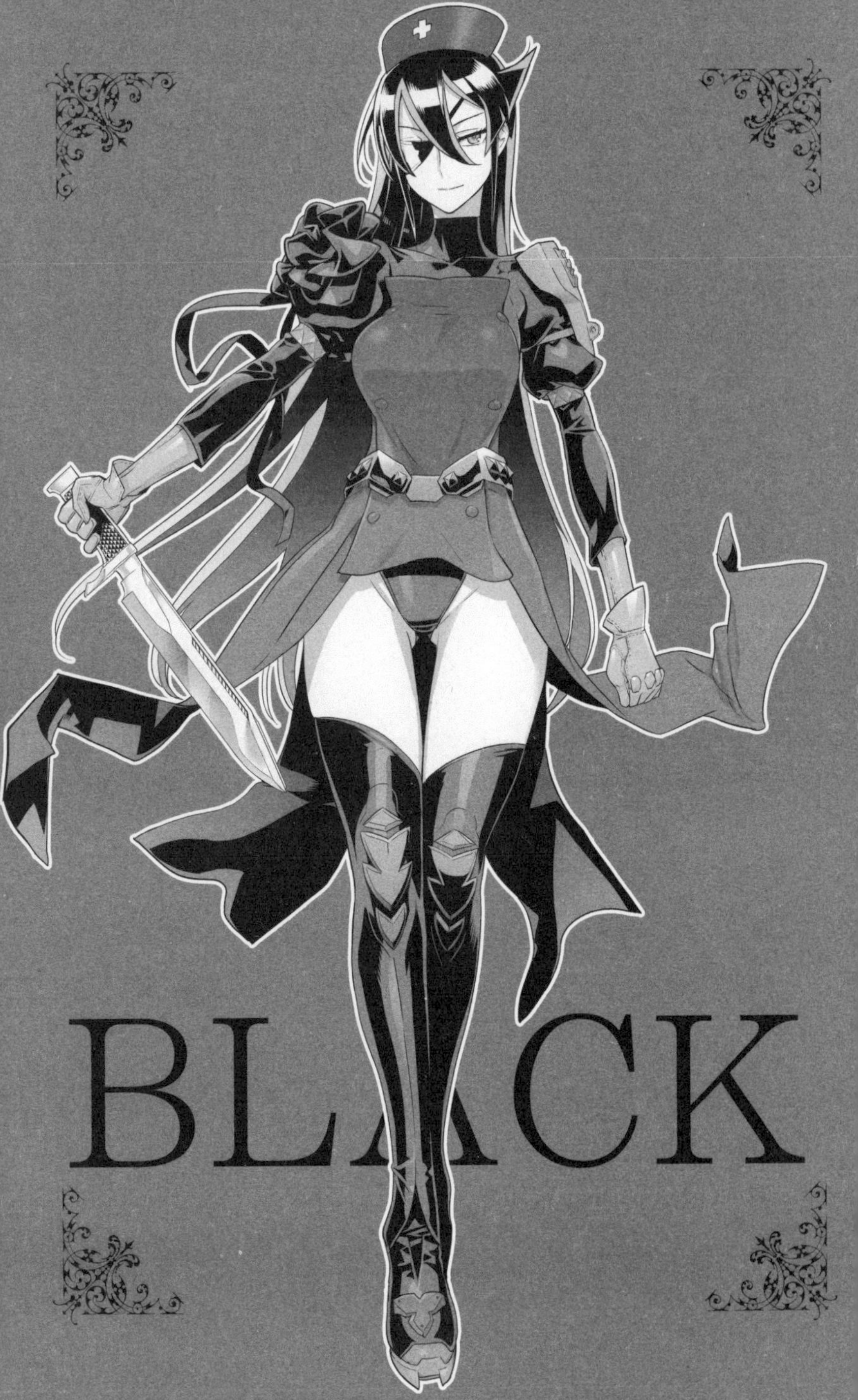
BLACK

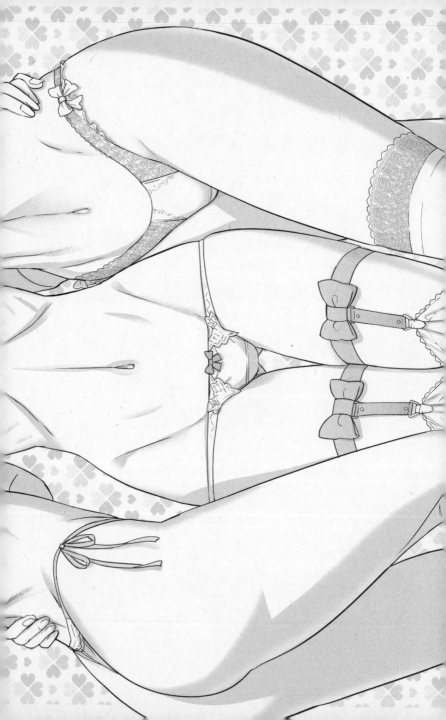

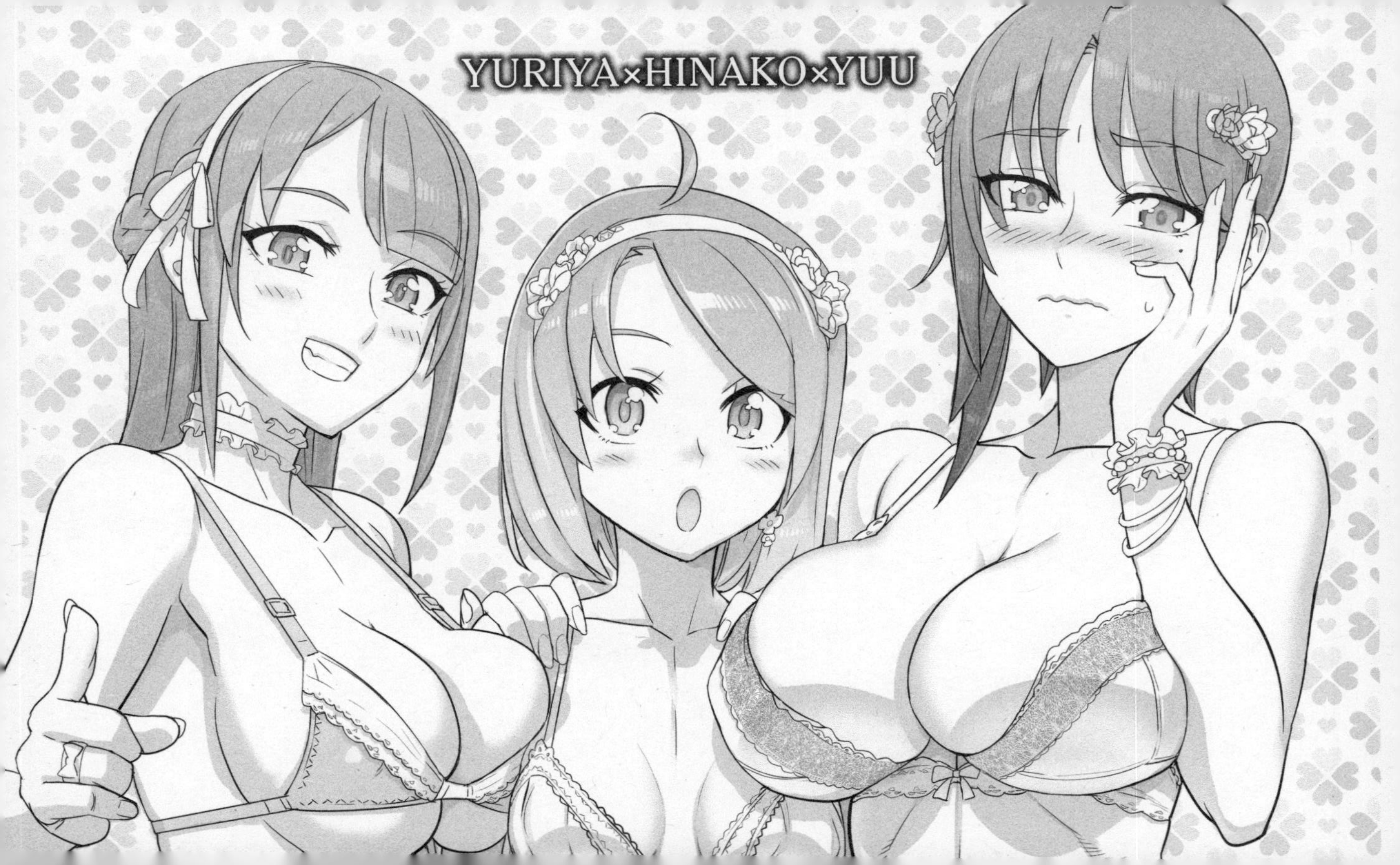
YURIYA×HINAKO×YUU

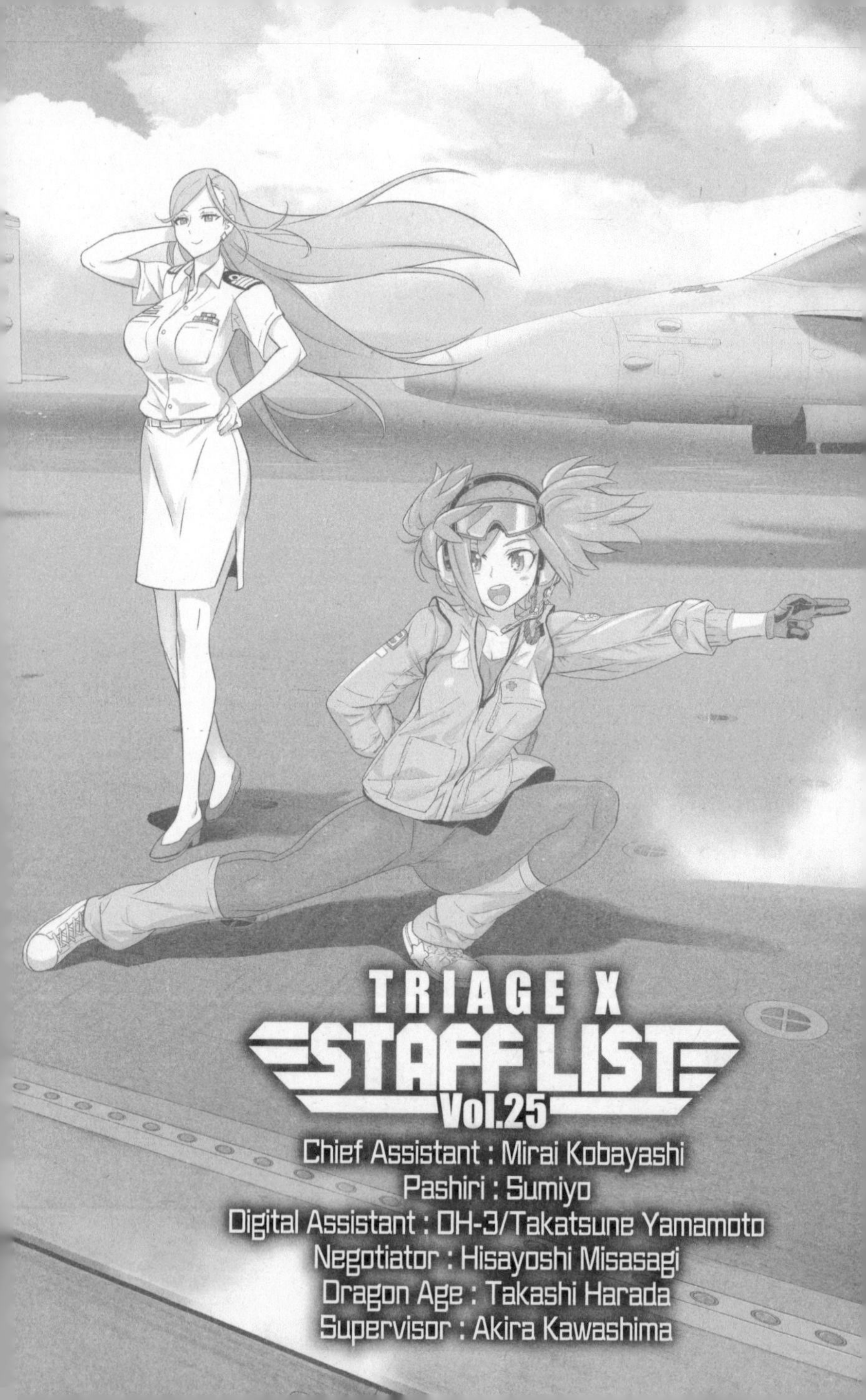

TRIAGE X
STAFF LIST
Vol.25

Chief Assistant : Mirai Kobayashi
Pashiri : Sumiyo
Digital Assistant : DH-3/Takatsune Yamamoto
Negotiator : Hisayoshi Misasagi
Dragon Age : Takashi Harada
Supervisor : Akira Kawashima

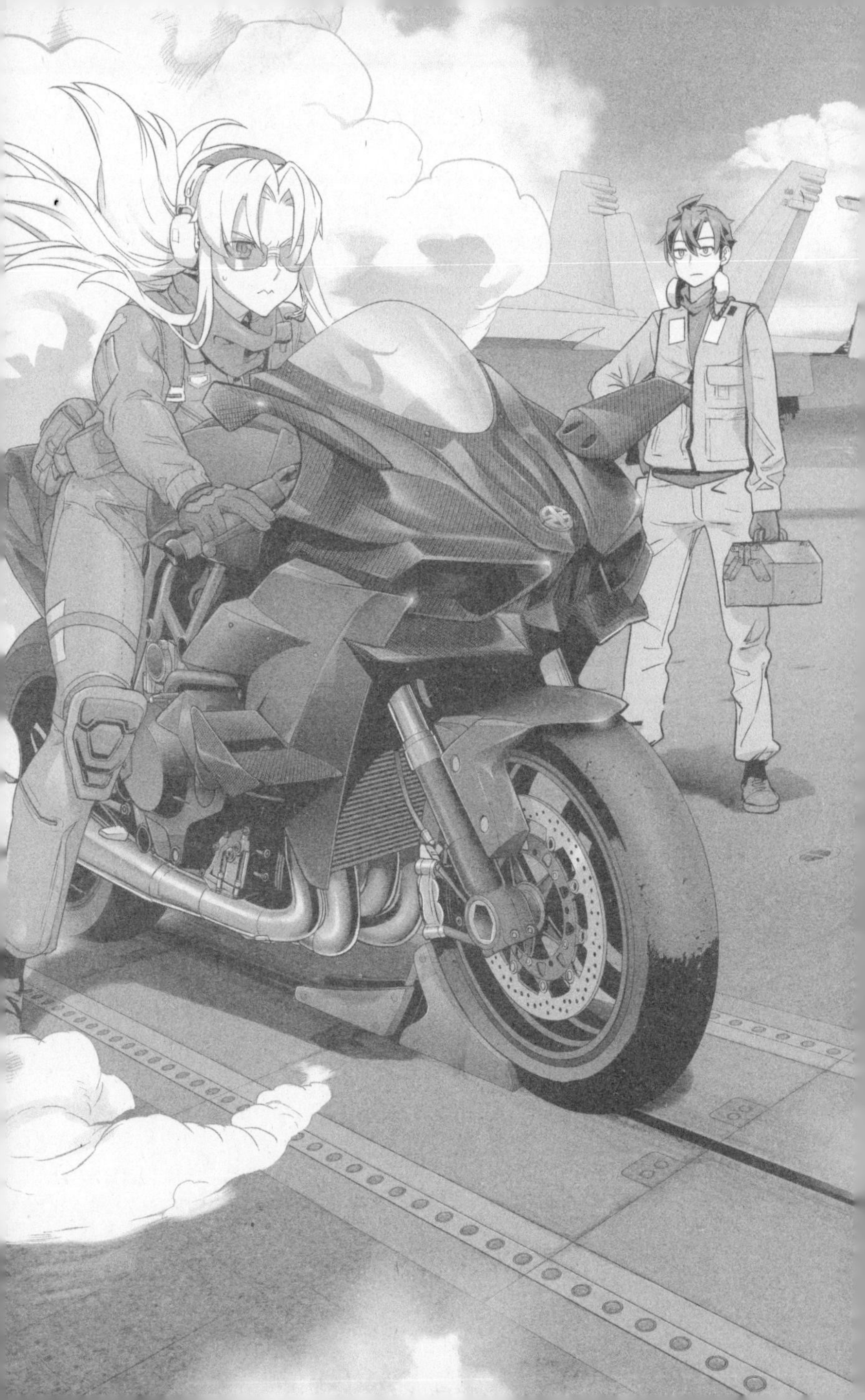

TRIAGE X ㉕

SHOUJI SATO

Translation: Christine Dashiell

Lettering: Abigail Blackman

TRIAGE X Volume 25 © Shouji Sato 2022. First published in Japan in 2022 by KADOKAWA CORPORATION, Tokyo. English translation rights arranged with KADOKAWA CORPORATION, Tokyo, through TUTTLE-MORI AGENCY, INC., Tokyo.

English translation © 2023 by Yen Press, LLC

Yen Press
150 West 30th Street, 19th Floor
New York, NY 10001

Visit us at yenpress.com
facebook.com/yenpress
twitter.com/yenpress
yenpress.tumblr.com
instagram.com/yenpress

First Yen Press Edition: June 2023
Edited by Abigail Blackman & Yen Press Editorial: Carl Li
Designed by Yen Press Design: Eddy Mingki, Wendy Chan

Yen Press is an imprint of Yen Press, LLC.
The Yen Press name and logo are trademarks of Yen Press, LLC.

Library of Congress Control Number: 2015952593

ISBNs: 978-1-9753-6483-0 (paperback)
978-1-9753-6484-7 (ebook)

10 9 8 7 6 5 4 3 2 1

WOR

Printed in the United States of America